Edward J. Lowell

The Eve of the French Revolution

Edward J. Lowell

The Eve of the French Revolution

ISBN/EAN: 9783337234812

Printed in Europe, USA, Canada, Australia, Japan

Cover: Foto ©ninafisch / pixelio.de

More available books at **www.hansebooks.com**

THE EVE

OF THE

FRENCH REVOLUTION

BY

EDWARD J. LOWELL

AUTHOR OF "THE HESSIANS AND THE OTHER GERMAN AUXILIARIES
OF GREAT BRITAIN IN THE REVOLUTIONARY WAR"

BOSTON AND NEW YORK
HOUGHTON, MIFFLIN AND COMPANY
The Riverside Press, Cambridge

PREFACE.

THERE are two ways in which the French Revolution may be considered. We may look at the great events which astonished and horrified Europe and America: the storming of the Bastille, the march on Versailles, the massacres of September, the Terror, and the restoration of order by Napoleon. The study of these events must always be both interesting and profitable, and we cannot wonder that historians, scenting the approaching battle, have sometimes hurried over the comparatively peaceful country that separated them from it. They have accepted easy and ready-made solutions for the cause of the trouble. Old France has been lurid in their eyes, in the light of her burning country-houses. The Frenchmen of the eighteenth century, they think, must have been wretches, or they could not so have suffered. The social fabric, they are sure, was rotten indeed, or it would never have gone to pieces so suddenly.

There is, however, another way of looking at that great revolution of which we habitually set the beginning in 1789. That date is, indeed, momentous; more so than any other in modern history. It marks the outbreak in legislation and politics of ideas which had already been working for a century, and which have changed the face of the civilized world. These ideas are not all true nor all noble. They have in them a large admixture of speculative error and of spiritual baseness. They require to-day to be modified and readjusted. But they represent sides of truth which in 1789, and still more in 1689, were too much overlooked and neglected. They suited the stage of civilization which the world had reached, and men needed to emphasize them. Their very exaggeration was perhaps necessary to enable them to fight, and in a measure to supplant, the older doctrines which were in possession of the human mind. Induction, as the sole method of reasoning, sensation as the sole origin of ideas, may not be the final and only truth; but they were very much needed in the world in the seventeenth and eighteenth centuries, and they found philosophers to elaborate them, and enthusiasts to preach them. They made their way chiefly on French soil in the decades preceding 1789.

The history of French society at that time has of late years attracted much attention in France. Diligent scholars have studied it from many sides. I have used their work freely, and acknowledgment will be found in the foot-notes; but I cannot resist the pleasure of mentioning in this preface a few of those to whom I am most indebted; and first M. Albert Babeau, without whose careful researches several chapters of this book could hardly have been written. His studies in archives, as well as in printed memoirs and travels, have brought much of the daily life of old France into the clearest light. He has in an eminent degree the great and thoroughly French quality of telling us what we want to know. His impartiality rivals his lucidity, while his thoroughness is such that it is hard gleaning the old fields after him.

Hardly less is my indebtedness to the late M. Aimé Chérest, whose unfinished work, "La Chute de l'ancien régime," gives the most interesting and philosophical narrative of the later political events preceding the meeting of the Estates General. To the great names of de Tocqueville and of Taine I can but render a passing homage. The former may be said to have opened the modern mind to the proper method of studying the eighteenth century in France, the latter is, perhaps, the most brilliant of writers on the subject; and no one has recently written, or will soon write, about the time when the Revolution was approaching without using the books of both of them. And I must not forget the works of the Vicomte de Broc, of M. Boiteau, and of M. Rambaud, to which I have sometimes turned for suggestion or confirmation.

Passing to another branch of the subject, I gladly acknowledge my debt to the Right Honorable John Morley. Differing from him in opinion almost wherever it is possible to have an opinion, I have yet found him thoroughly fair and accurate in matters of fact. His books on Voltaire, Rousseau, and the Encyclopædists, taken together, form the most satisfactory history of French philosophy in the eighteenth century with which I am acquainted.

Of the writers of monographs, and of the biographers, I will not speak here in detail, although some of their books have been of very great service to me. Such are those of M. Bailly, M. de Lavergne, M. Horn, M. Stourm, and M. Charles Gomel, on the financial history of France;

M. de Poncins and M. Desjardins, on the cahiers; M. Rocquain on the revolutionary spirit before the revolution, the Comte de Luçay and M. de Lavergne, on the ministerial power and on the provincial assemblies and estates; M. Desnoiresterres, on Voltaire; M. Scherer, on Diderot; M. de Loménie, on Beaumarchais; and many others; and if, after all, it is the old writers, the contemporaries, on whom I have most relied, without the assistance of these modern writers I certainly could not have found them all.

In treating of the Philosophers and other writers of the eighteenth century I have not endeavored to give an abridgment of their books, but to explain such of their doctrines as seemed to me most important and influential. This I have done, where it was possible, in their own language. I have quoted where I could; and in many cases where quotation marks will not be found, the only changes from the actual expression of the author, beyond those inevitable in translation, have been the transference from direct to oblique speech, or some other trifling alterations rendered necessary in my judgment by the exigencies of grammar. On the other hand, I have tried to translate ideas and phrases rather than words.

EDWARD J. LOWELL.

June 24, 1892.

CONTENTS.

CHAPTER		PAGE
	Introduction	1
I.	The King and the Administration	4
II.	Louis XVI. and his Court	11
III.	The Clergy	25
IV.	The Church and her Adversaries	40
V.	The Church and Voltaire	51
VI.	The Nobility	70
VII.	The Army	83
VIII.	The Courts of Law	103
IX.	Equality and Liberty	119
X.	Montesquieu	126
XI.	Paris	154
XII.	The Provincial Towns	175
XIII.	The Country	186
XIV.	Taxation	207
XV.	Finance	230
XVI.	"The Encyclopædia"	243
XVII.	Helvetius, Holbach, and Chastellux	261
XVIII.	Rousseau's Political Writings	274
XIX.	"La Nouvelle Héloïse" and "Emile"	303
XX.	The Pamphlets	322
XXI.	The Cahiers	342
XXII.	Social and Economical Matters in the Cahiers	359
XXIII.	Conclusion	377
Index of Editions cited		389
Index		399

THE EVE OF THE FRENCH REVOLUTION.

INTRODUCTION.

It is characteristic of the European family of nations, as distinguished from the other great divisions of mankind, that among them different ideals of government and of life arise from time to time, and that before the whole of a community has entirely adopted one set of principles, the more advanced thinkers are already passing on to another. Throughout the western part of continental Europe, from the sixteenth to the eighteenth century, absolute monarchy was superseding feudalism; and in France the victory of the newer over the older system was especially thorough. Then, suddenly, although not quite without warning, a third system was brought face to face with the two others. Democracy was born full-grown and defiant. It appealed at once to two sides of men's minds, to pure reason and to humanity. Why should a few men be allowed to rule a great multitude as deserving as themselves? Why should the mass of mankind lead lives full of labor and sorrow? These questions are difficult to answer. The Philosophers of the eighteenth century pronounced them unanswerable. They did not in all cases advise the establishment of democratic government as a cure for the wrongs which they saw in the world. But they attacked the things that were, proposing other things, more or less practicable, in their places. It seemed to these men no very difficult task to reconstitute society and civilization, if only the faulty arrangements of the past could be done away. They believed that men and things might be governed by a few simple laws, obvious and uniform. These natural laws they did not make any great effort to discover; they rather took them for granted; and while they disagreed in their statement of principles, they still believed their principles to be axiomatic. They therefore undertook to demolish simultaneously all established things which to their minds did not rest on absolute logical right. They bent themselves to their task with ardent faith and hope.

The larger number of people, who had been living quietly in the existing order, were amused and interested. The attacks of the Philosophers seemed to them just in many cases, the reasoning conclusive. But in their hearts they could not believe in the reality and importance of the assault. Some of those most interested in keeping the world as it was, honestly or frivolously joined in the cry for reform and for destruction.

At last an attempt was made to put the new theories into practice. The social edifice, slowly constructed through centuries, to meet the various needs of different generations, began to tumble about the astonished ears of its occupants. Then all who recognized that they had something at stake in civilization as it existed were startled and alarmed. Believers in the old religion, in old forms of government, in old manners and morals, men in fear for their heads and men in fear for their estates, were driven together. Absolutism and aristocracy, although entirely opposed to each other in principle, were forced into an unnatural alliance. From that day to this, the history of the world has been largely made up of the contests of the supporters of the new ideas, resting on natural law and on logic, with those of the older forms of thought and customs of life, having their sanctions in experience.

INTRODUCTION.

It was in France that the long struggle began and took its form. It is therefore interesting to consider the government of that country, and its material and moral condition, at the time when the new ideas first became prominent and forced their way toward fulfillment.

It is seldom in the time of the generation in which they are propounded that new theories of life and its relations bear their full fruit. Only those doctrines which a man learns in his early youth seem to him so completely certain as to deserve to be pushed nearly to their last conclusions. The Frenchman of the reign of Louis XV. listened eagerly to Voltaire, Montesquieu and Rousseau. Their descendants, in the time of his grandson, first attempted to apply the ideas of those teachers. While I shall endeavor in this book to deal with social and political conditions existing in the reign of Louis XVI., I shall be obliged to turn to that of his predecessor for the origin of French thoughts which acted only in the last quarter of the century.

CHAPTER I.

THE KING AND THE ADMINISTRATION.

WHEN Louis XVI. came to the throne in the year 1774, he inherited a power nearly absolute in theory over all the temporal affairs of his kingdom. In certain parts of the country the old assemblies or Provincial Estates still met at fixed times, but their functions were very closely limited. The *Parliaments*, or high courts of justice, which had claimed the right to impose some check on legislation, had been browbeaten by Louis XIV., and the principal one, that of Paris, had been dissolved by his successor. The young king appeared, therefore, to be left face to face with a nation over which he was to exercise direct and despotic power. It was a recognized maxim that the royal will was law.[1] Moreover, for more than two centuries, the tendency of continental governments had been toward absolutism. Among the great desires of men in those ages had been organization and strong government. A despotism was considered more favorable to these things than an aristocracy. Democracy existed as yet only in the dreams of philosophers, the history of antiquity, and the example of a few inconsiderable countries, like the Swiss cantons. It was soon to be brought into greater prominence by the American Revolution. As yet, however, the French nation looked hopefully to the king for government, and for such measures of reform as were deemed necessary. A king of France who had reigned justly and strongly would have received the moral support of the most respectable part of his subjects. These longed

[1] Si veut le roi, si veut la loi.

for a fair distribution of public burdens and for freedom from unnecessary restraint, rather than for a share in the government. The admiration for the English constitution, which was commonly expressed, was as yet rather theoretic than practical, and was not of a nature to detract from the loyalty undoubtedly felt for the French crown.

Every monarch, however despotic in theory, is in fact surrounded by many barriers which it takes a strong man to overleap. And so it was with the king of France. Although he was the fountain of justice, his judicial powers were exercised through magistrates many of whom had bought their places, and could therefore not be dispossessed without measures that were felt to be unjust and almost revolutionary. The breaking up of the Parliament of Paris, in the latter years of the preceding reign, had thrown the whole body of judges and lawyers into a state of discontent bordering on revolt. The new court of justice which had superseded the old one, the Parlement Maupeou as it was called, after the name of the chancellor who had advised its formation, was neither liked nor respected. It was one of the first acts of the government of Louis XVI. to restore the ancient Parliament of Paris, whose rights over legislation will be considered later, but which exercised at least a certain moral restraint on the royal authority.

But it was in the administrative part of the government, where the king seemed most free, that he was in fact most hampered. A vast system of public offices had been gradually formed, with regulations, traditions, and a professional spirit. This it was which had displaced the old feudal order, substituting centralization for vigorous local life.

The king's councils, which had become the central governing power of the state, were five in number. They were, however, closely connected together. The king himself was supposed to sit in all of them, and appears to have attended three with tolerable regularity. When there was a prime minister, he also sat in the three that were most important. The controller of the finances was a member of four of the councils, and the chancellor of three at least. As these were the most important men in the government, their presence in the several councils secured unity of action. The boards, moreover, were small, not exceeding nine members in the case of the first four in dignity and power: the Councils of State, of Despatches, of Finance, and of Commerce. The fifth, the Privy Council, or Council of Parties, was larger, and served in a measure as a training-school for the others. It comprised, beside all the members of the superior councils, thirty councilors of state, several intendants of finance, and eighty lawyers known as *maîtres des requêtes*.[1]

The functions of the various councils were not clearly defined and distinguished. Many questions would be submitted to one or another of them as chance or influence might direct. Under each there were a number of public offices, called bureaux, where business was prepared, and where the smaller matters were practically settled. By the royal councils and their subordinate public offices, France was governed to an extent and with a minuteness hardly comprehensible to any one not accustomed to centralized government.

The councils did nothing in their own name. The king it was who nominally settled everything with their advice. The final decision of every question was supposed to rest with the monarch himself. Every important matter was in fact submitted to him. Thus in the government of the country, the king could at any moment take as much of the burden upon his own shoulders as they were strong enough to bear.

The legislative power was exercised by the councils. It

[1] De Lucay, *Les Secrétaires d'Etat*, 418, 419, 424, 442, 448, 449.

was a question not entirely settled whether their edicts possessed full force of law without the assent of the high courts or parliaments. But with the councils rested, at least, all the initiative of legislation. The process of law-making began with them, and by them the laws were shaped and drafted.

They also possessed no small part of the judiciary power. The custom of removing private causes from the regular courts, and trying them before one or another of the royal councils, was a great and, I think, a growing one. This appellate jurisdiction was due in theory partly to the doctrine that the king was the origin of justice; and partly to the idea that political matters could not safely be left to ordinary tribunals. The notion that the king owes justice to all his subjects and that it is an act of grace, perhaps even a duty on his part, to administer it in person when it is possible to do so, is as old as monarchy itself. Solomon in his palace, Saint Louis under his oak, when they decided between suitors before them, were exercising the inherent rights of sovereignty, as understood in their day. The late descendants of the royal saint did not decide causes themselves except on rare occasions, but in questions between parties followed the decision of the majority of the council that heard the case. Thus the ancient custom of seeking justice from a royal judge merely served to transfer jurisdiction to an irregular tribunal.[1]

The executive power was both nominally and actually in the hands of the councils. Great questions of foreign and domestic policy could be settled only in the Council of State.[2] But the whole administration tended more and more in the same direction. Questions of detail were submitted from all parts of France. Hardly a bridge was built or a steeple repaired in Burgundy or Provence without a permission signed by the king in council and coun-

[1] De Lucay, *Les Secrétaires d'Etat*, 465.
[2] Sometimes called Conseil d'en haut, or Upper Council.

tersigned by a secretary of state. The Council of Despatches exercised disciplinary jurisdiction over authors, printers, and booksellers. It governed schools, and revised their rules and regulations. It laid out roads, dredged rivers, and built canals. It dealt with the clergy, decided differences between bishops and their chapters, authorized dioceses and parishes to borrow money. It took general charge of towns and municipal organization. The Council of Finance and the Council of Commerce had equally minute questions to decide in their own departments.[1]

Evidently the king and his ministers could not give their personal attention to all these matters. Minor questions were in fact settled by the bureaux and the secretaries of state, and the king did little more than sign the necessary license. Thus matters of local interest were practically decided by subordinate officers in Paris or Versailles, instead of being arranged in the places where they were really understood. If a village in Languedoc wanted a new parsonage, neither the inhabitants of the place, nor any one who had ever been within a hundred miles of it, was allowed to decide on the plan and to regulate the expense, but the whole matter was reported to an office in the capital and there settled by a clerk. This barbarous system, which is by no means obsolete in Europe, is known in modern times by the barbarous name of bureaucracy.

The royal councils and their subordinate bureaux had their agents in the country. These were the intendants, men who deserve attention, for by them a very large part of the actual government was carried on. They were thirty-two in number, and governed each a territory, called a *généralité*. The intendants were not great lords, nor the owners of offices that had become assimilated to

[1] De Lucay, *Les Secrétaires d'Etat*, 418. For this excessive centralization, see, also, De Tocqueville, *L'ancien Régime et la Révolution*, passim.

property; they were hard-working men, delegated by the council, under the great seal, and liable to be promoted or recalled at the royal pleasure. They were chosen from the class of *maîtres des requêtes*, and were therefore all lawyers and members of the Privy Council. Thus the unity of the administration in Versailles and the provinces was constantly maintained.

It had originally been the function of the intendants to act as legal inspectors, making the circuit of the provincial towns for the purpose of securing uniformity and the proper administration of justice in the various local courts.[1] They retained to the end of the monarchy the privilege of sitting in all the courts of law within their districts.[2] But their duties and powers had grown to be far greater than those of any officer merely judicial. The intendant had charge of the interests of the Catholic religion and worship, and the care of buildings devoted to religious purposes. He also controlled the Protestants, and all their affairs. He encouraged and regulated agriculture and commerce. He settled many questions concerning military matters and garrisons. The militia was entirely managed by him. He coöperated with the courts of justice in the control of the police. He had charge of post-roads and post-offices, stage coaches, books and printing, royal or privileged lotteries, and the suppression of illegal gambling. He was, in fact, the direct representative of the royal power, and was in constant correspondence with the king's minister of state. And as the power of the crown had constantly grown for two centuries, so the power of the intendant had constantly grown with it, tending to the centralization and unity of France and to the destruction of local liberties.

As the intendants were educated as lawyers rather than as administrators, and as they were often transferred

---

[1] Du Boys, i. 517.
[2] De Lucay, *Les Assemblées provinciales*, 31.

from one province to another after a short term of service, they did not acquire full knowledge of their business. Moreover, they did not reside regularly in the part of the country which they governed, but made only flying visits to it, and spent most of their time near the centre of influence, in Paris or Versailles. Yet their opportunities for doing good or harm were almost unlimited. Their executive command was nearly uncontrolled; for where there were no provincial estates, the inhabitants could not send a petition to the king except through the hands of the intendant, and any complaint against that officer was referred to himself for an answer.[1]

The intendants were represented in their provinces by subordinate officers called sub-delegates, each one of whom ruled his petty district or *élection*. These men were generally local lawyers or magistrates. Their pay was small, they had no hope of advancement, and they were under great temptation to use their extensive powers in a corrupt and oppressive manner.[2]

Beside the intendant, we find in every province a royal governor. The powers of this official had gradually waned before those of his rival. He was always a great lord, drawing a great salary and maintaining great state, but doing little service, and really of far less importance to the province than the new man. He was a survival of the old feudal government, superseded by the centralized monarchy of which the intendant was the representative.[3]

---

[1] For the intendants, see Necker, *De l'administration*, ii. 469, iii. 379. Ibid., *Mémoire au roi sur l'établissement des administrations provinciales*, passim. De Lucay, *Les Assemblées provinciales*, 29. Mercier, *Tableau de Paris*, ix. 85. The official title of the intendant was *commissaire départi*.

[2] De Lucay, *Les Assemblées provinciales*, 42, etc.

[3] The *généralité* governed by the intendant, and the *province* to which the royal governor was appointed, were not always coterminous.

CHAPTER II.

LOUIS XVI. AND HIS COURT.

A CENTRALIZED government, when it is well managed and carefully watched from above, may reach a degree of efficiency and quickness of action which a government of distributed local powers cannot hope to equal. But if a strong central government become disorganized, if inefficiency, or idleness, or, above all, dishonesty, once obtain a ruling place in it, the whole governing body is diseased. The honest men who may find themselves involved in any inferior part of the administration will either fall into discouraged acquiescence, or break their hearts and ruin their fortunes in hopeless revolt. Nothing but long years of untiring effort and inflexible will on the part of the ruler, with power to change his agents at his discretion, can restore order and honesty.

There is no doubt that the French administrative body at the time when Louis XVI. began to reign, was corrupt and self-seeking. In the management of the finances and of the army, illegitimate profits were made. But this was not the worst evil from which the public service was suffering. France was in fact governed by what in modern times is called "a ring." The members of such an organization pretend to serve the sovereign, or the public, and in some measure actually do so; but their rewards are determined by intrigue and favor, and are entirely disproportionate to their services. They generally prefer jobbery to direct stealing, and will spend a million of the state's money in a needless undertaking, in order to divert a few thousands into their own pockets.

They hold together against all the world, while trying to circumvent each other. Such a ring in old France was the court. By such a ring will every country be governed, where the sovereign who possesses the political power is weak in moral character or careless of the public interest; whether that sovereign be a monarch, a chamber, or the mass of the people.[1]

Louis XVI., king of France and of Navarre, was more dull than stupid, and weaker in will than in intellect. In him the hobbledehoy period had been unusually prolonged, and strangers at court were astonished to see a prince of nineteen years of age running after a footman to tickle him while his hands were full of dirty clothes.[2] The clumsy youth grew up into a shy and awkward man, unable to find at will those accents of gracious politeness which are most useful to the great. Yet people who had been struck at first only with his awkwardness were sometimes astonished to find in him a certain amount of education, a memory for facts, and a reasonable judgment.[3] Among his predecessors he had set himself Henry IV. as a model, probably without any very accurate idea of the character of that monarch; and he had fully determined that he would do what in him lay to make his people happy. He was, moreover, thoroughly conscientious, and had a high sense of the responsibility of his great calling. He was not indolent, although heavy, and his courage, which was sorely tested, was never broken. With these virtues he might have made a good king, had he possessed firmness of will enough to support a good minister, or to adhere to a good policy. But such strength

---

[1] "Quand, dans un royaume, il y a plus d'avantage à faire sa cour qu'à faire son devoir, tout est perdu." Montesquieu, vii. 176, (*Pensées diverses.*)

[2] Swinburne, i. 11.

[3] Campan, ii. 231. Bertrand de Moleville, *Histoire*, i. Introd.; *Mémoires*, i. 221.

had not been given him. Totally incapable of standing by himself, he leant successively, or simultaneously, on his aunt, his wife, his ministers, his courtiers, as ready to change his policy as his adviser. Yet it was part of his weakness to be unwilling to believe himself under the guidance of any particular person; he set a high value on his own authority, and was inordinately jealous of it. No one, therefore, could acquire a permanent influence. Thus a well-meaning man became the worst of sovereigns; for the first virtue of a master is consistency, and no subordinate can follow out with intelligent zeal to-day a policy which he knows may be subverted to-morrow.

The apologists of Louis XVI. are fond of speaking of him as "virtuous." The adjective is singularly ill-chosen. His faults were of the will more than of the understanding. To have a vague notion of what is right, to desire it in a general way, and to lack the moral force to do it, — surely this is the very opposite of virtue.

The French court, which was destined to have a very great influence on the course of events in this reign and in the beginning of the French Revolution, was composed of the people about the king's person. The royal family and the members of the higher nobility were admitted into the circle by right of birth, but a large place could be obtained only by favor. It was the court that controlled most appointments, for no king could know all applicants personally and intimately. The stream of honor and emolument from the royal fountain-head was diverted, by the ministers and courtiers, into their own channels. Louis XV. had been led by his mistresses; Louis XVI. was turned about by the last person who happened to speak to him. The courtiers, in their turn, were swayed by their feelings, or their interests. They formed parties and combinations, and intrigued for or against each other. They made bargains, they gave and took bribes. In all these intrigues, bribes, and bargains, the court ladies had a great share. They were as corrupt as the men, and as frivolous. It is probable that in no government did women ever exercise so great an influence.

The factions into which the court was divided tended to group themselves round certain rich and influential families. Such were the Noailles, an ambitious and powerful house, with which Lafayette was connected by marriage; the Broglies, one of whom had held the thread of the secret diplomacy which Louis XV. had carried on behind the backs of his acknowledged ministers; the Polignacs, new people, creatures of Queen Marie Antoinette; the Rohans, through the influence of whose great name an unworthy member of the family was to rise to high dignity in the church and the state, and then to cast a deep shadow on the darkening popularity of that ill-starred princess. Such families as these formed an upper class among nobles, and the members firmly believed in their own prescriptive right to the best places. The poorer nobility, on the other hand, saw with great jealousy the supremacy of the court families. They insisted that there was and should be but one order of nobility, all whose members were equal among themselves.[1]

The courtiers, on their side, thought themselves a different order of beings from the rest of the nation. The ceremony of presentation was the passport into their society, but by no means all who possessed this formal title were held to belong to the inner circle. Women who came to court but once a week, although of great family, were known as "Sunday ladies." The true courtier lived always in the refulgent presence of his sovereign.[2]

The court was considered a perfectly legitimate power, although much hated at times, and bearing, very properly,

---

[1] See among other places the Instructions of the Nobility of Blois to the deputies, *Archives parlementaires*, ii. 385.
[2] Campan, iii. 89.

a large share of the odium of misgovernment. The idea of its legitimacy is impressed on the language of diplomacy, and we still speak of the Court of St. James, the Court of Vienna, as powers to be dealt with. Under a monarchy, people do not always distinguish in their own minds between the good of the state and the personal enjoyment of the monarch, nor is the doctrine that the king exists for his people by any means fully recognized. When the Count of Artois told the Parliament of Paris in 1787 that they knew that the expenses of the king could not be regulated by his receipts, but that his receipts must be governed by his expenses, he spoke a half-truth; yet it had probably not occurred to him that there was any difference between the necessity of keeping up an efficient army, and the desirability of having hounds, coaches, and palaces. He had not reflected that it might be essential to the honor of France to feed the old soldiers in the Hôtel des Invalides, and quite superfluous to pay large sums to generals who had never taken the field and to colonels who seldom visited their regiments. The courtiers fully believed that to interfere with their salaries was to disturb the most sacred rights of property. In 1787, when the strictest economy was necessary, the king united his "Great Stables" and "Small Stables," throwing the Duke of Coigny, who had charge of the latter, out of place. Although great pains were taken to spare the duke's feelings and his pocket, he was very angry at the change, and there was a violent scene between him and the king. "We were really provoked, the Duke of Coigny and I," said Louis good-naturedly afterwards, "but I think if he had thrashed me, I should have forgiven him." The duke, however, was not so placable as the king. Holding another appointment, he resigned it in a huff. The queen was displeased at this mark of temper, and remarked to a courtier that the Duke of Coigny did not appreciate the consideration that had been shown him.

"Madam," was the reply, "he is losing too much to be content with compliments. It is too bad to live in a country where you are not sure of possessing to-day what you had yesterday. Such things used to take place only in Turkey."[1]

It is not easy, in looking at the French government in the eighteenth century, to decide where the working administration ended, and where the useless court that answered no real purpose began. The ministers of state were reckoned a part of the court. So were many of the upper civil-servants, the king's military staff, and in a sense, the guards and household troops. So were the "great services," partaking of the nature of public offices, ceremonial honors, and domestic labors. Of this kind were the Household, the Chamber, the Antechamber and Closet, the Great and the Little Stables, with their Grand Squire, First Squire and pages, who had to prove nobility to the satisfaction of the royal herald. There was the department of hunting and that of buildings, a separate one for royal journeys, one for the guard, another for police, yet another for ceremonies. There were five hundred officers "of the mouth," table-bearers distinct from chair-bearers. There were tradesmen, from apothecaries and armorers at one end of the list to saddle-makers, tailors and violinists at the other.

When a baby is at last born to Marie Antoinette (only a girl, to every one's disappointment), a rumor gets about that the child will be tended with great simplicity. The queen's mother, the Empress Maria Theresa, in distant Vienna, takes alarm. She does not approve of "the present fashion according to Rousseau" by which young princes are brought up like peasants. Her ambassador in Paris hastens to reassure her. The infant will not lack reasonable ceremony. The service of her royal person alone will employ nearly eighty attendants.[2]

[1] Besenval, ii. 255. [2] Mercy-Argenteau, iii. 283, 292.

The military and civil households of the king and of the royal family are said to have consisted of about fifteen thousand souls, and to have cost forty-five million francs per annum. The holders of many of the places served but three months apiece out of every year, so that four officers and four salaries were required, instead of one.

With such a system as this we cannot wonder that the men who administered the French government were generally incapable and self-seeking. Most of them were politicians rather than administrators, and cared more for their places than for their country. Of the few conscientious and patriotic men who obtained power, the greater number lost it very speedily. Turgot and Malesherbes did not long remain in the Council. Necker, more cautious and conservative, could keep his place no better. The jealousy of Louis was excited, and he feared the domination of a man of whom the general opinion of posterity has been that he was wanting in decision. Calonne was sent away as soon as he tried to turn from extravagance to economy. Vergennes alone, of the good servants, retained his office; perhaps because he had little to do with financial matters; perhaps, also, because he knew how to keep himself decidedly subordinate to whatever power was in the ascendant. The lasting influences were that of Maurepas, an old man who cared for nothing but himself, whose great object in government was to be without a rival, and whose art was made up of tact and gayety; and that of the rival factions of Lamballe and Polignac, guiding the queen, which were simply rapacious.

The courtiers and the numerous people who were drawn to Versailles by business or curiosity were governed by a system of rules of gradual growth, constituting what was known as "Etiquette." The word has passed into common speech. In this country it is an unpopular word, and there is an impression in many people's minds that the thing which it represents is unnecessary. This, however, is a great delusion. Etiquette is that code of rules, not necessarily connected with morals, by which mutual intercourse is regulated. Every society, whether civilized or barbarous, has such a code of its own. Without it social life would be impossible, for no man would know what to expect of his neighbors, nor be able promptly to interpret the words and actions of his fellow-men. It is in obedience to an unwritten law of this kind that an American takes off his hat when he goes into a church, and an Asiatic, when he enters a mosque, takes off his shoes; that Englishmen shake hands, and Africans rub noses. Where etiquette is well understood and well adapted to the persons whom it governs, men are at ease, for they know what they may do without offense. Where it is too complicated it hampers them, making spontaneous action difficult, and there is no doubt that the etiquette that governed the French court was antiquated, unadvisable and cumbrous. Its rules had been devised to prevent confusion and to regulate the approach of the courtiers to the king. As all honors and emoluments came from the royal pleasure, people were sure to crowd about the monarch, and to jostle each other with unmannerly and dangerous haste, unless they were strictly held in check. Every one, therefore, must have his place definitely assigned to him. To be near the king at all times, to have the opportunity of slipping a timely word into his ear, was an invaluable privilege. To be employed in menial offices about his person was a mark of confidence. Rules could not easily be revised, for each of them concerned a vested right. Those in force in the reign of Louis XVI. had been established by his predecessors when manners were different.

At the close of the Middle Ages privacy may be said to have been a luxury almost unknown to any man. There was not room for it in the largest castle. Solitude was seldom either possible or safe. People were crowded together without means of escape from each other. The greatest received their dependents, and often ate their meals, in their bedrooms. A confidential interview would be held in the embrasure of a window. Such customs disappeared but gradually from the sixteenth century to our own. But by the latter part of the eighteenth, modern ways and ideas were coming in. Yet the etiquette of the French court was still old-fashioned. It infringed too much on the king's privacy; it interfered seriously with his freedom. It exposed him too familiarly to the eyes of a nation overprone to ridicule. A man who is to inspire awe should not dress and undress in public. A woman who is to be regarded with veneration should be allowed to take her bath and give birth to her children in private.[1]

Madame Campan, long a waiting-woman of Marie Antoinette, has left an account of the toilet of the queen and of the little occurrences that might interrupt it. The whole performance, she says, was a masterpiece of etiquette; everything about it was governed by rules. The Lady of Honor and the Lady of the Bedchamber, both if they were there together, assisted by the First Woman and the two other women, did the principal service; but there were distinctions among them. The Lady of the Bedchamber put on the skirt and presented the gown. The Lady of Honor poured out the water to wash the queen's hands and put on the chemise. When a Princess of the Royal Family or a Princess of the Blood was present at the toilet, the Lady of Honor gave up the latter function to her. To a Princess of the Royal Family, that is to say to the sister, sister-in-law, or aunt of the king, she handed

---

[1] See the account of the birth of Marie Antoinette's first child, when she was in danger from the mixed crowd that filled her room, stood on chairs, etc., 19th Dec. 1778. Campan, i. 201. At her later confinements only princes of the blood, the chancellor and the ministers, and a few other persons were admitted. Ibid., 203.

the garment directly; but to a Princess of the Blood (the king's cousin by blood or marriage) she did not yield this service. In the latter case, the Lady of Honor handed the chemise to the First Woman, who presented it to the Princess of the Blood. Every one of these ladies observed these customs scrupulously, as appertaining to her rank.

One winter's day it happened that the Queen, entirely undressed, was about to put on her chemise. Madame Campan was holding it unfolded. The Lady of Honor came in, made haste to take off her gloves and took the chemise. While she still had it in her hands there came a knock at the door, which was immediately opened. The new-comer was the Duchess of Orleans, a Princess of the Blood. Her Highness's gloves were taken off, she advanced to take the shift, but the Lady of Honor must not give it directly to her, and therefore passed it back to Madame Campan, who gave it to the princess. Just then there came another knock at the door, and the Countess of Provence, known as Madame, and sister-in-law to the king, was ushered in. The Duchess of Orleans presented the chemise to her. Meanwhile the Queen kept her arms crossed on her breast, and looked cold. Madame saw her disagreeable position, and without waiting to take off her gloves, merely threw away her handkerchief and put the chemise on the Queen. In her haste she knocked down the Queen's hair. The latter burst out laughing, to hide her annoyance; and only murmured several times between her teeth: "This is odious! What a nuisance!"

This anecdote gives but an instance of the well-known and not unfounded aversion of Marie Antoinette to the etiquette of the French court. But the young queen made no attempt to reform that etiquette; she tried only to evade it. Much has been written about Marie Antoinette as a woman, her terrible misfortunes and the fortitude with which she bore them having evoked the sympathy of mankind. Her conduct as a queen-consort has been less considered. The woman was lively and amiable, possessing a great personal charm, which impressed those who approached her; but that mattered little to the nation, whose dealings were with the queen. What were the duties of her office and how did she fulfill them?

The first thing demanded of her was parade. She had to keep up the splendor and attractiveness of the French monarchy. This, in spite of her impatience of etiquette, was of all her public duties the one which she best performed. Her manners were dignified, gracious, and appropriately discriminating. It is said that she could bow to ten persons with one movement, giving, with her head and eyes, the recognition due to each separately.

She had also the art of talking to several people at once, so that each one felt as if her remarks had been addressed to himself, and the equally important art (sometimes called royal) of remembering faces and names. As she passed from one part of her palace to another, surrounded by the ladies of her court, she seemed to the spectator to surpass them all in the nobility of her countenance and the dignified grace of her carriage. She had the crowning beauty of woman, a well-poised and proudly carried head. Her gait was a gliding motion, in which the steps were not clearly distinguishable. Foreigners generally were enchanted with her, and to them she owes no small part of her posthumous popularity. The French nobility, on the other hand, complained, not unreasonably, that the queen was too exclusively devoted to the society of a few intimate companions, for whose sake she neglected other people. Her court, on this account, was sometimes comparatively deserted. But a young queen can hardly be very severely blamed if she often prefers her pleasures and her friends to the tedious duties of her position. Marie Antoinette had had little education or guidance. Her likes and dislikes were strong, nor was she entirely above petty spite. "You tell me," wrote Maria Theresa to her daughter on one occasion, "that for love of me you treat the Broglies well, although they have been disrespectful to you personally. That is another odd idea. Can a little Broglie be disrespectful to you? I do not understand that. No one was ever disrespectful to me, nor to any of your ten brothers and sisters." It was no fair-weather queen that wrote this most royal reproof. Marie Antoinette never rose to this height of dignity, where the great lady sits above the clouds. In her days of prosperity she certainly never approached it. Perhaps no mortal woman ever reached it in early life.[1]

It is one of the most important duties of a queen-consort to set a good example in morals. Here Marie Antoinette was deficient. Her private conduct has probably been slandered, but she brought the slanders on herself. Beside the code of morals, there is in every country a code of proprieties, and people who habitually do that which is considered improper have only themselves to thank if a harsh construction is put on their doubtful actions. The scandals concerning Marie Antoinette were numberless and public. The young queen of France chose for her intimate companions men and women of bad reputation. Her brother, Joseph II., was shocked when he visited her, at the familiar manners which she permitted. He wrote to her that English travelers compared her court to Spa, then a famous gambling-place, and he called the house of the Princess of Guémenée, which she was in the habit of frequenting, "a real gambling-hell." Accusations of cheating at cards flew about the palace, and one courtier had his pocket picked in the royal drawing-room. The queen was constantly surrounded by dissipated young noblemen, who on race days were allowed to come into

---

[1] Mercy-Argenteau, *passim*, and especially i. 218, 265, 279; ii. 218, 232, 312, 525; iii. 56, 113, 132 and n., 157, 265, 490. Tilly, *Mémoires*, 230. Goguel, 59, 84; Wraxall, i. 85; Walpole's *Letters*, vi. 245 (23d Aug. 1776), etc.

her presence in costumes which shocked conservative people. She herself was recognized at public masked balls, where the worst women of the capital jostled the great nobles of the court. When she had the measles, four gentlemen of her especial friends were appointed nurses, and hardly left her chamber during the day and evening, People asked ironically what four ladies would be appointed to nurse the king if he were ill. In her amusements she was seldom accompanied by her husband. It hardly told in her favor that the latter was a man for whom a young and high-spirited woman could not be expected to entertain any very passionate affection.

The country was deeply in debt, and during a part of the reign an expensive war was going on. It was obviously the queen's duty to retrench her own expenses, and to set an example of economy. Yet her demands on the treasury were very great. Her personal allowance was much larger than that of the previous queen, and she was frequently in debt. Her losses at play were considerable, in spite of her husband's well-known aversion to gambling. She increased the number of expensive and useless offices about her court. She was constantly accessible to rapacious favorites. The feeble king could at least recognize that he owed something to his subjects; the queen appears to have thought that the revenues of France were intended principally to provide means for the royal bounty to people who had done nothing to deserve it. On the other hand, she acknowledged the duty of private charity, and believed that thereby she was earning the gratitude of her subjects. That the taxpayer was entitled to any consideration is an idea that does not seem to have entered her mind.

Had Marie Antoinette been the wife of a strong and able king, she would probably have been quite right in avoiding interference in the government of the state. Being married to Louis XVI., it was inevitable that she should try to direct his vacillating will in public matters. It therefore becomes pertinent to ask whether her influence was generally exerted on the right side.

It is evident that in the earlier part of her reign the affairs of the state did not interest her, though her feelings were often strongly moved for or against persons. Her preference for Choiseul and his adherents, over Aiguillon and his party, was natural and well founded. The Duke of Choiseul was not only the author of the Austrian alliance and of the queen's marriage, but was also the ablest minister who had recently held favor in France. Had Marie Antoinette possessed as much influence over her husband in 1774 as she obtained later, she might perhaps have overcome what seems to have been one of his strongest prejudices, and have brought Choiseul back to power, to the benefit of the country. But her efforts in that direction were unavailing. In her relations with the other ministers, Turgot, Malesherbes, and Necker, her voice was generally on the side of extravagance and the court, and against economy and the nation. This, far more than the intrigues of faction, was the cause of the unpopularity that pursued her to her grave. If the court of France was a corrupt ring living on the country, Marie Antoinette was not far from being its centre.

CHAPTER III.

THE CLERGY.

The inhabitants of France were divided into three orders, differing in legal rights. These were the Clergy, the Nobility, and the Commons, or Third Estate. The first two, which are commonly spoken of as the privileged orders, contained but a small fraction of the population numerically, but their wealth and position gave them a great importance.

The clergy formed, as the philosophers were never tired of complaining, a state within a state. No accurate statistics concerning it can be obtained. The whole number of persons vowed to religion in the country, both regular and secular, would seem to have been between one hundred and one hundred and thirty thousand. They owned probably from one fifth to one quarter of the soil. The proportion was excessive, but it does not appear that the lay inhabitants of the country were thereby crowded. Like other landowners, the clergy had tenants, and they were far from being the worst of landlords. For one thing, they were seldom absentees. The abbot of a monastery might spend his time at Versailles, but the prior and the monks remained, to do their duty by their farmers. It is said that the church lands were the best cultivated in the kingdom, and that the peasants that tilled them were the best treated.[1] In any case the church was

---

[1] Barthélémy, *Erreurs et mensonges historiques*, xv. 40. Article entitled *La question des congrégations il y a cent ans*, quoting largely from Féroux, *Vues d'un Solitaire Patriote*, 1784. See also Genlis, *Dictionnaire des Etiquettes*, ii. 79. Mathieu, 324. Babeau, *La vie rurale*, 133.

rich. Its income from invested property, principally land, has been reckoned at one hundred and twenty-four million livres a year. It received about as much more from tithes, beside the amount, very variously reckoned, which came in as fees, on such occasions as weddings, christenings, and funerals.

Tithes were imposed throughout France for the support of the clergy. They were not, however, taken upon all articles of produce, nor did they usually amount to one tenth of the increase. Sometimes the tithe was compounded for a fixed rent in money; sometimes for a given number of sheaves, or measures of wine per acre. Oftener it was a fixed proportion of the crop, varying from one quarter to one fortieth. In some places wood, fruit, and other commodities were exempt; in other places they were charged. Tithe was in some cases taken of calves, lambs, chickens, sucking pigs, fleeces, or fish; and the clergy or the tithe owners were bound to provide the necessary bulls, rams, and boars. A distinction was usually made between the Great tithes, levied on such common articles as corn and wine, and the Small tithes, taken from less important crops. Of these the former were often paid to the bishops, the latter to the parish priest. The tithes had in some cases been alienated by the church and were owned by lay proprietors. In general, it is believed that this tax on the agricultural class in France amounted to about one eighteenth of the gross product of the soil.[1]

The whole body of the clergy, as it existed within the boundaries of the kingdom, was not subject to the same rules and laws. The larger part of it formed what was known as the "Clergy of France," and possessed peculiar rights and privileges presently to be described. Those

---

[2] Chassin, *Les cahiers du clergé*, 36. Bailly, ii. 414, 419. Boiteau, 41. Rambaud, ii. 58 n. Taine, *L'ancien Régime* (book i. chap. ii.). The livre of the time of Louis XVI. is commonly reckoned to have had at least twice the purchasing power of the franc of to-day.

ecclesiastics, however, who lived in certain provinces, situated principally in the northern and eastern part of the country, and annexed to the kingdom since the beginning of the sixteenth century, were called the "Foreign Clergy." These did not share the rights of the larger body, but depended more directly on the papacy. They paid certain taxes from which the Clergy of France were exempt. The mode of appointment to bishoprics and abbacies was different among them from what it was in the rest of the country. Throughout France, and in all affairs, ecclesiastical and secular, were anomalies such as these.

The Church of France enjoyed great and peculiar privileges, both among the churches of Christendom, and among the Estates of the French realm. By the Concordat, or treaty of 1516, made between Pope Leo X. and King Francis I., the nomination to bishroprics and to considerable ecclesiastical benefices had been given to the king, while the Holy Father kept only a right of veto on appointments. The *annates*, or first-fruits of the bishoprics, taxes equal in theory to one year's revenue on every change of incumbent, but in fact of less amount than that, were paid to the Pope, and these, with other dues, made up a sum of three or four million livres sent annually from France to Rome. On the other hand, the Clergy of France was the only body in the state which had undisputed constitutional rights independent of the throne. Its ordinary assemblies were held once in ten years. The country was divided into sixteen ecclesiastical provinces, each under the superintendence of an archbishop. In each of these provinces a meeting was held, composed of delegates of the various dioceses. Each of these provincial meetings elected two bishops and two other ecclesiastics, either regular or secular. These deputies received, from their constituents, instructions called *cahiers*, to be taken by them to the Ordinary Assembly of the clergy, which was held in Paris. This body granted subsidies to the king, managed the debt and other secular affairs of the clergy, and pronounced unofficially even in matters of doctrine. Smaller Assemblies, nearly equal in power, came together at least once during the interval which elapsed between the meetings of the Ordinary Assemblies; so that as often as once in five years the Church of France exercised a true political activity. The sum voted to the king was called a Free Gift,[1] and the name was not altogether inappropriate, for, although the amount required was stated by the king's ministers, conditions were not infrequently exacted of the crown. Thus in 1785, on the occasion of a gift of eighteen million livres, the suppression of the works of Voltaire was demanded. And once at least, as late as 1750, on the occasion of a squabble between the church and the court, the clergy had refused to make any grant whatsoever. The total amount of the Free Gift voted during the reign of Louis XVI. was 65,800,000 livres, or less than four and a half millions a year on an average. The grant was not annual, but was made in lump sums from time to time; a vote of two thirds of the assembly being necessary for making it. The assembly itself assessed the tax on the dioceses. A commission managed the affairs of the clergy when no assembly was sitting. The order had its treasury, and its credit was good. The king was its debtor to the extent of about a hundred million livres.

The clergy itself was in debt. Instead of raising directly, by taxation of its members, the money which it paid to the state, it had acquired the habit of borrowing the necessary sum. The debt thus incurred appears to have been about one hundred and thirty-four million livres. In addition to the amount necessary for interest on this debt, and for a provision for its gradual repayment, the order had various expenses to meet. For these

[1] Don Gratuit.

purposes it taxed itself to an amount of more than ten
million livres a year. On the other hand it received back
from the king a subsidy of two and a half million livres.
From most of the regular, direct taxes paid by Frenchmen the Clergy of France was freed.[1]

The bishops were not subject to the secular tribunals,
but other clerks came under the royal jurisdiction in temporal matters. In spiritual affairs they were judged by
the ecclesiastical courts.

The income of the clergy, had it been fairly distributed,
was amply sufficient for the support of every one connected
with the order. It was, however, divided with great partiality. There were set over the clergy, both French and
foreign, eighteen archbishops and a hundred and twenty-
one bishops, beside eleven of those bishops *in partibus
infidelium*, who, having no sees of their own in France,
might be expected to make themselves generally useful.
These hundred and fifty bishops were very highly, though
unequally paid. The bishoprics, with a very few exceptions, were reserved for members of the nobility, and this
rule was quite as strictly enforced under Louis XVI. as
under any of his predecessors. Nothing prevented the
cumulation of ecclesiastical benefices, and that prelate
was but a poor courtier who did not enjoy the revenue of
several rich abbeys. Nor was it in money and in ecclesiastical preferment alone that the bishops were paid for
the services which they too often neglected to perform.

---

[1] *Revue des questions historiques*, 1st July, 1890 (L'abbé L. Bour-
gain, *Contribution du clergé à l'impot*). Sciout, i. 35. Boiteau, 195.
Rambaud, ii. 44. Necker, *De l'Administration*, ii. 308. The financial
statement given above refers to the Clergy of France only. Its pecuniary affairs are as difficult and doubtful as those of every part of
the nation at this period, and have repeatedly been made the subject of confused statement and religious and political controversy.
The Foreign Clergy paid some of the regular taxes, giving the state
about one million livres a year on an income of twenty million livres.
Boiteau, 196.

Not a few of them were barons, counts, dukes, princes of the Holy Roman Empire, or peers of France by virtue of their sees. Several rose to be ministers of state. Even in that age they were accused of worldliness. It was a proverb that with Spanish bishops and French priests an excellent clergy could be made. But not all the French bishops were worldly, nor neglectful of their spiritual duties. Among them might be found conscientious and serious prelates, abounding both in faith and good works, living simply and bestowing their wealth in charity.[1]

After the bishops came the abbots. As their offices were in the gift of the king, and as no discipline was enforced upon them, they were chiefly to be found in the antechambers of Versailles and in the drawing-rooms of Paris. They were not even obliged to be members of the religious orders they were supposed to govern.[2] Leaving the charge of their monasteries to the priors, they spent the incomes where new preferment was to be looked for, and devoted their time to intrigues rather than to prayers. No small part of the revenues of the clergy was wasted in the dissipations of these ecclesiastic courtiers. They were imitated in their vices by a rabble of priests out of place, to whom the title of abbot was given in politeness, the little *abbés* of French biography and fiction. These men lived in garrets, haunted cheap eating-houses, and appeared on certain days of the week at rich men's tables, picking up a living as best they could. They were to be seen among the tradesmen and suitors who crowded the levees of the great, distinguishable in the throng by their black clothes, and a very small tonsure. They attended

---

[1] Rambaud, ii. 37. Mathieu, 151.

[2] The abbots of abbeys *en commende* were appointed by the king. These appear to have been most of the rich abbeys. There were also *abbayes régulières*, where the abbot was elected by the brethren. Rambaud, ii. 53. The revenues of the monasteries were divided into two parts, the *mense abbatiale*, for the abbot, the *mense conventuelle*, for the brethren. Mathieu, 73.

the toilets of fashionable ladies, ever ready with the last bit of literary gossip, or of social scandal. They sought employment as secretaries, or as writers for the press. The church, or indeed, the opposite party, could find literary champions among them at a moment's notice. Nor was hope of professional preferment always lacking. It is said that one of the number kept an ecclesiastical intelligence office. This man was acquainted with the incumbents of valuable livings; he watched the state of their health, and calculated the chances of death among them. He knew what patrons were likely to have preferment to give away, and how those patrons were to be reached. His couriers were ever on the road to Rome, for the Pope still had the gift of many rich places in France, in spite of the Concordat.[1]

Another large part of the revenues of the church was devoted to the support of the convents. These contained from sixty to seventy thousand persons, more of them women than men. Owing to various causes, and especially to the action of a commission appointed to examine all convents, and to reform, close, or consolidate such as might need to be so treated, the number of regular religious persons fell off more than one half during the last twenty-five years of the monarchy. Yet many of the functions which in modern countries are left to private charity, or to the direct action of the state, were performed in old France by persons of this kind. The care of the poor and sick and the education of the young were largely, although not entirely, in the hands of religious orders. Some monks, like the Benedictines of St. Maur, devoted their lives to the advancement of learning. But there were also monks and nuns who rendered no services to the public, and were entirely occupied with their own spiritual and temporal interests, giving alms, perhaps, but only incidentally, like other citizens. Against these

[1] Mercier, ix. 350.

the indignation of the French Philosophers was much excited. Their celibacy was attacked, as contrary to the interests of the state; they were accused of laziness and greed. How far were the Philosophers right in their opposition? It is impossible to discuss in detail here the policy of allowing or discouraging religious corporations in a state. Should men and women be permitted to retire from the struggles and duties of active life in the world? Is the monastery, with its steady and depressing routine, its religious observances, often mechanical, and its quiet life, more or less degrading than the wearing toil of the world without, and the coarse pleasures of the club or the tavern? Is it better that a woman, whom choice or necessity has deprived of every probability of governing a home of her own, should struggle against the chances and temptations of city life, or the constant drudgery of spinsterhood in the country; or that she should find the stupefying protection of a convent? These questions have seldom been answered entirely on their own merits. They have presented themselves in company with others even more important; with questions of freedom of conscience and of national existence. The time seems not far distant when they must be reconsidered for their own sake. Already in France the persons leading a monastic life are believed to be twice as numerous as they were at the outbreak of the Revolution. It is difficult to ascertain the number in our own country, but it is not inconsiderable.[1]

A pleasant life the inmates of some convents must have had of it. The incomes were large, the duties easy. Cer-

---

[1] Rambaud (ii. 52 and n.) reckons 100,000 in the 18th century and 158,500 to-day in France, but the figures for the last century are probably too high, at least if 1788 be taken as the point of comparison. Sadlier's *Catholic Directory*, 1885, p. 116, gives the number of Catholic religious in the Archdiocese of New York at 117 regular priests, 271 brothers, 2136 religious women, in addition to 279 secular priests.

tain houses had been secularized and turned into noble chapters. The ladies who inhabited them were freed from the vow of poverty. They wore no religious vestment, but appeared in the fashionable dress of the day. They received their friends in the convent, and could leave it themselves to reënter the secular life, and to marry if they pleased. Such a chapter was that of Remiremont in Lorraine, whose abbess was a princess of the Holy Roman Empire, by virtue of her office. Her crook was of gold. Six horses were harnessed to her carriage. Her dominion extended over two hundred villages, whose inhabitants paid her both feudal dues and ecclesiastical tithes. Nor were her duties onerous. She spent a large part of her time in Strasburg, and went to the theatre without scruple. She traveled a good deal in the neighborhood, and was a familiar figure at some of the petty courts on the Rhine. The canonesses followed her good example. Some of them were continually on the road. Others stayed at home in the convent, and entertained much good company. They dressed like other people, in the fashion, with nothing to mark their religious calling but a broad ribbon over the right shoulder, blue bordered with red, supporting a cross, with a figure of Saint Romaric. No lady was received into this chapter who could not show nine generations or two hundred and twenty-five years of chivalric, noble descent, both on the father's and on the mother's side.

Such requirements as this were extreme, but similar conditions were not unusual. The Benedictines of Saint Claude, transformed into a chapter of canonesses, required sixteen quarterings for admission; that is to say, that every canoness must show by proper heraldic proof, that her sixteen great-grandfathers and great-grandmothers were of noble blood. The Knights of Malta required but four quarterings. They had two hundred and twenty commanderies in France, with eight hundred Knights.

The Grand Priory gave an income of sixty thousand livres to the Prior, who was always a prince. The revenues of the order were 1,750,000 livres.

But very rich monasteries were exceptional after all. Those where life was hard and labor continuous were far more common. In some of them, forty men would be found living on a joint income of six thousand livres a year. They cultivated the soil, they built, they dug. They were not afraid of great undertakings in architecture or engineering, to be accomplished only after long years and generations of labor, for was not their corporation immortal? Then we have the begging orders, infesting the roads and villages, and drawing several million livres a year from the poorer classes, which supported and grumbled at them. And against the luxury of the noble chapters must be set the silence, the vigils, the fasts of La Trappe. This monastery stood in a gloomy valley, sunk among wooded hills. The church and the surrounding buildings were mostly old, and all sombre and uninviting. Each narrow cell was furnished with but a mattress, a blanket and a table, without chair or fire. The monks were clad in a robe and a hood, and wore shoes and stockings, but had neither shirt nor breeches. They shaved three times a year. Their food consisted of boiled vegetables, with salad once a week; never any butter nor eggs. Twice in the night they rose, and hastened shivering to the chapel. Never did they speak, but to their confessor; until, in his last hour, each was privileged to give to the prior his dying messages. Hither, from the active and gay world of philosophy and frivolity would suddenly retire from time to time some young officer, scholar, or courtier. Here, bound by irrevocable vows, he could weep over his sins, or gnash his teeth at the folly that had brought him, until he found peace at last in life or in the grave.

To enjoy the temporal privileges of the religious life

neither any great age nor any extensive learning was required. To hold a cure of souls or the abbacy of a "regular" convent (whose inmates chose their abbot), a man must be twenty-five years old. But an abbot appointed by the king need only be twenty-two, a canon of a cathedral fourteen, and a chaplain seven. It cannot be doubted that persons of either sex were obliged to make irrevocable vows, without any proof of free vocation, or any reason to expect a fixed resolution. Daughters and younger sons could thus be conveniently disposed of. A larger share was left for the family, for the religious were civilly dead, and did not take part in the inheritance. On the other hand, misfortune and want need not be feared for the inmate of the convent. If a nun were lost to the joys of the world, she was lost to its cares. To make such a choice, to commit temporal suicide, the very young should surely not be admitted. Yet it was not until 1768 that the time for taking final vows was advanced to the very moderate age of twenty-one for young men and eighteen for girls.[1]

The secular clergy was about as numerous as the regular. It was principally composed of the *curés* and *vicaires* who had charge of parishes.[2] These men were mostly drawn from the lower classes of society, or at any rate not from the nobility. They had therefore very little chance of promotion. Some of them in the country districts were very poor; for the great tithes, levied on the principal crops, generally belonged to the bishops, to the convents

[1] Rambaud, ii. 45. Mathieu, 43. Chassin, 25. Boiteau, 176. Bailly, 421. Mme. d'Oberkirch, 127. Mme. de Genlis, *Dict. des Etiquettes*, i. 111 *n.*, *Le Comte de Fersen et la Cour de France*, I. xxix. Mercier, xi. 358.

[2] The bishops, of course, belonged to the secular clergy. So, in fact, did the canons; who, on account of the similarity of their mode of life, have been treated with the regulars. In the French hierarchy the *curé* comes above the *vicaire*. The relation is somewhat that of parson and curate in the church of England.

of regulars, or to laymen; and only the lesser tithes, the occasional fees,[1] and the product of a small glebe were reserved for the parish priest, and the latter was liable to continual squabbles with the peasants concerning his dues. But the parish priest, with all other churchmen, was exempt from the state taxes, although obliged to pay a proportion of the *décimes*,[2] or special tax laid by the clergy on their own order. Moreover, the government set a minimum;[3] and if the income of the parish priest fell below it, the owner of the great tithes was bound to make up the difference. This minimum was set at five hundred livres a year for a *curé* in 1768, and raised to seven hundred in 1785. A *vicaire* received two hundred and three hundred and fifty. These amounts do not seem large, but they must have secured to the country priest a tolerable condition, for we do not find that the clerical profession was neglected.

Apart from considerations of material well being, the condition of the parish priest was not undesirable. He was fairly independent, and could not be deprived of his living without due process of law. His house was larger or smaller according to his means, but his authority and influence might in any case be considerable. He had more education and more dealings with the outer world than most of his parishioners. To him the intendant of the province might apply for information concerning the state of his village, and the losses of the peasants by fire, or by epidemics among their cattle. His sympathy with his

[1] *Casuel.*

[2] *Décime*, in the singular, was an extraordinary tax levied on ecclesiastical revenue for some object deemed important. *Décimes*, in the plural, was the tax paid annually by benefices. *Dime*, tithe (see Littré, *Décime*). It seems a question whether the proportion of the *décimes* paid by the parish priests was too large. See *Revue des questions historiques*, 1st July 1890, 102. Necker, *De l'Administration*, ii. 313.

[3] *Portion congrue.*

fellow-villagers was the warmer, that like them he had a piece of ground to till, were it only a garden, an orchard, or a bit of vineyard. Round his door, as round theirs, a few hens were scratching; perhaps a cow lowed from her shed, or followed the village herd to the common. The priest's servant, a stout lass, did the milking and the weeding. In 1788, a provincial synod was much disturbed by a motion, made by some fanatic in the interest of morals, that no priest should keep a serving-maid less than forty-five years of age. The rule was rejected on the ground that it would make it impossible to cultivate the glebes. Undoubtedly, the priests themselves often tucked up the skirts of their cassocks, and lent a hand in the work. They were treated by their flocks with a certain amount of respectful familiarity. They were addressed as *messire*. With the joys and sorrows of their parishioners, their connection was at once intimate and professional. Their ministrations were sought by the sick and the sad, their congratulations by the happy. No wedding party nor funeral feast was complete without them.[1]

The privileges and immunities which the Church of France enjoyed had given to her clergy a tone of independence both to the Pope and to the king. We have seen them accompanying their " free gifts " to the latter by requests and conditions. Toward the Holy See their attitude had once been quite as bold. In 1682 an assembly of the Church of France had promulgated four propositions which were considered the bulwarks of the Gallican liberties.

[1] Turgot, v. 364. This letter is very interesting, as showing the importance of the *curés* and their possible dealings with the intendant. Mathieu, 152. Babeau, *La vie rurale*, 157. A good study of the clergy before the Revolution is found in an article by Marius Sepet (*La société française à la veille de la révolution*), in the *Revue des questions historiques*, 1st April and 1st July, 1889.

(1.) God has given to Saint Peter and his successors no power, direct or indirect, over temporal affairs.

(2.) Ecumenical councils are superior to the Pope in spiritual matters.

(3.) The rules, usages and statutes admitted by the kingdom and the Church of France must remain inviolate.

(4.) In matters of faith, decisions of the Sovereign Pontiff are irrevocable only after having received the consent of the church.

These propositions were undoubtedly a part of the law of France, and were fully accepted by a portion of the French clergy. But the spirit that dictated them had in a measure died out during the corrupt reign of Louis XV. The long quarrel between the Jesuits and the Jansenists, which agitated the Gallican church during the latter part of the seventeenth and the earlier half of the eighteenth century, had tended neither to strengthen nor to purify that body. A large number of the most serious, intelligent and devout Catholics in France had been put into opposition to the most powerful section of the clergy and to the Pope himself. Thus the Church of France was in a bad position to repel the violent attacks made upon her from without.[1]

For a time of trial had come to the Catholic Church, and the Church of France, although hardly aware of its danger, was placed in the forefront of battle. It was against her that the most persistent and violent assault of the Philosophers was directed. Before considering the doctrines of those men, who differed among themselves very widely on many points, it is well to ask what was the cause of the great excitement which their doctrines created. Men as great have existed in other centuries, and have exercised an enormous influence on the human mind.

[1] Rambaud, ii. 40. For a Catholic account of the Jansenist quarrel, see Carné, *La monarchie française au* 18*me siècle*, 407.

But that influence has generally been gradual; percolating slowly, through the minds of scholars and thinkers, to men of action and the people. The intellectual movement of the eighteenth century in France was rapid. It was the nature of the opposition which they encountered which drew popular attention to the attacks of the Philosophers.

CHAPTER IV.

THE CHURCH AND HER ADVERSARIES.

THE new birth of learning in the fifteenth and sixteenth centuries had been followed by the strengthening and centralization of government, both in church and state. France had its full share of this change. Its civil government became the strongest in Europe, putting down every breath of opposition. Against the political conduct of Louis XIV. neither magistrate nor citizen dared to raise his voice. The Church of France, on the other hand, in close alliance with the civil power, became almost irresistible in her own sphere. The Catholic Church throughout Europe had been the great schoolmaster of civilization. It had fallen into the common fault of schoolmasters, the assumption of infallibility. It was, moreover, a state within all states. Its sovereign, the Pope, the most powerful monarch in Christendom, is chosen in accordance with a curious and elaborate set of regulations, by electors appointed by his predecessors. His rule, nominally despotic, is limited by powers and influences understood by few persons outside of his palace. His government, although highly centralized, is yet able to work efficiently in all the countries of the earth. It is served by a great body of officials, probably less corrupt on the whole than those of any other state. They are kept in order, not only by moral and spiritual sanctions, but by a system of worldly promotion. They wield over their subjects a tremendous weapon, sometimes borrowed, but seldom long or very skillfully used by laymen, and called, in clerical language, excommunication. This, when it is confined to the denial of religious privileges, may be considered a spiritual weapon. But in the eighteenth century the temporal power of Catholic Europe was still in great measure at the service of the ecclesiastical authorities. Obedience to the church was a law of the state. Although Frenchmen were no longer executed for heresy in the reign of Louis XVI., they still were persecuted. The property of Protestants was unsafe, their marriages invalid. Their children might be taken from them. Such toleration as existed was precarious, and the Church of France was constantly urging the temporal government to take stronger measures for the extirpation of heresy.

The church had succeeded in implanting in the minds of its votaries one opinion of enormous value in its struggle for power. Originally and properly an association for the practice and spreading of religion, the corporation had succeeded in making itself an object of worship. One great reason why atheism took root in France was the impossibility, induced by long habit, of distinguishing between religion and Catholicism, and of conceiving that the one may exist without the other. The by-laws of the church had become as sacred as the primary duties of piety; and the injunction to refrain from meat on Fridays was indistinguishable by most Catholics, in point of obligation, from the injunction to love the Lord their God.

The Protestant churches which separated themselves from the Church of Rome in the sixteenth century carried with them much of the intolerant spirit of the original body. It is one of the commonplace sneers of the unreflecting to say that religious toleration has always been the dogma of the weaker party. The saying, if it were true, which it is not, yet would not be especially sagacious. Toleration, like other things, has been most sought by those whose need of it was greatest. But they have not always recognized its value. It was no small step in the progress of the human mind that was taken when men came to look on religious toleration as desirable or possible. That the state might treat with equal favor all forms of worship was an opinion hardly accepted by wise and liberal-minded men in the eighteenth century. It may be that the fiery contests of the Reformation were still too near in those days to let perfect peace be safe or profitable.

Yet religious toleration was making its way in men's minds. Cautiously, and with limitations, the doctrine is stated, first by Locke, Bayle, and Fénelon in the last quarter of the seventeenth century, then by almost all the great writers of the eighteenth. The Protestants, with their experience of persecution, assert that those persons should not be tolerated who teach that faith should not be kept with heretics, or that kings excommunicated forfeit their crowns and kingdoms; or who attribute to themselves any peculiar privilege or power above other mortals in civil affairs; in short, they exclude the Catholics. Atheists also may be excluded, as being under no possible conscientious obligation to dogmatize concerning their negative creed. The Catholics maintain the right of the sovereign to forbid the use of ceremonies, or the profession of opinions, which would disturb the public peace. Montesquieu, a nominal Catholic only, declares that it is the fundamental principle of political laws concerning religion, not to allow the establishment of a new form if it can be prevented; but when one is once established, to tolerate it. He refuses to say that heresy should not be punished, but he says that it should be punished only with great circumspection. This left the case of the French Protestants to all appearances as bad as before; for the laws denied that they had been established in the kingdom, and the church always asserted that it was mild and circumspect in its dealings with heretics. Voltaire will not say that those who are not of the same religion as the prince should share in the honors of the state, or hold public office. Such limitations as these would seem to have deprived toleration of the greater part of its value, by excluding from its benefits those persons who were most likely to be persecuted. But the statement of a great principle is far more effectual than the enumeration of its limitations. Toleration, eloquently announced as an ideal, made its way in men's minds. "Absolute liberty, just and true liberty, equal and impartial liberty, is the thing we stand in need of," cries Locke, and the saying is retained when his exceptions concerning the Catholics are forgotten. "When kings meddle with religion," says Fénelon, "instead of protecting, they enslave her."[1]

The Church of France had long been cruel to her opponents. The persecution of the French Protestants, which preceded and followed the revocation of the Edict of Nantes in 1685, is known to most readers. It was long and bloody. But about the middle of the eighteenth century it began to abate. The last execution for heresy in France appears to have taken place in 1762. A Protestant meeting was surprised and attacked by soldiers in 1767. Some eight or ten years later than this, the last prisoner for conscience' sake was released from the galleys at Toulon. But no religion except the Roman Catholic was recognized by the state; and to its clergy alone were entrusted certain functions essential to the conduct of civilized life. No marriage could be legally solemnized but by a Catholic priest. No public record of births was kept but in the parish registers. As a consequence of this, no faithful Protestant could be legally married at

[1] Locke, vi. 45, 46 (*Letter on Toleration*). Bayle, *Commentary on the Text " Compelle intrare "* (for atheists), ii. 431, a., Fénelon, *Œuvres*, vii. 123 (*Essai philosophique sur le gouvernement civil*). Montesquieu, *Œuvres*, iv. 68 ; v. 175 (*Esprit des Lois*, liv. xii. ch. v. and liv. xxxv. ch. x.). Felice, Voltaire, xli. 247 (*Essai sur la tolérance*).

all, and all children of Protestant parents were bastards, whose property could be taken from them by the nearest Catholic relative. It is true that the courts did much to soften the execution of these laws; but the judges, with the best intentions, were sometimes powerless; and all judges did not mean to act fairly by heretics.

Slowly, during the lifetime of a generation, the Protestants gained ground. The coronation-oath contained a clause by which the king promised to exterminate heretics. When Louis XVI. was to be crowned at Rheims, Turgot desired to modify this part of the oath. He drew up a new form. The clergy, however, resisted the innovation, and Maurepas, the prime minister, agreed with them. The young king, with characteristic weakness, is said to have muttered some meaningless sounds, in place of the disputed portion of the oath.

In 1778, an attempt was made to induce the Parliament of Paris to interfere in behalf of the oppressed sectaries. It was stated that since 1740, more than four hundred thousand marriages had been contracted outside of the church, and that these marriages were void in law and the constant cause of scandalous suits. But the Parliament, by a great majority, rejected the proposal to apply to the king for relief. In 1775, and again in 1780, the assembly of the clergy protested against the toleration accorded to heretics. It is not a little curious that at a time when a measure of simple humanity was thus opposed by the highest court of justice in the realm, and by the Church of France in its corporate capacity, a foreign Protestant, Necker, was the most important of the royal servants.

The spirit of the church, or at least of her leading men, is expressed in the Pastoral Instruction of Lefranc de Pompignan, Archbishop of Vienne, perhaps the most prominent French ecclesiastic of the century. The church, he says, has never persecuted, although misguided men have done so in her name. The sovereign should maintain the true religion, and is himself the judge of the best means of doing it. But religion sets bounds to what a monarch should do in her defense. She does not ask for violent or sanguinary measures against simple heretics. Such measures would do more harm than good. But when men have the audacity to exercise a pretended and forbidden ministry, injurious to the public peace, it would be absurd to think that rigorous penalties applied to their misdeeds are contrary to Christian charity. And in connection with toleration, the prelate brings together the two texts, "Judge not, that ye be not judged;"—"but he that believeth not is condemned already." This plan of dealing gently with Protestants, while so maltreating their pastors as to make public worship or the administration of sacraments very difficult, was a favorite one with French churchmen.

The great Revolution was close at hand. On the last day of the first session of the Assembly of Notables, in the spring of 1787, Lafayette proposed to petition the king in favor of the Protestants. His motion was received with almost unanimous approval by the committee to which it was made, and the Count of Artois, president of that committee, carried a petition to Louis XVI. accordingly. His Majesty deigned to favor the proposal, and an edict for giving a civil status to Protestants was included in the batch of bills submitted to the Parliament of Paris for registration. The measure of relief was of the most moderate character. It did not enable the sectaries of the despised religion to hold any office in the state, nor even to meet publicly for worship. Yet the opposition to the proposed law was warm, and was fomented by part of the nobility and of the clergy. One of the great ladies of the court called on each counselor of the Parliament, and left a note to remind him of his duty to the Catholic religion and the laws. The Bishop of Dol told the king of France that he would be answerable to God and man for the misfortunes which the reëstablishment of Protestantism would bring on the kingdom. His Majesty's sainted aunt, according to the bishop, was looking down on him from that heaven where her virtues had placed her, and blaming his conduct. Louis XVI. resented this language and found manliness enough to send the Bishop of Dol back to his see. On the 19th of January, 1788, the matter was warmly debated in the Parliament itself. D'Esprémenil, one of the counselors, was filled with excitement and wrath at the proposed toleration. Pointing to the image of Christ, which hung on the wall of the chamber, "would you," he indignantly exclaimed, "would you crucify him again?" But the appeal of bigotry was unavailing. The measure passed by a large majority.[1]

It was not against Protestants alone that the clergy showed their activity. The church, in its capacity of guardian of the public morals and religion, passed condemnation on books supposed to be hostile to its claims. In this matter it exercised concurrent jurisdiction with the administrative branch of the government and with the courts of law. A new book was liable to undergo a triple ordeal. A license was required before publication, and the manuscript was therefore submitted to an official censor, often an ecclesiastic. Thence it became the custom to print in foreign countries, books which contained anything to which anybody in authority might object, and to bring them secretly into France. The presses of Holland and of Geneva were thus used. Sometimes, instead of this, a book would be published in Paris with a foreign

[1] For the last persecution of the Protestants, see Felice, 422. Howard, *Lazzarettos*, 55. Coquerel, 93. Geffroy, i. 406. Chérest, i. 45, 382. For the oath, Turgot, i. 217; vii. 314, 317. See also Dareste, vii. 20, *Lefranc de Pompignan*, i. 132. Geffroy, i. 410; ii. 85. Droz, ii. 38. Sallier, *Annales françaises*, 136 *n*. The majority was 94 to 17. Seven counselors and three bishops retired without voting.

imprint. Thus "Boston" and "Philadelphia" are not infrequently found on the title-pages of books printed in France in the reign of Louis XVI. Such books were sold secretly, with greater or less precautions against discovery, for the laws were severe; an ordinance passed as late as 1757 forbade, under penalty of death, all publications which might tend to excite the public mind. So loose an expression gave discretionary power to the authorities. The extreme penalty was not enforced, but imprisonment and exile were somewhat capriciously inflicted on authors and printers.

But a book that had received the *imprimatur* of the censor was not yet safe. The clergy might denounce, or the Parliament condemn it. The church was quick to scent danger. An honest scholar, an upright and original thinker, could hardly escape the reproach of irreligion or of heresy. Nor were the laws fairly administered. It might be more dangerous to be supposed to allude disagreeably to the mistress of a prince, than to attack the government of the kingdom. Had a severe law been severely and consistently enforced, slander, heresy, and political thought might have been stamped out together. Such was in some measure the case in the reign of Louis XIV. But under the misrule of the courtiers of his feeble successors, no strict law was adhered to. There was a common tendency to wink at illegal writings of which half the public approved. Malesherbes, for instance, was at one time at the head of the official censors. He is said to have had a way of warning authors and publishers the day before a descent was to be made upon their houses. Under laws thus enforced, authors who held new doctrines learned to adapt their methods to those of the government. Almost all the great French writers of the eighteenth century framed some passages in their books for the purpose of satisfying the censor or of avoiding punishment. They were profuse in expressions of loyalty to church and state, in passages sometimes sounding ludicrously hollow, sometimes conveying the most biting mockery and satire, and again in words hardly to be distinguished from the heartfelt language of devotion. They became skillful at hinting, and masters of the art of innuendo. They attacked Christianity under the name of Mahometanism, and if they had occasion to blame French ministers of state, would seem to be satirizing the viziers of Turkey. Politics and theology are subjects of unceasing and vivid interest, and their discussion cannot be suppressed, unless minds are to be smothered altogether. If any measure of free thought and speech is to be admitted, the engrossing topics will find expression. If people are not allowed pamphlets and editorials, they will bring out their ideas in poems and fables. Under Louis XV. and Louis XVI., politics took possession of popular songs, and theology of every conceivable kind of writing. There was hardly an advertisement of the virtues of a quack medicine, or a copy of verses to a man's mistress, that did not contain a fling at the church or the government. There can be no doubt that the moral nature of authors and of the public suffered in such a course. Books lost some of their real value. But for a time an element of excitement was added to the pleasure both of writers and readers. The author had all the advantage of being persecuted, with the pleasing assurance that the persecution would not go very far. The reader, while perusing what seemed to him true and right, enjoyed the satisfaction of holding a forbidden book. He had the amusement of eating stolen fruit, and the inward conviction that it agreed with him.[1]

The writers who adopted this course are mostly known as the "Philosophers." It is hard to be consistent in the

---

[1] Loménie, *Vie de Beaumarchais*, i. 324. Montesquieu, i. 464 (*Lettres persanes*, cxlv.). Mirabeau, *L'ami des hommes*, 238 (pt. ii. ch. iv.). *Anciennes Lois*, xxii. 272. Lanfrey, 193.

use of this word as applied to Frenchmen of the eighteenth century. The name was sometimes given to all those who advocated reform or alteration in church or state. In its stricter application, it belongs to a party among them; to Voltaire and his immediate followers, and especially to the Encyclopædists.

"Never," says Voltaire, in his "English Letters," "will our philosophers make a religious sect, for they are without enthusiasm." This was a favorite idea with the disciples of the great cynic, but the event has disproved its truth. The Philosophers in Voltaire's lifetime formed a sect, although it could hardly be called a religious one. The Patriarch of Ferney himself was something not unlike its pontiff. Diderot and d'Alembert were its bishops, with their attendant clergy of Encyclopædists. Helvetius and Holbach were its doctors of atheology. Most reading and thinking Frenchmen were for a time its members. Rousseau was its arch-heretic. The doctrines were materialism, fatalism, and hedonism. The sect still exists. It has adhered, from the time of its formation, to a curious notion, its favorite superstition, which may be expressed somewhat has follows: "Human reason and good sense were first invented from thirty to fifty years ago." "When we consider," says Voltaire, "that Newton, Locke, Clarke and Leibnitz, would have been persecuted in France, imprisoned at Rome, burnt at Lisbon, what must we think of human reason? It was born in England within this century."[1] And similar expressions are frequent in his writings. The sectaries, from that day to this, have never been wanting in the most glowing enthusiasm. In this respect they generally surpass the Catho-

[1] Voltaire (Geneva ed. 1771) xv. 99 (Newton). Also (Beuchot's ed.) xv. 351 (*Essai sur les Mœurs*) and *passim*. The date usually set by Voltaire's modern followers is that of the publication of the *Origin of Species;* although no error is more opposed than this one to the great theory of evolution.

lics; in fanaticism (or the quality of being cocksure) the Protestants. They hold toleration as one of their chief tenets, but never undertake to conceal their contempt for any one who disagrees with them. The sect has always contained many useful and excellent persons, and some of the most dogmatic of mankind.

CHAPTER V.

THE CHURCH AND VOLTAIRE.

THE enemies of the Church of France were many and bitter, but one man stands out prominent among them. Voltaire was a poet, much admired in his day, an industrious and talented historian, a writer on all sorts of subjects, a wit of dazzling brilliancy; but he was first, last, and always an enemy of the Catholic Church, and although not quite an atheist, an opponent of all forms of religion. For more than forty years he was the head of the party of the Philosophers. During all that time he was the most conspicuous of literary Frenchmen. Two others, Rousseau and Montesquieu, may rival him in influence on the modern world, but his followers in the regions of thought are numerous and aggressive to-day.

Voltaire was born in 1694, the son of a lawyer named Arouet. There are doubts as to the origin of the name he has made so famous; whether it was derived from a fief possessed by his mother, or from an anagram of AROUET LE JEUNE. At any rate, the name was adopted by the young poet, at his own fancy, a case not without parallel in the eighteenth century.[1]

Voltaire began early to attract public attention. Before he was twenty-five years old he had established his reputation as a wit, had spent nearly a year in the Bastile on a charge of writing satirical verses, and had produced a successful tragedy. In this play a couplet sneering at priests might possibly have become a familiar quotation

[1] As in the case of D'Alembert. For Voltaire's name, see Desnoiresterres, *Jeunesse de Voltaire*, 161.

even had it been written by another pen.[1] For several years Voltaire went on writing, with increasing reputation. In 1723, his great epic poem, "La Henriade," was secretly circulated in Paris.[2] The author was one of the marked men of the town. At the same time his reputation must have been to some extent that of a troublesome fellow. And in December of that year an event occurred which was destined to drive the rising author from France for several years, and add bitterness to a mind naturally acid.

The details of the story are variously told. It appears that Voltaire was one evening at the theatre behind the scenes, and had a dispute with the Chevalier de Chabot, of the family of Rohan. "Monsieur de Voltaire, Monsieur Arouet, what's your name!" the chevalier is said to have called out. "My name is not a great one, but I am no discredit to it," answered the author. Chabot lifted his cane, Voltaire laid his hand on his sword. Mademoiselle Lecouvreur, the actress, for whose benefit, perhaps, the little dispute was enacted, took occasion to faint. Chabot went off, muttering something about a stick.

A few days later, Voltaire was dining at the house of the Duke of Sulli. A servant informed him that some one wanted to see him at the door. So Voltaire went out, and stepped quietly up to a coach that was standing in front of the house. As he put his head in at the coach door, he was seized by the collar of his coat and held fast, while two men came up behind and belabored him with sticks. The Chevalier de Chabot, his noble adversary, was looking on from another carriage.

When the tormentors let him go, Voltaire rushed back into the house and appealed to the Duke of Sulli for ven-

[1] *Œdipe*, written in 1718.

"Nos prêtres ne sont point ce qu'un vain peuple pense;
Nôtre crédulité fait toute leur science."
Act IV., Scene I.

[2] Desnoiresterres, *Jeunesse*, 297.

geance, but in vain. It was no small matter to quarrel with the family of Rohan. Then the poet applied to the court for redress, but got none. It is said that Voltaire's enemies had persuaded the prime minister that his petitioner was the author of a certain epigram, addressed to His Excellency's mistress, in which she was reminded that it is easy to deceive a one-eyed Argus. (The minister had but one eye.) Finally Voltaire, seeing that no one else would take up his quarrel, began to take fencing lessons and to keep boisterous company. It is probable that he would have made little use of any skill he might have acquired as a swordsman. Voltaire was not physically rash. The Chevalier de Chabot, although he held the commission of a staff-officer, was certainly no braver than his adversary, and was in a position to take no risks. Voltaire was at first watched by the police; then, perhaps after sending a challenge, locked up in the Bastile. He remained in that state prison for about a fortnight, receiving his friends and dining at the governor's table. On the 5th of May, 1726, he was at Calais on his way to exile in England.[1]

Voltaire spent three years in England, years which exercised a deep influence on his life. He learned the English language exceptionally well, and practiced writing it in prose and verse. He associated on terms of intimacy with Lord Bolingbroke, whom he had already known in France, with Swift, Pope, and Gay. He drew an epigram from Young. He brought out a new and amended edition of the "Henriade," with a dedication in English to Queen Caroline. He studied the writings of Bacon, Newton, and Locke. Thus to the Chevalier de Chabot, and his shameful assault, did French thinkers owe, in no small measure, the influence which English writers exercised upon them.

While in England, Voltaire was taking notes and writ-

[1] Desnoiresterres, *Jeunesse*, 345.

ing letters. These he probably worked over during the years immediately following his return to France. The "Lettres Philosophiques," or "Letters concerning the English Nation," were first published in England in 1733. They were allowed to slip into circulation in France in the following year. Promptly condemned by the Parliament of Paris as "scandalous and contrary to religion and morals, and to the respect due to the powers that be," they were "torn and burned at the foot of the great staircase," and read all the more for it.

It is no wonder that the church, and that conservative if sometimes heterodox body, the Parliament of Paris, should have condemned the "English Letters." A bitter satire is leveled at France, with her religion and her government, under cover of candid praise of English ways and English laws. What could the Catholic clergy say to words like these, put into the mouth of a Quaker? "God forbid that we should dare to command any one to receive the Holy Ghost on Sunday to the exclusion of the rest of the faithful! Thank Heaven we are the only people on earth who have no priests! Would you rob us of so happy a distinction? Why should we abandon our child to mercenary nurses when we have milk to give him? These hirelings would soon govern the house and oppress mother and child. God has said: 'Freely ye have received; freely give.' After that saying, shall we go chaffer with the Gospel, sell the Holy Ghost, and turn a meeting of Christians into a tradesman's shop? We do not give money to men dressed in black, to assist our poor, to bury our dead, to preach to the faithful. Those holy occupations are too dear to us to be cast off upon others."[1]

Having thus attacked the institution of priesthood in general, Voltaire turns his attention in particular to the priests of France and England. In morals, he says, the Anglican clergy are more regular than the French. This

[1] Voltaire, xxxvii. 124.

is because all ecclesiastics in England are educated at the universities, far from the temptations of the capital, and are called to the dignities of the church at an advanced age, when men have no passions left but avarice and ambition. Advancement here is the recompense of long service, in the church as well as in the army. You do not see boys becoming bishops or colonels on leaving school. Moreover, most English priests are married men. The awkward manners contracted at the university, and the slight intercourse with women usual in that country, generally compel a bishop to be content with his own wife. Priests sometimes go to the tavern in England, because custom allows it; but if they get drunk, they do so seriously, and without making scandal.

"That indefinable being, who is neither a layman nor an ecclesiastic, in a word, that which we call an *abbé*, is an unknown species in England. Here all priests are reserved, and nearly all are pedants. When they are told that in France young men known for their debauched lives and raised to the prelacy by the intrigues of women make love publicly, amuse themselves by composing amorous songs, give long and dainty suppers every night, and go thence to ask the enlightenment of the Holy Spirit, and boldly call themselves successors of the apostles, they thank God that they are Protestants; — but they are vile heretics, to be burned by all the devils, as says Master François Rabelais. Which is why I have nothing to do with them."[1]

While the evil lives of an important part of the French clergy are thus assailed, the doctrines of the Church are not spared. The following is from the letter on the Socinians. "Do you remember a certain orthodox bishop, who in order to convince the Emperor of the consubstantiality [of the three Persons of the Godhead] ventured to chuck the Emperor's son under the chin, and to pull

[1] Voltaire, xxxvii. 140.

his nose in his sacred majesty's presence? The Emperor was going to have the bishop thrown out of the window, when the good man addressed him in the following fine and convincing words: 'Sir, if your Majesty is so angry that your son should be treated with disrespect, how do you think that God the Father will punish those who refuse to give to Jesus Christ the titles that are due to Him?' The people of whom I speak say that the holy bishop was ill-advised, that his argument was far from conclusive, and that the Emperor should have answered: 'Know that there are two ways of showing want of respect for me; the first is not to render sufficient honor to my son, the other is to honor him as much as myself.'"[1] Such words as these were hardly to be borne. But the French authorities recognized that there was a greater and more insidious danger to the church in certain other passages by which Frenchmen were made to learn some of the results of English abstract thought.

Among the French writers of the eighteenth century are several men of eminent talent; one only whose sinister but original genius has given a new direction to the human mind. I shall treat farther on of the ideas of Rousseau. The others, and Voltaire among them, belong to that class of great men who assimilate, express, and popularize thought, rather than to the very small body of original thinkers. Let us then pause for a moment, while studying the French Philosophers and their action on the church, and ask who were their masters.

Montaigne, Bayle, and Grotius may be considered the predecessors on the Continent of the French Philosophic movement, but its great impulse came from England. Bacon had much to do with it; Hooker and Hobbes were not without influence; Newton's discoveries directed men's minds towards physical science; but of the metaphysical and political ideas of the century, John Locke

[1] Voltaire, xxxvii. 144.

was the fountain-head. Some Frenchmen have in modern times disputed his claims. To refute these disputants it is only necessary to turn from their books to those of Voltaire and his contemporaries. The services rendered by France to the human race are so great that her sons need never claim any glory which does not clearly belong to them. All through modern history, Frenchmen have stood in the front rank of civilization. They have stood there side by side with Englishmen, Italians, and Germans. International jealousy should spare the leaders of human thought. They belong to the whole European family of nations. The attempt to set aside Locke, Newton, and Bacon, as guides of the eighteenth century belongs not to that age but to our own.

The works of Locke are on the shelves of most considerable libraries; but many men, now that the study of metaphysics is out of fashion, are appalled at the suggestion that they should read an essay in three volumes on the human understanding, evidently considering their own minds less worthy of study than their bodies or their estates. It may be worth while, therefore, to give a short summary of those theories, or discoveries of Locke which most modified French thought in the eighteenth century. The great thinker was born in 1632 and died in 1704. His principal works were published shortly after the English Revolution of 1688, but had been long in preparation; and the "Essay on the Human Understanding" is said to have occupied him not less than twenty years.

It is the principal doctrine of Locke that all ideas are derived from sensation and reflection. He acknowledges that "it is a received doctrine that men have native ideas and original characters stamped upon their minds in their very first being;" but he utterly rejects every such theory. It is his principal business to protest and argue against the existence of such "innate ideas." Virtue he believes to be generally approved because it is profitable not on account of any natural leaning of the mind in its direction. Conscience "is nothing else but our own opinion or judgment of the moral rectitude or pravity of our own actions." Memory is the power in the mind to revive perceptions which it once had, with this additional perception annexed to them, that it has had them before. Wit lies in the assemblage of ideas, judgment in the careful discrimination among them. "Things are good or evil only in reference to pleasure or pain;" . . . "our love and hatred of inanimate, insensible beings is commonly founded on that pleasure or pain which we receive from their use and application any way to our senses, though with their destruction; but hatred or love of beings capable of happiness or misery is often the uneasiness or delight which we find in ourselves, arising from a consideration of their very being or happiness. Thus the being and welfare of a man's children or friends, producing constant delight in him, he is said constantly to love them. But it suffices to note that our ideas of love and hatred are but dispositions of the mind in respect of pleasure or pain in general, however caused in us."

We have no clear idea of substance nor of spirit. Substance is that wherein we conceive qualities of matter to exist; spirit, that in which we conceive qualities of mind, as thinking, knowing, and doubting. The primary ideas of body are the cohesion of solid, and therefore separate parts, and a power of communicating motion by impulse. The ideas of spirit are thinking and will, or a power of putting body into motion by thought, and, which is consequent to it, liberty. The ideas of existence, mobility, and duration are common to both.

Locke's intelligence was clear enough to perceive that these two ideas, spirit and matter, stand on a similar footing. Less lucid thinkers have boldly denied the existence of spirit while asserting that of matter. Locke's system would not allow him to believe that either conception depended on the nature of the mind itself. He therefore rejected the claims of substance as unequivocally as those of spirit, declaring it to be "only an uncertain supposition of we know not what, *i. e.*, of something whereof we have no particular, distinct, positive idea, which we take to be the substratum or support of those ideas we know." Yet he inclines on the whole toward materialism. "We have," he says, "the ideas of matter and thinking, but possibly shall never be able to know whether any mere material being thinks, or no; it being impossible for us, by the contemplation of our own ideas, without revelation, to discover whether omnipotency has not given to some system of matter, fitly disposed, a power to perceive and think, or else joined and fixed to matter so disposed a thinking immaterial substance, it being, in respect of our notions, not much more remote from our comprehension to conceive that God can, if he pleases, superadd to matter a faculty of thinking, than that he should superadd to it another substance, with a faculty of thinking; since we know not wherein thinking consists, nor to what sort of substances the Almighty has been pleased to give that power, which cannot be in any created being, but merely by the good pleasure and power of the Creator." . . . "All the great ends of morality and religion," he adds, "are well secured without philosophical proof of the soul's immateriality." As to our knowledge "of the actual existence of things, we have an intuitive knowledge of our own existence, and a demonstrative knowledge of the existence of God; of the existence of anything else, we have no other but a sensitive knowledge, which extends not beyond the objects present to our senses."[1]

[1] Is not an intuitive knowledge suspiciously like an innate idea? Locke's *Works*, i. 38, 39, 72, 82, 137, 145, 231; ii. 10, 11, 21, 331, 360, 372 (Book i. ch. 3, 4, Book ii. ch. 1, 10, 11, 20, 23, Book iv. ch. 3).

The eulogy of Locke in Voltaire's "Lettres Philosophiques" gave especial offense to the French churchmen. Voltaire writes to a friend that the censor might have been brought to give his approbation to all the letters but this one. "I confess," he adds, "that I do not understand this exception, but the theologians know more about it than I do, and I must take their word for it."[1] The letter to which the censor objected was principally taken up with the doctrine of the materiality of the soul. "Never," says Voltaire, "was there perhaps a wiser or a more methodical spirit, a more exact logician, than Locke." . . "Before him great philosophers had positively decided what is the soul of man; but as they knew nothing at all about it, it is very natural that they should all have been of different minds." And he adds in another part of the letter, "Men have long disputed on the nature and immortality of the soul. As to its immortality, that cannot be demonstrated, since people are still disputing about its nature; and since, surely, we must thoroughly know a created being to decide whether it is immortal or not. Human reason alone is so unable to demonstrate the immortality of the soul, that religion has been obliged to reveal it to us. The common good of all men demands that we should believe the soul to be immortal; faith commands it; no more is needed, and the matter is almost decided. It is not the same as to its nature; it matters little to religion of what substance is the soul, if only it be virtuous. It is a clock that has been given us to regulate, but the maker has not told us of what springs this clock is composed."[2]

[1] Voltaire, li. 356 (*Letter to Thieriot*, 24 Feb. 1733).
[2] Voltaire, xxxvii. 177, 182 (*Lettres philosophiques*. In the various editions of Voltaire's collected works published in the last century these letters do not appear as a series, but their contents is distributed among the miscellaneous articles, and those of the *Dictionnaire philosophique*. The reason for this was that the letters, having been

The "Lettres philosophiques" may be considered the first of Voltaire's polemic writings. They exhibit his mordant wit, his clear-sightedness and his moral courage. There is in them, perhaps, more real gayety, more spontaneous fun, than in his later books. Voltaire was between thirty-five and forty years old when they were written, and although he possessed to the end of his long life more vitality than most men, yet he was physically something of an invalid, and his many exiles and disappointments told upon his temper. From 1734, when these letters first appeared in France, to 1778, when he died, worn out with years, labors, quarrels, and honors, his activity was unceasing. He had many followers and many enemies, but hardly a rival. Voltaire was and is the great representative of a way of looking at life; a way which was enthusiastically followed in his own time, which is followed with equal enthusiasm to-day. This view he expressed and enforced in his numberless poems, tragedies, histories, and tales. It formed the burden of his voluminous correspondence. As we read any of them, his creed becomes clear to us; it is written large in every one of his more than ninety volumes. It may almost be said to be on every page of them. That creed may be stated as follows: We know truth only by our reason. That reason is enlightened only by our senses. What they do not tell us we cannot know, and it is mere folly to waste time in conjecturing. Imagination and feeling are blind leaders of the blind. All men who pretend to supernatural revelation or inspiration are swindlers, and those who believe them are dupes. It may be desirable, for political or social purposes, to have a favored religion in the state, but freedom of opinion and of expression

judicially condemned, might have brought their publishers into trouble if they had appeared under their own title. Bengesco, ii. 9. Desnoiresterres, *Voltaire à Cirey*, 28, Voltaire, xxxvii. 113. In Beuchot's edition the letters appear in their original form).

should be allowed to all men, at least to all educated men; for the populace, with their crude ideas and superstitions, may be held in slight regard.

Voltaire's hatred was especially warm against the regular clergy. "Religion," he says, "can still sharpen daggers. There is within the nation a people which has no dealings with honest folk, which does not belong to the age, which is inaccessible to the progress of reason, and over which the atrocity of fanaticism preserves its empire, like certain diseases which attack only the vilest populace." The best monks are the worst, and those who sing the "Pervigilium Veneris" in place of matins are less dangerous than such as reason, preach, and plot. And in another place he says that "a religious order should not form a part of history." But it is well to notice that Voltaire's hatred of Catholicism and of Catholic monks is not founded on a preference for any other church. He thinks that theocracy must have been universal among early tribes, "for as soon as a nation has chosen a tutelary god, that god has priests. These priests govern the spirit of the nation; they can govern only in the name of their god, so they make him speak continually; they set forth his oracles, and all things are done by God's express commands." From this cause come human sacrifices and the most atrocious tyranny; and the more divine such a government calls itself, the more abominable it is.

All prophets are impostors. Mahomet may have begun as an enthusiast, enamored of his own ideas; but he was soon led away by his reveries; he deceived himself in deceiving others; and finally supported a doctrine which he believed to be good, by necessary imposture. Socrates, who pretended to have a familiar spirit, must have been a little crazy, or a little given to swindling. As for Moses, he is a myth, a form of the Indian Bacchus. The Koran (and consequently the Bible) may be judged by the ignorance of physics which it displays. "This is the touchstone of the books which, according to false religions, were written by the Deity, for God is neither absurd nor ignorant." Several volumes are devoted by Voltaire to showing the inconsistencies, absurdities and atrocities of the Old and New Testaments, and the abominations of the Jews.

The positive religious opinions of Voltaire are less important than his negations, for the work of this great writer was mainly to destroy. He was a theist, of wavering and doubtful faith. He was well aware that any profession of atheism might be dangerous, and likely to injure him at court and with some of his friends. He thought that belief in God and in a future life were important to the safety of society, and is said to have sent the servant out of the room on one occasion when one of the company was doubting the existence of the Deity, giving as a reason that he did not want to have his throat cut. Yet it is probable that his theism went a little deeper than this. He says that matter is probably eternal and self-existing, and that God is everlasting, and self-existing likewise. Are there other Gods for other worlds? It may be so; some nations and some scholars have believed in the existence of two gods, one good and one evil. Surely, nature can more easily suffer, in the immensity of space, several independent beings, each absolute master of its own portion, than two limited gods in this world, one confined to doing good, the other to doing evil. If God and matter both exist from eternity, "here are two necessary entities; and if there be two there may be thirty. We must confess our ignorance of the nature of divinity."

It is noticeable that, like most men on whom the idea of God does not take a very strong hold, Voltaire imagined powers in some respects superior to Deity. Thus he says above that nature can more easily suffer several independent gods than two opposed ones. Having supposed one or several gods to put the universe in order, he supposes an order anterior to the gods. This idea of a superior order, Fate, Necessity, or Nature, is a very old one. It is probably the protest of the human mind against those anthropomorphic conceptions of God, from which it is almost incapable of escaping. Voltaire and the Philosophers almost without exception believed that there was a system of natural law and justice connected with this superior order, taught to man by instinct. Sometimes in their system God was placed above this law, as its origin; sometimes, as we have seen, He was conceived as subjected to Nature. "God has given us a principle of universal reason," says Voltaire, " as He has given feathers to birds and fur to bears; and this principle is so lasting that it exists in spite of all the passions which combat it, in spite of the tyrants who would drown it in blood, in spite of the impostors who would annihilate it in superstition. Therefore the rudest nation always judges very well in the long run concerning the laws that govern it; because it feels that these laws either agree or disagree with the principles of pity and justice which are in its heart." Here we have something which seems like an innate idea of virtue. But we must not expect complete consistency of Voltaire. In another place he says, "Virtue and vice, moral good and evil, are in all countries that which is useful or injurious to society; and in all times and in all places he who sacrifices the most to the public is the man who will be called the most virtuous. Whence it appears that good actions are nothing else than actions from which we derive an advantage, and crimes are but actions that are against us. Virtue is the habit of doing the things which please mankind, and vice the habit of doing things which displease it. Liberty, he says elsewhere, is nothing but the power to do that which our wills necessarily require of us.[1]

[1] Voltaire, xx. 439 (*Siècle de Louis XIV.*, ch. xxxvii.), xxi. 369 (*Louis XV.*, ch. xxxviii.), xv. 34, 40, 123, 316 (*Essai sur les mœurs*),

The Church of France was both angered and alarmed by the writings of Voltaire and his friends, and did her feeble best to reply to them. But while strong in her organization and her legal powers, her internal condition was far from vigorous. Incredulity had become fashionable even before the attacks of Voltaire were dangerous. An earlier satirist has put into the mouth of a priest an account of the difficulties which beset the clergy in those days. "Men of the world," he says, "are astonishing. They can bear neither our approval nor our censure. If we wish to correct them, they think us ridiculous. If we approve of them, they consider us below our calling. Nothing is so humiliating as to feel that you have shocked the impious. We are therefore obliged to follow an equivocal line of conduct, and to check libertines not by decision of character but by keeping them in doubt as to how we receive what they say. This requires much wit. The state of neutrality is difficult. Men of the world, who venture to say anything they please, who give free vent to their humor, who follow it up or let it go according to their success, get on much better.

"Nor is this all. That happy and tranquil condition which is so much praised we do not enjoy in society. As soon as we appear, we are obliged to discuss. We are forced, for instance, to undertake to prove the utility of prayer to a man who does not believe in God; the necessity of fasting to another who all his life has denied the immortality of the soul. The task is hard, and the laugh is not on our side."[1]

xliii. 74 (*Examen important de Lord Bolingbroke*), xxxi. 13 (*Dict. philos. Liberté*) xxxvii. 336 (*Traité de métaphysique*). For general attacks on the Bible and the Jews, see *Œuvres*, xv. 123–127, xliii. 39–205, xxxix. 454–464. Morley's *Diderot*, ii. 178. Notice how many of the arguments that are still repeated nowadays concerning the Mosaic account of the creation, etc. etc., come from Voltaire. Notice also that Voltaire, while too incredulous of ancient writers, was too credulous of modern travelers.

[1] Montesquieu, *Lettres persanes*, i. 210, 211, Lettre lxi.

The prelates appointed to their high offices by Louis XV. and his courtiers were not the men to make good their cause by spiritual weapons. There was no Bossuet, no Fénelon in the Church of France of the eighteenth century. Her defense was intrusted to far weaker men. First we have the archbishops, Lefranc de Pompignan of Vienne and Elie de Beaumont of Paris. Then come the Jesuit Nonnotte and the managers of the Mémoires de Trévoux, the Benedictine Chaudon, the Abbé Trublet, the journalist Fréron, and many others, lay and clerical. The answers of the churchmen to their Philosophic opponents are generally inconclusive. Lefranc de Pompignan declared that the love of dry and speculative truth was a delusive fancy, good to adorn an oration, but never realized by the human heart. He sneered at Locke and at the idea that the latter had invented metaphysics. His objections and those of the Catholic church to that philosopher's teachings were chiefly that the Englishman maintained that thought might be an attribute of matter; that he encouraged Pyrrhonism, or universal doubt; that his theory of identity was doubtful, and that he denied the existence of innate ideas. All these matters are well open to discussion, and the advantage might not always be found on Locke's side. But in general the Catholic theologians and their opponents were not sufficiently agreed to be able to argue profitably. They had no premises in common. If one of two disputants assumes that all ideas are derived from sensation and reflection, and the other, that the most important of them are the result of the inspiration of God, there is no use in their discussing minor points until those great questions are settled. The attempt to reconcile views so conflicting has frequently been made, and no writings are more dreary than those which embody it. But men who are too far apart to cross swords in argument may yet hurl at each other the missiles of vituperation, and there were plenty of combatants to engage in that sort of warfare with Voltaire, Rousseau, and the Encyclopædists.

On the two sides, treatises, comedies, tales, and epigrams were written. It was not difficult to point out that the sayings of the various opponents of the church were inconsistent with each other; that Rousseau contradicted Voltaire, that Voltaire contradicted himself. There were many weak places in the armor of those warriors. Pompignan discourses at great length, dwelling more especially on the worship which the Philosophers paid to physical science, on their love of doubt, and on their mistaken theory that a good Christian cannot be a patriot. Chaudon, perhaps the cleverest of the clerical writers, sometimes throws a well directed shaft. "That same Voltaire," he says, "who thinks that satires against God are of no consequence, attaches great importance to satires written against himself and his friends. He is unwilling to see the pen snatched from the hands of the slanderers of the Deity; but he has often tried to excite the powers that be against the least of his critics." This was very true of Voltaire, who was as thin-skinned as he was violent; and who is believed to have tried sometimes to silence his opponents by the arbitrary method of procuring from some man in power a royal order to have them locked up. Palissot, in a very readable comedy, makes fun of Diderot and his friends. As for invective, the supply is endless on both sides. The Archbishop of Paris condemns the "Emile" of Rousseau as containing a great many propositions that are "false, scandalous, full of hatred of the church and her ministers, erroneous, impious, blasphemous, and heretical." The same prelate argues as follows: "Who would not believe, my very dear brethren, from what this impostor says, that the authority of the church is proved only by her own decisions, and that she proceeds thus: 'I decide that I am infallible, therefore so I am.' A calumnious imputation, my very dear brethren! The constitution of Christianity, the spirit of the Scriptures, the very errors and the weakness of the human mind tend to show that the church established by Jesus Christ is infallible. We declare that, as the Divine Legislator always taught the truth, so his church always teaches it. We therefore prove the authority of the church, not by the church's authority, but by that of Jesus Christ, a process as accurate as the other, with which we are reproached, is absurd and senseless."

The arguments of the clerical writers were not all on this level. Chaudon and Nonnotte prepared a series of articles, arranged in the form of a dictionary, in which the Catholic doctrine is set forth, sometimes clearly and forcibly. But it is evident that the champions of Catholicism in that age were no match in controversy for her adversaries.

The strength of a church does not lie in her doctors and her orators, still less in her wits and debaters, though they all have their uses. The strength of a church lies in her saints. While these have a large part in her councils and a wide influence among her members, a church is nearly irresistible. When they are few, timid and uninfluential, knowledge and power, nay, simple piety itself, can hardly support her. In the Church of France, through the ages, there have been many saints; but in the reigns of Louis XVI. and his immediate predecessor there were but few, and none of prominence. The persecution of the Jansenists, petty as were the forms it took, had

[1] Lefranc de Pompignan, i. 27 (*Instruction pastorale sur la prétendue philosophie des incrédules*). *Dictionnaire antiphilosophique*, republished and enlarged by Grosse under the title *Dictionnaire d'antiphilosophisme*. Palissot, *Les philosophes*. Beaumont's "*mandement*" given in Rousseau, *Œuvres*, vii. 22, etc. See also Barthélemy, *Erreurs et mensonges*, 5me, 13me, 14me Série, articles on *Fréron, Nonnotte, Trublet*, and *Patrouillet*. *Confessions de Fréron*. Nisard, *Les ennemis de Voltaire*. The superiority of the Philosophers over the churchmen in argument is too evident to be denied. Carné, 408.

turned aside from ardent fellowship in the church many of the most earnest, religious souls in France. The atmosphere of the country was not then favorable to any kind of heroism. Such self-devoted Christians as there were went quietly on their ways; their existence to be proved only when, in the worst days of the Revolution, a few of them should find the crown of martyrdom.

CHAPTER VI.

THE NOBILITY.

THE second order in the state was the Nobility. It is a mistake, however, to suppose that this word bears on the Continent exactly the same meaning as in England. Where all the children of a nobleman are nobles, a strict class is created. An English peerage, descending only to the eldest son, is more in the nature of an office. The French *noblesse* in the latter years of the old monarchy comprised nearly all persons living otherwise than by their daily toil, together with the higher part of the legal profession. While the clergy had political rights and a corporate existence, and acted by means of an assembly, the nobility had but privileges. This, however, was true only of the older provinces, the "Lands of Elections," whose ancient rights had been abolished. In some of the "Lands of Estates," which still kept a remnant of self-government, the order was to some extent a political body with constitutional rights.

The nobility have been reckoned at about one hundred thousand souls, forming twenty-five or thirty thousand families, owning one fifth of the soil of France. Only a part of this land, however, was occupied by the nobles for their gardens, parks, and chases. The greater portion was let to farmers, either at a fixed rent, or on the *métayer* system, by which the landlord was paid by a share of the crops. And beside his rent or his portion, the noble received other things from his tenants: payments and services according to ancient custom, days of labor, and occasional dues. He could tramp over the ploughed lands with his servants in search of game, although he might destroy the growing corn. The game itself, which the peasant might not kill, was still more destructive. Such rights as these, especially where they were harshly enforced, caused both loss and irritation to the poor. Although there were far too many absentees among the great families, yet the larger number of the nobles spent most of their time at home on their estates, looking after their farms and their tenants, attending to local business, and saving up money to be spent in visits to the towns, or to Paris. When they were absent, their bailiffs were harder masters than themselves. Unfortunately the eyes of the noble class were turned rather to the enjoyments of the city and the court than to the duties of country life on their estates, an inevitable consequence of their loss of local power.

If the nobles had few political rights, they had plenty of public privileges. They were exempt from the most onerous taxes, and the best places under the government were reserved for them. Therefore every man who rose to eminence or to wealth in France strove to enter their ranks, and since nobility was a purchasable commodity, through the multiplication of venal offices which conferred it, none who had much money to spend failed to secure the coveted rank. Thus the order had come to comprise almost all persons of note, and a great part of the educated class. To describe its ideas and aspirations is to describe those of most of the leaders of France. Nobility was no longer a mark of high birth, nor a brevet of distinction; it was merely a sign that a man, or some of his ancestors, had had property. Of course all persons in the order were not equal. The descendants of the old families, which had been great in the land for hundreds of years, despised the mushroom noblemen of yesterday, and talked contemptuously of "nobility of the gown." Theirs was of the sword, and dated from the Crusades. And under

Louis XVI., after the first dismissal of Necker, there was a reaction, and ground gained by the older nobility over the newer, and by both over the inferior classes. As the Revolution draws near and financial embarrassment grows more acute, the pickings of the favored class have become scarcer, while the appetite for them has increased. Preferment in church or state must no longer go to the vulgar.

There is a distinction among nobles quite apart from the length of their pedigree. We find a higher and a lower nobility, with no clear line of division between them. They are in fact the very rich, whose families have some prominence, and the moderately well off. For it may be noticed that among nobles of all times and countries, although wealth unaided may not give titles and place, it is pretty much a condition precedent for acquiring them. A man may be of excellent family, and poor; but to be a great noble, a man must be rich. In old France the road to preferment was through the court; but to shine at court a considerable income was required; and so the *noblesse de cour* was more or less identical with the richer nobility.

In this small but influential part of the nation, both the good and the bad qualities which are favored by court life had reached a high degree of development. The old French nobility has sometimes been represented as exhibiting the best of manners and the worst of morals. I believe that both sides of the picture have been painted in too high colors. The courtier was not always polite, nor were all great nobles libertines. Faithful husbands and wives were by no means exceptional; although, as in other places, well behaved people did not make a parade of their morality. There is such a thing as a French prig; but prigs are neither common nor popular in France. Before the Revolution the art of pleasing was more studied than it is to-day, — that art by which men and women make themselves agreeable to their acquaintance.

"In old times, under Louis XV. and Louis XVI.," says the Viscount of Ségur, "a young man entering society made what was called a *début*. He cultivated accomplishments. His father suggested and directed this work, for work it was; but the mother, the mother only, could bring her son to that last degree of politeness, of grace and amiability, which completed his education. Beside her natural tenderness, her pride was so much at stake that you may judge what care, what studied pains, she used in giving her children, on their entrance into society, all the charm that she could develop in them, or bestow upon them. Thence came that rare politeness, that exquisite taste, that moderation in speech and jest, that graceful carriage, in short that combination which characterized what was called good company, and which always distinguished French society even among foreigners. If a young man, because of his youth, had failed in attention to a lady, in consideration for a man older than himself, in deference for old age, the mother of the thoughtless young fellow was informed of it by her friends the same evening; and on the following day he was sure to receive advice and reproof."[1]

The instruction thus early given was not confined to forms. Indeed, French society in that day was probably less formal in some ways than any other European society; and in Paris people were more free than in the provinces. Although making a bow was a fine art, although a lady's curtsey was expected to be at once "natural, soft, modest, gracious, and dignified," ceremonious greetings were considered unnecessary, and few compliments were paid. To praise a woman's beauty to her face would have been to disparage her modesty. Good manners

[1] The Viscount of Ségur was brother to the Count of Ségur, from the preface to whose Memoirs this extract is taken.

consisted in no small part in distinguishing perfectly what was due to every one, and in expressing that distinction with lightness and grace. Different modes of address were appropriate toward parents, relations, friends, acquaintances, strangers, your superiors in rank, your poor dependents, yet all must be treated with courtesy and consideration. Such manners are possible only where social distinctions are positively ascertained. In old France, at least, every man had his place and knew where he was.

But it was in their dealings with ladies that the Frenchmen of that day showed the perfection of their system. Vicious they might be, but discourteous they were not. No well-bred man would then appear in a lady's room carelessly dressed, or in boots. In speech between the sexes, the third person was generally used, and a gentleman in speaking to a lady dropped his voice to a lower tone than he employed to men. Gentlemen were careful before ladies not to treat even each other with familiarity. Still less would one of them, however intimate he might be with a lady's husband or brother, speak to her of his friend by any name less formal than his title. These habits have left their mark in France and elsewhere to this day; but the mark is fast disappearing, not altogether to the advantage of social life.[1]

Friendship between men was sometimes carried so far as to interfere with the claims of domestic affection. At least it was faithful and sincere, and the man on whom fortune had frowned, the fallen minister, or the disgraced courtier, was followed in his adversity by the kindness of his friends. Of all the virtues this is perhaps the one which in our hurried age tends most to disappear. It is left for the occupation of idle hours, and the smallest piece of triviality which can be tortured into the name of business, is allowed to crowd away those constantly repeated

[1] Genlis, *Dictionnaire des Etiquettes*, i. 94, 218 ; ii. 194, 347.

attentions which might add a true grace and refinement to the lives of those who gave and of those who received them. It is often said that friendships are formed only in youth. Is not this partly because youth alone will take time to form them? In France, before the Revolution, men of all ages made friendships, and supported them by the consideration for others which is at the bottom of all politeness. The Frenchman is nervous and irritable. When he lets his temper get beyond his control, he is fierce and violent. He has little of the easy-going good-nature under inconveniences, which some branches of the Teutonic race believe themselves to possess. He has less kindly merriment than the Tuscan. But he has trained himself for social life; and has learned, when on his good behavior, to make others happy about him. And it is part of the well-bred Frenchman's pride and happiness to be almost always on his good behavior.

In one respect Paris in the eighteenth century was more like a provincial town than like a great modern capital. Acquaintanceship had not swallowed up intimacy. A man or a woman did not undertake to keep on terms of civility with so many people that he could not find time to see his best friends oftener than once or twice a year. The much vaunted *salons* of the old monarchy were charming, in great measure because they were reasonably organized. An agreeable woman would draw her friends about her; they would meet in her parlor until they knew each other, and would be together often enough to keep touch intellectually. The talker knew his audience and felt at home with it. The listener had learned to expect something worth hearing. The mistress of the house kept language and men within bounds, and had her own way of getting rid of bores. But even French wit and vivacity were not always equal to the demands upon them. "I remember," says Montesquieu, "that I once had the curiosity to count how many times I should hear a little story, which certainly did not deserve to be told or remembered; during three weeks that it occupied the polite world, I heard it repeated two hundred and twenty-five times, which pleased me much."[1]

Beside the tie of friendship we may set that of the family. In old France this bond was much closer than it is in modern America. If a man rose in the world, the benefit to his relations was greater than now; and there was no theory current that a ruler, or a man in a position of trust, should exclude from the places under him those persons with whom he is best acquainted, and of whose fidelity to himself and to his employers he has most reason to be sure. On the other hand, a disgrace to one member of a family spread its blight on all the others, and the judicial condemnation of one man might exclude his near relations from the public service — a state of things which was beginning to be repugnant to the public conscience, but which had at least the merit of forming a strong band to restrain the tempted from his contemplated crime.

In fact, the old idea of the family as an organic whole, with common joys, honors, and responsibilities, common sorrows and disgraces, was giving way to the newer notion of individualism. In France, however, the process never went so far as it has done in some other countries, including our own.

Good manners were certainly the rule at the French court, but there were exceptions, and not inconspicuous ones, for Louis XV. was an unfeeling man, and Louis XVI. was an awkward one. When Mademoiselle Genet, fifteen years old, was first engaged as reader to the former king's daughters, she was in a state of agitation easy to imagine. The court was in mourning, and the great rooms hung with black, the state armchairs on platforms, several steps above the floor, the feathers and the shoul-

[1] *Œuvres*, vii. 179 (*Pensées diverses*).

der-knots embroidered with tinsel made a deep impression on her. When the king first approached, she thought him very imposing. He was going a-hunting, and was followed by a numerous train. He stopped short in front of the young girl and the following dialogue took place: —

"Mademoiselle Genet, I am told that you are very learned; that you know four or five foreign languages."

"I know only two, sir," trembling.

"Which are they?"

"English and Italian."

"Do you speak them fluently?"

"Yes, sir, very fluently."

"That's quite enough to put a husband out of temper;" and the king went on, followed by his laughing train, and left the poor little girl standing abashed and disconsolate.[1]

The memoirs of the time are full of stories proving that the rigorous enforcement of etiquette and the general training in good manners had not done away with eccentricity of behavior. The Count of Osmont, for instance, was continually fidgeting with anything that might come under his hand, and could not see a snuff-box without ladling out the snuff with three fingers, and sprinkling it over his clothes like a Swiss porter. He sometimes varied this pleasant performance by putting the box itself under his nose, to the great disgust of whomever happened to be its owner. He once spent a week at the house of Madame de Vassy, a lady who was young and good-looking enough, but stiff and ceremonious. This lady wore a skirt of crimson velvet over a big panier, and was covered with pearls and diamonds. Madame de Vassy would not reprove Monsieur d'Osmont in words for his method of treating her magnificent golden snuff-box; but used to get up from her place at the card-table as soon as he had so used it, empty all the snuff into the fireplace, and ring for more. D'Osmont, meanwhile, would go on

[1] Campan, i. pp. vi. viii.

without noticing her, laugh and swear over his cards, and get in a passion with himself if the luck ran against him. Yet when he was not playing, the man was lively, modest and amiable, and except for his fidgety habits, had the tone of the best society.[1]

That which above all things distinguished the French nobility, and especially the highest ranks of it, from the rest of mankind was the amount of leisure which it enjoyed. Most people in the world have to work, most aristocracies to govern. The English gentleman of the eighteenth century farmed his estates, acted as a magistrate, took part in politics. Living in the country, he was a mighty hunter. The French nobleman, unless he were an officer in the army (and even the officers had inordinately long leave of absence), had nothing to do but to kill time. Only the poorer country gentlemen ever thought of farming their own lands. For the unemployed nobles of Paris, there was but occasional sport to be had. Indeed, the Frenchman, although he likes the more violent and tumultuous kinds of hunting, is not easily interested in the quieter and more lasting varieties of sport. He will joyfully chase the wild boar, when horses, dogs, and horns, with the admiration of his friends and servants, concur to keep his blood boiling; but he will not care to plod alone through the woods for a long afternoon on the chance of bringing home a brace of woodcock; nor can he mention fishing without a sneer. Being thus deprived of the chief resource by which Anglo-Saxons combine activity and indolence, the French nobility cultivated to their highest pitch those human pleasures which are at once the most vivid and the most delicate. They devoted themselves to society and to love-making. Too quick-witted to fall into sloth, too proud to become drunkards or gluttons, they dissipated their lives in conversation and stained their souls with intrigue. Never, probably, have the arts which

[1] Dufort, ii. 46.

make social intercourse delightful been carried to so high a degree of excellence as among them. Never perhaps, in a Christian country, have offenses against the laws of marriage been so readily condoned, where outward decency was not violated, as in the upper circles of France in the century preceding the Revolution.

The vice of Parisian society under Louis XV. and his grandson presented a curious character. Adultery had acquired a regular standing, and connections dependent upon it were openly, if tacitly recognized. Such illicit alliances were even governed by a morality of their own, and the attempt to induce a woman to be unfaithful to her criminal lover might be treated as an insult.[1] But this pedantry of vice was not always maintained. There were men and women in high life who changed their connections very frequently, yielding to the caprice of the moment, as the senses or the wit might lead them. Such people were not passionate, but simply depraved; yet the mass of the community, deterred partly by fear of ridicule, and partly by the Philosophic spirit which had decided that chastity was not a part of natural morals, did not visit them with very severe condemnation.

If eccentricity sometimes overrode etiquette and even politeness, good morals and religion not infrequently made a stand against corruption. There were loving wives and careful mothers among the highest nobility. Of the Duchess of Ayen we get a description from her children. Her mansion was in the Rue St. Honoré, and had a garden running back almost to that of the Tuileries (for the Rue de Rivoli was not then in existence). The house was known for the beauty of its apartments, and for the superb

[1] Witness Rousseau and Mme. d'Houdetot in the *Confessions*. Mlle. d'Aydie was accounted very virtuous for dissuading her lover from marrying her, even after the birth of her child, for fear of injuring his prospects. Yet the match would not seem, to modern ideas, to have been a very unequal one.

collection of pictures which it contained. After dinner, which was served at three o'clock, the duchess would retire to her bedchamber, a large room hung with crimson damask, and take her place in a great armchair by the fire. Her books, her work, her snuff-box, were within reach. She would call her five girls about her. These, on chairs and footstools, squabbling gently at times for the places next their mother, would tell of their excursions, their lessons, the little events of every day. There was nothing frivolous in their education. Their old nurse had not filled their minds with fairy tales, but with stories from the Old Testament and with anecdotes of heroic actions.

The pleasures of these girls were simple. Once or twice in a summer they went on a visit to their grandfather, the Marshal de Noailles at Saint Germain en Laye. In the autumn they spent a week with their other grandfather, Monsieur d'Aguesseau at Fresnes. An excursion into the suburbs, a ride on donkeys on the slopes of Mont Valérien, made up their innocent dissipations. Their most frivolous excitement was to see their governess fall off her donkey.

The piety of the duchess might in some respects appear extravagant. Her fourth daughter had two beggars of the parish for god-parents, as a constant reminder of humility. The same child was of a violent and willful disposition, but was converted at the age of eleven and became mild, patient, and studious. The conversion of so young a sinner, and the seriousness with which the event was treated by the family, seem rather to belong to the atmosphere of Puritanism than to that of the Catholicism of the eighteenth century. But if the religion of the Duchess of Ayen sometimes led her to fantastic extremes, these were not its principal characteristics. Her piety was applied to the conduct of her daily life and to the education of her daughters in honesty, reasonableness, and self-devotion. Their faith and hers were to be tested by the hardest trials, and to be victorious both in prison and on the scaffold. We are fortunate in possessing their biographies. In how many cases at the same time and in the same country did similar virtues go unrecorded?[1]

As for the smaller nobility, the "sparrow hawks,"[2] living in the country, they dwelt among their less exalted neighbors, doing good or evil as the character of each one of them directed. Sometimes we find them on friendly terms with the villagers, acting as godfathers and godmothers to the children, summoning the peasants to take part in the chase, or to dance in the courtyard of the castle. We find them endowing hospitals, giving alms, keeping an eye on the conduct of the village priest. A continual interchange of presents goes on between the cottage and the great house. A new lord is welcomed by salvos of musketry, the ladies of his family are met by young girls bearing flowers. Such relations as these are said to have grown less common as the great Revolution drew near. It has often been remarked of the Vendée and Brittany, where a larger proportion of lords resided on their estates than was the case elsewhere, that a friendlier feeling was there cultivated between the upper and the lower classes; and that it was in those provinces that a stand was made by lords and peasants alike for the maintenance of the old order of things. In some parts of the country the peasants and their lords were continually quarreling and going to law. The royal intendant was besieged with complaints. The poor could not get their pay for their work. They received blows instead of money. Arrogance and injustice on the one side were met by impudence and fraud on the other. The old leadership had passed away. The upper class had lost its power and its responsibility; it insisted the

[1] Vide Madame de Lafayette, Mme. de Montagu.
[2] *Hobéraux.*

more tenaciously on its privileges. Exemption from certain taxes was the chief of these, but there were others as irritating if less important. Quarrels arose with the priest about the lord's right to be first given the holy water. One vicar in his wrath deluged his lordship's new wig.

In general, we may conceive of the lesser nobles, deprived of their useful function of regulating and administering the country, leading somewhat penurious and useless lives. They hunted a good deal, they slept long. Generally they did not eat overmuch, for gluttony is not a vice of their race. They grumbled at the ascendency of the court, and at the new army-regulations. They preserved in their families the noble virtues of dignity and obedience. Children asked their parents' blessing on their knees before they went to bed. The elder Mirabeau, the grim Friend of Men, still knelt nightly before his mother in his fiftieth year. The children honored their parents in fact as well as in form, and took no important step in life without paternal consent. The boys ran rather wild in their youth, but settled down at the approach of middle life; the oldest inheriting the few or barren paternal acres; the younger sons equally noble, and thus debarred from lucrative occupations, pushing their fortunes in the army. The girls were married young or went into a convent. Marriages were arranged entirely by the parents. "My father," said a young nobleman, "I am told that you have agreed on a marriage for me. Would you be kind enough to tell me if the report be true, and what is the name of the lady?" "My son," answered his parent, "be so good as to mind your own business, and not to come to me with questions." [1]

[1] Babeau, *Le Village*, 158. Ch. de Ribbe, 169. Mme. de Montagu, 57. Genlis, *Dictionnaire des Etiquettes*, i. 71. Lavergne, *Les Economistes*, 127.

CHAPTER VII.

THE ARMY.

THE nobility of France was essentially a military class. Its privileges were claimed on account of services rendered in the field. The priests pray, the nobles fight, the commons pay for all; such was the theory of the state. It is true that the nobility no longer furnished the larger part of the armies; that the old feudal levies of ban and rearban, in which the baron rode at the head of his vassals, were no longer called out. But still the soldier's life was considered the proper career of the nobleman. A large proportion of the members of the order were commissioned officers, and most officers were members of the order.

The rule which required proofs of nobility as a prerequisite to obtaining a commission was not severely enforced in the reign of Louis XV., and in the earlier years of his successor. In many regiments it was usual to promote one or two deserving sergeants every year. In others the necessary certificate of birth could be signed by any nobleman and was often obtained from greed or good-nature. Moreover, an order of 1750 had provided that officers of plebeian extraction should sometimes be ennobled for distinguished services. But in 1781, a new rule was established. No one could thenceforth receive a commission as second lieutenant who could not show four generations of nobility on his father's side, counting himself. Thus were all members of families recently ennobled excluded from the service, and no door was left open to the military ambition of people belonging to the middle class; although that class was yearly increasing in importance. Moreover, strict genealogical proofs were required, the candidate for a commission having to submit his papers to the royal herald. Exceptions were made in favor of the sons of members of the military order of Saint Louis.[1]

But all nobles were not on the same footing in the army. Among the regimental officers two classes might be distinguished. There were, on the one hand, the ensigns, lieutenants, captains, majors, and lieutenant-colonels, who generally belonged to the poorer nobility. They served long and for small pay, with little hope of the more brilliant rewards of the profession. They did their work and stayed with their regiments, although leave of absence was not difficult to obtain in time of peace. Their lives were hard and frugal, a captain's pay not exceeding twenty-five hundred livres, which was perhaps doubled by allowances. On the other hand were the colonels and second colonels, young men of influential families, who, at most, passed through the lower ranks to learn something of the duties of an officer. Their commissions were procured by favor. There was scarce a bishop about the court who did not have a candidate for a colonelcy, scarcely a pretty woman who did not aspire to make her friend a captain. The rich young men, thus promoted, threw their money about freely in camp and garrison. Thus if the nobility had exclusive privileges, the court had privileges that excluded those of the rest of the nobility, and in the very last days of the old monarchy, these also were enhanced. The Board of War in 1788, decided that no one should become a general officer who had not

---

[1] Ségur, i. 82, 158. Chérest, i. 14. *Anciennes lois françaises*, 22d May, 1781. The regiments to which the regulation applies are those of French infantry (not foreign regiments), cavalry, light horse, dragoons, and *chasseurs à cheval*. This would seem to exclude the artillery and engineers. The foreign regiments appear to have been included in a later order. Chérest, i. 24.

previously been a colonel; and colonels' commissions, besides being very expensive, were given, as above stated, by favor alone. Thus on the eve of the Revolution were the bands of privilege drawn tighter in France.[1]

The colonels thus appointed were generally not wanting in courage. The French nobility of all degrees was ready enough to give its blood on the battle-field. Thus the son of the Duke of Boufflers, fourteen years old, had been made colonel of the regiment which bore the name of his family. The duke served as a lieutenant-general in the same army. Fearing that the boy might not know how to behave in battle, the father, on the first occasion, obtained permission from the Marshal, Maurice de Saxe, commander of the army, to accompany his son as a volunteer. The boy's regiment was ordered to attack the intrenched village of Raucoux. The young colonel and his father, followed by two pages, led their men against the intrenchments. When they reached the works, the duke took his son in his arms and threw him over the parapet. He himself followed, and both came off unhurt, but the two pages were shot dead.[2]

In America, as in Europe, the young favorites of fortune were ready enough to fight. Such men as Lauzun, Ségur, or the Viscount of Noailles asked nothing better than adventures, whether of war or love; but in peace they could not be looked on as satisfactory or hard-working officers. Yet they and their like continued to get advancement. Ordinances might be passed from time to time, requiring age or length of service, but ordinances in old France did not apply to the great. The poorer nobility might grumble, but the court families continued to get the good places. The lieutenant-colonels and the other working officers of the army had but little chance of rising to be general officers. Even before the order of 1788, promotion fell to the courtier colonels. The baton

[1] Ségur, i. 154. Chérest, ii. 90. [2] Montbarey, i. 38.

of the marshals of France was placed in the hands only of the very highest nobility. All over Europe in the seventeenth and eighteenth centuries, armies were often commanded by men born to princely rank. That this did not necessarily mean that they were ill commanded may be shown by the names of Turenne and Condé, Maurice de Saxe and Eugene of Savoy, Prince Henry of Prussia and Frederick the Great.

While the higher commands were thus monopolized (or nearly so) by the rich and powerful, the poorer nobility flocked into the army, to occupy the subordinate ranks of commissioned officers. Sometimes they came through the military schools. The most important of these had been founded at Paris in 1750, by the financier Paris-Duverney. Here several hundred young gentlemen, mostly born poor and preferably the sons of officers, received a military education. The boys came to the school from their homes in the country between the ages of nine and eleven, rustic little figures sometimes, in wooden shoes and woolen caps, like the peasant lads who had been their early playmates. They were taught the duties of gentlemen and officers, cleanliness, an upright carriage, the manual and tactics, and something of military science. Other schools, kept by monks, existed in the provinces where the young aspirants for commissions learned engineering and the theory of artillery. But many young noblemen entered their career by a process more in accordance with youthful tastes. We find boys in camp in time of war, evading the orders which forbade entering the service before the age of sixteen. Children of twelve and thirteen are wounded in battle.[1]

As the only form of active life in which most nobles could take part was found in the army, there was always too large a number of officers, and too great a proportion of the military expenses was devoted to them. In 1787

[1] Babeau, *Vie militaire*, ii. 7, 45. Montbarey, i. 18.

hardly more than one in three of those holding commissions was in active service. The number of soldiers under Louis XVI. was less than a hundred and fifty thousand actually with the colors. There were thirty-six thousand officers, on paper; thirteen thousand actively employed. The soldiers cost the state 44,100,000 livres a year, the officers 46,400,000 livres.[1]

The relation between the officers and the soldiers of the old French army was more intimate and kindly than that existing in any other European army of the time. For both, their regiment was a home, and the military service a lifelong profession. They had entered it young, and they hoped to die in it. Their relation to each other had become a part of the structure of their minds; a condition of coherent thought. A soldier might rise from the ranks and become a lieutenant, or even a captain, but such promotion was infrequent; few common soldiers had the education or the means to aspire to it. On the other hand, the command of a company was sometimes almost hereditary. The captain might be lord of the village in which his soldiers were born. In that case he would care for them in sickness, and perhaps even grant a furlough when the private was much needed by his family at home. His own chance of promotion was small. He expected to do the work of his life in that company, among those soldiers, with perhaps his younger brother, or, in time, his son, as his lieutenant. It would seem that in the years immediately preceding the French Revolution these kindly relations were in some measure dying out. The captain was no longer so closely connected with his company as he had been. Officialism was taking the place of those personal connections which had characterized the feudal system. The gulf between soldiers and officers, if not harder to cross for the ambitious, separated the com-

[1] Babeau, *Vie militaire*, i. 15; ii. 90, 145. Necker, *De l'Administration*, ii. 415, 418.

monplace members of each group more widely from those of the other.¹

The private soldiers of King Louis XVI., who stood in long white lines on parade at Newport, while their many colored flags floated above and the officers brandished their spontoons in front, or who rushed in night attack on the advanced redoubt at Yorktown, were not, like modern European soldiers, brought together by conscription. They were, nominally at least, volunteers. Unruly lads, mechanics out of work, runaway apprentices, were readily drawn into the service by skillful recruiting officers. Thirty years before, it had been the custom of these landsharks to cheat or bully young men into the service. The raw youth, arriving in Paris from the country, had been offered by a chance acquaintance a place as servant in a gentleman's family, and after signing an engagement had found himself bound for eight years to serve His Majesty, in one of his regiments of foot. The young barber-surgeon had waked from a carouse with the king's silver in his pocket. Such things were still common in Germany. In France some effort had been made to regulate the activity of the recruiting officers. Complaints of force or fraud in enlistment received attention from the authorities. The soldiers of Louis XVI., therefore, were engaged with comparative fairness. The infantry came mostly from the towns, the cavalry and artillery from the country. The soldiers were derived from the lowest part of the population. Whether they improved or deteriorated in the service depended on their officers. In any case they became entirely absorbed in it. The soldier did not keep even the name by which he had been known in common life. He assumed, or was given, a *nom de guerre* such as La Tulippe, La Tendresse, Pollux, Pot-de-Vin, Vide-bouteille, or Va-de-bon-cœur. His term of service

¹ Babeau, *Vie militaire*, i. 43, 189. Montbarey, ii. 272. Moore's *View*, i. 365.

was seven or eight years, but he was by no means sure of getting a fair discharge at the end of it; and was in any case likely to reënlist. Thus the recruit had in fact entered upon the profession of his life.[1]

The uniforms of the day were ill adapted to campaigning. The French soldier of the line wore white clothes with colored trimmings, varying according to his regiment. On his head was perched the triangular cocked hat of the period, standing well out over his ears, but hardly shading his eyes. Beneath it his hair was powdered, or rather, pasted; for the powder was sifted on to the wet hair, and caked in the process. The condition of the mass after a rainy night at the camp-fire may be imagined. In some regiments the wearing of a moustache was required, and those soldiers whom nature had not supplied with such an ornament were obliged to put on a false one, fastened with pitch, which was liable to cause abcesses on the lip. Sometimes a fine, uniform color was produced in the moustaches of a whole regiment by means of boot-blacking. Broad white belts were crossed upon the breast. The linen gaiters, white on parade, black for the march, came well above the knee, and a superfluous number of garters impeded the step. It was a tedious matter to put these things on; and if a pebble got in through a button-hole, the soldier was tempted to leave it in his shoe, until it had made his foot sore. Uniforms were seldom renewed. The coat was expected to last three years, the hat two, the breeches one.[2]

All parts of the soldier's uniform were tight and close fitting. I think that this was learned from the Prussians. The ideal of the army as a machine seems to have origi-

---

[1] Babeau, *Vie militaire*, i. 55, 136, 182. Mercier, x. 273. Ségur, i. 222; *Encyc. méth. Art milit.* ii. 177 (*Désertion*).

[2] Babeau, *Vie militaire*, i. 93. *Encyc. méth. Art milit.* i. 589 (*Chaussure*) ii. 179. Susane, ix. (*Plates*). See also a very interesting little book by a great man, Maurice de Saxe, *Les Rêveries*.

nated, or at least to have been first worked out in Germany. Such an ideal was a natural consequence of the military system of the age. Of the soldiers of Frederick the Great only one-half were his born subjects. Other German princes enlisted as many foreigners as they could. In the French army were many regiments of foreign mercenaries. Nowhere was the pay high, or the soldier well treated. Desertion was very common. Under these circumstances mechanical precision became an invaluable quality. The soldier must be held in very strict bands, for if left free he might turn against the power that employed him.

The connection between a rigid system in which nothing is left to the soldier's intelligence or initiative, and a tight uniform, which confines his movements, is both deep and evident. If a man is never to have his own way, his master will inevitably find means to make him needlessly uncomfortable. As the modern owner of a horse sometimes diminishes the working power of the animal by check-reins and martingales, so the despot of the eighteenth century buckled and buttoned his military cattle into shape, and made them take unnatural paces. But even under these disadvantages the French soldiers surpassed all others in grace and ease of bearing. Officers were sometimes accused of sacrificing the efficiency of their commands to appearances. The evolutions of the troops involved steps more appropriate to the dancing-master than to the drill sergeant.[1] Such criticisms as these have often been made on the French soldier by his own countrymen and by foreigners. But those who think he can be trifled with on this account, are apt to find themselves terribly mistaken.

The food of the soldiers was coarse and barely sufficient. The pay was so absorbed by the requirements of the uniform, many of the smaller parts of which were at

[1] Montbarey, ii. 272.

THE ARMY. 91

the expense of the men, and by the diet, that little was left for the almost necessary comforts of drink and tobacco. The barracks, handsome outside, were close and crowded within. During this reign orders were given that only two men should sleep in a bed. In some garrisons soldiers were still billeted on the inhabitants. In sickness they were better cared for than civilians, the military hospitals being decidedly better than those open to the general public.[1]

If we compare the material condition of the French soldier in the latter years of the old monarchy with that of other European soldiers of his day, we shall find him about as well treated as they were. If we compare those times with these, we shall find that he is now better clothed, but not better fed than he was then.[2]

"The soldiers are very clean," writes an English traveler in France in the year 1789; "so far from being meagre and ill-looking fellows, as John Bull would persuade us, they are well-formed, tall, handsome men, and have a cheerfulness and civility in their countenances and manner which is peculiarly pleasing. They also looked very healthy, great care is taken of them."[3]

The period of twenty-five years that preceded the Revolution was a time of attempted reform in the French army. The defeats of the Seven Years' War had served as a lesson. The Duke of Choiseul, the able minister of Louis XV., abolished many abuses. The manœuvres of the troops became more regular, the discipline stricter and more exact for a time. The Duke of Aiguillon ousted Choiseul, by making himself the courtier of the strumpet

[1] Lafayette told the Assembly of Notables in 1787 that the food of the soldiers was insufficient for their maintenance. *Mémoires*, i. 215. Ségur, i. 161.
[2] Babeau, *Vie militaire*, i. 374.
[3] Rigby, 13.

Du Barry, and things appear to have slipped back. Then the old king died, and Aiguillon followed his accomplice into exile. Louis XVI. found his finances in disorder, his army and navy demoralized. The death of the minister of war in 1775 gave him the opportunity to make one of his well-meant and feeble attempts at reform. He called to the ministry an old soldier, the Count of Saint-Germain, who had for some time been living in retirement. The count had seen much foreign service, was in full sympathy neither with the French army nor with the French court, and was moreover a man who had little knack at getting on with anybody. He had written a paper on military reforms, and thus attracted notice. In vain, when in office, he attacked some crying abuses, especially the privileges granted to favored regiments and favored persons. While he disgusted the court in this way, he raised a storm of indignation in the army by his love of foreign innovations, and especially of one practice considered deeply degrading. This was the punishment of minor offenses by flogging with the flat of the sword; using a weapon especially made for that purpose. The arguments in favor of this punishment are obvious. It is expeditious; it is disagreeable to the sufferer, but does not rob the state of his services, nor subject him to the bad influences and foul air of the guard-house. The objections are equally apparent. Flogging, which seems the most natural and simple of punishments to many men in an advanced state of civilization, is hated by others, hardly more civilized, with a deadly hatred. In the former case it inflicts but a moderate injury upon the skin; in the latter, it strikes deep into the mind and soul. It would be hard to say beforehand in which way a nation will take it. The English soldier of Waterloo, like the German of Rossbach, received the lash almost as a joke. The Frenchman, their unsuccessful opponent on those fields, could hardly endure it. Grenadiers wept at inflicting the sword stroke, and their colonel mingled his tears with theirs. "Strike with the point," cried a soldier, "it hurts less!"

To some of the foreigners in the French service this sensitiveness seemed absurd. The Count of Saint-Germain consulted, on the subject, a major of the regiment of Nassau, who had risen from the ranks. "Sir," said the veteran, "I have received a great many blows; I have given a great many, and all to my advantage."[1]

The spirit of reform was in the air, and ardent young officers would let nothing pass untried. The Count of Ségur tells a story of such an one; and although no name be given, he seems to point to the brother-in-law of Lafayette, the brave Viscount of Noailles.

"One morning," says Ségur, "I saw a young man of one of the first families of the court enter my bedroom. I had been his friend from childhood. He had long hated study, and thought only of pleasure, play, and women. But recently he had been seized with military ardor, and dreamed but of arms, horses, school of theory, exercises, and German discipline.

"As he came into my room, he looked profoundly serious; he begged me to send away my valet. When we were alone: 'What is the meaning, my dear Viscount,' said I, 'of so early a visit and so grave a beginning? Is it some new affair of honor or of love?'

"'By no means,' said he, 'but it is on account of a very important matter, and of an experiment that I have absolutely resolved to make. It will undoubtedly seem very strange to you; but it is necessary in order to en-

---

[1] Ségur, i. 80. Mercier, vii. 212. Besenval, ii. 19. Allonville. *Mém. sec.* 84. Montbarey, i. 311. Flogging in some form and German ways in general seem to have been introduced into the French army as early as Choiseul's time, and more or less practiced through the reign of Louis XVI.; but the great discontent appears to date from the more rigorous application of such methods by Saint-Germain. Montbarey. Dumouriez, i. 370 (liv. ii. ch. iii.).

lighten me on the great subject we are all discussing; we can judge well only of what we have ourselves undergone. When I tell you my plan you will feel at once that I could intrust it only to my best friend, and that none but he can help me to execute it. In a word, here is the case: I want to know positively what effect strokes with the flat of the sword may have on a strong, courageous, well-balanced man, and how far his obstinacy could bear this punishment without weakening. So I beg you to lay on until I say "Enough."'

"Bursting out laughing at this speech, I did all I could to turn him aside from his strange plan, and to convince him of the folly of his proposal; but it was useless. He insisted, begged and conjured me to do him this pleasure, with as many entreaties as if it had been a question of getting me to render him some great service.

"At last I consented and resolved to punish his fancy by giving him his money's worth. So I set to work; but, to my great astonishment, the sufferer, coldly meditating on the effect of each blow, and collecting all his courage to support it, spoke not a word and constrained himself to appear unmoved; so that it was only after letting me repeat the experiment a score of times that he said: 'Friend, it is enough. I am contented; and I now understand that this must be an efficacious method of conquering many faults.'

"I thought all was over; and up to that point the scene had seemed to me simply comic; but just as I was about to ring for my valet to dress me, the Viscount, suddenly stopping me, said: 'One moment, please; all is not finished; it is well that you should make this experiment, too.'

"I assured him that I had no desire to do so, and that it would by no means change my opinion, which was entirely adverse to an innovation so opposed to the French character.

" 'Very well,' answered he, 'but I ask it not for your sake but for mine. I know you; although you are a perfect friend, you are very lively, a little fond of poking fun, and you would perhaps make a very amusing story of what has just happened between us, at my expense, among your ladies.'

" 'But is not my word enough for you?' I rejoined.

" 'Yes,' said he, 'in any more serious matter; but anyway, if I am only afraid of an indiscretion, that fear is too much. And so, in the name of friendship, I beg you, set me completely at ease on that point by taking back what you have been kind enough to lend me so gracefully. Moreover, I repeat it, believe me, you will profit by it and be glad to have judged for yourself this new method that is so much discussed.'

"Overcome by his prayers, I let him take the fatal weapon; but after he had given me the first stroke, far from imitating his obstinate endurance, I quickly called out that it was enough, and that I considered myself sufficiently enlightened on this grave question. Thus ended this mad scene; we embraced at parting; and in spite of my desire to tell the story, I kept his secret as long as he pleased."[1]

The discipline of the French army, like that of other bodies, military and civil, depended much less on regulations than on the individual character of the men in command for the time being. France was engaged in but one war during the reign of Louis XVI., and in that war the land forces were occupied only in America. "The French discipline is such," writes Lafayette to Washington from Newport, "that chickens and pigs walk between the lines without being disturbed, and that there is in the camp a cornfield of which not one leaf has been touched." And Rochambeau tells with honest pride of apples hanging on

[1] Ségur, i. 84.

the trees which shaded the soldier's tents. "The discipline of the French army," he says, "has always followed it in all its campaigns. It was due to the zeal of the generals, of the superior and regimental officers, and especially to the good spirit of the soldier, which never failed." But Rochambeau was a working general, and Lafayette had done his best in France that, as far as was possible, the French commander in America should have working officers under him. Neither in war nor in peace have the French always been famous for their discipline; and the discontent which had been caused by the changes above mentioned had not tended to strengthen it in the closing years of the monarchy. "Whatever idea I may have formed of the want of discipline and of the anarchy which reigned among the troops," says Besenval, "it was far below what I found when I saw them close," and circumstances confirm the testimony of this not over-trustworthy witness.[1]

It was in the latter part of the previous reign that the adventure of the Count of Bréhan had taken place; but the story is too characteristic to be omitted, and the spirit which it showed continued to exist down to the very end of the old monarchy.

The Count of Bréhan, after serving with distinction in the Seven Years' War, had retired from the army, and devoted his time to society and the fine arts. He was called to Versailles one day by the Duke of Aiguillon, prime minister to Louis XV., his friend and cousin. "I have named you to the king," said the duke, "as the only man who would be able to bring the Dauphiny regiment into a state of discipline. The line officers, by their insubordinate behavior, have driven away several colonels in succession. If I were offering you a favor, you might refuse; but this is an act of duty, and I have assured the king that you would undertake it."

[1] *Washington*, vii. 518. Rochambeau, i. 255, 314. Fersen, i. 39, 57. Besenval, ii. 36.

"You do me justice," answered Bréhan. "I will take the command of the regiment, but I must make three conditions. I must have unlimited power to reward and punish; I must be pardoned if I overstep the regulations; and if I succeed in bringing the regiment into good condition, I am not to be obliged to keep it for more than a year."

His conditions granted, Bréhan set out for Marseilles, where the regiment was quartered. On his arrival in that city, he put up at a small and inconspicuous inn, and, dressed as a civilian, made his way on foot to a coffee-house, which was said to be a favorite lounging-place of the officers of the Dauphiny regiment. Taking a seat, he listened to the conversation going on about him, and soon made out that the insubordinate subalterns were talking about their new colonel, and of the fine tricks they would play him on his arrival. Picking out two young officers who were making themselves particularly conspicuous, he interrupted their conversation.

"You do not know," he says, "the man whom you want to drive away. I advise you to mind what you do, or you may get into a scrape."

"Who is this jackanapes that dares to give us advice?"

"A man who will not stand any rudeness, and who demands satisfaction!" cries Bréhan, unbuttoning his civilian's coat and showing his military order of Saint Louis.

So he goes out with the young fellows, and all the way to the place where they are to fight, he chaffs and badgers them. This puts them more and more out of temper, so that when they reach the ground they are very much excited, while he is perfectly cool. He wounds them one after the other; then, turning to the witnesses: "Gentlemen," says he, "I believe I have done enough, for a man who has been traveling night and day all the way from Paris. If anybody wants any more, he can easily find me. I am not one of the people who get out of the way."

Thereupon he leaves them, goes back to his inn, puts on his uniform, calls on the general commanding the garrison, and sends orders to the officers of the Dauphiny regiment to come and see him. These presently arrive, and are thoroughly astonished when they recognize the man whom they met in the coffee-house, and who has just wounded two of their comrades. But Bréhan pretends not to know any of them, speaks to all kindly, tells them of the severe orders that he bears in case of insubordination, and expresses the hope and conviction that there will be no trouble. He then asks if all the officers of the regiment are present. They answer that two gentlemen are ill. "I will go to see them," says the new colonel, "and make sure that they are well taken care of." He does in fact visit his late adversaries, and finds them in great trepidation. They try to make excuses, but Bréhan stops them. "I do not want to know about anything that happened before I took command," he says, "and I am quite sure that henceforth I shall have only a good report to make to the king of all the officers of my regiment, with whom I hope to live on the best of terms."

By this firm and conciliatory conduct, the Count of Bréhan inspired the Dauphiny regiment with respect and affection. He restored its discipline and left it when his service was over, much regretted by all its officers.[1]

The lieutenants of the French army were united in an association called the Calotte. The legitimate object of this society was to lick young officers into shape, by obliging them to conform to the rules of politeness and proper behavior, as understood by their class. For this purpose the senior lieutenant of each regiment was the chief of the regimental club, and there was a general chief for the whole army. Offenses against good manners, faults of meanness, or oddity of behavior, were discour-

[1] Allonville, i. 162.

aged by admonitions, given privately by the chief, or publicly in the convivial meetings of the club. Moral pressure might be carried so far in an aggravated case, as to cause the culprit to resign his commission. The society in fact represented an organized professional spirit; and although not recognized by the regulations, was favored by the superior officers.[1]

When discipline was relaxed, the Calotte assumed too great powers. Not content with moral means, it undertook to enforce its decrees by physical ones; and it extended its jurisdiction far above the rank of lieutenant.

At the outbreak of the war between France and England in 1778, two camps were formed in Normandy and Brittany for the purpose of training the army, and perhaps with some intention of making a descent on the English coast. The young French officers swarmed to these camps and divided their time between drill and pleasure. On one occasion, seats had been reserved on a hill for some Breton ladies, who were to see the manœuvres. Two colonels, escorting two ladies of the court who had recently arrived from Paris, undertook to appropriate the chairs for their companions. A squabble such as is common on such occasions was the result.

The Count of Ségur, above mentioned, was acting as aide-de-camp to the commanding general. A few days after the quarrel about the chairs, just as he was going to begin a game of prisoners' base, two officers who were his friends informed him privately that the Calotte had ordered the two colonels who had given offense on that occasion to be publicly tossed in blankets and that the sentence was about to be carried out. Ségur, to gain time, ordered the drummers to beat an alarm. The game

---

[1] Calotte = scull cap, here fool's-cap. Concerning this society, see a series of *feuilletons* in the *Moniteur Universel*, Nov. 25th to 30th, 1864 by Gen. Ambert; also *Encyclopédie méthodique*, *Art militaire. Militaire*, iv. 101–103 (article *Calotte*); Ségur, i. 132.

was broken up, every officer ran to his colors, and the aide-de-camp hastened to explain the matter to the astonished general. The proposed punishment was deferred and finally prevented; but the escape from a scandalous breach of discipline had been a narrow one.

As the Revolution drew nearer, its spirit became evident in the army. The Count of Guibert, the most talented and influential member of the Board of War in 1788, was the object of satire and epigram. The younger officers conspired to spoil the success of his manœuvres. The experiments that had been tried, the frequent changes in the regulations, had unsettled their ideas. In their reaction against the disagreeable rigor of German discipline, they protested that English officers alone, and not the machine-like soldiers of a despot, were the models for freemen. The common soldiers caught the spirit of insubordination from those who commanded them. Especially, the large regiment of French Guards, a highly privileged body, permanently quartered in Paris, was infected with the spirit of revolt. Its men were conspicuous in the early troubles of the Revolution, acting on the side of the mob.[1]

The militia of old France does not call for a long notice. It consisted of from sixty to eighty thousand men, whose chief duty was in garrison in time of war, and who during peace were not kept constantly together, but asembled from time to time for drill. As the term of service was six years, the number of men drawn did not exceed fifteen thousand annually. This was surely no great drain on a population of twenty-six millions. Militia duty was greatly hated, however. This appears to have been because men did not volunteer for it, but were drafted; and because many persons were exempted from the draft. This immunity covered not only the sons of aged parents who were dependent on them for support, but privileged

[1] Chérest, i. 552. Miot de Mélito, i. 3.

persons of all sorts, from apothecaries to advocates, gentlemen and their servants and game-keepers. The burden was thus thrown entirely on the poorer peasantry.[1]

The navy in the time of Louis XVI. reached a high state of efficiency. The war of 1778 to 1783 was in great measure a naval war, and although the French and their allies were worsted in some of the principal actions, the general result may be held to have been favorable to them. The navy at the outbreak of hostilities consisted of about seventy ships of the line, and as many frigates and large corvettes, with a hundred smaller vessels. These ships were built on admirable models, for the French marine architects were well-trained and skillful; but the materials and the construction were not equal in excellence to the design. The invention of coppering the ships' bottoms, and thus adding to their speed, although generally practiced in England, had been applied in France only to the smaller part of the navy. The French, however, had an advantage over the English in the fact that ships of the same nominal class were in reality larger and broader of beam among the former than among the latter, so that the French were sometimes able to fight their lower batteries in rough water, when the English had to keep their lower ports closed.

The naval officers of France were almost all noblemen, and received a careful professional training. Yet the practice of transferring officers of high rank from the army to the navy had not been completely abandoned. Thus d'Estaing, who commanded with little distinction on the North American coast in 1778, was no sailor, but a lieutenant-general, artificially turned into a vice-admiral. Such cases, however, were not common, and in general the French commanders erred rather by adhering too closely to naval rule, than by want of professional training. In the navy, as elsewhere, no great original talent

[1] Broc, i. 117; Babeau, Le Village, 259.

was developed during this reign, which was a time of expectation rather than of action.

The men, like the officers, were good and well-trained, except when the lack of sailors obliged the government to employ soldiers on shipboard. It is noticeable that the seamen bore the rope's end with equanimity, although the landsmen were so much offended at flogging with the flat of the sword. Nor do I find any complaint of want of discipline at sea.

The administration of naval affairs was less satisfactory than the ships or the crews. The magazines were not well provided; and the stores were probably bad, for the fleets were subject to epidemics.[1]

In general the navy appears to have suffered less than the army from the fermentation of the public mind. Marine affairs must always remain the concern of a special class of men, cut off by absorbing occupations from the interests and sympathies of the rest of mankind.

[1] Chabaud - Arnault, 189, 196, 214.   Charnock, iii. 222, 282. Ségur, i. 138.   Chevalier.

CHAPTER VIII.

THE COURTS OF LAW.

WHILE the greater and more conspicuous part of the French nobility lived by the sword, a highly respectable portion of the order wore the judicial gown. Prominent in French affairs in the eighteenth century we find the Parliaments, a branch of the old feudal courts of the kings of France, retaining the function of high courts of justice, and playing, moreover, a certain political part. In the Parliament of Paris, on solemn occasions, sat those few members of the highest nobility who held the title of Peers of France. With these came the legal hierarchy of First President, presidents à mortier and counselors, numbering about two hundred. The members were distributed, for the purposes of ordinary business, among several courts, the Great Chamber, five courts of Inquest, two courts of Petitions, etc.[1] The Parliament of Paris possessed original and appellate jurisdiction over a large part of central France, — too large a part for the convenience of suitors, — but there were twelve provincial parliaments set over other portions of the kingdom. The members of these courts, and of several other tribunals of inferior jurisdiction, formed the magistracy, a body of great dignity and importance.

We have seen that the church possessed certain political rights; that it held assemblies and controlled taxes. The political powers of the Parliaments were more limited, amounting to little more than the right of solemn remonstrance. Under a strong monarch, like Louis XIV., this

[1] Grand' Chambre, Cour des Enquêtes, Cour des Requêtes.

power remained dormant; under weak kings, like his successors, it became important.

The method of passing a law in the French monarchy was this. The king, in one of his councils, issued an edict, and sent it to the Parliament of Paris, or to such other Parliaments as it might concern, for registration. If the Parliament accepted the edict, the latter was entered in its books, and immediately promulgated as law. If the Parliament did not approve, and was willing to enter on a contest with the king and his advisers, it refused to register. In that case the king might recede, or he might force the registration. This was done by means of what was called a *bed of justice*. His Majesty, sitting on a throne (whence the name of the ceremony), and surrounded by his officers of state, personally commanded the Parliament to register, and the Parliament was legally bound to comply. As a matter of fact, it did sometimes continue to remonstrate; it sometimes adjourned, or ceased to administer justice, by way of protest; but such a course was looked on as illegal, and severe measures on the part of the king and his counselors — the court, as the phrase went, — were to be expected. These measures might take the form of imprisonment of recalcitrant judges, or of exile of the Parliament in a body. Sometimes new courts of justice, more closely dependent on the king's pleasure, were temporarily established. Such were the Royal Chamber and the famous Maupeou Parliament under Louis XV., the Plenary Court of Louis XVI. Had these monarchs been strong men, the new courts would undoubtedly have superseded the old Parliaments altogether; as it was, they led only to confusion and uncertainty.[1]

Throughout the reign of Louis XV. the Parliament of Paris was fighting against the church, while the court repeatedly changed sides, but oftener inclined to that of the clergy. The controversy was theological in its origin,

[1] Du Boys, *Hist. du droit criminel de la France*, ii. 225, 239.

the magistrates being Jansenist in their proclivities, while the Church of France was largely controlled by the Molinist, or Jesuit party. The contest was long and doubtful, neither side obtaining a full victory. It was the fashion in the Philosophic party to represent the whole matter as a miserable squabble. Yet, apart from the importance of the original controversy, which touched the mighty but insoluble questions of predestination and free-will, the quarrel had a true interest for patriotic Frenchmen. The Roman Church was contending for the absolute and unlimited control of religious matters; the Parliament for the supremacy of law in the state.

In the reign of Louis XVI. the Parliament was principally engaged in struggles of another character. The magistrates were members of a highly privileged class. Their battle was arrayed for vested rights against reforms. From the time of Turgot to that of Loménie de Brienne and the Notables, the Parliament of Paris, sometimes in sympathy with the nation, sometimes against it, was vigorously resisting innovations. Yet so great was the irritation then felt against the royal court that the Parliament generally gained a temporary popularity by its course of opposition.

The courts of justice, and especially the Parliaments, were controlled by men who had inherited or bought their places.[1] This, while offering no guarantee of capacity, assured the independence of the judges. As the places were looked on as property, they were commonly transmitted from father to son, and became the basis of that nobility of the gown which played a large part in French

---

[1] Under Louis XIV. the price of a place of *président à mortier* was fixed at 350,000 livres, that of a *maitre des requêtes* at 150,000 livres, that of a counselor at 90,000 to 100,000 livres. The place of First President was not venal, but held by appointment. Martin, xiii. 53 and *n*. The general subject of the venality of offices is considered in the chapter on Taxation.

affairs. The owner of a judicial place was obliged to pass an examination in law, before he could assume its duties and emoluments. This examination differed in severity at different times and in the different Parliaments. In the latter part of the eighteenth century it would appear to have been very easy at Paris, but harder in some of the provinces. The Parliaments, in any case, retained control over admission to their own bodies. Although they could not nominate, they could refuse certificates of capacity and morality. They insisted that none but counselors should be admitted to the higher places, and that candidates should be men of means, "so that, in a condition where honor should be the only guide, they might be able to live independently of the profits accessory to their labors, which should never have any influence." This caution was especially necessary as the judges were paid in great measure by the fees, or costs, which under the quaint name of spices were borne by the parties. Originally these fees had in fact consisted of sugar plums, not more than could be eaten in a day, but subsequently they had been commuted and increased until they amounted to considerable sums.[1]

By requiring pecuniary independence and social position, together with a certain amount of learning and of personal character, the tone of the upper courts was kept good, the magistrates being generally among the most learned, solid, and respectable men in France. They seem also to have been hard-working and honest, although prejudiced in favor of their own privileged class. As the Revolution drew near, they fell into the common weakness of their age and country, the worship of public opinion, and the love of popularity. We find the Parliament of Paris undergoing, and even courting, the applause of the mob in its own halls of justice. Like the great Assembly which was soon to have in its hands the destinies of

---

[1] Bastard d'Estang, i. 122, 245; Du Boys, 535.

France, the most dignified court of justice in the land failed to perceive that the deliberative body that allows itself to be influenced or even interrupted by spectators, will soon, and deservedly, lose respect and power.[1]

When we pass from the consideration of the political functions of the Parliaments, and of their composition, to that of the ordinary administration of justice, we are struck by the diversity of the law in civil matters, and by its severity in criminal affairs. The kingdom of France, as it existed in the eighteenth century, was made up of many provinces and cities, various in their history. Each one had its local customs and privileges. The complication of rules of procedure and rights of property was almost infinite. The body of the law was derived from sources of two distinct kinds, from feudal custom and from Roman jurisprudence. The customs which arose, or were first noted, in the Middle Ages, originating as they did in the manners of barbarian tribes, or in the exigencies of a rude state of society, were products of a less civilized condition of the human mind than the laws of Rome. From a very early period, therefore, the most intelligent and educated lawyers all over Europe were struggling, more or less consciously, to bring customary feudal law into conformity with Roman ideas. These legists recognized that in many matters the custom had definitely fixed the law; but whenever a doubtful question arose, they looked for guidance to the more perfect system. "The Roman law," they said, "is observed everywhere, not by reason of its authority, but by the authority of reason." This idea was peculiarly congenial to the tone of thought current in the eighteenth century.

[1] De Tocqueville praises the independence of the old magistrates, who could neither be degraded nor promoted by the government, Œuvres, iv. 171 (*Ancien Régime*, ch. xi.). Montesquieu, iii. 217 (*Esp. des lois*, liv. v. ch. xix.). Mirabeau, *L'Ami des hommes*, 212, 219. Bastard d'Estang, ii. 611, 621. Grimm, xi. 314.

Even in England the common and customary law was enlarged at that time and adapted to new conditions in accordance with Latin principles, by the genius of Lord Mansfield and other eminent lawyers. In France the process began earlier and lasted longer. Domat, d'Aguesseau, and Pothier were but the successors of a long line of jurists. By the time of Louis XVI., some uniformity of principle had been introduced; but everywhere feudal irregularity still worried the minds of Philosophers and vexed the temper of litigants. The courts were numerous and the jurisdiction often conflicting. The customs were numberless, hardly the same for any two lordships. To the subjects of Louis XVI., believing as they did that there was a uniform, natural law of justice easily discoverable by man, this state of things seemed anomalous and absurd. "Shall the same case always be judged differently in the provinces and in the capital? Must the same man be right in Brittany and wrong in Languedoc?" cries Voltaire. And the inconvenience arising from this excessive variety of legal rights, together with the vexatious nature of some of them, did more perhaps than any other single cause to engender in the men of that time their too great love of uniformity.[1]

It has been said that the judges of the higher courts were generally honest. In the lower courts, and especially in those tribunals which still depended on the lords, oppression and injustice appear to have been not uncommon. The bailiffs who presided in them were often partial where the interests of the lords whose salaries they received were concerned. And even when we come to

---

[1] "Servatur ubique jus romanum, non ratione imperii, sed rationis imperio." Laferriere, i. 82, 532. See Ibid., i. 553 n., for a list of eighteen courts of extraordinary jurisdiction, and of five courts of ordinary jurisdiction, viz.; 1, Parlemens, 2, Présidiaux, 3, Baillis et sénéchaux royaux, 4, Prévôts royaux, 5, Juges seigneuriaux. Voltaire, xxi. 419 (*Louis XV.*), Sorel, i. 148.

the practice before the Parliaments, the American reader will sometimes be struck with astonishment at the extent to which members of those high tribunals were allowed by custom to be influenced by the private and personal solicitation of parties. The whole spirit of the continental system of civil and criminal law is here at variance with that of the Anglo-Saxon system. English and American judges are like umpires in a conflict; French judges like interested persons conducting an investigation. The latter method is perhaps the better for unraveling intricate cases, but the former would seem to expose the bench to less temptation. A judge who is long closeted with each of the contestants alternately must find it harder to keep his fingers from bribes and his mind from prejudice than a judge who is prevented by strict professional etiquette from seeing either party except in the full glare of the court-room, and from listening to any argument of counsel, save where both sides are represented. Accusations of bribery, even of judges, were common in old France. The lower officers of the court took fees openly. Thick books, under the name of *mémoires*, were published, with the avowed intention of influencing the public and the courts in pending cases.[1]

One judicial abuse especially contrary to fair dealing had become very common. Powerful and influential persons could have their cases removed from the tribunals in which they were begun, and tried in other courts where from personal influence they might expect a more favorable result. It was not only the royal council that could draw litigation to itself. The practice was widespread. By a writ called *committimus*, the tribunal by which an action was to be tried could be changed.

[1] For a statement that influential persons went unpunished in criminal matters and got the better of their adversaries in civil matters by means of *lettres de cachet*, and for instances, see Bos. 148; a long list of iniquitous judgments, Ibid., 190, etc.

This appears to have been a frequent cause of failure of justice.

As for the criminal proceedings of the age, there was hardly a limit to their cruelty. Under Louis XV. the prisons were filthy dens, crowded and unventilated, true fever-holes. A private cell ten feet square, for a man awaiting trial, cost sixty francs a month. Large dogs were trained to watch the prisoners and to prevent their escape. Twice a year, in May and September, the more desperate convicts left Paris for the galleys. They made the journey chained together in long carts, so that eight mounted policemen could watch a hundred and twenty of them. The galleys at Toulon appear to have been less bad than the prisons in Paris. They were kept clean and well-aired, and the prisoners were fairly well fed and clothed; but some of them had been imprisoned for forty, fifty, or even sixty years. They were allowed to work for themselves and to earn a little money. They were divided into three classes, deserters, smugglers, and thieves, distinguished by the color of their caps.[1]

Torture was regarded as a regular means for the discovery of crime. It was administered in various ways, the forms differing from province to province. They included the application of fire to various parts of the body, the distension of the stomach and lungs by water poured into the mouth, thumbscrews, the rack, the boot. These were but methods of investigation, used on men and women whose crime was not proved. They might be repeated after conviction for the discovery of accomplices. The greater part of the examination of accused persons was carried on in private, and during it they were not allowed counsel for their defense. They were confronted but once with the witnesses against them, and that only after those witnesses had given their evidence and were liable to the penalties of perjury if they retracted it. Many

[1] Mercier, iii. 265, x. 151. Howard, *Lazarettos*, 54.

offenses were punishable with death. Thieving servants might be executed, but under Louis XVI. public feeling rightly judged the punishment too severe for the offense, so that masters would not prosecute nor judges condemn for it.[1]

Other criminals did not escape so easily. A most barbarous method of execution was in use. The wheel was set up in the principal cities of France. The voice of the crier was heard in the streets as he peddled copies of the sentence. The common people crowded about the scaffold, and the rich did not always scorn to hire windows overlooking the scene. The condemned man was first stretched upon a cross and struck by the executioner eleven times with an iron bar, every stroke breaking a bone. The poor wretch was then laid on his back on a cart wheel, his broken bones protruding through his flesh, his head hanging, his brow dripping bloody sweat, and left to die. A priest muttered religious consolation by his side. By such sights as these was the populace of the French cities trained to enjoy the far less inhuman spectacle of the guillotine.[2]

It was not until the middle of the century that men's minds were fairly turned toward the reform of the criminal law. Yet eminent writers had long pointed out the

[1] Counsel were not allowed in France for that important part of the proceedings which was carried on in secret. Voltaire, xlviii. 132. In England, at that time, counsel were not allowed of right to prisoners in cases of felony; but judges were in the habit of straining the law to admit them. Strictly they could only instruct the prisoner in matters of law. Blackstone iv. fol. 355 (ch. 27). The English seem for a long time to have entertained a wholesome distrust of confessions. Blackstone, *ubi supra*. How far is the Continental love of confessions derived from the church; and how far is the love of the church for confessions a result of the ever present busybody in human nature?

[2] Mercier, iii. 267. Howard says that the gaoler at Avignon told him that he had seen prisoners under torture sweat blood. *Lazarettos*, 53.

inutility of torture. "Torture-chambers are a dangerous invention, and seem to make trial of patience rather than of truth," says Montaigne; but he thinks them the least evil that human weakness has invented under the circumstances. Montesquieu advanced a step farther. He pointed out that torture was not necessary. "We see to-day a very well governed nation [the English] reject it without inconvenience." . . . "So many clever people and so many men of genius have written against this practice," he continues, "that I dare not speak after them. I was about to say that it might be admissible under despotic governments, where all that inspires fear forms a greater part of the administration; I was about to say that slaves among the Greeks and Romans, — but I hear the voice of nature crying out against me." Voltaire attacked the practice in his usual vivacious manner; but, with characteristic prudence suggested that torture might still be applied in cases of regicide.[1]

Such scattered expressions as these might long have remained unfruitful. But in 1764 appeared the admirable book of the Milanese Marquis Beccaria, and about thirteen years later the Englishman John Howard published his first book on the State of the Prisons. Beccaria shared the ideas of the Philosophers on most subjects. Where he differed from them, it was as Rousseau differed, in the direction of socialism. But in usefulness to mankind few of them can compare with him. From him does the modern world derive some of its most important ideas concerning the treatment of crime. Extreme, like most of the Philosophers of his age; unable, like them, to recognize the proper limitations of his theories, he has yet transformed the thought of civilized men on one of the

---

[1] Montaigne, ii. 36 (liv. ii. ch. v). So I interpret the last words of the chapter. Montesquieu, iii. 260 (*Esprit des Lois*, liv. vi. ch. 17). Voltaire, xxxii. 52 (*Dict. philos. Question*), xxxii. 391 (*Ibid., Torture*).

most momentous subjects with which they have to deal. So great is the change wrought in a hundred years by his little book, that it is hard to remember as we read it that it could ever have been thought to contain novelties. "The end of punishment ... is no other than to prevent the criminal from doing farther injury to society, and to prevent others from committing the like offense." "All trials should be public." "The more immediately after the commission of a crime the punishment is inflicted, the more just and useful it will be." "Crimes are more effectually prevented by the *certainty* than by the severity of punishment." These are the commonplaces of modern criminal legislation. The difficulty lies in applying them. In the eighteenth century their enunciation was necessary. "The torture of a criminal during his trial is a cruelty consecrated by custom in almost every nation," says Beccaria. Indeed it seems to have been legal in his day all over the Continent, although restricted in Prussia and obsolete in practice in Holland. Beccaria opposed torture entirely, on broad grounds. As to torture before condemnation he holds it a grievous wrong to the innocent, "for in the eye of the law, every man is innocent whose crime has not been proved. Besides, it is confounding all relations to expect that a man should be both the accuser and the accused, and that pain should be the test of truth; as if truth resided in the muscles and sinews of a wretch in torture. By this method the robust will escape and the weak will be condemned." The penalties proposed by Beccaria are generally mild, — he would have abolished that of death altogether, — his reliance being on certainty and not on severity of punishment.[1]

It was not to be expected that Beccaria's book should work an immediate change in the manners of Christendom. The criminal law remained unaltered at first, in theory and practice. But the consciences of the more

[1] Beccaria, *passim*. Lea, *Superstition and Force*, 515.

advanced thinkers were affected. In 1766, at Abbeville, a young man named La Barre was convicted of standing and wearing his hat while a religious procession was passing, singing blasphemous songs, speaking blasphemous words, and making blasphemous gestures. There was much popular excitement at the time on account of the mutilation of a crucifix standing on a bridge in the town, but La Barre was not shown to have been concerned in this outrage. The judges at Abbeville appear to have laid themselves open to the accusation of personal hostility to him. The young man, having been tortured, was condemned to make public confession with a rope round his neck, before the church of Saint Vulfran, where the injured crucifix had been placed, to have his tongue cut out, to be beheaded, and to have his body burned. This outrageous sentence was confirmed by the Parliament of Paris. The superstitious king, Louis XV., would not grant a pardon. The capital sentence was executed, but the cutting out of the tongue was omitted, the executioner only pretending to do that part of his work. La Barre's head fell, amid the applause of a cruel crowd which admired the skillful stroke of the headsman. A thrill of indignation, not unmixed with fear, ran through the liberal party in France. The anger and grief of Voltaire were loudly expressed. It was at least an improvement on the state of public feeling in former generations that such severity should not have met with universal acquiescence.[1]

The practice of torture was not without defenders. One of them asked what could be done to find stolen money if the thief refused to say where he had hidden it. But this was not his only argument. "The accused himself," he said, "has a guarantee in torture, which makes him a judge in his own case, so that he becomes able to

---

[1] The best account of the affair of La Barre which I have met is in Desnoiresterres, *Voltaire et Rousseau*, 465.

avoid the capital punishment attached to the crime of which he is accused." And this writer confidently asserts that for a single example which might be cited in two or three centuries of an innocent man yielding to the violence of torture, a million cases of rightful punishment could be mentioned.[1]

Yet the march of progress was fairly rapid in the latter part of the eighteenth century. In the jurisprudence of that age a distinction was made between preparatory torture, which was administered to suspected persons to make them confess, and previous torture, which was inflicted on the condemned, previous to execution, to obtain the accusation of accomplices. The former of these, by far the greater disgrace to civilization, was abolished in France on the 24th of August, 1780; the latter not until 1788, and then only provisionally. Thus was one of the greatest of modern reforms accomplished before the Revolution. About the same time many ordinances were passed for the amelioration of French prisons. They were about as bad as those of other countries, and that was very bad indeed.[2]

The courts of law did not act against persons alone. The Parliament of Paris was in the habit of passing condemnation on books supposed to contain dangerous matter. The suspected volume was brought to the bar of the court by the advocate general, the objectionable passages were read, and the book declared to be "heretical, schismatical, erroneous, blasphemous, violent, impious," and con-

[1] Muyard de Vougland, quoted in Du Boys, ii. 205.
[2] *Question préparatoire ; question préalable*, sometimes called *q. définitive*. Desmaze, *Supplices*, 177. Desjardins, p. xx. Howard, *passim*. The English have long boasted that torture is not allowed by their law ; and although the *peine forte et dure* was undoubted torture, the boast is in general not unfounded. Torture was abolished in several parts of Germany in the eighteenth century, but lingered in other parts until the nineteenth. It was not done away in Baden until 1831. Lea, *Superstition and Force*, 517.

demned to be burned by the public executioner. Then a fagot was lighted at the foot of the great steps which may still be seen in front of the court-house in Paris. The street boys and vagabonds ran to see the show. The clerk of the court, if we may believe a contemporary, threw a dusty old Bible into the fire, and locked the condemned book, doubly valuable for its condemnation, safely away in his book-case.[1]

As for the author, the Parliament would sometimes proceed directly against him, but oftener he was dealt with by an order under the royal hand and seal, known as a *lettre de cachet*.[2] Arbitrary imprisonment, without trial, is a thing so outrageous to Anglo-Saxon feelings that we are apt to forget that it has until recent years formed a part of the regular practice of most civilized nations. It is considered necessary to what is called the *police* of the country, a word for which we have in English no exact equivalent. Police, in this sense, not only punishes crime, but averts danger. Acts which may injure the public are prevented by guessing at evil intentions; and criminal enterprises are not allowed to come to action.

This sort of protection is a part of the function of every government; but on the Continent, in old times, and still in some countries, long and painful imprisonment of men who had never been convicted of any crime was considered one of the proper methods of police. It was justified in some measure in French eyes by the fact that secrecy saved the feelings of innocent families, which thus did not suffer in the public estimation for the misdeeds of one unruly member. In France, where the family is much

---

[1] Mercier, iv. 241.

[2] The *lettre de cachet* was written on paper, signed by the king, and countersigned by a minister. It was so sealed that it could not be opened without breaking the seal. It was reputed a private order. Larousse.

more of a unit than in English-speaking countries, the disgrace of one person belonging to it affects the others far more seriously. The *lettre de cachet* of old France, confining its victim in a state prison, was too elaborate a method to be used with the turbulent lower classes — for them there were less dignified forms of proceeding; but it was freely employed against persons of any consequence. Spendthrifts and licentious youths were shut up at the request of their relations. Authors of dangerous books were readily clapped into the Bastille, Vincennes or Fors l'Evêque. Voltaire, Diderot, Mirabeau, and many others underwent that sort of confinement; and the first of them is said to have procured by his influence the incarceration of one of his own literary enemies. Fallen statesmen were fortunate when they did not pass from the cabinet to the prison, but were allowed the alternative of exile, or of seclusion in their own country houses. But this was not the worst. The *lettre de cachet* was too often the instrument of private hate. Signed carelessly, or even in blank, by the king, it could be procured by the favorite or the favorite's favorite, for his own purposes. And if the victim had no protector to plead his cause, he might be forgotten in captivity and waste a lifetime.

For such abuses as this, there is no remedy but publicity. If, on the one hand, too much has been made of the romantic story of the Bastille, which was certainly not a standing menace to most peaceable Frenchmen, too great stress, on the other hand, may be laid on the undoubted fact that under Louis XVI. the grim old fortress contained but few prisoners, and that some of them were persons who might have been cast into prison under any system of government. In the reign of that king's immediate predecessor great injustice had been committed. Nor had arbitrary proceedings been entirely renounced by the government of Louis XVI. itself. In the very last year before that in which the Estates General met at

Versailles, the royal ministers imprisoned in the Bastille twelve Breton gentlemen, whose crime was that they importunately presented a petition from the nobles of their province. The apartments which they were to occupy were filled with other prisoners, so room was made by removing these unhappy occupants to the madhouse at Charenton, whence they were released only in the following year by order of a committee of the National Assembly.[1]

[1] Barère, i. 281. Perhaps the most terrifying thing about the Bastille was that no one really knew what went on inside. Mercier thinks that the common people were not afraid of it, iii. 287, 289.

CHAPTER IX.

EQUALITY AND LIBERTY.

It was as a privileged order that the Nobility of France principally excited the ill-will of the common people. The more thoughtful Frenchmen of the eighteenth century, all of them at least who have come to be known by the name of Philosophers, set before themselves two great ideals. These were equality and liberty. The aspiration after these was accompanied in their minds by contempt for the past and its lessons, misunderstanding of the benefits which former ages had bequeathed to them, and hatred of the wrongs and abuses which had come down from earlier times. Among them the word gothic was a violent term of reproach, aimed indiscriminately at buildings, laws, and customs. History, with the exception of that of Sparta, was thought to consist far more of warnings than of models. Just before the Revolution, a number of persons who had met in a lady's parlor were discussing the education of the Dauphin. "I think," said Lafayette, "that he would do well to begin his History of France with the year 1787."

This tendency to depreciate the past was due in a measure to the preference, natural to lively minds, for deductive over inductive methods of thought. It is so much easier and pleasanter to assume a few plausible general principles and meditate upon them, than to amass and compare endless series of dry facts, that not by long chastening will the greater part of the world be brought to the more arduous method. Nor should enthusiasm for one of the great processes of thought cause contempt of the other. Even the great inductive French philosopher of the eighteenth century, Montesquieu, failed in a measure to grasp the continuity of history; and drew the facts for his study rather from China and from England than from France, rather from the Roman republic than the existing monarchy. Fear of the censor and of the civil and ecclesiastical tribunals, which would not bear the open discussion of questions of present interest, doubtless added to this tendency.

The idea of equality at first seems simple, but equality may be of many kinds. Absolute equality in all respects between two human beings, no one has ever seen, and no one perhaps has ever thought of desiring. All the relations of life are founded on inequality. By their differences husband and wife, friend and friend, are made necessary and endeared to each other; the parent protects and serves the child, the child obeys and helps the parent; the citizen calls on the magistrate to guard his rights, the magistrate enforces the laws which have their sanction in the consent of the body of citizens. Equality as a political ideal is therefore a limited equality. It may extend to condition, it may be confined to civil rights, or to opportunities.

The Philosophers of the eighteenth century, followed by a school in our day, universally assumed that an approximate equality of condition was desirable. Rousseau agreed with Montesquieu, in believing that a small republic, none of whose citizens were either very rich or very poor, was likely to be in a desirable condition. Virtue, they thought, would be its especial characteristic. In some of the Swiss cantons, and later in the struggling American colonies of Great Britain, Frenchmen discovered communities approaching their ideal in respect to the equal distribution of wealth; and their discovery in the latter case was not without great results. This kind of equality has since passed away from large portions of

America, as it must always disappear where civilization increases. Good people mourn its departure; some few, perhaps, would patiently endure its return. They are about as numerous as those who abandon city life to dwell permanently in the country, also the home of comparative equality of condition. The theoretic admiration for this sort of equality was shared by a large and enlightened part of the French nobility. Thus the order was weakened by the fact that many of its own members did not believe in its claims.

Another kind of equality is that of civil rights. Before the Revolution, France was ruled by law, but all Frenchmen were not ruled by the same law. There were privileged persons and privileged localities. Of these anomalies, sometimes working hardship, the minds of intelligent men at that time were especially impatient. They believed, as has been said, in natural laws, implanted in every breast, finding their expression in every conscience; and many of them entertained a crude notion that such laws could easily be applied to the enormously complicated facts of actual life. Assuming such laws to exist, as absolute as mathematical axioms and far easier of application, all variation was error, all anomaly absurd, all claims of a privileged class unfair and unfounded.

Equality of civil rights is also desired from the fear of oppression; a very important motive in the eighteenth century, when the great still had the power to be very oppressive at times. We have seen the treatment which Voltaire received at the hands of a member of one of the great families. Outrages still more flagrant appear to have been not uncommon in the reign of Louis XV., and although there had probably never been a time in France so free from them as that of his sucesssor, their memory was still fresh. It is in their decrepitude that political abuses are most ferociously attacked. When young and lusty they are formidable.

Again, there is equality of opportunity. This is desired as a means of subverting equality of condition to our own advantage, as a chance to be more than equal to our fellow-men. This kind is longed for by the able and ambitious. Where it is denied, the strongest good men will be less useful to the state, unless they happen to be favorably placed at birth; the strongest bad men perhaps more dangerous, because more discontented. It is this sort of equality, more than any other, which the French Philosophers and their followers actually secured for Frenchmen, and in a less degree for other Europeans of to-day. By their efforts, the chance of the poor but talented child to rise to power and wealth has been somewhat increased. This chance, when they began their labors, was not so hopeless as it is often represented. It is not now so great as it is sometimes assumed to be. Still, there has been one decided advance. We have seen that under the old monarchy many important places were reserved for members of the noble class, and practically for a few families among them. Since that monarchy passed away, the opportunity to serve the state, with the great prizes which public life offers to the strong and the aspiring, has been thrown open, theoretically at least, to all Frenchmen.

If the idea of equality be comparatively simple, that of liberty is very much the reverse. The word, in its general sense, signifies little more than the absence of external control. In politics it is used, in the first place, for the absence of foreign conquest, and in this sense a country may be called free although it is governed by a despot. The next signification of liberty is political right, and this is the sense in which it has been most used until recent years. When a tyrant overthrew the liberties of a Greek city, he substituted his own personal rule for the rights of an oligarchy. The mass of the inhabitants may have been neither better nor worse off than before. When

Hampden resisted the encroachments of King Charles I., he was fighting the battle of the upper and middle classes against despotism, and we hold him one of the principal champions of liberty. Indeed, liberty in this sense is so far from being identical with equality, that many of those who have been foremost in its defense have been members of aristocracies and holders of slaves. To accuse them of inconsistency is to be misled by the ambiguous meaning of a word. They fought for rights which they believed to be their own; they denied that the rights of all men were identical. During the eighteenth century in France, certain bodies, such as the clergy and the Parliament of Paris, were struggling for political liberties in this older sense, and before the outbreak of the French Revolution many of the most enlightened of the nobility hoped to acquire such liberties. Much blood and confusion might have been spared, and many useful reforms accomplished, had Frenchmen clutched less wildly at the phantom of equality, and sought the safer goal of political liberty.

Another sort of liberty, although it has undoubtedly been desired by individuals in all ages, is almost entirely modern as an ideal for civilized communities. This is the absence of interference, not only of a foreign power, or of a lawless oppressor, but of the very law itself. The desire for such freedom as this, would in almost all ages of the world have been held inconsistent with proper respect for order and security. It would have been considered no more than the wicked longing of an unchastened spirit, the temptation of the Evil One himself. In the eighteenth century, however, we see the rise of new opinions. It may be that order had become so firmly established in the European world that a reaction could safely set in. At any rate we find a new way of looking at things. "Independence," a word which had been often used by the clerical party, and always as a term of reproach, is treated by the Philosophers with favor. Toleration of all kinds of opinions, and of most kinds of spoken words, is making way.[1] A new school of thinkers is adapting the new form of thought to economical matters. *Laissez faire; laissez passer.* Restrict the functions of government. Order will arise from the average of contending interests; the right direction is produced by the sum of conflicting forces. The doctrine has exerted enormous influence since the French Revolution in resisting the claims of socialism, — that new form of tyranny in which all are to be the despot and each the slave. But few of the Philosophers accepted it entirely. Most of them desired the constant interference of the government for one purpose or another, and many believed in the power, almost the omnipotence, of a mythical personage, borrowed in part from Plutarch and commonly called the Legislator.

The history and action of this personage may be roughly stated as follows. Every nation now civilized was in early days in a barbarous condition. Once upon a time, a great man came from somewhere, and brought a complete set of laws, morals, and manners with him. To these laws and customs he generally ascribed a divine origin. The nation to which they were proclaimed adopted them, and the people's subsequent happiness and prosperity were in proportion to their excellence. The reasons which are supposed to have induced the barbarous tribe to change all its habits at the bidding of one man are seldom given, or if given, are ludicrously inadequate. The theory of the legislator is now out of date. It is generally held that the institutions of every race have grown up with it, that they are appropriate to its nature and history, gradually modified sometimes by act of the national will, and more or less changed under foreign influences, but that their general character cannot sud-

---

[1] In spite of the impatience shown by Voltaire of any criticism of himself, he and his followers did more than any other men that ever lived to make criticism free to all writers.

denly be subverted. Its institutions thus as truly belong to a civilized race, as the skin without fur or the erect position belong to mankind. There is some evidence in support of either theory, and the truth will probably be found to lie between them, although nearer to the latter. Yet the effect of a higher civilization implanted on a lower one seems at times singularly rapid. The story of the legislator is a part of most early histories and mythologies. The classical model has generally been held to be either Minos or Lycurgus. There were few clever men in France between the years 1740 and 1790 who did not dream of trying on the sandals of those worthies.

While the ideas attached to equality and to liberty were vague and indefinite, it was generally assumed that they would coincide. Liberty and equality, however, have tendencies naturally opposed to each other. Remove the exterior forces which control the wills of men, overturn foreign domination, give every citizen political rights, reduce the interference of laws to a minimum, and the natural differences and inequalities of physical, mental, and moral strength, or power of will, inherent in mankind, will have the fuller opportunity to act. The strong improve their natural advantage, they acquire dominion over their weaker neighbors, they monopolize opportunities for themselves, their friends and their children. Only by keeping all men in strict subjection to something outside of themselves can all be kept in comparative equality. This fact was instinctively apprehended by one school of French thinkers. We shall see that the followers of Rousseau, while posing as champions of Liberty, were in fact the founders of a system which is the very antithesis of individual freedom.[1]

---

[1] It is perhaps needless to remark that I have touched here only on the political meanings of the word Liberty. In the eighteenth century the word was much used in its philosophical sense, and the eternal problem of necessity and free-will was warmly discussed.

CHAPTER X.

MONTESQUIEU.

ONE man stands out among the French nobility of the gown in the eighteenth century, influencing human thought beyond the walls of the court-room; one Philosopher who looks on existing society as something to be saved and directed. The work of Voltaire and his followers was principally negative. Their favorite task was demolition. The ugly and uninhabitable edifices of Rousseau's genius required for their erection a field from which all possible traces of civilized building had been removed. But Montesquieu, while he satirized the vices of the society which he saw about him, yet appreciated at their full value the benefits of civilization. He recognized that change is always accompanied by evil, even if its preponderating result be good, and that it should be attempted only with care and caution. His ideas influenced the leading men of the second half of the century somewhat in proportion to their judgment and in inverse proportion to their enthusiasm.

Charles Louis de Secondat, Baron of Montesquieu, born in 1689, was by inheritance one of the presidents of the Parliament of Bordeaux.[1] He was recognized in early life as a rising man, a respectable magistrate, sensible and brilliant rather than learned; a man of the world, rich and thrifty, not very happily married, and fond of

[1] In his youth he was known as Charles Louis de la Brède, the name being taken from a fief of his mother. The name of Montesquieu he inherited from an uncle, together with his place of president à mortier. Vian, *Histoire de Montesquieu*, 16, 30.

the society of ladies. In appearance he was ugly, with a large head, weak eyes, a big nose, a retreating forehead and chin. In temperament he was calm and cheerful. "I have had very few sorrows," he says, "and still less ennui." — "Study has been to me a sovereign remedy against the troubles of life, and I have never had a grief that an hour's reading would not dissipate." He was shy, he tells us, but less among bright people than among stupid ones. Good-natured he appears to have been, and somewhat selfish; easily amused, less by what people said than by their way of saying it. He was a good landlord and a kind master. It is told of him that one day, while scolding one of his servants, he turned round with a laugh to a friend standing by. "They are like clocks," said he, "and need winding up now and then.[1]

Montesquieu set himself a high standard of duty. In a paper intended only for his son, he writes: "If I knew something which was useful to myself and injurious to my family, I should reject it from my mind. If I knew of anything which was useful to my family and which was not so to my country, I should try to forget it. If I knew something useful to my country, which was injurious to Europe and the human race, I should consider it a crime."[2]

Montesquieu's first book appeared in 1721, a book very different from those which followed it. It is witty and licentious after a rather stately fashion, full of keen observation and cutting satire. In contrast to the books of other famous writers of the century, the "Persian Letters" are eminently the work of a gentleman; — of a French gentleman, when the Duke of Orleans was Regent.

[1] See the medallion given in Vian, and said by the *Biographie universelle* to be the only authentic portrait. Also Montesq. vii. 150, (*Pensées diverses. Portrait de M. par lui-même*, apparently written when he was about forty). Also Vian, 141.
[2] Montesq., vii. 157.

The "Lettres Persanes" are, as their name suggests, the supposed correspondence of two rich Persians, Usbek and Rica, traveling in France and exchanging letters with their friends and their eunuchs in Persia. The letters which the travelers receive, containing the gossip of their harems, form but the smaller portion of the book, and are evidently intended to give it variety and lightness. In the letters which they write to their Persian correspondents we have the satirical picture of French society. How far had the ruling, infallible church sunk in the minds of Frenchmen, when a well-placed and rather selfish man could write what follows.

"The Pope is the chief of the Christians. He is an old idol, to which people burn incense from the force of habit. In old times he was formidable even to princes; for he deposed them as easily as our magnificent Sultans depose the kings of Irimette and of Georgia. But he is no longer feared. He calls himself the successor of one of the earliest Christians, known as Saint Peter; and it is certainly a rich inheritance, for he has enormous treasures and a rich country under his dominion."

The bishops are legists, subordinate to the Pope. They have two functions. When assembled they make articles of faith as he does. When separate, they dispense people from obeying the law. For the Christian religion is full of difficult observances; and it is thought to be harder to do your duty than to have bishops to give you dispensation. The doctors, bishops, and monks are constantly raising questions on religious subjects, and dispute for a long time, until at last an assembly is held to decide among them. In no kingdom have there been as many civil wars as in that of Christ.[1]

Farther on we have a picture of the way in which religion is regarded in French society. It is less a subject of sanctification than of dispute. Courtiers, soldiers, even

---

[1] Montesq., i. 124. Letter xxix.

women, rise up against ecclesiastics and ask them to prove what the others have resolved not to believe. This is not because people have determined their minds by reason, nor that they have taken the trouble to examine the truth or falsehood of this religion which they reject. They are rebels who have felt the yoke and who have shaken it off before they have known it. They are, therefore, no firmer in their unbelief than in their faith. They live in an ebbing and flowing tide, which unceasingly carries them from one to the other.[1] Making a large allowance for satire, we have yet an interesting and doleful picture of a small but important part of the French nation. And it is noticeable that the Persian Letters precede by thirteen years Voltaire's "Philosophical," or "English Letters."[2]

Montesquieu argues that it is well to have several sects in a country, as they keep a watch on each other, and every man is anxious not to disgrace his party. But it is for toleration and not for equality that the author pleads. A state church seemed almost necessary to thought in the early part of the eighteenth century. Yet Montesquieu has no great liking for any form of dogmatic religion; in this he belongs distinctly with the Philosophers; morality is, in his eyes, the great, perhaps the only thing to be desired; obedience to law, love to men, filial piety, these he says are the first acts of all religions; ceremonies are good only on the supposition that God has commanded them; but about the commands of God it is easy to be mistaken, for there are two thousand religions, each of which puts in its claim. Thus was the great argument of the Catholics, that the multiplicity of Protestant sects proved their falsity, turned against its inventors.[3]

[1] Montesq., i. 251. Letter lxxv.   [2] 1721-1734.
[3] Ibid., i. 164. Letter xlvi. Compare with Montesquieu's opinion, expressed in the *Spirit of the Laws*, that the sovereign should neither

The licentiousness of the "Persian Letters" has been mentioned. It is one of the most noticeable features of the writings of the Philosophers of the eighteenth century that the whole subject of sexual morality is viewed by them from a standpoint different from that taken by ourselves. The thinking Frenchmen of that age believed that there was a system of natural morals, imposed on man by his own nature and the nature of things. They believed that there was also an artificial system resting only on positive law, or on the ordinances of the church. It was the tendency of the ecclesiastical mind to ignore that distinction. That tendency had been pushed too far and had produced a reaction.

The distinction is one which is not quite disregarded even by men of those races which have most respect for law. Nobody feels that the injunction to keep off the grass in a public park, or the rule to pass to the right in driving, is of quite the same sort of obligation as the precept to keep your hands from picking and stealing. A far greater amount of odium is incurred by the known breach of a rule of natural morals, than by that of a rule depending solely on the ordinance of the legislative power. Smuggling may be mentioned as a crime coming near the dividing line in the popular feeling of most countries. Few men would feel as much disgraced at being caught by a custom-house officer, with a box of cigars hidden under the trowsers at the bottom of their trunk, as at being seized in the act of stealing the same box from the counter of a tobacconist. In countries where the laws are arbitrary and the law-making power distrusted, this distinction is more strongly marked than where the government has the full confidence and approbation of the community. The more progressive Frenchmen of a hundred and fifty years ago believed the laws of their country allow the establishment of a new form of religion, nor persecute one already established.

to be bad in many respects. They therefore thought that there was a great difference between what jurists call *prohibited wrong* and *wrong in itself.*

Now, admitting this distinction to exist in men's minds, there is one large class of crimes and vices which is put in one category by most Anglo-Saxons and which was put in the other by the French Philosophers. These are the breaches of the sexual laws. It is one of the greatest services of the church to Christendom that she has always laid particular emphasis on the duty of chastity. It is one of her greatest errors, that she has exalted the practice of celibacy over that of conjugal fidelity. The Philosophers, as was their custom, looked abroad on the practice of various nations. They found that some of the ancients granted divorce freely at the request of either party. They learned that Orientals generally allowed polygamy. They saw in their own country a low state of sexual morals among the highest classes, partly due perhaps to the example of a depraved court. Observation and desire concurred with hatred of the clergy to warp their judgments. They forgot, at least in part, that chastity is the foundation of the family and the civilized state; that divorce and polygamy, although of momentous importance, are but secondary questions; that on sexual self-restraint civilization rests, as much as on respect for life and property. On the false theory that unchastity is but an artificial crime, the delusive invention of an ascetic church, will, I think, be found to depend much that has been worst in the practice of Frenchmen, much that is most disgusting in their literature.[1]

This theory is seldom held unreservedly. In the "Persian Letters" it goes no farther than an elaborate apol-

[1] The commandment "Thou shalt not commit adultery" is equally applicable to polygamists and monogamists. It was originally promulgated to the former, and to a nation in which a man could put away his wife.

ogy for divorce, a scathing denunciation of celibacy, and a general licentiousness of tone. The later writings of Montesquieu are free from indecency. But it is noticeable of him, perhaps the most high-minded of the Philosophers, and of the rest of them, that while they constantly insist on the importance of virtue, they hardly rank chastity among the virtues.[1]

The monarchy fares little better than the church in the "Persian Letters." "The King of France," says Rica, "is the most powerful prince in Europe. He has no goldmines like his neighbor the King of Spain; but he has more wealth than the latter, for he draws it from the vanity of his subjects, more inexhaustible than mines. He has been known to undertake and carry on great wars, with no other resource than titles of honor to sell; and by a prodigy of human pride, his troops were paid, his forts furnished, his fleets equipped."

"Moreover, this king is a great magician; he rules the very minds of his subjects; he makes them think as he pleases. If he has only one million dollars in his treasury and needs two, he has but to assure them that one dollar is worth two, and they believe him. If he has a difficult war to carry on, and has no money, he has but to put it into their heads that a piece of paper is bullion, and immediately they are convinced. He even goes so far as to make them believe that he cures them of all manner of diseases by touching them. Such is the strength and power that he has over their minds."[2]

"What I tell you of this prince need not astonish you. There is another magician stronger than he; who is no

---

[1] See the story of a Guebir who marries his sister, Montesq., i. 226, Letter lxvii. The point appears to be that the laws forbidding marriage in cases of consanguinity are arbitrary.

[2] Ibid., i. 110, Letter xxiv. Referring to the sale of offices and titles, to the habit of debasing the coinage, and to that of touching for scrofula.

less master of the king's spirit, than the king himself is of that of others. This magician is called the Pope. Sometimes he makes the king believe that three are only one; that the bread people eat is not bread, that the wine that they drink is not wine, and many things of the same kind."

Rica has seen the young king, Louis XV. His countenance is majestic and charming; a good education, added to a good natural disposition, gives promise of a great sovereign. But Rica is informed that you cannot tell about these western kings until you know of their mistress and their confessor. Under a young prince these exercise rival powers; under an old one, they are united. The strength of a young king makes the dervish weak; but the mistress turns both strength and weakness to account."[1]

The Christian princes long ago freed all the slaves in their states; saying that Christianity made all men equal. This religious action was very useful to them, for it abridged the power of their chief lords. Since then, they have conquered new countries where slavery was profitable. They have forgotten their religion and allowed slaves to be bought and sold.[2]

The French are more governed by the laws of honor than the Persians, because they are more free. But the sanctuary of honor, reputation, and virtue seems to be built in republics, where a man may feel that he has indeed a country. In Greece and Rome a crown of leaves, a statue, the praise of the state, were recompense enough for a battle won or a city taken. Switzerland and Holland, with the poorest soil in Europe, are the most populous countries for their area. Liberty — and opulence, which always follows it — draws strangers to the country. Political equality among citizens generally produces equality of fortune, and scatters abundance and life.

---

[1] Montesq., i. 339, Letter cvii.
[2] Ibid., i. 252, Letter lxxv.

But under an arbitrary government, the prince, his courtiers, and a few individuals, possess all the wealth, while the rest of the country suffers from extreme poverty.[1]

The satirical character of the "Persian Letters" is sufficiently evident from the extracts given above. But Montesquieu is far more widely and justly known as a wise and learned writer on government than as a satirist. The book we have been considering was by far the lightest, as it was the earliest, of his considerable writings. The good sense, caution, and conservatism of his nature appear in the "Persian Letters" less conspicuously than in his later works; yet, even there, are in marked contrast to the haste and shallowness of many of the Philosophers. "It is true," he says, "that laws must sometimes be altered, but the case is rare; and when it happens, they should be touched with a trembling hand; and so many solemnities should be observed, and so many precautions used, that the people may naturally conclude that the laws are very sacred, since so many formalities are necessary to abrogate them."[2]

Here is an opinion, overstated perhaps, but not without its frequent illustrations since he wrote it. "It seems . . . that the largest heads grow narrow when they are assembled, and that where there are most wise men, there is least wisdom. Large bodies are always deeply attached to details, to vain customs; and essential matters are always postponed. I have heard that a king of Aragon, having assembled the Estates of Aragon and Catalonia, the first meetings were taken up in deciding in what language the deliberations should be held. The dispute was lively, and the Estates would have broken up a thousand times, had not an expedient been hit upon,

[1] Montesq., i. 291, Letter lxxxix. See also pp. 381, 386, Letters cxxii., cxxiv.
[2] Ibid., i. 401, Letter cxxix.

which was that the questions should be put in Catalonian and the answers given in Aragonese."[1]

"I have never heard people talk about public law," he says in another letter, "that they did not inquire carefully what was the origin of society; which strikes me as absurd. If men did not form a society, if they separated and fled from each other, we should have to ask the reason of it, and to seek out why they kept apart. But they are created all bound to each other, the son is born near his father and stays there; this is society, and the cause of society."[2]

A satirical book, like the "Persian Letters," could not have been openly published in France under Louis XV. The first edition was in fact printed at Amsterdam, although Cologne appeared on the title-page as the place of publication. The book was anonymous, but Montesquieu was well known to be the author, and speedily acquired a great reputation. After several years, for things did not move fast in Old France, he was proposed for election to the Academy. To be one of the forty members of that body is the legitimate ambition of the literary Frenchman. The Cardinal de Fleury, who was prime minister, is said to have announced that the king would never consent to the election of the author of the "Persian Letters." He added that he had not read the book, but that people in whom he had confidence assured him that it was dangerous. According to Voltaire, Montesquieu thereupon had a garbled edition of the Letters hastily printed, himself took a copy to the Cardinal, induced His Eminence to read a part of it, and, with the help of friends, pre-

---

[1] Montesq., i. 344, Letter cix. See several of the principal deliberative bodies of the world so bound by their own rules that they can scarcely move; and compare with them in point of efficiency the small legislatures and boards which manage many important and complicated interests promptly, sitting with closed doors.

[2] Ibid., i. 301, Letter xciv.

vailed on him to alter his decision. Such a trick is more worthy of Voltaire, who continually denied his own works, than of Montesquieu, who, I believe, never did so. D'Alembert tells the story in a way entirely creditable to the latter. He says that Montesquieu saw the minister, told him that for private reasons he did not give his name to the "Persian Letters," but that he was far from disowning a book of which he did not think he had cause to be ashamed. He then insisted that the Letters should be judged after reading them, and not on hearsay. Thereupon the Cardinal read the book, was pleased with it and with its author, and withdrew his opposition to the latter's election to the Academy.[1]

A little before this time Montesquieu resigned his place as one of the presidents of the Parliament of Bordeaux, selling the life estate in it, but reserving the reversion for his son. Having thus obtained leisure, he set out on a long course of travel, lasting three years. "In France," said he later, "I make friends with everybody; in England with nobody; in Italy I make compliments to every one; in Germany I drink with every one." "When I go into a country, I do not look to see if there are good laws, but whether they execute those they have; for there are good laws everywhere."[2]

Montesquieu arrived in England in the autumn of 1729, sailing from Holland in the yacht of Lord Chesterfield,

---

[1] *Nouvelle Biographie Universelle.* Voltaire (*Siècle de Louis XIV. Liste des écrivains*). D'Alembert, vi. 252. The date of Montesquieu's election was Jan. 24, 1728. See a discussion of the whole story in Vian, 100. Montesquieu is there said to have threatened to leave France, and to have declined a pension at this time. Montesquieu tells the story of the pension, but without fixing a date: "Je dis que n'ayant pas fait de bassesse, je n'avais pas besoin d'être consolé par des graces," vii. 157. Voltaire was always jealous of Montesquieu's reputation ; and also, at this time, out of temper with the Academy, to which he was elected only in 1746.

[2] Vian, 90. Montesq. vii. 186, 189.

whose acquaintance he had made on the Continent. He spent seventeen months in the country, and, in spite of his epigram about making friends with nobody, saw some of the most eminent men, including Swift and Pope, was received by the Royal Society, and presented at Court. At a time when England and the English language were little known in France, he studied them in a way which deeply influenced all his views of government. "In London," he says, "liberty and equality. The liberty of London is the liberty of the best people,[1] in which it differs from the liberty of Venice," which is the liberty of debauchery. "The equality of London is also the equality of the best people, in which it differs from the liberty of Holland, which is the liberty of the populace."

"England is at present the most free country in the world; I do not except any republic. I call it free because the prince can do no conceivable harm to anybody; because his power is controlled and limited by a law. But if the lower chamber should become the mistress, its power would be unlimited and dangerous, because it would have executive power also; whereas now unlimited power is in the parliament and the king, and the executive power in the king, whose power is limited. A good Englishman must, therefore, seek to defend liberty equally against the attacks of the crown and those of the chamber."[2]

Montesquieu brought back from England an admiration of what he had seen there as genuine, and far more discriminating than that of Voltaire. While the studies of Montesquieu were principally directed to the political institutions of the country, those of Voltaire embraced the philosophy and social life of England. Through

[1] *Honnestes gens*, which cannot be exactly translated. Montesq., vii. 185. Vian, 112.

[2] Montesq., vii. 195 (*Notes sur l'Angleterre*).

these two great men, more perhaps than through any others, English ideas were spread in France in the middle of the eighteenth century.[1]

Montesquieu now went on with his studies with an enlarged mind. He would appear, before he started on his travels, to have already formed the project of writing a great work on the Spirit of the Laws. But in 1734 he published a smaller book, the "Greatness and Decadence of the Romans." It is said that this essay was composed of a part of the material collected for the Spirit of the Laws, and was published separately in order not to give the Romans too large a place in the more important work. This has been doubted, but there is nothing either in the subject or in the treatment to make it improbable. Nor is it important, so long as between the two books there is unity of purpose and agreement of method.

The "Greatness and Decadence of the Romans" is a study of philosophic history. In form it is not unlike Machiavelli's Discourses on the first ten books of Livy. That remarkable work would have been most profitable reading for Frenchmen of the eighteenth century, as it must be in all times for students of the science of politics. Of republics Machiavelli had more experience than Montesquieu. Both considered the republican form of government the most desirable; both thought it impossible without the preservation of substantial equality of property among the citizens. Montesquieu, who knew more of monarchy than Machiavelli, had also more faith in it. Both hated the rule of the Roman Church.[2] The Frenchman excels the Italian in practical wisdom; he is also more brilliant. By his brilliancy he may sometimes have been led away, but I think not often. While we feel in reading Voltaire that the sparkling point is often

---

[1] Voltaire returned from England a few months before Montesquieu went there in 1729.

[2] Machiavelli, ii. 210. Montesq., ii. 136, 140. Mach., ii. 130.

the cause of the saying, with Montesquieu we are generally struck with the weight of thought in what we read.

"The tyranny of a prince," says Montesquieu, "does not bring him nearer to ruin, than indifference to the public good brings a republic. The advantage of a free state is that the revenues are better administered — but how if they are worse? The advantage of a free state is that there are no favorites; but when that is not the case, and when instead of enriching the prince's friends and relations, all the friends and relations of all those who share in the government have to be enriched, all is lost; the laws are evaded more dangerously than they are violated by a prince, who, being always the greatest citizen of a state, has the most interest in its preservation."[1]

Kings, as Montesquieu points out, are less envied than aristocracies; for the king is too far above most of his subjects to excite comparisons, while the nobility is not so placed. Republics, where birth confers no privileges, are, he thinks, happier in this respect than other countries; for the people can envy but little an authority which it grants and withdraws at its pleasure. Montesquieu forgets that every chance to rise which excites in the strong and virtuous a noble emulation, will cause in the weak and sour the corresponding base passion of envy. Complete despotism he believes to be impossible. There is in every nation a general spirit on which all power is founded. Against this, the ruler is powerless. It is wise not to disturb established forms and institutions, for the very causes which have made them last hitherto may maintain them in the future, and these causes are often complicated and unknown. When the system is changed, theoretic difficulties may be overcome, but drawbacks remain which only use can show. It is folly in conquer-

[1] Montesq., ii. 139.

ors to wish to make the conquered adopt new laws and customs, and it is useless; for under any form of government, subjects can obey. Men are never more offended than when their ceremonies and customs are interfered with. Oppression is sometimes a proof of the esteem in which they are held; interference with their customs is always a mark of contempt.[1]

Such are some of the general opinions of Montesquieu, found in the "Greatness and Decadence of the Romans." In the same book occurs the expression of an idea (afterwards repeated and worked out), which was to be perhaps the most fruitful of his teachings. "The laws of Rome," he says, "had wisely divided the public power among a great number of offices, which sustained, arrested, and moderated each other; and as each had but a limited power, every citizen was capable of attaining to any one of them; and the people, seeing several persons pass before it one after the other, became accustomed to none of them."[2]

This idea that the division of power was highly desirable, that a system of checks and balances in government would tend to secure freedom, never took firm root in France. Indeed, Montesquieu, as he himself had partly foreseen, was more praised than read in his own country.[3] But in the distant colonies of America the "Greatness and Decadence of the Romans" and the "Spirit of the Laws" found eager students. The thoughts of Montesquieu were embodied in the constitutions of new states, whose social and economic condition was not far removed from that which he considered the most desirable. In these states the doctrine of the division of powers was consciously and carefully adopted, with the most beneficent results. This division was not a new idea to the

---

[1] Montesq., ii. 181, 315, 316, 266, 174, 209.
[2] Ibid., ii. 200.
[3] Ibid., vii. 157 (*Pensées diverses. Portrait de M. par lui-même*).

American colonists; it was already in a measure a part of their institutions. But there can be little doubt that the idea was enforced in their minds by being clearly stated by one of the writers on political subjects whom they most admired.[1]

Fourteen years had passed from the time of the publication of the "Greatness and Decadence of the Romans," when in 1748 appeared the great work of Montesquieu, the "Spirit of the Laws." The book is announced by its author as something entirely original, "a child without a mother."[2] Nor is the claim altogether unfounded, although any reader familiar with the "Politics" of Aristotle can hardly fail to observe the resemblance between that great book and the other. Nor is it a detraction from the genius of Montesquieu to say that the comparison will not be altogether in his favor.

Montesquieu's scheme is announced in the title originally given to his book. "Of the Spirit of the Laws, or of the relation which the laws should have to the constitution of every government, manners, climate, religion, commerce, etc. To which the author has added new researches into the Roman laws concerning inheritance, into French laws, and into feudal laws." Thus we see that the principal subject of the book is the relation of laws to the circumstances of the country in which they exist. In this also is its chief value and its claim to originality. The Philosophers of the eighteenth century, following the example of the churches, believed that there

[1] We have seen that Montesquieu had arrived at this idea from the study of the English Constitution as it existed in his day. In respect to the division of powers, the government of the United States conforms far more nearly to his idea than does the present government of England, in which the system of balanced powers has been superseded by that of government by the Lower Chamber, of which he pointed out the danger. The full results of this change will be known only to future generations.

[2] *Prolem sine matre creatam*, on the title-page.

was an absolute standard of justice to which all laws could easily be referred, independently of the country in which the laws existed. If the laws of Naples differed from those of Prussia, the laws which governed the phlegmatic Dutchman from those which contained the excitable inhabitant of Marseilles, one or the other set of laws, or both of them, must be wrong. The Civil Law of the Latin races, the Common Law of England, each claimed to be the expression of perfect abstract reason. The church with its canon, the same for all races and climates, confirmed the theory. To all these came Montesquieu with a teaching that would reconcile their claims.

"Law in general is human reason, in so far as it governs all the nations of the earth; and the political and civil laws of each nation should be but the particular cases to which that human reason is applied."

"They should be so adapted to the people for whom they are made, that it is a very great chance if those of one nation will apply to another."

"They must be in relation to the nature and the principle of the government which is established, or about to be established; whether they form it, as do political laws; or maintain it, as do civil laws."

"They must be in relation to the *physical* nature of the country; to the frozen, burning, or temperate climate; to the quality of the soil, the situation and size of the country; to the style of life of the people, as farmers, hunters, or shepherds; they should be in relation to the amount of liberty which the constitution may allow; to the religion of the inhabitants, their inclinations, their wealth, their numbers, their customs, their morals, and their manners. Finally, they have relations to each other; they have them to their own origin, to the object of the legislator, to the order of things on which they are established. They should be considered from all these points of view."

"This is what I undertake to do in this work. I will examine all these relations. They form together what is called 'the Spirit of the Laws.'"[1]

It will be noticed that Montesquieu by no means denies that there are general principles of justice. On the contrary, he positively asserts it.[2] But the great value of his teaching consists in the other lesson. "It is better to say that the government most in conformity with nature is that whose particular disposition is most in relation to the disposition of the people for which it is established." This principle may certainly be deduced from Aristotle; but it was none the less necessary to teach it in the eighteenth century; it is none the less necessary to teach it to-day.[3]

The conception was a great one, so simple that it seems impossible that it could ever have been missed; but it was combated with violence on its announcement, and many brilliant and learned men have failed to grasp it.[4] Such are the persons in our own time who praise despotism in France, or who would set up parliamentary government in India. Montesquieu probably carried his theories too far. To the north he assigned energy and valor, as if the most widely conquering nations that Europe had then known had been the Norwegian and the Finn, instead of the Macedonian, the Italian, and the Spaniard. Sterility of soil he considered favorable to republics, fertility to monarchies. It was natural that a man in revolt against the long spiritual tyranny that had oppressed thought in Europe should have attributed excessive importance to material causes. Not the less did the idea contain its share of truth. Nor was his statement of this, which we may call his favorite theory, always excessive. "Several

---

[1] Montesq., iii. 99 (liv. i. c. 3).
[2] Ibid., iii. 91 (liv. i. c. 1).
[3] Ibid., iii. 99 ; Aristotle, *Politics*, liv. vii. c. ii.
[4] Montesq., iv. 145 n.

things," he says, "govern man; climate, religion, laws, the maxims of government, the examples of things past, morals, manners; whence comes a general spirit which is their result. "Sometimes one of these forces dominates and sometimes another."[1]

It may be noted of Montesquieu, and as often of Voltaire, that each of them is constantly led astray by imperfect knowledge of foreign, and especially of barbarous and savage nations. Since the voyages and conquests of the Renaissance, accounts of strange countries had abounded in Europe, written in many cases by men anything but accurate, if not, in the words of Macaulay, "liars by a double right, as travellers and as Jesuits."[2] The writers of a hundred and fifty years ago could use no better material than was to be had. They wished to draw instruction from distant objects, and their spy-glasses distorted shapes and modified colors. Imperfect knowledge of foreign countries sometimes led Montesquieu into curious mistakes; yet these affected his illustrations oftener than his theories.

Having stated his general doctrine, Montesquieu proceeds to apply it. As laws should be adapted to the nature of the government of each country, it is essential to study that nature, and to consider what is the *principle*, or motive force of each form of government. "There is this difference," he says, "between the nature of the government and its principle: that its nature is what makes it such as it is, and its principle what makes it act. One is its especial structure, and the other the human passions which cause it to operate."[3]

Four kinds of government are recognized by Montesquieu: democratic, aristocratic, monarchical, and despotic. The principle of democracy he holds to be *virtue*, without

---

[1] Montesq., iv. 307 (liv. xix. c. 4).
[2] *Essay on Machiavelli*.
[3] Montesq., iii. 120 (liv. iii. c. 1).

which popular government cannot continue to exist.[1] An aristocratic state needs less virtue, because the people is kept in check by the nobles. But the nobility can with difficulty repress the members of their own order, and do justice for their crimes. In default of great virtue, however, an aristocratic state can exist if the ruling class will practice *moderation*.[2] In monarchies great things can be done with little virtue, for in them there is another moving principle, which is *honor*.[3] This sort of government is founded on the prejudice of each person and each sort of men; it rests on ranks, preferences, and distinctions, so that emulation often supplies the place of virtue. In a monarchy there will be many tolerable citizens, but seldom a very good man, who loves the state better than himself. The motive principle of a despotism is *fear*;[4] for in despotic states virtue is unnecessary, and honor would be dangerous. These qualities of virtue, honor, and fear, may not exist in every republic, monarchy, and despotism; but they should do so, if the government is to be perfect of its kind.[5]

It is worth while to remember, when considering the "Spirit of the Laws," that Montesquieu oftenest had in his mind, when speaking of democratic republics, those of Greece; when speaking of aristocratic republics, early Rome and Venice; of monarchies, France and England; of despotisms, the East.[6]

Under each form of government, education and the laws should work together to strengthen the motive principle belonging to that form. Especially is this necessary in republics, for honor, which sustains monarchies, is

---

[1] Montesq., iii. 122 (liv. iii. c. 3).   [2] Ibid., iii. 126 (liv. c. 4).
[3] Ibid., iii. 128 (liv. iii. c. 5, 6, and 7).
[4] Ibid., iii. 135 (liv. iii. c. 9).   [5] Ibid., iii. 140 (liv. iii. c. 11).
[6] But he sometimes refers to England as a country where a republic is hidden under the forms of a monarchy. Montesq., iii. 216 (liv. v. c. 19).

favored by the passions; but virtue, on which democracies depend, implies renunciation of self. Virtue, in a republic, is love of the republic itself, which leads to good morals; the public good is set above private gratification. Thus we see that monks love their order the more, the more austere is its rule. The love of the state, in a democracy, becomes the love of equality, and thus limits ambition to the desire to render great services to the republic. The love of equality and frugality are principally excited by equality and frugality themselves, when both are established by law. The laws of a democratic state should encourage equality in every way; as by forbidding last wills, and preventing the acquisition of large landed estates. In a democracy all men contract an enormous debt to the state at their birth, and, do what they may, they can never repay it. There should be no great wealth in the hands of private persons, because such wealth confers power and furnishes delights which are contrary to equality. Domestic frugality should make public expenditure possible. Even talents should be but moderate. But if a democratic republic be founded on commerce, individuals may safely possess great riches; for the spirit of commerce brings with it that of frugality, economy, moderation, labor, wisdom, tranquillity, and order.

It is very important in a democracy to keep old laws and customs; for things tend to degenerate, and a corrupted nation seldom does anything great. To maintain an aristocratic republic, moderation is necessary. The nobles should be simple in their lives and hardly distinguishable from plebeians. Distinctions offensive to pride, such as laws forbidding intermarriage, are to be avoided. Privileges should belong to the senate as a body and simple respect only be paid to the individual senators.[1]

[1] Montesq., iii. 151 (liv. iv. c. 5). Ibid., iii. 165–183 (liv. v. c. 2–8).

As honor is the motive principle of monarchy, the laws should support it, and be adapted to sustain that *nobility* which is the parent and the child of honor. Nobility must be hereditary; it must have prerogatives and rights; it forms the link between the prince and the nation. Monarchical government has the great advantage over the republican form, that, as affairs are in a single hand, there is the greater promptitude of execution. But there should still be something to moderate the will of the prince. This is best found, not in the nobility itself, but in such bodies as courts of law with constitutional rights, like the French Parliaments.[1]

Montesquieu has been much blamed, both in his own age and since, for his partiality to the monarchy as he found it existing in France. While recognizing that a republic was a more just and equal form of government, he thought that monarchy was that best suited to his time and country. Many people who have watched the history of France since his day will be found to agree with him. While defending some practices which are now considered among the flagrant abuses of old France, he recommended some reforms which would have been very salutary. It is often wiser to find excuses for retaining an old custom than reasons for introducing a new one; and Montesquieu was a conservative, made so by his nature, his social position, his wealth, his education as a lawyer, his age and his experience. When he wrote the "Persian Letters" he might possibly have been willing to overthrow the principal institutions of his country for the sake of remedying abuses; but when he had spent twenty years over the "Spirit of the Laws," when he had realized the complication of life, and the interdependence of things, he was more ready to reform than to destroy.

In a despotic government the motive principle is fear. The governor of the town must be absolutely responsible

[1] Montesq., iii. 191 (liv. v. c. 10).

to the governor of the province, or the latter cannot be entirely responsible to the sovereign. Thus absolutism extends throughout the state. As there is no law but the will of the prince, and as that law cannot be known in detail to every one, there must be a great number of petty tyrants dependent on those immediately above them.[1]

After a not very successful attempt to define liberty, which he decides to be the power to do that which we ought to desire and not to do that which we ought not to desire,[2] Montesquieu tells us that political liberty is found only in limited governments, for all men who have power will tend to abuse it, and will go on until they meet with obstacles; as virtue itself needs to be restrained. Various nations, he then says, have various objects: conquest was that of Rome, war of Sparta, commerce of Marseilles; there is a country the direct object of whose constitution is political liberty. That country is England.[3]

There are in every state three kinds of power, the legislative, the executive, and the judicial. Political liberty in a citizen is the tranquillity of mind which comes from the opinion he has of his own security; and to give him this liberty the government must be such that no citizen can be afraid of another. Now this security can exist only where the legislative, executive, and judicial powers are in different hands. In most of the monarchies of Europe the goverment is limited, because the prince, who has the first two powers, leaves the third to others; he makes laws and executes them, but he appoints other men to act as judges in his place. In the republics of Italy all three powers are united. The same body of magistrates

---

[1] Montesq., iii. 209 (liv. v. c. 16).
[2] Ibid., iv. 2-4 (liv. xi. c. 2, 3).
[3] Montesquieu, here and elsewhere, avoids mentioning England or France by name ; a curious affectation. The references, however, are unmistakable.

makes the laws, executes them, and judges every citizen according to its pleasure; such a body is as despotic as an eastern prince.[1] The judicial power, says Montesquieu (with the English jury in his mind), should not be given to a permanent senate, but exercised by persons drawn from the body of the people, forming a tribunal which lasts only as long as necessity may require it. In serious cases the criminal should combine with the law to choose his judges, or at least should have a right of challenge. The legislative and executive powers can with less danger be given to permanent bodies, because they are not exercised against individuals. He then commends representative government and the freedom left to members of Parliament in the English system. He believes the people more capable of choosing representatives wisely than of deciding questions, an opinion on which modern experience may have thrown some doubt. He approves of the existence of a second chamber, composed of persons distinguished by birth, wealth, or honors; for if such were mixed with the people and given only one vote apiece like the others, the common liberty would be their slavery, and they would have no interest in defending it, because it would oftenest be turned against themselves.[2]

The government of France, says Montesquieu, has not, like that of England, liberty for its direct object; it tends only to the glory of the citizen, the state, and the prince. But from this glory comes a spirit of liberty, which in France can do great things, and can contribute as much to happiness as liberty itself. The three powers are not there distributed as in England; but they have a distribution of their own, according to which they approach more or less to political liberty; and if they did not

[1] This judgment is somewhat softened as to Venice. The most conspicuous example in modern times of the tyranny of a single popular body is that of France under the Convention.

[2] Montesq., iv. 7 (liv. xi. c. 6).

approach it, the monarchy would degenerate into despotism.[1] This sounds somewhat like an empty phrase; yet there undoubtedly were in Montesquieu's time some checks on the absolutism of a French monarch. "If subjects owe obedience to kings, kings on their part owe obedience to the laws," said the Parliament of Paris in 1753. And outside of its own boundaries France had long been considered a limited monarchy.[2] Apart from the limitations imposed by the privileges of the church and of the Parliaments, there appear to have been some acknowledged fundamental laws (the succession of the crown in the male line was one of them) which it would have been beyond the power of the sovereign for the time being to destroy. And public opinion, as Montesquieu has already told us, has power even in the most despotic countries. In a European nation, not broken in spirit by long-continued tyranny, and possessing the printing-press, this power must always be very great.

As for Montesquieu's admiration of the English form of government, it doubtless concurred with other causes to encourage on the Continent the study of English political methods. Those methods have since been adopted by many continental states, with hardly as many modifications to adapt them to local circumstances as might have been desirable. But it is the modern English constitution, in which power lies almost entirely in the House of Commons, and is exercised by its officers, that has been thus copied. In America the principle of the division of powers has been carried farther than it ever was in England; and is, of all parts of their form of government, that from which many intelligent Americans would be most loath to part.

We have seen enough of Montesquieu's attacks on the

[1] Montesq., iv. 24. (liv. xi. c. 7).
[2] Rocquain, 170. Machiavelli, ii. 140, 215, 322 (*Discourses on the first ten books of Livy*).

church. The most violent of them were made in his youth, and in a book avowedly satirical. In mature life, writing in a more philosophical spirit, his language is temperate and wise. "It is bad reasoning against religion," he says, "to bring together in a great work a long enumeration of the evils which she has produced, unless you also recount the good she has done. If I should tell all the harm which civil laws, monarchy, or republican government have done in the world, I should say frightful things."[1] This idea was far beyond the reach of Voltaire.

Montesquieu goes on to argue about different forms of religion. Mahometanism he holds especially suited to despotism, Christianity to limited governments. Catholicism is adapted to monarchies, Protestantism, and especially Calvinism, to republics. Where fatalism is a religious dogma, the penalties imposed by law must be more severe, and the watch kept on the community more vigilant, so that men may be driven by these motives who otherwise would abandon self-restraint; but if the dogma of liberty be established, the case is otherwise. Climate is not without influence on religion. The ablutions required of a Mahometan are useful in his warm country. The Protestant of Northern Europe has to work harder for a living than the Catholic of the South, and therefore desires fewer religious holidays. If a state can prevent the establishment of a new form of religion within its borders, it will find it well to do so; but if several religions are established, they should not be allowed to interfere with each other. Penal laws in religious matters should be avoided; for each religion has its own spiritual penalties, and to put a man between the fear of temporal punishment, on the one hand, and the fear of spiritual punishment on the other, degrades his soul. The possessions of the clergy should be limited by laws of mortmain.[2]

[1] Montesq., v. 117 (liv. xxiv. c. 2).
[2] Ibid., v. 124–136 (liv. xxiv. c. 5–14).

The spirit of moderation should be the spirit of the legislator. This Montesquieu declared to be the great theme of his book. Political good, like moral good, is always found between extremes.[1]

It was this moderation which made the "Spirit of the Laws" distasteful to the more ardent Philosophers. Sharing in many of the feelings of his contemporaries, and especially in their distrust of the church, Montesquieu was yet unwilling to go to the same extremes as they. His chapter on Uniformity and the criticisms made on it by Condorcet, form an admirable instance of this.

"There are certain ideas of uniformity," says Montesquieu, "which sometimes take possession of great minds (for they touched Charlemagne), but which invariably strike small ones. These find in them a kind of perfection which they recognize, because it is impossible not to see it; the same weights in matters of police, the same measures in commerce, the same laws in the state, the same religion in all its parts. But is this always desirable without exceptions? Is the evil of changing always less than the evil of suffering? And would not the greatness of genius rather consist in knowing in what case uniformity is necessary, and in what case difference? In China, the Chinese are governed by the Chinese ceremonies, and the Tartars by Tartar ceremonies; yet this is the nation in all the world which is most devoted to tranquillity. So long as the citizens obey the law, what matters it that they shall all obey the same?"

This chapter (the whole of it is given above, and it may pass in the "Spirit of the Laws" for one of middling length), is, according to Condorcet, "one of those which have acquired for Montesquieu the indulgence of all prejudiced people, of all who hate intellectual light; of all protectors of abuses, etc." And after going on with his invective for some time, Condorcet states the substance of his

[1] Montesq., v. 379 (liv. xxix. c. 1).

argument as follows: "As truth, reason, justice, the rights of men, the interest of property, of liberty, of security, are the same everywhere, we do not see why all the provinces of one state, or even why all states should not have the same criminal laws, the same civil laws, the same laws of commerce, etc. A good law must be good for all men, as a true proposition is true for all. The laws which appear as if they should be different for different countries, either pronounce on objects which should not be regulated by laws, like most commercial regulations, or are founded on prejudices and habits which should be uprooted; and one of the best means of destroying them is to cease to sustain them by laws."[1]

In these two passages we have the issue between Montesquieu and the Philosophic party fairly joined. He alone of the great Frenchmen of his century recognized the enormous complication of human life and human affairs. Not denying that there are fundamental principles of justice, he saw that those principles are hard to formulate truly, harder to apply wisely. For their application he offered many valuable suggestions. These were lost in the rush and hurry of approaching revolution. The superb simplicity of mind which could ignore the diversities of human nature was perhaps necessary for the uprooting of old abuses. But the delicate task of constructing a permanent government cannot succeed unless the differences as well as the resemblances among men be taken into account.

[1] Montesq., v. 412 (liv. xxix. c. 18). Condorcet, i. 377. Yet Condorcet speaks elsewhere of Montesquieu as having made a revolution in men's minds on the subject of law. D'Alembert, i. 64 (Condorcet's *Eloge de d'Alembert*). Rousseau also teaches that all laws and institutions are not adapted to all nations, but it is because he considers most nations childish or effete.

CHAPTER XI.

PARIS.

THE members of the Third Estate differed among themselves far more than did those of the Clergy or the Nobility. This order comprised the rich banker and the beggar at his gate, the learned encyclopædist and the water-carrier that could not spell his name. Every layman, not of noble blood, belonged to the Third Estate. And although this was the unprivileged order, there were privileged bodies and privileged persons within it. Corporations, guilds, cities, and whole provinces possessed rights distinct from those of the rest of the country.

In the reign of Louis XVI. the city of Paris held a position in the world even more prominent than that which it holds to-day. For France was then incontestably the first European power, and Paris was then, as it is now, not only the capital and the metropolis, but the heart and centre of life in France. The population was variously estimated at from six to nine hundred thousand. The city was growing in size, and new houses were continually erected. There was so much building at times during this reign, that masons worked at night, receiving double wages. Architects and master masons were becoming rich, and rents were high when compared to those of other places. Strangers and provincials flocked to Paris for the winter and returned to the country during the fine season. Sentimentalists read the works of Rousseau and praised a country life, but then as now few people that could afford to stay in the city, and had once been caught by its fascination, cared to live permanently out of town.[1]

The public buildings and gardens were worthy of the first city in Europe. With some of them travelers of to-day are familiar. The larger number of the remarkable churches now standing were in existence before the Revolution. Of the palaces then in the city, the three most famous have met with varied fates. The Luxembourg, which was the residence of the king's eldest brother, is the least changed. To the building itself but small additions have been made. Its garden was and is a quiet, orderly place where respectable family groups sit about in the shade. The Louvre has been much enlarged. Under Louis XVI. it consisted of the buildings surrounding the eastern court, of a wing extending toward the river (the gallery of Apollo), and of a long gallery, since rebuilt, running near the river bank and connecting this older palace with the Tuileries. About one-half of the space now enclosed between the two sides of the enormous edifice, and known as the Place du Carrousel, was then covered with houses and streets. The land immediately to the east of the Tuileries palace was not built upon, but part of it was enclosed by a tall iron railing. Such a railing, either the original one or its successor, was to be seen in the same place until recent times and may be standing to-day. The Place du Carrousel, as it then existed outside of this railing, was a square of moderate size surrounded by houses.

The Palace of the Tuileries itself has had an eventful history since Louis XVI. came to the throne, and has only in recent years been utterly swept from the ground. But the gardens which bear its name are little changed. The long raised terraces ran along their sides then as now; although there was no Rue de Rivoli, and the only

[1] Mercier, iv. 205, vii. 190. Babeau, *Paris en 1789*, 27.

access to the gardens on the north side was by two or three streets or lanes from the Rue Saint-Honoré. Within the garden the arrangement of broad, sunny walks and of shady horse-chestnuts was much the same as now. Well-dressed persons walked about or sat under the trees, and the unwashed crowd was admitted only on two or three holidays every year. In consequence of this exclusion the wives of respectable citizens used to come unattended to take the air in the gardens. They were brought in sedan-chairs, from which they alighted at the gate. What is now the Place de la Concorde was then the Place Louis Quinze, with an equestrian statue of that "well-beloved" monarch where the obelisk stands. Not far from the pedestal of that statue overturned, — not far from the entrance of the street called Royal, — near the place where many people had been crushed to death in the crowd assembled to see the fireworks in honor of the marriage of the Dauphin and the Princess Marie Antoinette of Austria, — was to stand the scaffold on which that Dauphin and that princess, after reaching the height of earthly splendor, were to pay for their own sins and weaknesses and for those of their country.

To the west of the square came the Champs Elysées, still somewhat rough in condition, but with people sitting on chairs even then to watch the carriages rolling by, as they still do on any fine afternoon. The Boulevards stretched their shady length all round the city, and were a fashionable drive and walk, near which the smaller theatres rose and throve, evading the monopoly of the opera and the Français. But the boulevards were almost the only broad streets. Those interminable, straight avenues, which even the brilliancy and movement of Paris can hardly make anything but tiresome, had not yet been cut. The streets were narrow and shady; most of them not very long, nor mathematically straight, but keeping a general direction and widening here and there into a little square before a church door, or curving to follow an irregularity of the ground. Such streets were not in accordance with the taste of the age and caused progressive people to complain of Paris. Rousseau, who had seen Turin, was disappointed in the French capital. On arriving he saw at first only small, dirty, and stinking streets, ugly black houses, poverty, beggars, and working people; and the impression thus made was never entirely effaced from his mind, in spite of the magnificence which he recognized at a later time. Young thought that Paris was not to be compared with London; and Thomas Jefferson wrote that the latter, though handsomer than Paris, was not so handsome as Philadelphia. But the Parisian liked his uneven streets well enough. There were fine things to be seen in them. Although the city was crowded, there were gardens in many places, belonging to convents and even to private persons. And once in your walk you might come out upon a bridge, where, if there were not houses built upon it, you might catch a breath of the fresh breeze, and watch the sun disappearing behind the distant village of Chaillot; for nowhere does he set more gloriously than along the Seine.[1]

The houses were tall and dark, and the streets narrow and muddy. There was little water to use, and none to waste, for the larger part of the city depended upon wells or upon the supply brought in buckets from the Seine. The scarcity was hardly to be regretted, for there were few drains to carry dirty water away, and the gutter was full enough already. It ran down the middle of the street, which sloped gently toward it, and there were no sidewalks. When it rained, this street-gutter would rise and overflow, and enterprising men would come out with little wooden bridges on wheels and slip them in between

[1] *Paris à travers les ages.* Babeau, *Paris en* 1789. Cognel, 27, 74. Rousseau, xvii. 274 (*Confessions,* Part i. liv. iv.). Young, i. 60; Randall's *Jefferson,* i. 447.

the carriages, and give the quick-footed walker an opportunity to cross the torrent, if he did not slip in from the wet plank; while a pretty woman would sometimes trust herself to the arms of a burly porter.[1] The houses had gutters along the eaves, but no conductors coming down the walls, so that the water from the roofs was collected and came down once in every few yards in a torrent, bursting umbrellas, and deluging cloaks and hats. The manure spread before sick men's doors to deaden the sound of wheels was washed down the street to add to the destructive qualities which already characterized the mud of Paris. An exceptionally heavy fall of snow would entirely get the better of the authorities, filling the streets from side to side with pools of slush, in which fallen horses had been known to drown. When the sun shone again all was lively as before; the innumerable vehicles crowded the streets from wall to wall, with their great hubs standing well out beyond the wheels, and threatened to eviscerate the pedestrian, as he flattened himself against the house. The carriages of the nobility dashed through the press, the drivers calling out to make room; they were now seldom preceded by runners in splendid livery, as had been the fashion under the former reign, but sometimes one or two huge dogs careered in front, and the Parisians complained that they were first knocked down by the dogs and then run over by the wheels. At times came street cleaners and swept up some of the mud, and carted it away, having first freely spattered the clothes of all who passed near them. In some streets were slaughter-houses, and terrified cattle occasionally made their way into the neighboring shops. The signs swung merrily overhead. They appealed to the most careless eye, being often gigantic boots, or swords, or gloves, marking what was for sale within; or if in words, they might be

[1] See the print in Fournel, 539, after Granier. Conductors were coming into use before the Revolution. *Encyc. meth. Jurisp.*, x. 716.

misspelt, and thus adapted to a rude understanding. Large placards on the walls advertised the theatres. Street musicians performed on their instruments. Ballad-singers howled forth the story of the last great crime. Amid all the hubbub, the nimble citizen who had practiced walking as a fine art, picked his careful way in low shoes and white silk stockings; hoping to avoid the necessity of calling for the services of the men with clothes-brush and blacking who waited at the street corners.[1]

They were a fine sight, these citizens of Paris, before the male half of the world had adopted, even in its hours of play, the black and gray livery of toil. The Parisians of the latter part of King Louis XVI.'s reign affected simplicity of attire, but not gloom. The cocked hat was believed to have permanently driven out the less graceful round hat. It was jauntily placed on the wearer's own hair, which was powdered and tied behind with a black ribbon. For the coat, stripes were in fashion, of light blue and pink, or other brilliant colors. The waistcoat and breeches might be pale yellow, with pink bindings and blue buttons; the garters and the clocks of the white stockings, blue; the shoes black, with plain steel buckles. This would be an appropriate costume for the street; although many people wore court-mourning from economy, and forgot to take it off when the court did. A handsome snuff-box, often changed, and a ring, were part of the costume of a well-dressed man; and it was usual to wear two watches, probably from an excessive effort after symmetry; while it is intimated by the satirist that clean lace cuffs were sometimes sewn upon a dirty shirt.[2]

---

[1] Mercier, xii. 71, i. 107, 123, 215, 216. Young, i. 76. In 1761 the signs in the principal streets were reduced to a projection of three feet. Later, they were ordered to be set flat against the walls. Babeau, *Paris*, 42 ; but see Mercier. Names were first put on the street corners in 1728. Babeau, *Paris*, 43. Franklin, *L'Hygiène*.

[2] Babeau, *Paris*, 214. Fashion plates in various books. For

The costume of gentlemen in this reign was as graceful in shape as any that has been worn in modern Europe. The coat and waistcoat were rather long and followed the lines of the person; the tight breeches met the long stockings just below the knee, showing the figure to advantage. The dress of ladies, on the other hand, was stiff, grotesque, and ungainly; waists were worn very long, and hoops were large and stiff. But the most noticeable thing was the huge structure which, almost throughout the reign, was built upon ladies' heads. As it varied between one and three feet in height, and was very elaborate in design, it could not often be taken down. No little skill was required to construct it, and poor girls could sometimes earn a living by letting out their heads by the hour to undergo the practice of clumsy barbers' apprentices. At one time red hair came into fashion and was simulated by the use of red powder. The colors for clothes varied with the invention of the milliners, and the habit of giving grotesque names to new colors had already arisen in Paris. About 1782, "fleas' back and belly," "goose dung," and "Paris mud" were the last new thing. Caps "à la Boston," and "à la Philadelphie," had gone out. Instead of the fashion-plates with which Paris has since supplied the world, but which under Louis XVI. were only just coming into use, dolls were dressed in the latest style by the milliners and sent to London, Berlin, and Vienna.[1]

The dress of the common people was more brilliant and varied than it is in our time, but probably less neat. Cleanliness of person has never been a leading virtue

evening dress, suits all of black were beginning to come in towards 1789. In the street gentlemen were beginning to dress like grooms, aping the English. The sword was still worn at times, even by upper servants, but the cane was fast superseding it. Women also carried canes, which helped them to walk in their high-heeled shoes. Mercier, xi. 229, i. 293.

[1] Franklin, *Les soins de toilette.* Mercier, viii. 295, ii. 197, 198, 213.

among the French poor. Although there were elaborate bathing establishments in the river, a large proportion of the people hardly knew what it was to take a bath.[1] The sentimental milkmaids of Greuze are no more like the tanned and wrinkled women that sold milk in the streets of Paris, than the court-shepherdesses of Watteau and Boucher were like the rude peasants that watched their sheep on the Jura mountains. But the Parisian cockney was fond of dress, and would rather starve his stomach than his back. The milliners' shops, where the pretty seamstresses sat sewing all day in sight of the street, reminding the Parisians of seraglios, were never empty of those who had money to spend. For leaner purses, the women who sat under umbrellas in front of the Colonnade of the Louvre had bargains of cast-off clothing; and there were booths along the quays on Sunday, and a fair in the Place de la Grève on Monday.[2]

It is sometimes said of our own times that the rich have become richer and the poor poorer than in former days. I believe that this is entirely untrue, and that in the second half of the nineteenth century a smaller proportion of the inhabitants of civilized countries suffers from hunger and cold than ever before. Whatever be the figures by which fortunes are counted, there is no doubt that the visible difference between the rich and the poor was greater in the reign of Louis XVI. than in our own time.[3] In spite of the fashion of simplicity which was one of the affecta-

[1] But Young says, "In point of cleanliness I think the merit of the two nations is divided ; the French are cleaner in their persons, and the English in their houses." Young, i. 291. The whole comparison there given of French and English customs is most interesting.
[2] Mercier, viii. 269, ix. 294, v. 281, ii. 267.
[3] Mercier mentions fortunes varying from 100,000 to 900,000 livres income, and speaks of the former as common, i. 172. Meanwhile clerks got from 800 to 1500 livres and even less. Those with 1200 wore velvet coats, ii. 118.

tions of those days, the courtier still on occasion glittered in brocade. His liveried servants waited about his door. His lackeys climbed behind his coach, and awoke the dimly lighted streets with the glare of their torches, as the heavy vehicle bore him homeward from the supper and the card-table. The luxuries of great houses were relatively more expensive. A dish of early peas might cost six hundred francs. Six different officials (a word less dignified would hardly suit the importance of the subject), had charge of the preparation of his lordship's food and drink, and bullied the numerous train of serving-men, kitchen-boys, and scullions. There was the *maître d'hôtel*, or housekeeper, who attended to purchases and to storing the food; the chief cook, for soups, *hors d'œuvre*, *entrées*, and *entremets;* the pastry-cook, with general charge of the oven; the roaster, who fattened the poultry and larded the meat before he put the turnspit dog into the wheel; an Italian confectioner for sweet dishes; and a butler to look after the wine. Bread was usually brought from the bakers, even to great houses, and was charged for by keeping tally with notches on a stick. Baking was an important trade in Paris, and in times of scarcity the bakers were given the first chance to buy wood. For delicacies, there was the great shop at the Hôtel d'Aligre in the Rue Saint Honoré, a "famous temple of gluttony," where truffles from Périgord, potted partridges from Nérac, and carp from Strasbourg were piled beside dates, figs, and pots of orange jelly; and where the foreigner from beyond the Rhine, or the Alps, could find his own sauerkraut or macaroni.[1]

At the tables of the rich it was usual to entertain many guests; not in the modern way, by asking people for a particular day and hour, but by general invitation. The host opened his house two or three times a week for din-

[1] Mercier, x. 208, xi. 229, 346, xii. 243.

ner or supper, and anybody who had once been invited was always at liberty to drop in. Thus arose a class of respectably dressed people who were in the habit of dining daily at the cost of their acquaintance. After dinner it was the fashion to slip away; the hostess called out a polite phrase across the table to the retreating guest, who replied with a single word.[1] It was of course but a small part of the inhabitants of Paris that ate at rich men's tables. The fare of the middle classes was far less elaborate; but it generally included meat once or twice a day. The markets were dirty, and fish was dear and bad. The duties which were levied at the entrance of the town raised the price of food, and of the wine which Frenchmen find equally essential. Provisions were usually bought in very small quantities, less than a pound of sugar at a time. Enough for one meal only was brought home, in a piece of printed paper, or an old letter. Unsuccessful books thus found their use at the grocer's. Before dinner the supply for dinner was bought; before supper, that for supper. After the meal nothing was left. The poorer citizens carried their dinners to be baked at the cook-shops, and saved something in the price of wood. The lower classes had their meat chopped fine and packed in sausages, as is still done in Germany, an economical measure by which many shortcomings are covered up and no scrap is lost.[2]

The use of coffee had become universal. It was sold about the streets for two sous a cup, including the milk and a tiny bit of sugar. While the rich drank punch and ate ices, the poor slaked their thirst with liquorice water,

---

[1] Mercier, i. 176, ii. 225. *La Robe dine, La finance soupe.* Mercier says that a man who was a whole year without calling at a house where he had once been admitted had to be presented over again, and make some excuse, as that he had traveled, etc. This the hostess pretended to believe.

[2] Ibid., i. 219, xii. 128.

drawn from a shining cylinder carried on a man's back. The cups were fastened to this itinerant fountain by long chains, and were liable to be dashed from thirsty lips in a crowd by any one passing between the drinker and the water-seller.[1]

For the very poor there was second-hand food, the rejected scraps of the rich. In Paris they were nasty enough; but at Versailles, where the king and the princes lived, even people that were well to do did not scorn to buy dishes that had been carried untouched from a royal table. Near the poultry market in Paris, a great pot was always hanging on the fire, with capons boiling in it; you bought a boiled fowl with its broth, a savory mess. In general the variety of food was increasing. Within forty years the number of sorts of fruit and vegetables in use had almost doubled.[2]

The population was divided into many distinct classes, but there was a good deal of intercourse from class to class, nor was it extremely difficult for the able and ambitious to rise in the world. The financiers had become rich and important, but were regarded with jealousy. In an aristocratic state the nobles think it all wrong that any one else should have as much money as themselves. This is not strange; but it is more remarkable that the common people are generally of the same opinion, and that, while the profusion of the great noble is looked on as no more than the liberality which belongs to his station, the extravagance of the mere man of money is condemned and derided. This tendency was increased in France by the fact that many of the greatest fortunes were made by the farmers of the revenue, who were hated as publicans

---

[1] Mercier, viii. 270, n., iv. 154, xii. 296, v. 310. See plates in Fournel, 509, 516.

[2] Ibid., v. 85, 249. Genlis, *Dictionnaire des Etiquettes*, ii. 40, n., citing Buffon. Scraps of food are still sold in the Central Market of Paris.

even more than they were envied as rich men. Yet one financier, Necker, although of foreign birth, was perhaps the most popular man in France during this reign, and it was not the least of Louis's follies or misfortunes that he could not bring himself to share the admiration of his people for his Director General of the Treasury.

The mercantile class in Paris did not hold a high position. The merchant was too much of a shopkeeper, and the shopkeeper was too much of a huckster. The smallest sale involved a long course of bargaining. This was perhaps partly due to the fact, admirable in itself, that the wife was generally united with her husband in the management of the shop. The customary law of Paris was favorable to the rights of property of married women; and the latter were associated with their husbands in commerce and consulted in all affairs. This habit is still observed in France. It tends to draw husband and wife together, by uniting their occupations and their interests. Unfortunately it tends also to the neglect of children, especially in infancy, when their claims are exacting. Thus the Frenchwoman of the middle class is in some respects more of a wife and less of a mother than the corresponding Anglo-Saxon. The babies, even of people of very moderate means, were generally sent out from Paris into the country to be nursed. Later in the lives of children, girls were kept continually with their mothers, watched and guarded with a care of which we have little conception. Boys were much more separated from their parents, and left to schoolmasters. Neither boys nor girls were trusted or allowed to gain experience for themselves nearly as much as we consider desirable.[1]

Marriages were generally left to the discretion of parents, except in the lowest classes; and parents were too often governed by pecuniary, rather than by personal considerations in choosing the wives and husbands of their

[1] Mercier, i. 53, v. 231, ix. 173, vi. 325.

sons and daughters. Such a system of marriage would seem unbearable, did we not know that it is borne and approved by the greater part of mankind. It is possible that the chief objection to it is to be found less in the want of attachment between married people, which might be supposed to be its natural result, than in the diminution of the sense of loyalty. In England and America it is felt to be disgraceful to break a contract which both parties have freely made, with their eyes open; and this feeling greatly reënforces the other motives to fidelity. Yet while the rich and idle class in France, if the stories of French writers may be trusted, has always been honeycombed with marital unfaithfulness, there are probably no people in the world more united than the husbands and wives of the French lower and middle classes. Working side by side all the week with tireless industry, sharing a frugal but not a sordid life, they seek their innocent pleasures together on Sundays and holidays. The whole neighborhood of Paris is enlivened with their not unseemly gayety, as freely shared as the toil by which it was earned. The rowdyism of the sports in which men are not accompanied by women, the concentrated vulgarity of the summer boarding-house, where women live apart from the men of their families, are almost equally unknown in France. In the latter part of the eighteenth century many of the comfortable burghers of Paris owned little villas in the suburbs, whither the family retired on Sundays, sometimes taking the shop-boy as an especial favor. The common people also were to be found in great numbers in the suburban villages, such as Passy, Auteuil, or in the Bois de Boulogne, dancing on the green; although in the reign of Louis XVI. they are said to have been less gay than before.[1]

Artists, artisans, and journeymen, in their various degrees, formed classes of great importance, for Paris was

[1] Mercier, iii. 143, iv. 162, xii. 101.

famous for many sorts of manufactures, and especially for those which required good taste. But it was noticed that on account of the abridgment of the power of the trade-guilds, and the consequent rise of competition, French goods were losing in excellence, while they gained in cheapness; so that it was said that workmanship was becoming less thorough in Paris than in London.

The police of Paris was already remarkable for its efficiency. The inhabitants of the capital of France lived secure in their houses, or rode freely into the country, while those of London were in danger of being stopped by highwaymen on suburban roads, or robbed at night by housebreakers in town. From riots, also, the Parisians had long been singularly free, and for more than a century had seen none of importance, while London was terrified, and much property destroyed in 1780 by the Gordon riots. In spite of the forebodings of some few pessimists, people did not expect any great revolution, but rather social and economic reforms. It was believed that the powers of repression were too strong for the powers of insurrection. The crash came at last, not through the failure of the ordinary police, but from demoralization at the centre of government and in the army. While Louis still reigned in peace at Versailles, the administration of Paris went on efficiently. Correspondence was maintained with the police of other cities. Criminals and suspected persons, when arrested, could be condemned by summary process. The Lieutenant General of Police had it in his discretion to punish without publicity. The more scandalous crimes were systematically hidden from the public; a process more favorable to morality than to civil liberty. For the criminal classes in Paris arbitrary imprisonment was the common fate, and disreputable men and women were brought in by bands.[1]

The liability to arbitrary arrest affected the lives of but

[1] Mercier, vi. 206. Monier, 396.

a small proportion of the citizens after all. To most Parisians it was far more important that the streets were safe by day and night; that fire-engines were provided, and Capuchin monks trained to use them, while soldiers hastened to the fire and would press all able-bodied men into the service of passing buckets; that small civil cases were promptly and justly disposed of.[1]

The increase of humane ideas which marked the age was beginning in the course of this reign to affect the hospitals and poor-houses as well as the prisons, and to diminish their horrors. At the Hôtel Dieu, the greatest hospital in Paris, six patients were sometimes wedged into one filthy bed. Yet even there, some improvement had taken place. And while Howard considered that hospital a disgrace to Paris, he found many other charitable foundations in the city which did it honor. Here as elsewhere there was no uniformity.[2]

In the medical profession, the regular physicians held themselves far above the surgeons, many of whom had been barbers' apprentices; but it would appear that the science of surgery was better taught and was really in a more advanced state than that of medicine. More than eight hundred students attended the school of surgery. In medicine, inoculation was slowly making its way, but was resorted to only by the upper classes. Excessive bleeding and purgation were going out of fashion, but the poor still employed quacks, or swallowed the coarse drugs which the grocers sold cheaper than the regular apothecaries, or relied on the universal remedy of the lower classes in Paris, a cordial of black currants.[3]

---

[1] Mercier, i. 197, 210, ix. 220, xii. 162 (*Jurisdiction consulaire*).
[2] Mercier, vii. 7, iii. 225. Howard, *State of the Prisons*, 176, 177. Babeau, *La Ville*, 435. Cognel, 88. A horrible description of the Hôtel Dieu, written in 1788 by Tenon, a member of Academy of Sciences, is given in A. Franklin, *L'Hygiène*, 181.
[3] It was called *Cassis*. Mercier, xii. 126, vii. 126.

Near the Hôtel Dieu was the asylum for foundlings, whither they were brought not only from Paris, but from distant towns, and whence they were sent out to be nursed in the country. They were brought to Paris done up tightly in their swaddling clothes, little crying bundles, packed three at a time into wadded boxes, carried on men's backs. The habit of dressing children loosely, recommended by Rousseau, had not yet reached the poor; as the habit of having babies nursed by their own mothers, which he had also striven to introduce, had been speedily abandoned by the rich. The mortality among the foundlings was great, for two hundred of them were sometimes kept in one ward during their stay at the asylum.[1]

Although some falling off in the ardor of religious practices was noticed as the Revolution drew near, the ceremonies of the church were still visible in all their splendor. On the feast of Corpus Christi a long procession passed through the streets, where doors and windows were hung with carpets and tapestry. The worsted pictures, it is true, were adapted rather to a decorative than to a pious purpose, and over-scrupulous persons might be shocked at seeing Europa on her bull, or Psyche admiring the sleeping Cupid, on the route of a religious procession. Such anomalies, however, could well be disregarded. Around the sacred Host were gathered the dignitaries of the state and the city in their robes of office, marshaled by the priests, who for that day seemed to command the town. In some cases, it is said, the great lords contented themselves with sending their liveried servants to represent them. Soldiers formed the escort. The crowd in the street fell on its knees as the procession passed. Flowers, incense, music, the faithful with their foreheads in the dust, all contributed to the picturesqueness of the

[1] Mercier, iii. 239, viii. 188. Cognel found the asylum very clean, Cognel, 87.

scene. A week later the ceremony was repeated with almost equal pomp. On the Sunday following, there was another procession in the northern suburbs. Naked boys, leading lambs, represented Saint John the Baptist; Magdalens eight years old, walking by their nurses' side, wept over their sins; the pupils of the school of the Sacred Heart marched with downcast eyes. The Host was carried under a dais of which the cords were held by respected citizens, and was escorted by forty Swiss guards. A hundred and fifty censers swung incense on the air. The diplomatic corps watched the procession from the balcony of the Venetian ambassador, even the Protestants bowing or kneeling with the rest.[1]

From time to time, through the year, these great ceremonies were renewed, either on a regularly returning day, or as occasion might demand. On the 3d of July the Swiss of the rue aux Ours was publicly carried in procession. There was a legend that a Swiss Protestant soldier had once struck the statue of the Holy Virgin on the corner of this street with his sword, and that blood had flowed from the wounded image. Therefore, on the anniversary of the outrage, a wicker figure was carried about the town, bobbing at all the sacred images at the street corners, with a curious mixture of piety and fun. Originally it had been dressed like a Swiss, but the people of Switzerland, who were numerous and useful in Paris, remonstrated at a custom likely to bring them into contempt; and the grotesque giant was thereupon arrayed in a wig and a long coat, with a wooden dagger painted red in his hand. The grammarian Du Marsais once got into trouble on the occasion of this procession. He was walking in the street when one woman elbowed another in trying to get near the statue. "If you want to pray," said the woman who had been pushed, "go on your knees where you are; the Holy Virgin is everywhere." Du

[1] Mercier, iii. 78. Cognel, 101.

Marsais was so indiscreet as to interfere. Being a grammarian, he was probably of a disputatious turn of mind. "My good woman," said he, "you have spoken heresy. Only God is everywhere; not the Virgin." The woman turned on him and cried out: "See this old wretch, this Huguenot, this Calvinist, who says that the Holy Virgin is not everywhere!" Thereupon Du Marsais was attacked by the mob and forced to take refuge in a house, whence he was rescued by the guard, which kept him shut up for his own safety until after nightfall.[1]

For an occasional procession, we have one in October, 1785, when three hundred and thirteen prisoners, redeemed from slavery among the Algerines, were led for three days about the streets with great pomp by brothers of the orders of the Redemption. Each captive was conducted by two angels, to whom he was bound with red and blue ribbons, and the angels carried scrolls emblazoned with the arms of the orders. There was the usual display of banners and crosses, guards and policemen; there were bands of music and palm-branches. The long march required frequent refreshment, which was offered by the faithful, and it is said that many of the captives and some of the professionally religious persons indulged too freely. A drunken angel must have been a cheerful sight indeed. The object of this procession was to raise money to redeem more prisoners from slavery, for the Barbary pirates were still suffered by the European powers to plunder the commerce of the Mediterranean and to kidnap Christian sailors.[2]

Nor was it in great festivals alone that the religious spirit of the people was manifested. On Sundays all

---

[1] Mercier, iv. 97. Fournel, 176. This procession was abolished by order of the police, June 27, 1789. Fournel, 177.

[2] Bachaumont, xxx. 24. Compare Lesage, i. 347 (*Le diable boiteux*, ch. xix). For a procession of persons delivered by charity from imprisonment for not paying their wet nurses, see Mercier, xii. 85.

shops were shut, and the common people heard at least the morning mass, although they were getting careless about vespers. Every spring for a fortnight about Easter, there was a great revival of religious observance, and churches and confessionals were crowded. But throughout the year, one humble kind of procession might be met in the streets of Paris. A poor priest, in a worn surplice, reverently carries the Host under an old dirty canopy. A beadle plods along in front, with an acolyte to ring the bell, at the sound of which the passers-by kneel in the streets and cabs and coaches are stopped. Louis XV. once met the "Good God," as the eucharistic wafer was piously called, and earned a short-lived popularity by going down on his silken knees in the mud. All persons may follow the viaticum into the chamber of the dying. The watch, if it meets the procession on its return, will escort it back to its church.[1]

Let us follow it in the early morning, and, taking our stand under the porch where the broken statues of the saints are still crowned with the faded flowers of yesterday's festival, or wandering thence about the streets of the city, let us watch the stream of life as it flows now stronger, now more gently hour by hour.

It is seven o'clock. The market gardeners, with their empty baskets, are jogging on their weary horses toward the suburbs. Already they have supplied the markets. They meet only the early clerks, fresh shaven and powdered, hastening to their offices. At nine, the town is decidedly awake. The young barber-surgeons ("whiting" as the Parisians call them), sprinkled from head to foot with hair powder, carry the curling-iron in one hand, the wig in the other, on their way to the houses of their customers. The waiters from the lemonade-shops are bringing coffee and cakes to the occupants of furnished

[1] *Ordonnance de la police du Chatelet concernant l'observation des dimanches et fêtes*, du 18 *Novembre*, 1782. Monin, 403.

lodgings. On the boulevards, young dandies, struck with Anglomania, contend awkwardly with their saddle-horses.

At ten lawyers in black and clients of all colors flock to the island in the river where are the courts of law. The Palace, as the great court-house is called, is a large and imposing pile of buildings, with fine halls and strong prisons, and the most beautiful of gothic chapels. But the passages are blocked with the stalls of hucksters who sell stationery, books, and knicknacks.[1]

In the rue Neuve des Petits Champs they are drawing the royal lottery. The Lieutenant-General of Police, accompanied by several officers, appears on a platform. Near him is the wheel of fortune. The wheel is turned, it stops, and a boy with blindfolded eyes puts his hand into an opening in the wheel, and pulls out a ticket, which he hands to the official. The latter opens it, holding it up conspicuously in front of him to avert suspicion of foul play. The ticket is then posted on a board, and the boy pulls out another. The crowd is noisy and excited at first, then sombre and discouraged as all the chances are exhausted.

Noon is the time when the Exchange is most active, and when lazy people hang about the Palais Royal, whose gardens are the centre of news and gossip. The antechambers of bankers and men in place are crowded with anxious clients. At two the streets are full of diners-out, and all the cabs are taken. They are heavy and clumsy vehicles, dirty inside and out, and the coachmen are drunken fellows. Clerks and upper servants dash about in cabriolets, and sober people are scandalized at seeing women in these frivolous vehicles unescorted. "They go alone; they go in pairs!" cries one, "without any men. You would think they wanted to change their sex." Dandies drive the high-built English "whiski." All are blocked among carts and drays, with sacks, and

[1] Mercier, vi. 72, iv. 146, ix. 171. Cognel, 41.

beams, and casks of wine. For people that would go out of town there are comfortable traveling chaises, or the cheap and wretched *carrabas*, in which twenty persons are jolted together, and the rate of travel is but two or three miles an hour; while on the road to Versailles, the active postillions known as *enragés* will take you to the royal town and back, a distance of twenty miles, and give you time to call on a minister of state, all within three hours.[1]

Between half past two and three, people of fashion are sitting down to dinner, following the mysterious law of their nature which makes them do everything an hour or two later in the day than other mortals. At quarter past five the streets are full again. People are on their way to the theatre, or going for a drive in the boulevards, and the coffee-houses are filling. As daylight fails, bands of carpenters and masons plod heavily toward the suburbs, shaking the lime from their heavy shoes. At nine in the evening people are going to supper, and the streets are more disorderly than at any time in the day. The scandalous scenes which have disappeared from modern Paris, but which are still visible in London, were in the last century allowed early in the evening; but long before midnight the police had driven all disorderly characters from the streets. At eleven the coffee-houses are closing; the town is quiet, only to be awakened from time to time by the carriages of the rich going home after late suppers, or by the tramp of the beasts of burden of the six thousand peasants who nightly bring vegetables, fruit, and flowers into the great city.[2]

[1] Mercier, vii. 114, 228, ix. 1, 266, xi. 17, xii. 253. Chérest, ii. 166.
[2] Ibid., iv. 148.

CHAPTER XII.

THE PROVINCIAL TOWNS.

THE provincial towns in France under Louis XVI. were only beginning to assume a modern appearance. Built originally within walls, their houses had been tall, their streets narrow, crooked, and dirty. But in the eighteenth century most of the walls had been pulled down, and public walks or drives laid out on their sites. The idea that the beauty of cities consists largely in the breadth and straightness of their streets had taken a firm hold on the public mind. This idea, if not more thoroughly carried out than it can be in an old town, has much in its favor. Before the French Revolution the broad, dusty, modern avenues, which allow free passage to men and carriages and free entrance to light and air, but where there is little shade from the sun or shelter from the wind, were beginning to supersede the cooler and less windy, but malodorous lanes where the busy life of the Middle Ages had found shelter. Large and imposing public buildings were constructed in many towns, facing on the public squares. With the artistic thoroughness which belongs to the French mind, the fronts of the surrounding private houses were made to conform in style to those of their prouder neighbors. The streets were lighted, although rather dimly; their names were written at their corners, and in some instances the houses were numbered.

But such innovations did not touch every provincial town, nor cover the whole of the places which they entered. More commonly, the old appearance of the streets was little changed. The houses jutted out into the narrow way, with all manner of inexplicable corners and angles. The shop windows were unglazed, and shaded only by a wooden pent-house, or by the upper half of a shutter. The other half might be lowered to form a shelf, from which the wares could overrun well into the roadway. Near the wooden sign which creaked overhead stood a statue of the Virgin or a saint. Glancing into the dimly-lighted shop, you might see the master working at his trade, with a journeyman and an apprentice. The busy housewife bustled to and fro; now chaffering with a customer at the shop-door, now cooking the dinner, or scolding the red-armed maid, in the kitchen.[1]

The house was only one room wide, but several stories high. Upstairs were the chambers and perhaps a sitting-room. Even among people of moderate means the modern division of rooms was coming into fashion, and beds were being banished from kitchens and parlors. There were more beds also, and fewer people in each, than in former years. On the walls of the rooms paint and paper were taking the place of tapestry, and light colors, with brightness and cleanliness, were displacing soft dark tones, dirt, and vermin.[2]

Houses were thinly built and doors and windows rattled in their frames. The rooms in the greater part of France were heated only by open fires, although stoves of brick or glazed pottery were in common use in Switzerland and Germany; and wood was scarce and dear. In countries where the winter is short and sharp, people bear it with what patience they may, instead of providing against it, as is necessary where the cold is more severe and prolonged. Thicker clothes were worn in the house than when moving about in the streets. Wadded slippers protected the feet against the chill of the brick floors, and

---

[1] Babeau, *La Ville*, 363. Ibid., *Les Artisans*, 73, 82. Viollet le Duc, *Dict. d'Architecture* (Boutique.)

[2] Babeau, *Les Bourgeois*, 9, 19, 37.

the old sat in high-backed chairs to cut off the draft, with footstools under their feet. Chilblains were, and are still, a constant annoyance of European winter. The dressing-gown was in fashion in France as in America, where we frequently see it in portraits of the last century. Similar garments had been in use in the Middle Ages. They belong to cold houses.[1]

The dress of the working-classes, which had been very brilliant at the time of the Renaissance, had become sombre in the seventeenth century, but was regaining brilliancy in the eighteenth. The townspeople dressed in less bright colors than the peasants of the country, but not cheaply in proportion to their means. Already social distinctions were disappearing from costume, and it was remarked that a master-workman, of a Sunday, in his black coat and powdered hair, might be mistaken for a magistrate; while the wife of a rich burgher was hardly distinguishable from a noblewoman.[2]

Great thrift was practiced by the poorer townspeople of the middle class, but their lives were not without comfort. We read of a family in a small town of Auvergne before the middle of the century, composed of a man and his wife, with a large number of children, the wife's mother, her two grandmothers, her three aunts, and her sister, all sitting about one table, and living on one modest income. The husband and father had a small business and owned a garden and a little farm. In the garden almost enough vegetables were raised for the use of the family. Quinces, apples, and pears were preserved in honey for the winter. The wool of their own sheep was spun by the women, and so was the flax of their field, which the neighbors helped

---

[1] Babeau, *Les Artisans*, 123. In 1695 the water and wine froze on the king's table at Versailles, *Les Bourgeois*, 23.

[2] Babeau, *Les Artisans*, 13, 199. Handiwork was very cheap. Babeau gives the bill for a black gown costing 210 livres 15 sous, of which only 3 livres was for the making ; *Les Bourgeois*, 169 n.

them to strip of an evening. From the walnuts of their trees they pressed oil for the table and for the lamp. The great chestnuts were boiled for food. The bread also was made of their own grain, and the wine of their own grapes.

In the country towns, among people of small means, a healthy freedom was allowed to boys and girls. There were moonlight walks and singing parties. Love matches resulted from thus throwing the young people together, and were found not to turn out worse than other marriages. But in large towns matches were still arranged by parents, and the girls were educated rather to please the older people than the young men, for it was the elders who would find husbands for them.[1]

Amusements were simple and rational in the cultivated middle class. People in the provinces were not above enjoying amateur music and recitation, and the fashion of singing songs at table, which was going out of vogue in Paris, still held its own in smaller places. A literary flavor, which has now disappeared, pervaded provincial society. People wrote verses and made quotations. But this did not prevent less intellectual pleasures. Players sometimes spent eighteen out of the twenty-four hours at the card-table. Balls were given either by private persons or by subscription. Dancing would begin at six and last well into the next morning; for the dwellers in small towns will give themselves up to an occupation or an amusement with a thoroughness which the more hurried life of a capital will not allow. The local nobility, and the upper ranks of the burgher class, the officers, magistrates, civil functionaries and their families, met at these balls; for social equality was gaining ground in France. The shopkeepers and attorneys contented themselves, as a rule, with quieter pleasures, excursions into the country, theatres, visits, and little supper par-

[1] Marmontel, i. 10, 51. Babeau, *Les Bourgeois*, 315.

ties. Dancing in the open air and street shows, in which once all classes had taken part, were now left to the poor.[1]

The journeyman sometimes lived with his master, sometimes had a room of his own in another part of the town. He dressed poorly and lived hard; but generally had his wine. Bread and vegetables formed the solid part of his diet, beans being a favorite article of food. Wages appear to have been about twenty-six sous a day for men, and fifteen for women on an average, the value of money being perhaps twice what it is now, but the variations were great from town to town. The hours of work were long. People were up at four in the summer mornings, in provincial towns, and did not stop working until nine at night. But the work was the varied and leisurely work of home, not the monotonous drudgery of the great factory. Moreover, holidays were more than plenty, averaging two a week throughout the year. The French workman kept them with song and dance and wine; but drunkenness and riot were uncommon.[2]

The workman's chance of rising in his trade was far better than it is now. There were not twice as many journeymen as masters.[3] The capital required for setting up in business was small, although the fees were relatively large; the police had to be paid for a license; and the guilds for admission.

These guilds regulated all the trade and manufactures of the country. They held strict monopolies, and no man was allowed to exercise any handicraft as a master without being a member of one of them. The guilds were

[1] Babeau, *Les Bourgeois*, 209, 225, 241, 305.
[2] Babeau, *Les Artisans*, 21, 34. A. Young, i. 565.
[3] Babeau, *Les Artisans*, 63. Perhaps more workmen under Louis XVI. Manufactures on a larger scale were coming in. At Marseilles, 65 soap factories employed 1000 men ; 60 hatters, 800 men and 400 women. Julliany, i. 85. But Marseilles was a large city. In smaller places the old domestic trades still held their ground.

continually squabbling. Thus it was an unceasing complaint of the shoemakers against the cobblers that the latter sold new shoes as well as second-hand, a practice contrary to the high privileges of the shoemakers' corporation. Sometimes the civil authorities were called on to interfere. We find the trimming-makers of Paris, who have the right to make silk buttons, obtaining a regulation which forbids all persons wearing buttons of the same cloth as their coats, or buttons that are cast, turned or made of horn.

Minute regulations governed manufactures exercised within the guilds. The number of threads to the inch in cloth of various names and kinds was strictly regulated. New inventions made their way with difficulty against the vested rights of these corporations. Thus Le Prévost, who invented the use of silk in making hats, was exposed to all sorts of opposition from the other hatters, who said that he infringed their privileges; but he overcame it by perseverance, and finally made a large fortune. The regulations served to keep up the standard of excellence in manufacture, which probably fell in some respects on their abolition. They were often made to benefit the masters at the expense of the workmen, who on their side formed secret combinations of their own, fighting by much the same methods as such unions employ to-day. Thus in 1783 the journeymen paper-makers instituted a system of fines on their masters, which they enforced by deserting in a body the service of those who resisted them.[1]

The successful master of a trade, as he grew rich, might pass into the upper middle class, the *haute bourgeoisie*. He became a manufacturer, a merchant, perhaps even, when he retired on his fortune, a royal secretary, with a patent of hereditary nobility. His children, instead of

[1] Babeau, *Les Artisans*, 51, 108, 202, 239. Levasseur, ii. 353. Turgot, iii. 328, 347. (*Eloge de M. de Gournay*), Mercier, xi. 363.

leaving school when they had learned to read, write and cipher, and had taken their first communion, stayed on, or were promoted to a higher school, to learn Latin and Greek. His wife was called Madame, like a duchess. She had probably assisted in his rise, not only by good advice and domestic frugality, but by the arts of a saleswoman and by her talent for business. Should he die while his sons were young, she understood his affairs and could carry them on for her own benefit and for that of her children. No longer a single maidservant, red in the face and slatternly about the skirts, clatters among the pots in the little dark kitchen behind the shop, or stands with her arms akimbo giving advice to her mistress. The successful man has mounted his house on a larger scale, and if the insolent lackeys of the great do not hang about his door, there are at least one or two of those quiet and attentive old men-servants, whose respectful and self-respecting familiarity adds at once to the comfort and the dignity of life.[1]

It was not within the walls of his own house alone that the burgher might be a man of importance. The towns retained to the end of the monarchy a few of the rights for which they had struggled in earlier and rougher times. Assemblies differently composed in different places, but sometimes representing the guilds and fraternities and sometimes made up of the whole body of citizens, took a part in the government of the town. They voted on loans, on the conduct of the city's lawsuits, and on municipal business generally. Officers were chosen in various ways, some of them by very complicated forms of election, and some by throwing of lots. These officers bore different titles in different places, as consuls, échevins, syndics, or jurats. They sometimes exercised considerable executive and judicial powers, controlling the ordinary police of the city. Their perquisites and privileges varied from town

[1] Babeau, *Les Artisans*, 158, 167, 181, 204, 271.

to town, with the color of their official robes, and the ceremonies of their installation. The cities valued their ancient rights, shorn as they were of much substantial importance by the centralizing servants of the crown; and repeatedly bought them back from the king, as time after time the old offices were abolished, and new-fashioned purchasable mayoralties set up in their stead.[1]

The municipal authorities shared with the clergy the control of education and the care of the poor and the sick. The last were collected in large hospitals, many of which were inefficiently managed.[2] It must always be borne in mind, when thinking of the daily life of the past, that in old times, and even so late as the second half of the last century, a high degree of civilization and a great deal of luxury were not inconsistent with an almost entire disregard of what we are in the habit of considering essential conveniences. Comfort, indeed, has been well said to be a modern word for a modern idea. Dirt and smells were so common, even a hundred years ago, as hardly to be noticed, and diseases arising from filth and foul air were borne as unavoidable dispensations of divine wrath. Yet some advance had been made. Baths had been absolutely essential in the Middle Ages when every one wore wool; the result of the common use of linen had been at first to put them out of fashion; under Louis XVI. they were coming in again. The itch, so common in Auvergne early in the century that in the schools a separate bench

[1] Babeau, *La Ville*, 39. When the towns bought in the office of mayor, they had to name an incumbent, and the town owned the office only for his lifetime and had to buy it in again on his death. *Ibid.*, 81. This looks as if the royal office of mayor were not hereditary, in spite of the *Edit de la Paulette*. Where no other purchaser came forward, the towns were obliged to buy the office. *Ibid.*, 79.

[2] There were great differences from place to place. Howard, *passim*. The hospital, poor-house, etc., at Dijon were good; the hospital at Lyons large, but close and dirty. Rigby, 102, 113. Muirhead, 156.

was set apart for the pupils who had it, was almost unknown in 1786. Leprosy had nearly disappeared from France before the end of the seventeenth century. The plague was still an occasional visitant in the first quarter of the eighteenth, in spite of rigorous quarantine regulations. On its approach towns shut their gates and manned their walls, and the startled authorities took to cleansing and whitewashing. In 1722, the doctors of Marseilles went about dressed in Turkey morocco, with gloves and a mask of the same material; the mask had glass eyes, and a big nose full of disinfectants. How the sight of this costume affected the patients is not mentioned. When the plague was over, the Te Deum was sung, and processions took their way to the shrine of Saint Roch.[1]

Schools were established in every town. The schoolmasters formed a guild, the writing-masters another, and neither was allowed to infringe the prerogatives of its rival. The schoolmasters in towns were generally appointed by the clergy, but the municipal government kept a certain control. A good deal of the teaching of boys was done by Brotherhoods, while that of girls was almost entirely entrusted to Sisters. In many places primary instruction was free and obligatory, at least in name. The law making it so had been passed under Louis XIV., for the purpose of bringing the children of Protestants under Catholic teaching; but this law was not always enforced. In northern France, there were evening schools for adults, and Sunday schools where reading and writing was taught, probably to children employed in trades during the week. A certain amount of religious instruction preceded the ceremony of the "first communion." As to secondary or advanced schools, they are said to have been more numerous and accessible in the eighteenth century than now, when they have mostly been consolidated in the larger cities. There were five hundred and sixty-

[1] Babeau, *Les Bourgeois*, 177. Ibid., *La Ville*, 443.

two establishments reckoned as secondary in France in 1789, about one third of them being in the hands of Brotherhoods. There were also many private schools licensed by the municipal authorities. The boys when away from home lived very simply indeed. Marmontel, who was sent from his own little town to attend the school at a neighboring one, has left a description of his mode of life. "I was lodged according to the custom of the school with five other scholars, at the house of an honest artisan of the town; and my father, sad enough at going away without me, left with me my package of provisions for the week. They consisted of a big loaf of rye-bread, a small cheese, a piece of bacon and two or three pounds of beef; my mother had added a dozen apples. This, once for all, was the allowance of the best fed scholars in the school. The woman of the house cooked for us; and for her trouble, her fire, her lamp, her beds, her lodging and even the vegetables from her little garden which she put in the pot, we gave her twenty-five sous apiece a month; so that all told, except for my clothing, I might cost my father from four to five louis a year." This was about 1733, and the style of living may have risen a little, even for schoolboys, during the following half century. The sons of professional men and people of the middle class were better off in respect to education than most young nobles; as the former were sent to good schools, while the latter were brought up at home by incompetent tutors. It would appear to have been easy enough for a boy to get an education; harder for a girl. But no one who has glanced at the literature of the time will imagine that France was then destitute of clever women.[1]

In the eighteenth century great changes were taking place in the national life. Simple artisans presumed to be more comfortable in 1789 than the first people of the

[1] Babeau, *La Ville*, 482. Ibid., *Les Bourgeois*, 369. Marmontel, i. 16. Montbarey, i. 280. Ch. de Ribbe, i. 320.

town had been fifty years before. The middle class lived in many respects like the nobility, with material luxuries and intellectual pleasures. Yet the artificial barriers were still maintained. The citizen, unless of noble birth, was excluded not only from the army, but from the higher positions in the administration and in the legal profession. The nobility of the gown was liable to be treated with alternate familiarity and impertinence by that of the sword or by that of the court. The last held most of the positions which strongly appealed to vanity, many of those which bore the largest profit. Jealousy is possible only where persons or classes come near each other, and before the Revolution the various classes in France were rapidly drawing together.

CHAPTER XIII.

THE COUNTRY.

THERE is perhaps no great country inhabited by civilized man more favored by nature than France. Possessing every variety of surface from the sublime mountain to the shifting sand-dune, from the loamy plain to the precipitous rock, the land is smiled upon by a climate in which the extremes of heat and cold are of rare occurrence. The grape will ripen over the greater part of the country, the orange and the olive in its southeastern corner. The deep soil of many provinces gives ample return to the labor of the husbandman. If the inhabitants of such a country are not prosperous, surely the fault lies rather with man than with nature.

It has been the fashion to represent the French peasant before the Revolution as a miserable and starving creature. "One sees certain wild animals, male and female, scattered about the country; black, livid and all burnt by the sun; attached to the earth in which they dig with invincible obstinacy. They have something like an articulate voice, and when they rise on their feet they show a human face; and in fact they are men. They retire at night into dens, where they live on black bread, water, and roots. They spare other men the trouble of sowing, digging and harvesting to live, and thus deserve not to lack that bread which they have sown." This description, eloquently written by La Bruyère, has been quoted by a hundred authors. Some have used it to embellish their books with a sensational paragraph; others, and they are many, to show from what wretchedness the French nation has been delivered by its Revolution.

The advances of the last hundred years are many and great, but it is not necessary therefore to believe that in three generations a great nation has emerged from savagery. Let us see what part of La Bruyère's description may be set down to rhetoric, and to the astonishment of the scholar who looks hard at a countryman for the first time. Undoubtedly the peasant is sunburnt; unquestionably he is dirty. His speech falls roughly on a town-bred ear; his features have been made coarse by exposure. His hut is far less comfortable than a city house. His food is coarse, and not always plentiful. All these things may be true, and yet the peasant may be intelligent and civilized. He may be as happy as most of the toilers upon earth. He may have his days of comfort, his hours of enjoyment.

While the French writers of the eighteenth century find fault with many things in the condition of the peasant, their general opinion of his lot is not unfavorable. Voltaire thinks him well off on the whole. Rousseau is constantly vaunting not only the morality but the happiness of rural life. Mirabeau the elder says that gayety is disappearing, perhaps because the people are too rich, and argues that France is not decrepit but vigorous.[1]

"The general appearance of the people is different to what I expected," writes an English traveler, to his family, in 1789; "they are strong and well made. We saw many most agreeable scenes as we passed along in the evening before we came to Lisle: little parties sitting at their doors; some of the men smoking, some playing at cards in the open air, and others spinning cotton. Everything we see bears the mark of industry, and all the people look happy. We have indeed seen few signs of opulence in individuals, for we do not see so many gen-

---

[1] La Bruyère, *Caractères*, ii. 61 (*de l'homme*). Voltaire, *passim*, xxxi. 481, *Dict. philos.* (*Population*). Mirabeau, *L'ami des hommes*, 316, 325, 328.

tlemen's seats as in England, but we have seen few of the lower classes in rags, idleness, and misery. What strange prejudices we are apt to take concerning foreigners! I will own that I used to think that the French were a trifling, insignificant people, that they were meagre in their appearance, and lived in a state of wretchedness from being oppressed by their superiors. What we have already seen contradicts this;[1] the men are strong and athletic, and the face of the country shows that industry is not discouraged. The women, too, — I speak of the lower class, which in all countries is the largest and the most useful, — are strong and well made, and seem to do a great deal of labor, especially in the country. They carry great loads and seem to be employed to go to market with the produce of the fields and gardens on their backs. An Englishwoman would, perhaps, think this hard, but the cottagers in England are certainly not so well off; I am sure they do not look so happy. These women with large and heavy baskets on their backs have all very good caps on, their hair powdered, earrings, necklaces, and crosses. We have not yet seen one with a hat on. What strikes me most in what I have seen is the wonderful difference between this country and England. I don't know what we may think by and by, but at present the difference seems to be in favor of the former; if they are not happy they look at least very like it."

"We have now traveled between four and five hundred miles in France," says the same traveler in another place, "and have hardly seen an acre uncultivated, except two forests and parks, the one belonging to the Prince of Condé, as I mentioned in a former letter, the other to the king of France at Fontainebleau, and these are covered with woods. In every place almost every inch has been ploughed or dug, and at this time appears to be pressed

[1] Observe that this was written in French Flanders. Note by Dr. Rigby.

with the weight of the incumbent crop. On the roads, to the very edge where the travelers' wheels pass, and on the hills to the very summit, may be seen the effects of human industry. Since we left Paris we have come through a country where the vine is cultivated. This grows on the sides and even on the tops of the highest hills. It will also flourish where the soil is too poor to bear corn, and on the sides of precipices where no animal could draw the plough." [1]

Let us now turn to the other end of France, and hear another traveler, one generally less enthusiastic than the last. "The vintage itself," says Arthur Young, "can hardly be such a scene of activity and animation, as this universal one of treading out the corn, with which all the towns and villages in Languedoc are now alive. The corn is all roughly stacked around a dry, firm spot, where great numbers of mules and horses are driven on a trot round a centre, a woman holding the reins, and another, or a girl or two, with whips drive; the men supply and clear the floor; other parties are dressing, by throwing the corn into the air for the wind to blow away the chaff. Every soul is employed, and with such an air of cheerfulness, that the people seem as well pleased with their labor, as the farmer himself with his great heaps of wheat. The scene is uncommonly animated and joyous. I stopped and alighted often to see their method; I was always very civilly treated, and my wishes for a good price for the farmer, and not too good a one for the poor, well received." [2]

These descriptions would give too favorable an idea if they were taken for the whole of France. All peasant women did not powder their hair and wear earrings. Those of France did much more field-work than those of England. Their figures became bent, their general

[1] Dr. Rigby, 11, 96. See also Sir George Collier, 21.
[2] Arthur Young, i. 45 (July 24, 1787).

appearance worn; an English observer, accustomed to the more ruddy faces of his countrywomen, might set them down for twice their age. They often went barefoot, and on their way to market carried their shoes on a stick until they drew near the town. They had to be thrifty, and might be seen picking weeds on the wayside into their aprons, to feed their cows. All provinces were not so rich as Flanders. There were vast stretches of waste land in France, given up to broom and heath. Wolves and bears were still a terror to remote farms. There were, moreover, times of famine, which the foolish regulations of the government aggravated, by preventing the free movement of provisions within the country. In some provinces these seasons of famine were often repeated. Then the wretched inhabitants sank into despair. Young people would refuse to marry, saying that it was not worth while to bring unfortunate children into the world. But in general the country people were laborious and happy, with enough for their daily needs, and often merry, — resembling in that respect the English before the Puritan revival rather than the Anglo-Saxons of more modern times.[1]

In the country, as in the towns, prosperity and material well-being were slowly increasing. The latter years of King Louis XIV. had been years of depression and misery. External wars, and the persecution of the Protestants at home, heavy taxation and bad government, had reduced the numbers and the wealth of the French nation. But with the accession of Louis XV. in 1715, a time of

[1] A. Young, i. 6 (May 22, 1787). Ibid., i. 45 (July 24, 1787), i. 18, (June 10, 1787), i. 28 (June 28, 1787). D'Argenson, vi. 49 (Oct. 4, 1749), vi. 322 (Dec. 28, 1850), vii. 55 (Dec. 22, 1751), viii. 8, 35, 233, ix. 160. Turgot (iv. 274) reckons that in Limousin, 1766, the laborers' families did not have more than 25 to 30 livres per person per annum for their support, counting all they got. This is but $1\frac{64}{100}$ sou a day, and bread cost $2\frac{1}{2}$ sous per lb. A. Young, i. 439. This does not seem possible. The people lived partly on chestnuts.

recuperation had begun. During the seventy years that followed, the population increased from about sixteen to about twenty-six millions. The rent of land rose also. The natural excellence of the soil, the natural intelligence of the people, were bringing about a slow and uneven improvement.[1]

One third of the soil was covered with small farms, which at the death of every proprietor were subdivided among his children. By a curious custom (arising in I know not what form of jealousy or caprice), the subdivision was wantonly made more disastrous. It was usual to divide not only the whole estate, but every part of it among the heirs. Thus, if a peasant died possessed of six fields and left three children, it was not the custom that each child should take two fields, and that he who got the best should make up the difference in money to his brethren. Perhaps cash was too scarce for that. But every one of the six fields would be divided into three parts, one of which was given to each child, so that instead of six separate plots of ground, there were now eighteen. This process had been repeated until a farm might almost be shaded by a single cherry-tree.[2]

The class of middling proprietors was very small. The incidents to the holding of land by all who were not noble drove rising families to the towns. The great change that has come over the French country during the last hundred years consists, in a measure, in the formation of a class of men owning farms of moderate size.

A large part of the soil belonged to the nobles and the

---

[1] Clamageran, iii. 464. Bois-Guillebert, 179, and *passim*. Horn, 1. The improvement was not universal. Lorraine is said to have lost prosperity from the time of its union with France in 1737. Mathieu, 316.

[2] Sybel, i. 22. Chérest, ii. 532. Turgot, iv. 260. English writers, from Arthur Young to Lady Verney, wax eloquent over the evils of small holdings.

clergy. The exact proportion cannot be ascertained. It has been stated as high as two thirds; but this is probably an exaggeration. These proprietors of the privileged classes seldom cultivated any very large part of their land themselves, by hired workmen, although certain privileges and exemptions were allowed to such as chose to keep their farms in their own hands. A few of them let their lands for a fixed rent in money. But the greater part of the cultivated soil which was owned by the nobility and clergy was in the hands of *métayers*, lessees who paid their rent in the shape of a proportionate part of the crops. Sometimes the landlord made himself responsible for a portion of the taxes; sometimes he furnished cattle or farming implements. His share of the gross crop was usually one half. The system, which is still common in some parts of France, is considered a good one neither for the landlord nor for the tenant, but is devised principally to meet the want of capital on the part of the latter.[1]

We may imagine the country-houses of the nobles scattered over the face of the country so that the traveler would come upon one of them once in two or three miles. Sometimes the seat of the lord was an ancient castle, with walls eight feet thick, rising above the surrounding forest from the top of a steep hill, dark and threatening,

---

[1] Young reckons that the price of arable land and its rent are about the same in France as in England. The net revenue is larger in France, because there are no poor-rates and the tithe is more moderate in that country. The price of arable land he calculates to be on an average £20 per acre; rent 15 shillings 7d. per acre $= 3\frac{9}{16}$ per cent. of the salable value. From this deduct the two vingtièmes and 4 sous per livre (taxes paid by the landlord) and other expenses, and the net revenue remains between 3 and $3\frac{1}{4}$ per cent. The product of wheat in France is, however, much worse than in England, so that the proportion obtained by the landlord is greater and that of the tenant less. In France the landlord gets one half of the crop; in England, one fourth to one sixth, sometimes only one tenth. A. Young, i. 353.

but no longer formidable. Within, the great hall was stone-paved. Its walls were hung with dusky portraits and rusty armor. From the hall would open a spacious bedroom, with tapestried walls and a monumental bedstead. Curtains and coverlets showed the delicate embroidery of some ancestress, long since laid to rest in the family chapel. The very sheets had perhaps been woven by her shuttle. This bedroom, according to old custom, was still the living-room of the family. Sometimes the lord's house was modern, elegant, and symmetrical; it was flanked with pavilions and in front of it was a stone terrace, with a balustrade, on which stood vases for growing plants. Inside the house were high-studded rooms with white walls and gilded mouldings. High-backed, crooked-legged chairs, in the style of the last reign, were ranged against the walls; and near the middle of the dark, slippery, well-waxed floor, were lighter seats and stools. The grandmother's armchair with its footstool stood at the chimney corner, where the fire was religiously lighted on All Saints and put out at Easter, regardless of weather. Through the tall windows that opened down to the ground might be seen the long straight garden-walks, none too well kept, and clipped shrubs, with here and there a marble nymph, moss-grown and broken, or a fountain out of repair. The family did not spend much money in the place. There was little to do except in the season for shooting.[1]

In order that this last occupation may be left to the lord and his friends, game is strictly preserved, to the great detriment of the crops. Poachers are sharply dealt with, and the peasant may not have a gun to protect him from wolves. There are laws enough against the wrongs wrought by landlords and gamekeepers, against the trampling down of young wheat, against vexatious complaints and fines, but the country people say that such laws are

[1] Taine, *L'ancien régime*, 17. Mme. de Montagu, 59.

not fairly enforced. Especially is the case hard of those who live near the *capitaineries* or royal hunting-grounds. Here rural proprietors may not raise a new wall without permission, lest the hares be restrained of their liberty of eating cabbages. No crops can be cut until the appointed day, that the young partridges be not disturbed. Deer and rabbits live at free quarters in the cultivated fields. They are the peasants' personal enemies, and among the first unlawful acts of the Revolution will be their wholesale destruction.[1]

In every village there is a church, sometimes even in small places a beautiful gothic building, oftener modest in size and of plain architecture. Once or twice in a day's ride the red roofs and high walls of a convent come in sight, not very different in appearance from a group of farm buildings, — were it not for the chapel and its belfry; — for here in France the farms are surrounded by high walls. The interminable straight roads, fine pieces of engineering, but little traveled, stretch out between the ploughed fields, with rows of Lombardy poplars on either hand, that tantalize the sun-baked traveler with a suggestion of shade.

The peasants live in villages oftener than in detached farms, and the village itself is apt to have a rudely fortified appearance. The fields that stretch about it belong to the peasants, but with a modified ownership. Over them the lords exercise their feudal rights. There is the *cens*, a fixed rent, annual, perpetual, inseparably attached to the soil. It is paid sometimes in money, sometimes in grain, fruits, or chickens, according to deed, or to long established custom. There is the *champart*, a rent proportional to the crop, also payable to the lord; and there

---

[1] Olivier, 78, mentions the laws protecting the crops. The universal complaint of the *cahiers* proves the grievance. See the chapter on the *cahiers*. The *capitainerie* of Chantilly was said to be over 100 miles in circumference. A. Young, i. 8 (May 25, 1787).

is the tithe which must be given to the clergy. Should the peasant wish to sell his holding, a fine called *lods et ventes*, amounting in some cases to one sixth of the price, must be paid to the lord by the purchaser, and on some estates the lord has also the right to refuse to accept the new tenant, and to take the bargain on his own account.[1]

These are the common incidents of feudal tenure. Rights analogous to them may be found in England or in Germany, wherever that system has existed. And the vestiges of a state of things far older than feudalism have not entirely disappeared. The commons of wood and of pasturage yet recall the time when agricultural lands were held by a common tenure. Even that tenure itself, with its annual redistribution of the fields, may be found in Lorraine.[2]

There were, moreover, many irksome restrictions on the peasant. In the lord's mill he must grind his corn; in the lord's oven he must bake his bread; to the lord's bull his cow must be taken. Days of labor on the lord's land might be demanded of him. Ridiculous customs, offensive to his dignity or his vanity, might be enforced. Newly married couples were in some parishes made to jump over the churchyard wall. In other places, on certain nights in the year, the peasants were obliged to beat the water in the castle ditch to keep the frogs quiet. These customs have been considered very grievous by democratic writers, nor were they so indifferent to the peasants themselves as the lovers of the good old times would have us believe.[3]

It was not always the lord of the soil who enjoyed and

---

[1] Prudhomme, 37, 137, 515.

[2] Mathieu, 322.

[3] See the rural *cahiers, passim*. Mathieu gives the text of a customary right of *banalité*. The fee of the *four banal* was $\frac{1}{24}$ of the bread by weight; the *moulin banal*, $\frac{1}{17}$ of the flour; the *pressoir*

exercised the feudal rights. He had sometimes sold them to strangers, in whose hands they were merely revenue, and who demanded them harshly.

The origin of these customs lay in a form of civilization that had long passed away. To understand the conditions on which the French peasants held their lands little more than a hundred years ago, we must glance back over many centuries. Feudalism began in military conquest. When the barbarians overran the Roman Empire, the victorious chiefs divided the land among their principal followers; and the titles thus conferred, although personal at first, soon became hereditary. The man who received or inherited land was expected to appear in the field with his followers at the call of his chief. The tenant, in his turn, distributed the land among his friends on conditions similar to those on which he had himself received it; and the process might be indefinitely repeated. Thus there came to be a hierarchy in the state, in which every member was responsible to his immediate superiors and obliged within certain limits to obey the man next above him, rather than the king who was supposed to rule them all. The obligations were various, according to the conditions on which the lands had been granted, but they always involved military service on the part of the grantee, and protection on the part of the grantor. The services being mutual, and the tenure the usual, or fashionable one, most persons who held land in any other way saw fit to conform to the feudal method; and absolute, or allodial owners, where the tide of conquest had left any, generally, in the course of time, surrendered their lands to some neighboring lord, and received them back again on feudal conditions.

banal, $\frac{1}{16}$ to $\frac{1}{12}$ of the wine ; but the fees varied in different places even in one province. It was complained that presses enough for the work were not furnished, and that grapes spoiled in consequence. Mathieu, 285.

But the tenure here described existed only among the comparatively rich and great. When the last feudal division had been accomplished, when the chief had made his last grant to his captains and the soil was divided among them, there still remained by far the larger part of the population which owed no feudal duty and held no feudal estate. The common soldiers of the invading army, the native people of the conquered country and their descendants, inextricably mixed together, remained upon the soil and cultivated it as free tenants, or as serfs. They paid for the use of the land on which they lived in money or in a share of the crops, or in services. They acknowledged the title of the feudal lords over them, and while struggling to make good bargains with their masters, they seldom set up a claim to equality, or to independence. The peasants came to think it the natural and divinely appointed order of things that they should obey and serve their lords, with a partial obedience and a limited service. To ask why they were content so to serve, would be to open one of the greatest problems of history. Whatever the reason, over a large part of the world, and through the greater part of historical time, men have consented to obey other men whom they have not selected, and have generally preferred the hereditary principle to any other in determining to whom they would look up as their rulers.

So the French peasants and their lords went on for centuries, living side by side, rendering each other mutual services, sometimes quarreling and sometimes making bargains. The peasants were called on for military service, but they and their families took refuge in the lord's castle when the frequent wars swept over the land. The mill, whose rough machinery was still an improvement on the rude hand-mill, or on the yet more primitive mortar and pestle; the oven where the peasant could bake his bread without lighting a fire on his own hearth, after the toil of the long summer's day; the bull of famous breed in all the country-side, were the lord's, and all his tenants must use them and pay for them, at rates fixed by immemorial custom, or perhaps by some long forgotten bargain, made when these conveniences were first furnished to the dwellers in the land. The lord led his peasants to battle, he protected them from the inhabitants of the next valley, he decided their differences in his court, where the more considerable of his tenants sat beside him; he governed his people, well or ill, according to his character, but on the whole to their reasonable satisfaction. His government, such as it might be, was their only refuge from anarchy. The lord was governed, not very strictly, by a greater lord, who in his turn owed duty to a greater than he; until, after one or more steps, came the king, or overlord of the land.

The long struggle by which the kings of France had transformed this loose chain of allegiance into the tightened band of almost absolute monarchy, is not to be told here. From the tenth century to the seventeenth the combat was waged with varied success. The feudal lords lost much of their power, but kept much of their wealth and many of their privileges. The dukes and counts, whose fathers, in their own domains, had been as powerful as the king himself, retained their titles, and drew their incomes, but they spent their time in attendance on their sovereign. The petty lord still held his court of justice, over which his bailiff usually presided, but its functions had been gradually usurped by the royal judges. The castle, no longer needed for protection, was transformed into a country house. But many old customs and old rights were maintained, although their origin was forgotten. The peasants still worked for several days in the year on the lands of their lord, or paid a part of their crops in rent for their farms, although these had been in the possession of their forefathers for a thousand years.

This rent, or some rent, the peasants under Louis XVI. believed to be just, for they did not claim absolute ownership, but they considered the services onerous and degrading. Their ideas on these subjects were not very definite, but of late years a general sense of wrong had been growing in their minds. The long-lived quarrels which ever exist in the country-side were envenomed by stronger suspicions of injustice. It was a common complaint that the last survey and apportionment of rent had been unfair. The lords were no longer so far removed from their poorer neighbors as to be above envy. They were no longer so useful as to be considered necessary evils, as a large part of the community everywhere is prone to think of its governors.

Let us look at the life of the peasant. His cottage is not attractive; a low thatched building, perhaps without a floor. The barn is close against it, and the family is not averse to seeking the warmth of the cattle and of the dunghill. The windows are without glass, and pigs and chickens wander in and out at the open door. But the house belongs to the peasant, and is his home. He dares not improve it for fear of increased taxes. He cares not much to do so. It keeps him warm at night and dry when it rains; daylight and fine weather will find him out of doors. If he can hide away a few pieces of silver in an old stocking, he will more readily bring them out to buy another bit of ground, than waste them in useless comforts and luxuries of building.

The furniture was generally better than the house. A great bedstead, with curtains of green serge, was the principal piece, the centre of family life, the birthplace of the children, the death-bed of the parents. It was made as high as possible, to lift the sleepers above the damp ground. A feather-bed helped to keep them warm. A few cupboards and chests stood about the walls of the room, dark with age and grime. They were made of oak, or pear wood, and sometimes rudely carved. In the eighteenth century comfort had much increased in the towns, but the country had seen little change. The dress, again, was generally better than the furniture. The costumes of the provinces are often the copy of some long-forgotten fashion of the court, simplified or changed to adapt it to rural skill and country needs. To be well dressed is a sign of respectability; to be modestly housed may pass for a sign of thrift. On Sundays, bright coats, blue, gray, or olive, made their appearance. The women came out in good gowns and clean caps. There were flowered damask waists, sleeves of white serge, wine-colored petticoats. A gold cross was a sign of comparative wealth, but silver jewelry was common. Leather shoes were worn by both sexes. On week days there were wooden shoes, or bare feet in the southern provinces, and overalls of gray linen. Under Louis XVI., cotton began to drive out the linen and woolen cloths of former years. Being cheaper and less strong, clothes were oftener renewed. The change was contrary to beauty, but favorable to cleanliness.

The food of the peasant depended much on his harvest. In good years and on good soils he was well fed; in bad years and in poor districts, ill. Bread, the chief article of his diet, was cheaper and less good than in England, the wheat flour being mixed with rye, barley, oats, chestnuts or pease. The women made a soup, or porridge, by boiling this bread in water, adding milk perhaps, or a little bit of pork for a relish. Cheese and butter were fairly plenty, for common lands were extensive. Beef and mutton would be eaten at Easter-tide or at the festival of the patron saint, and most at wedding-feasts. Wine appears to have been considered a luxury, but a common one. It would seem that a peasant who did not taste it several times a week was accounted poor; one who drank it freely but temperately twice a day would have been called rich. Tobacco, the comforter of the poor, was in common use. This description of the food of the country people applies rather to the poorer peasants, or to those whose condition was not above the average, than to those who were best off. In Normandy, good bread, meat, eggs, vegetables, and fruit, with plenty of cider, formed the daily fare in prosperous farm-houses.[1]

The peasants were not cut off from all social and political activity. Every rural parish formed a separate little community, very restricted in its rights and functions, yet not without valuable corporate powers.[2] It could hold property, both real and personal; it could sue and be sued; it could elect its own officers and manage its own affairs. In the eighteenth century it became the fashion in France, as in many other countries, to divide the common lands, but many parishes still held large tracts in the reign of Louis XVI. The sale of their woods, the letting of their pastures, of fishing rights, or of the office of wine-taster in grape-growing districts, formed the revenues of the rural community. Its expenses were many and various. It repaired the nave of the church, the choir being kept in order at the cost of the priest. The parsonage and the wall round the churchyard were maintained by the parish. The drawing for the militia was at the expense of the community. So were some of the roads. It paid the schoolmaster and the syndic. Then there were incidental expenses, such as the annual mass, the carriage of letters, the keeping in order of the church clock. Sometimes the accounts of a community show a charge for a present to some influential person, capable of helping in a lawsuit, or of effecting a reduction of the taxes assessed on the parish. It was a

[1] This description of the condition of the peasants is taken chiefly from Babeau, *La vie rurale*.
[2] The parish and the community were generally coterminous, but were not always so. Ibid., *Le Village*, 97.

notable feature of the communal expenses, that the lord of the village shared them with his poorer neighbors. Into these rural matters privilege did not extend.[1]

The public meetings of these little communities were held on certain Sundays of the year after mass, or after vespers. Sometimes the meeting took place in the church itself, oftener in front of it, on the green. There the men of the village, streaming from the porch, stood or sat in groups on the grass, under the trees. Their own elected syndic presided. Ten was a quorum for ordinary business, but two thirds of the whole number was necessary to confirm a loan. A fine could be imposed for absence, or for leaving the assembly before adjournment.

In these town meetings the affairs of the community were discussed and decided. Sales were made, land was let, repairs of public buildings or of roads were voted. The syndic was elected. A record of the proceedings was kept, and was afterwards submitted to the royal intendant for his approval, without which no action was valid. This system lasted to the eve of the Revolution, but was at that time giving way to another. Under pretense that the public meetings were disorderly, they were gradually obliged to surrender their functions to boards partly or wholly elected. But certain important matters, such as the election of a schoolmaster, were still left to the general assembly. At the same time the right of suffrage was somewhat curtailed. Voters were required to be twenty-five years old and to pay certain taxes.

The village had its elected head, the syndic,[2] whose functions were not unlike those of an American selectman.

---

[1] But this was not always the case. See the *cahier* of the Artignose in Provence, *Archives parlementaires*, vi. 249. "Clochers et autres bâtiments généraux. (Les seigneurs n'en payent rien, même pour leurs biens roturiers, pour les différentes charges des communantés)."

[2] So called in the north of France. In the south, *consul*. Babeau, *Le Village*, 45.

He was the executive officer of the community, who conducted its business and had charge of its papers. The central government of the country also laid tasks upon him. He had to attend to the drawing of the militia, to report epidemics among the cattle, to enforce the laws for the destruction of caterpillars. Beside him were other officers, also elected by the inhabitants, but more directly the servants of the central power than he. These were the collectors of taxes. The syndics and collectors had much work and responsibility, with little pay and no chance of promotion. Honest and capable men were much averse to taking such places and often tried to escape it. The dishonest acquired illicit gain in them, at the expense of their fellow-subjects. Serving the community was considered less an honor than a duty, and service could be forced on the unwilling citizen; but the inhabitants in easy circumstances often found means to avoid the task, and the syndics and collectors were then chosen from among the poorer and less educated peasants. Some of them could neither read nor write.[1] A public body that wishes to be well-served must not make public service too disagreeable. France suffered at once from overpaid courtiers, and from ill-treated syndics and collectors.

The chief layman of the village was the lord's steward (*bailli*), who exercised the judicial functions of his master. He held himself above the common peasants and his wife was called "Madame." Her kitchen showed a greater array of pots and pans than that of her neighbors; her linen and her jewelry were more abundant than theirs. The steward and the parish priest were the most important persons in the hamlet.[2]

---

[1] The above description of the political life of the village is taken chiefly from Babeau, *Le Village*. See also the *cahier* of the village of Pin (*Paris extra muros, Archives parlementaires*, v. 22, § 1).

[2] Babeau, *La vie rurale*, 156.

The schoolmaster came far below the priest, who had over him a right of supervision. The main control of the schools, however, was in the hands of the communities, which elected the masters from candidates approved by the clergy. The latter insisted more strongly on orthodoxy than on competence. The position of the village schoolmaster was not brilliant. His house usually consisted of two rooms, one for the school and one for the family; his books were few, his clothes shabby. He was paid in part by the scholars, at the rate of three or five sous a month for reading, higher for writing and arithmetic. In some cases a tax of a hundred and fifty livres was laid on the parish for his benefit. But school was not held during the whole year; the scholars would desert in a body early in Lent, and be kept busy in the fields until November. The master might act as surgeon, or attorney, or surveyor; he might cultivate a plot of ground. He was expected to assist the priest at divine service, to lead the choir, or even to ring the bells. Simple primary schools were abundant in the country, especially in some of the northern provinces. In some villages the boys and girls went together, but the higher civil and ecclesiastical authorities, the king and the bishops, more familiar with the manners of the court than with those of the village, looked on these mixed schools with disfavor. In general it was harder for girls to get an education than for boys.[1]

The ambitious lad found means by which to rise. In

[1] Babeau, *La vie rurale*, 143. Ibid., *Le Village*, 277. Ibid., *L'Ecole de village*, 17, 18. Mathieu, 262. *Cahier* of the "*Instituteurs des petites villes, bourgs, et villages de Bourgogne*," Rev. des deux Mondes, April 15, 1881, 874. Statistics are imperfect, but from an examination of marriage registers, Babeau gathers that the proportion of persons married who could sign their names varied from nearly 89 per cent. of the men and nearly 65 per cent. of the women in Lorraine, to 13 per cent. of the men and nearly 6 per cent. of the women in the Nivernois. The central provinces and Brittany were the most illiterate parts of the country. *L'Ecole*, 3 n. 187. *Le Village*, 282 n. 3.

spite of the heavy and badly levied taxes, he might grow rich, add new fields to his father's farm, attain in some degree to comfort and to that consideration in his neighborhood which is perhaps the most legitimately dear to the heart of all the worldly consequences of success. Nor was it necessary to confine himself entirely to agriculture. The lower walks of the law and of medicine might be attained by the son of a peasant, and if one generation of labor were hardly long enough to reach the higher, no career, except the few reserved for the upper nobility, was beyond the aspiration of the rising man for his children or his children's children. There was more modest promotion nearer at hand. The blacksmith and the innkeeper stood in the eyes of their poorer neighbors as instances of prosperity. The studious boy, with good luck, might become a schoolmaster, even a parish priest. The active and pushing might, with favor, aspire to some petty place under the central government; or to stewardship for the lord. To what eminence of fortune might not these prove the paths.[1]

Meanwhile for the unambitious, for the mass of rural mankind, there were simpler pleasures, the dance on the green of a Sunday afternoon, the weddings with their feasts and merry-makings, the fairs and the festival of the patron saint of the village. There were games, ploughing matches, grinning matches. Holidays were frequent, — too frequent, said the learned; but probably they did not often come amiss to the peasants. On those days they could throw off their cares and play as heartily as they had worked. It is generally believed that the Frenchman, and especially the French peasant, was livelier before the Revolution than he has ever been since.[2]

[1] Babeau, *La vie rurale*, 128, etc.
[2] *Ibid.*, 187. See Goldsmith's *Traveller*, the lines beginning: —

"To kinder skies, where gentler manners reign,
I turn ; and France displays her bright domain."

There was much that was hard in the condition of the rural classes, but it was better than that of the greater part of mankind. On the continent of Europe only the inhabitants of some small states equaled in prosperity those of the more fortunate of the French provinces.[1] And in France prosperity was growing. The peasant's taxes were constantly getting heavier, but his means of bearing them increased faster yet. The rising tide of material prosperity, the great change of modern times, could be felt, though feebly as yet, in the provinces of France.

[1] Holland and Lombardy were the richest countries in Europe. Tuscany was especially well governed just then. A. Young, i. 480. Serfdom still existed in some remote French provinces, especially in the Jura mountains. Its principal characteristic was the escheating to the lord of the property of all serfs dying childless.

CHAPTER XIV.

TAXATION.[1]

THE gross amount paid in taxes by the French nation before the Revolution will never be accurately known; the subject is too vast and complicated, and the accounts were too loosely kept. Necker in his work on the "Administration of the Finances" reckons the sum annually paid by the people at five hundred and eighty-five million livres. Bailly (whose book appeared in 1830 and has not been superseded) makes the gross amount eight hundred and eighty millions. But from this should be deducted feudal dues and fees for membership of trade guilds, which Bailly includes in his estimate, and which were certainly private property, however objectionable in their character. There will remain less than eight hundred and thirty-seven million livres as the amount paid by about twenty-six million Frenchmen, in general and local taxation, including tithes; an average of about thirty-two livres a head. Was this amount excessive? Probably not, if the load had been rightly distributed. If we allow the franc of to-day one half of the purchasing power of the livre of 1789, the modern Frenchman yet pays more than his great-grandfather did. But there can be little doubt that he pays it more easily to himself. In the eighteenth century the Englishman was probably better off than his French neighbor, but his advantage was not

---

[1] "I must again remark that clear accounts are not to be looked for in the complex mountain of French finances." A. Young, i. 578. Young reckons the revenue at the entire command of Louis XVI. at 680,664,943 livres, i. 575. See also Stourm, ii. 182.

undoubted. Grenville, in 1769, speaks of the comparative lightness of taxes and cheapness of living which, he says, must make France an asylum for British manufacturers and artificers. Young, twenty years later, asserts that the taxes in England are much more than double those in France, but more easily borne. Necker says that England bears as large a burden of taxation as France, in spite of a smaller number of inhabitants and a less amount of money in circulation; but bears it more readily because it is better distributed. And Chastellux, while arriving at a similar conclusion, remarks that after all the French is, of all nations, the one that suffers most from taxation.[1]

Under the old monarchy the taxes were unequally assessed in two ways. There were differences of places and differences of persons. This is pretty sure to be true of all countries, but in France the differences were very large and were not sanctioned by the popular conscience. In a country which had become strongly conscious of its unity, and which was full of national feeling, some provinces were taxed much more heavily than others, not for their own local purposes, but for the support of the central government. In the first place came those provinces which were included in the general assessment of taxes. These were divided into twenty-four districts (*généralités*), over each of which was an intendant. Twenty of these districts formed the heart of old France, extending irregularly from Amiens on the north to Bordeaux on the south, and from Grenoble on the east to the sea. To

---

[1] Necker, *De l'Administration*, i. 35, 51. Bailly, ii. 275. Grenville, *The Present State of the Nation*, 35 ; but this statement is made in a political pamphlet, answered and apparently refuted by Burke, *Observations on a Late State of the Nation*. A. Young, i. 596. Chastellux, ii. 169. For 1891 the average taxation per head amounts to 86 francs, for 1789 to 34 livres, *Statesman's Year Book*, 1891, p. 472, and Bailly.

these were added the conquered or ceded provinces: Alsace, Lorraine, Bar, the Three Bishoprics, Franche Comté, Flanders, and Hainault, forming among them four districts and enjoying privileges superior to those of old France. All these formed the Lands of Election (*pays d'Election*). On the other hand were the Lands of Estates (*pays d'Etats*), provinces which had retained their assemblies, and with them some of their ancient rights of taxing themselves, or at least of levying in their own way those taxes which the central government imposed. This was a privilege highly prized by the provinces which possessed it. These provinces formed a fringe round France, and included Languedoc, Provence, the duchy of Burgundy, Artois, Brittany, and some others. The central administration was so oppressive, at the same time that it was clumsy and inefficient, that every province and city was anxious to compound for its taxes, and to settle them at a fixed rate, though a high one. This was accomplished on the largest scale by the Lands of Estates, but similar privileges, to a greater or less extent, were maintained by most of the cities. We must remember, here as elsewhere, that France had not sprung into being as a homogeneous nation with her modern boundaries. From the accession of the House of Capet in the tenth century, province after province had been added to the dominions of the crown. Many of them had preserved ancient rights. Customs and tolls differed among them, duties were exacted in passing from one to the other. Privileges, the prizes of old wars, rights assured in some cases by solemn treaties, had to be regarded. The wars of the Middle Ages were waged chiefly concerning legal claims. The end of the period found all Europe full of privileged territories, persons, or corporations. Privileges and rights were regarded as property. Modern struggles have been for ideas, and among the most cherished of these have been equality and uniformity. The sacredness of property and of contract have in a measure gone down before them.[1]

Although the Provincial Estates differed in the various provinces which possessed them, they included in almost every case members of the three orders. The Clergy were usually represented by bishops, abbots, and persons deputed by chapters; the Nobility either by all nobles whose title was not less than a hundred years old, or by the possessors of certain fiefs; the third estate, or Commons, by the mayors and deputies of the towns. The three Orders sometimes sat apart, sometimes together. In the intervals between their sessions their powers were delegated to intermediate commissions, small boards for the regulation of current affairs. There was nothing democratic in such a constitution. Even the representatives of the commonalty were taken from among the most privileged members of their order. Nor were the powers of the Estates extensive. They bargained with the royal intendants for the gross amount of the taxes to be assessed on their provinces. They divided this sum and charged it to the various subdivisions of their territory. They levied it by taxes similar to those of the general government.[2]

But in spite of all drawbacks the Provincial Estates were much valued by the provinces which possessed them. They were at least a guarantee that some local knowledge and local patriotism would be applied to local affairs. Moreover, they had the right of petition, a right essential to good government, both for the information of rulers and for giving vent to the feelings of subjects. This right is, and has long been, so nearly free in English-speaking

---

[1] Necker, *De l'Administration*, i. ix. Bailly, ii. 276. Horn, 258. Bois-Guillebert, 207. (*La détail de la France Partie*, ii. c. vii.); Stubbs *Lectures*, 217. Walloon Flanders was in the anomalous position of forming part of a *généralité*, but possessing Estates. *Bailly*, ii. 327.

[2] Luçay, *Les assemblées provinciales*, 111. Necker, *Mémoire au roi sur l'établissement des administrations provinciales*, passim.

countries, that it is hard to realize that there are civilized lands where men may not quietly and respectfully express their wishes. Yet in old France, as in a large part of Continental Europe to-day, the citizen who publicly gave an opinion on public matters, or who pointed out a well-known public grievance, was considered a disturber of the peace. Under such circumstances, a body of men who were allowed to discuss and recommend might render a great service to their country by simply using that freedom. The complaints of the Estates of each province were transmitted to the king in council, by a document known as a *cahier*, and the wishes thus expressed often formed a basis of legislation, or of administrative orders.

Among the spasmodic efforts at reform made under Louis XVI. were two attempts to extend the system of local self-government. The first was made by Necker in 1778 and 1779. Provincial assemblies were established in those years by way of experiment in two provinces, Berry and Haute Guyenne. These assemblies were composed of forty-eight and fifty-two members respectively, one half being taken from among the clergy and nobility, one half from the Third Estate of the towns and the country. A third of the members of the Assembly of Berry were appointed by the king, and these elected their fellow-members, care being taken to preserve the equality of classes. One third of the members were to be renewed by the assembly itself once in three years. The body was, therefore, in no way dependent on popular election. The assembly met and voted as one chamber. Its functions were almost purely administrative, the assessment of taxes, the care of roads and the management of charitable institutions. All this was done under close supervision of the intendant and, through him, of the minister. The assembly sat only once in two years, for a time not exceeding one month, but an intermediate commission carried on its work between its sessions. The general plan of the

Assembly of Haute Guyenne was similar to that of the Assembly of Berry.

Eight years passed between the establishment of these experimental assemblies and the convocation of the first Assembly of Notables at Versailles, — eight important years in French history. Necker was driven from power, but the two new bodies survived the reactionary policy of his successors, and did some good service. The fallen minister kept his popularity and his influence with the public at large. His great book on the "Administration of the Finances" was in all hands, eighty thousand copies having been rapidly sold. In it he expounds his favorite scheme of Provincial Assemblies, and praises the working of the two that have been established. He points out that they are not representative bodies, empowered to make bargains with the king and to impede the government, but administrative boards, entrusted by the sovereign with the duty of watching over the interests of the people of their districts. The Assembly of Notables of 1787 and the minister Brienne adopted Necker's views, but not completely. They established provincial assemblies throughout France on a plan of their own. One half of the members of these new bodies were to be chosen in the first place by the king; the second half being elected by the first. But at the end of three years one quarter part of the assembly was to retire, and its place was to be filled by a true election. This, however, was not to be direct, but in three stages. A parochial board was to be created in every village, composed of the lord and the priest ex officio, and of several elected members. These parochial boards were to elect the district boards, (*assemblées d'élection*) and the latter were to elect the new members of the Provincial Assembly. The march of events after 1787 prevented these elections from taking place. But the nominated assemblies met twice, once for organization and once for business. They came too late to prevent a catastrophe, but lasted long enough to give well-founded hopes of usefulness. The great National Assembly of 1789 and its successors might have had a far less stormy history, had all France been accustomed, though only for one generation, to political bodies restrained by law.[1]

Within a given province or district, there was no proportional equality among persons in the matter of taxation. It was sometimes said that the noble paid with his blood, the villein with his money. But the order of the Nobility had come to include many persons who never thought of shedding their blood for their country; to include, in fact, the rich and prosperous generally. These were not (as they are sometimes represented to have been), quite free from taxation. Something like one half of the taxes were indirect, and might be supposed to be paid by all classes in proportion to their consumption. Yet even for the indirect taxes, privileged persons managed to find ways partially to escape. Some of the direct taxes were deducted from salaries, or imposed on incomes, but it was said that the rich and powerful often succeeded in having their incomes lightly assessed. By way of increasing the inequality of taxation, the government had a habit, when in need of more money than usual, of adding a percentage to some old tax, instead of devising a new one, thus bearing most heavily with the new impost on those classes which were most severely taxed already.

First among French taxes, both in blundering unfairness and in evil fame, came the Land Tax or *Taille*, producing for the twenty-four districts a revenue of about forty-five million livres, or with its accessory taxes, of about seventy-five millions.[2]

---

[1] Necker, *Compte rendu*, 74. Ibid., *De l'Administration*, ii. 225, 292. Lavergne, *Les Assemblées provinciales sous Louis XVI.* Luçay, *Les Assemblées provinciales sous Louis XVI.*, 163.

[2] Bailly, ii. 307. Necker, *De l'Administration*, i. 6, 35, puts the

The taille was of feudal origin, and in the Middle Ages was paid to the lord by his tenants. In the fifteenth century, however, it had already been diverted to the royal treasury, and its product was employed in the maintenance of troops. It was therefore paid only by villeins, for the nobles served in person, and the clergy by substitute, if at all.

The exemption of the upper orders from liability to the taille clung to that tax after the reason for such freedom had ceased to exist. The tax itself early grew to be of two kinds, real and personal. The *taille réele*, common in the southern provinces of France, was a true land-tax, assessed according to a survey and valuation on all lands not accounted noble, nor belonging to the church, nor to the public. The distinction between noble and peasant lands was an old one; and the peasant lands paid the tax even when owned by privileged persons.[1]

Over the greater part of France, however, the *taille réele* did not exist, and only the *taille personelle* was in force. This bore on the profits of the land and on all forms of industry; but the churchmen and the nobles were exempt, at least in part.[2] Owing to its personal nature, the tax was payable at the residence of the person taxed. If a peasant lived in one parish and derived most of his income from land situated in another, he was taxable at the place of his residence, at a rate perhaps entirely different from that of the parish in which his farm was situated. It might happen that a large part of the lands of a parish were owned by non-residents, and that the ability of the parish to pay its taxes was thus reduced. But there were exceptions to the rule by which the tax fol-

taille at 91 millions, but I think he includes the *tailles abonnées*, paid by the *Pays d'etats*, although not those paid by cities.

[1] Turgot, iv. 74.

[2] There appears to have been a limit to the exemption of nobles cultivating their own lands.

lowed the person, and the whole matter was so complicated as to be a fertile cause of dispute and of double taxation.[1]

The method of assessment and levy was peculiar. The gross amount of the taille was determined twice a year by the royal council, and apportioned arbitrarily among the twenty-four districts (*généralités*) of France, and then subdivided by various officials among the sub-districts (*élections*) and the parishes. The divisions thus made were very unequal; some provinces, sub-districts, and parishes being treated much more severely than others, apparently rather by accident or custom than for any equitable reason. An influential person could often obtain a diminution of the tax of his village. When the work of subdivision was completed, the syndics and other parish officers were notified of the tax laid on their parishes, which were thenceforth liable for the amount. But the taille had still to be apportioned among the inhabitants. For this purpose from three to seven collectors were elected in every rural community by popular vote. The collectors assessed their neighbors at their own discretion, and were personally responsible to the government for the whole amount assessed on the parish. In consideration of this, and of their labor, they were allowed to collect a percentage in addition to the taille, for their own pay.[2] The whole process was the cause of endless bickerings and disputes, lawsuits and appeals, and the collectors were frequently ruined in spite of all their efforts. They were ignorant peasants, unused to accounts, sometimes unable to read. In some of the mountain parishes of the Pyrenees their accounts were kept on notched sticks to a period not very long before the Revolution.[3]

[1] Turgot, iv. 76.
[2] "Six deniers par livre" $= 2\frac{1}{2}$ per cent. Turgot, vii. 125. Sometimes 5 per cent. Babeau, *Le Village*, 225.
[3] Bailly, ii. 159. Horn, 224. Babeau, *Le Village*, 222, 224. Turgot,

The liability to the taille was joint. A gross sum was laid on the parish, and if one person escaped, or was unable to pay, his share had to be borne by the rest. On the other hand, if one man were overcharged, the burden of his neighbors was lightened. Thus it was every one's interest to seem poor. And the taxes were so important a matter, taking so large a part of the yearly income, that they modified the whole conduct of life. People dared not appear at their ease, lest their shares should be increased. They hid their wealth and took their luxuries in secret. One day, Jean Jacques Rousseau, traveling on foot, as was his wont, entered a solitary farm-house, and asked for a meal. A pot of skimmed milk and some coarse barley bread were set before him, the peasant who lived in the house saying that this was all he had. After a while, however, the man took courage on observing the manners and the appetite of his guest. Telling Rousseau that he was sure he was a good, honest fellow, and no spy, he disappeared through a trap-door, and presently came back with good wheaten bread, a little dark with bran, a ham, and a bottle of wine. An omelet was soon sizzling in the dish. When the time came for Rousseau to pay and depart, the peasant's fears returned. He refused money, he was evidently distressed. Rousseau made out that the bread and the wine were hidden for fear of the tax-gatherer; that the man believed he would be ruined, if he were known to have anything.[2]

As it was for the advantage of individuals to be thought poor, so it was best for villages to appear squalid. The Marquis of Argenson writes in his journal: "An officer of the *élection* has come into the village where my coun-

---

vii. 122, iv. 51. *Encyclopédie*, xv. 841 (*Taille*). A similar practice existed in the English Court of Exchequer, to a later date.

[2] Rousseau, xvii. 281 (*Confessions*, Part i. liv. iv.). Vauban, 51, and *passim*. Bois-Guillebert, 191.

try-house is, and has said that the taille of the parish would be much raised this year; he had noticed that the peasants looked fatter than elsewhere, had seen hens' feathers lying about the doors, that people were living well and were comfortable, that I spent a great deal of money in the village for my household expenses, etc. This is what discourages the peasants. This is what causes the misfortunes of the kingdom. This is what Henry IV. would weep over were he living now."[1]

The country people had grown to be very distrustful and suspicious wherever officials of the government were concerned. " I remember a singular feature of this subject," says Necker. "I think it was twenty years ago that an intendant, with the laudable intention of encouraging the manufacture of honey and the cultivation of bees, began by asking for statistics as to the number of hives kept in the province. The people did not understand his intentions, they were, perhaps, suspicious of them, and in a few days almost all the hives were destroyed."[2]

No one could be induced to pay promptly, lest he should be thought to have money. The tax was due in four payments, from the first of October to the last of April, but the collection of one instalment was seldom completed before the following one was due; that of one year seldom made before the next had come. The peasants obliged the collectors to wring out the hard-earned copper pieces one or two at a time. The tardy were vexed with fines and distraints. Furniture, doors, the very rafters and floors were sold for unpaid taxes. In the time of Louis XV., if a whole village fell too much behindhand, its four principal inhabitants might be seized and carried off to jail. This corporal joint-liability was ended by a

---

[1] D'Argenson, vi. 256 (Sept. 12, 1750). See also vi. 425, vii. 55, viii. 8, 35, 53.

[2] *De l'Administration*, iii. 232.

law passed under the ministry of Turgot, and apparently not repealed on his fall.[1]

The assessment and collection of the taille presented many anomalies. In some places commissioners had been appointed by the intendant, for the purpose of assessing estates and of reckoning the value of day's labor of artisans. This method worked well and gave satisfaction, but it extended only to a few provinces.[2]

From the land tax we pass to the Twentieths (*vingtièmes*[3]), which, as their name implies, were in theory taxes of five per cent. on incomes. From these the clergy only were freed (having bought of the crown a perpetual exemption). Two twentieths and four sous in the livre of the first twentieth, or eleven per cent., was the regular rate in the reign of Louis XVI., and was expected to bring in from fifty-five to sixty million livres a year. A third twentieth was laid in 1782, to last for three years after the end of the war of the American Revolution, then in progress. This twentieth brought in twenty-one and a half millions only, on account of various exemptions that were allowed. The liability to the twentieths was not joint but individual; so that when a deduction was made from the amount charged to one tax-payer, the sum demanded of the others was not increased.

An attempt was made to levy the twentieths on the various sorts of income. The product of agriculture paid the largest part, but a percentage was retained on salaries and pensions paid by the government, and the incomes of public officers receiving fees was estimated. In spite of the desire to include every income in the operation of this

[1] Horn, 238; Vauban; Bailly, ii. 203; Stourm, i. 52; Turgot, vii. 119.

[2] Babeau, *Le Village*, 214.

[3] Not to be confounded with the *Droit de vingtième*, an indirect tax on wine. Kaufmann, 33. Notice that the two *vingtièmes* are constantly spoken of as the *dixième*.

tax, it was generally believed that valuations were habitually made too low, and that unfair discrimination took place. The inhabitants of some provinces, on the other hand, were thought to be overcharged. Attempts at rectification were resisted by the courts of law, the doctrine being asserted that the valuation of a man's income for the purposes of this tax could not legally be increased. It is instructive to compare the interest thus shown in the rights of the upper classes, who shared in the payment of the twentieths, with the indifference manifested to the arbitrary manner in which the common people were treated in levying the Land Tax.[1]

The poll tax (*capitation*) was one only in name. It was in fact a roughly reckoned income tax, and the inhabitants of France were for its purposes divided into twenty-two classes, according to their supposed ability to pay. In the country, the amount demanded for this tax was usually proportioned to that of the personal taille. People who paid no taille were assessed according to their public office, military rank, business, or profession. The rules were complicated, giving rise to endless disputes. In theory the very poor were exempt, but the exemption was not very generous, for maid-servants were charged at the rate of three livres and twelve sous a year, and there were yet poorer people who paid less than half that amount. If the poor man failed to pay, a garrison (*garnison*) was lodged upon him. A man in blue, with a gun, came and sat by his fire, slept in his bed, and laid hands on any money that might come into the house, thus collecting the

---

[1] Necker reckons the two *vingtièmes* and four sous at 55,000,000 livres. *De l'Administration*, i. 5, 6. *Compte rendu*, 61. Ibid., *Mémoire au roi sur l'établissement des administrations provinciales*, 25. Necker abolished the *vingtième d'industrie* applied to manufactures and commerce. *Compte rendu*, 64. In his later book he speaks of it as subsisting in a few provinces only. *De l'Administration*, i. 159. Turgot, iv. 289. Stourm, i. 54.

tax and his own wages. The amount levied by the poll-tax and accessories was from thirty-six to forty-two million livres a year.[1]

The indirect taxes of France were mostly farmed. Once in six years the Controller General of the Finances for the time being entered into a contract, nominally with a man of straw, but actually with a body of rich financiers, who appeared as the man's sureties, and who were known as the Farmers General. The first operation of the Farmers, after entering into the contract, was to raise a capital sum for the purpose of buying out their predecessors, of taking over the material on hand, and of paying an advance to the government; for although many individual Farmers General held over from one contract to the next, the association was a new one for each lease. In 1774, just before the death of King Louis XV., a new contract was made, and the capital advanced amounted to 93,600,000 livres. The Farmers were allowed interest on this sum at the rate of ten per cent. for the first sixty millions, and of seven per cent. for the remaining 33,600,000 livres. This interest was, however, taxed by the government for the two twentieths.

The rent paid by the Farmers under this contract was 152,000,000 livres a year, for which consideration they were allowed to collect the indirect taxes and keep the product. This system, which is at least as old as the New Testament, is now generally condemned, but in the eighteenth century it found defenders even among liberal writers.

The Farmers General in the contract of 1774 were sixty in number, but they did not divide among themselves all

---

[1] Bailly, ii. 307. Necker, *De l'Administration*, i. 8. Mercier, iii. 98, xi. 96. Mercier thinks that the *capitation* was more feared than the *dixième*, and than the *entrées*, because it attached more directly to the individual and to his person. Does this mean greater severity in collection? Notice that he writes of Paris, where there is no taille.

the profits of the enterprise. It was the habit to accord to many people a share in the operations of the farm, without any voice in its management. The people thus favored were called croupiers; king Louis XV. himself was one of them. His Controller General, the Abbé Terray, received a fee of three hundred thousand livres on concluding the contract, and the promise of one thousand livres for every million of profits. When the bargain had been struck and the advance paid, he announced to the Farmers that further croupes would be granted, and that sundry payments must be made to the treasury. The profits of the undertaking were thus materially reduced. The Farmers at first threatened to throw up their bargain, but the Controller told them that if they did so he would not return their advances, but only pay interest on them. In spite of this swindle, the lease turned out on the whole much to the benefit of the Farmers.

In 1780, when the lease above mentioned expired, Necker was Director of the Finances. He introduced reforms into the General Farm, cutting down the number of Farmers from sixty to forty, and reducing their gains. The collection of certain taxes was taken from them, and entrusted to new companies. His contract was for a rent of 122,900,000 livres and the advance was forty-eight millions, for which the Farmers received seven per cent. Moreover, the latter were not to take the whole profit above the rent of the Farm. The first three millions of that profit went to the treasury, which also received one half of the remaining gains, but croupes and pensions on the Farm were totally abolished. Necker reckons the total sum drawn yearly by the Farmers from the people under his administration at 184,000,000 livres, and the sums collected by the two new companies of his own devising, for the collection of the excise on drinkables and for the administration of the royal domains at 92,000,000 more.

The Farmers General were the most conspicuous representatives in France of the moneyed class, which was just rising into importance beside the old aristocracy, by whose members it was despised but courted. Many of the Farmers were of low origin and had risen to fortune by their own abilities. Others belonged to families which had long made a mark in the financial world. Their luxurious style of life was admired by the vulgar and derided by the envious. The offices of the Farm occupied several historic houses in Paris. In the chief of these the French Academy had once held its sittings under the presidency of Séguier, and the walls and ceilings shone with pictures from the brushes of Lebrun and Mignard. The warehouses and offices for the monopoly of tobacco occupied a fine building between the Louvre and the Tuileries, where once the duchesses of Chevreuse and of Longueville had prosecuted their political and amorous intrigues. The discontented tax-payers grumbled the louder at seeing the hated publicans so handsomely lodged.[1]

The first and most dreaded of the indirect taxes was the Salt Tax (*gabelle*). As salt is necessary for all, it has from early days been considered by some governments a good article for a tax, no one being able to escape payment by going entirely without it. To make the revenue more secure, every householder in certain parts of France was obliged to buy seven pounds of salt a year at the warehouses of the Farm, for every member of his family more than seven years old. In spite of this, a certain economy in the use of the article became the habit of the

[1] The total receipts of the Farm, according to Necker, were 186,000,000 livres. Against this sum must be set 2,000,000 for salt and tobacco sold to foreigners; 16,000,000 for the cost of salt and tobacco, and 8,000,000 for the cost of other articles to the Farm. The amount of actual taxation collected by the Farm would therefore seem to have been about 160,000,000. Necker, *De l'Administration*, i. 9, 14, iii. 122. Lemoine, *Les derniers fermiers généraux*, *passim*. Bailly, ii. 185, n. and *passim*. *Encyclopédie*, vi. 515 (*Fermes, Cinq grosses*) vi. 513, etc. (*Fermes du roi*). Bertin, 480. Mercier, xii. 89.

French nation, and the traveler of the nineteenth century may bless the government of the Bourbons when for once in his life he finds himself in a country where the cooks do not habitually oversalt the soup.

The unfortunate Frenchmen of the eighteenth century had to pay dear for this culinary lesson. But in this matter as in others they did not all pay alike. The whole product of the salt tax to the treasury was about sixty million livres, of which two thirds, or forty millions, was taken from provinces containing a little more than one third of the population of the kingdom. Necker, who much desired to equalize the impost, mentions six principal categories of provinces in regard to the salt tax; varying from those in which the sale was free, and the article worth from two to nine livres the hundred weight, to those where it was a monopoly of the Farm, and the salt cost the consumer about sixty-two livres. Salt being thus worth thirty times as much in one province as in another, it was possible for a successful smuggler to make a living by a very few trips. The opportunity was largely used; children were trained by their parents for the illicit traffic, but the penalties were very severe. In the galleys were many salt-smugglers; people were shut up on mere suspicion, and in the crowded prisons of that day were carried off by jail-fevers.[1]

Of all known stimulants, tobacco is perhaps the most agreeable and the least injurious to the person who takes it; but no method of taking it has yet been devised which is not liable to be offensive to the delicate nerves of some bystander. It is probably on this account that a certain

---

[1] Necker, *De l'Administration*, ii. 1. Ibid., *Compte rendu*, 82, and see the map of France divided according to the *gabelle* in the same volume. Bailly, ii. 163. Clamageran, iii. 84 *n.*, 296, 406. For the numerous officers and complicated system of the *gabelle*, see *Encyclopédie*, vii. 942 (*Grenier à sel*); Quintal = 100 French pounds; but which of the numerous French pounds, I know not.

discredit has always attached to this most soothing herb, and that it seldom gets fair treatment in the matter of taxation. Over a large part of France, containing some twenty-two millions of inhabitants, tobacco had been subject to monopoly for a hundred years when Louis XVI. came to the throne,[1] yet the use of the article had become so general that this population bought fifteen million pounds yearly, or between five eighths and three quarters of a pound per head. Of this amount about one twelfth was used for smoking in pipes, and the remainder was consumed in the pleasant form of snuff. Three livres fifteen sous a pound was the price set by the government and collected by the Farmers, and the tobacco was often mouldy.[2]

The excise on wine and cider (*aides*) was levied not only on the producer, but also on the consumer, in a most vexatious manner, so that the revenue officers were continually forcing their way into private houses, and so that the poor peasant who quietly diluted his measure of cider with two measures of water was lucky if he got off with a triple tax, and did not undergo fine and forfeiture for having untaxed cider in his house. It was moreover a principle with the officers of the excise that wine was never given away; and as a tax was due on every sale the poor vine-dresser could not give a part of the produce of his vineyard to his married children, or even bestow a few bottles in alms on a poor, sick woman without getting into trouble, and all this notwithstanding the fact that in France in the eighteenth century, when tea and coffee were unknown to the rural classes, and when drinking water was often taken from polluted wells, wine or cider was generally considered necessary to health and to life.

It is needless to consider in detail the duties on imports

---

[1] With an interval of two years, during which it was subject to a high duty. Stourm, i. 361.

[2] Necker, *De l'Administration*, ii. 100. Babeau, *La vie rurale*, 78.

and exports (*traites*). From the beginning of the eighteenth century until three years after the end of the American War, commerce between France and England was totally prohibited as to most articles, and subjected to prohibitory duties in the case of the few that remained. This state of things was tempered by a great system of smuggling, so successfully conducted that insurance in many cases was as low as ten and even as five per cent. Goods were sometimes taken directly from one coast to the other on dark nights, and no reader of the literature of the last century will need to be reminded that the "free traders" who brought them were favorably received by the people among whom they might come to land. Sometimes the articles were sent by circuitous routes through Holland or Germany, on whose frontiers the same walls of prohibition did not exist. But there were many things which could not conveniently be smuggled, and in their case the want of competition, and still more the lack of standards of comparison, tended to retard and injure production. While improved machinery for spinning and weaving was common in England, the old spindle, wheel, and house-loom still held their own in France.

In the year 1786, a commercial treaty was signed between the two countries. By its provisions French wines were put on a better footing, and many manufactured articles, as hardware, cutlery, linen, gauze, and millinery were to pay but ten or twelve per cent. The confusion of business which was the natural result of so great a change had not ceased to be felt when the great Revolution began to disturb all commercial relations.

It was not at the frontiers alone that commerce was subject to tolls and duties. Trade was hampered on every road and river in the kingdom, and so complicated were these local dues that it was said that not more than two or three men in a generation understood them thoroughly.

Duties on food were then as now collected at the entrance of many French cities (*octrois*). In the last century they were often partial in their operation; such of the burghers as owned farms or gardens outside the walls being allowed to bring in their produce without charge, while their poorer neighbors were obliged to pay duties on all they ate. In Paris some kinds of food, and notably fish, were both bad and dear, because the charges at the city gate were many times as great as the original value.[1]

There was another burden which shared with the taille and the gabelle the especial hatred of the French peasantry. This was the villein service (*corvée*) which was exacted of the farmers and agricultural laborers. The service was of feudal origin, and, while still demanded in many cases by the lords, in accordance with ancient charters or customs, was now also required by the state for the building of roads and the transportation of soldiers' baggage. The demand was based on no general law, but was imposed arbitrarily by intendants and military commanders. The amount due by every parish was settled without appeal by the same authorities. The peasant and his draft-cattle were ordered away from home, perhaps just at the time of harvest. On the roads might be seen the overloaded carts, where the tired soldiers had piled themselves on top of their baggage, while their comrades goaded the slow teams with swords and bayonets, and jeered at the remonstrances of the unhappy owner. The oxen were often injured by unusual labor and harsh treatment, and one sick ox would throw a whole team out of work. The burden, imposed on the parish collectively,

---

[1] See the pathetic *cahier* of the village of Pavaut, *Archives parlementaires*, v. 9. Vauban, *Dime royale*, 26, 51. Montesquieu, iv. 122 (*Esprit des Lois*, liv. xiii. c. 7). Necker, *De l'Administration*, ii. 113. *Encylopédie méthodique*, *Finance*, iii. 709 (*Traites*). Turgot, vii. 37. Mercier, xi. 100. Stourm, i. 325.

was distributed among the peasants by their syndics, political officers, often partial, who were sometimes accompanied in their work of selection by files of soldiers, equally rough and impatient with the refractory peasants and the wretched official. Turgot, who was keenly alive to the hardships of the *corvée*, abolished it during his short term of power, substituting a tax, but it was restored by his successor immediately on his fall, and was not discontinued until the end of the monarchy.[1]

It is entirely impossible to discover, even approximately, what proportion of a Frenchman's income was taken in taxes by the government of Louis XVI. We may guess that the burden was too large, we may be sure that it was ill distributed, yet under it prosperity and population were slowly increasing.

Let us take the figures of Necker, as the most moderate. It is the fashion to make light of Necker, and he certainly was not a man of sufficient strength and genius to overcome all the difficulties with which he was surrounded, but he probably knew more about the condition of France than any other man then living. Let us then take his figures and suppose that the two twentieths, and the four sous per livre of the first twentieth, produced the eleven per cent. which they should theoretically have given. In that case eleven per cent. of the country's income was equal to fifty-five million livres. But at that rate the direct taxes and tithes would have taken more than half the income, and the indirect taxes more than the other half, and French subjects would have been left

[1] The *corvées* owned by the lords were limited by legal custom to twelve days a year. *Encyclopédie*, iv. 280 (*Corvée*). I can find no such limitations of *corvées* imposed by the government. Some regard seems to have been paid to peasants' convenience in fixing the season of *corvées* of road building, but none in those of military transportation. Compensation was given for the latter, but it was inadequate, hardly amounting to one fourth of the market price of such labor. Turgot, iv. 367. Bailly, ii. 215.

with less than nothing to live on. Clearly, then, the twentieths did not produce anything like the theoretical eleven per cent.

M. Taine has gone into the question with apparent care, and his figures are adopted by recent writers, but they would seem to be open to the same objection. He reckons that some of the peasants paid over eighty per cent. of their income. But if a man could pay that proportion to the government year after year and not die of want, how very prosperous a man living on the same land must be to-day if his taxes amount only to one quarter or one third of his income. The real difficulty is one of assessment. We can tell approximately how much the country paid; we can never know the amount of its wealth.

How far did the rich escape taxation? The clergy of France as a body did so in a great measure. They paid none of the direct taxes levied on their fellow subjects. They made gifts and loans to the state, however, and borrowed money for the purpose. For this money they paid interest, which must be looked on as their real contribution to the expenses of the state. But in this again they were assisted by the treasury. The amount which finally came out of the pockets of the clergy by direct taxation would appear to have been less than ten per cent. of their income from invested property.

The nobility bore a larger share. The only great tax from which the members of that order were exempted was the taille, forming less than one half of the direct taxation, less than one sixth of the whole. But in the other direct taxes, their wealth and influence sometimes enabled them to escape a fair assessment.

The indirect taxes also bore heavily on the poor. They were levied largely on necessaries, such as salt and food, or on those simple luxuries, wine and tobacco, on which Frenchmen of all classes depend for their daily sense of well-being. The gabelle, with its obligatory seven pounds of salt, approached a poll-tax in its operation.

The worst features of French taxation were the arbitrary spirit which pervaded the financial administration, the regulations never submitted to public criticism, and the tyranny and fraud of subordinates, for which redress was seldom attainable.[1] We groan sometimes, and with reason, at the publicity with which all life is carried on to-day. We turn wearily from the wilderness of printed words which surrounds the simplest matters. But only publicity and free discussion will prevent every unscrupulous assessor and every arbitrary clerk in the customhouse from being a petty tyrant. They will not by themselves procure good government, but they will prevent bad government from growing intolerable. In France, as we have seen, to print anything which might stir the public mind was a capital offense; and while the writer of an abstract treatise subversive of religion and government might hope to escape punishment, the citizen who earned the resentment of a petty official was likely to be prosecuted with virulence.

[1] Horn, 254.

CHAPTER XV.

FINANCE.

CERTAIN financial practices, not immediately connected with taxation, call for a short notice; for they are among the most famous errors of the government of old France. One of these was the habit of issuing what were called anticipations.[1] These were securities with a limited time to run, payable from a definite portion of the future revenue. They were a favorite form of investment with certain people, and a great convenience to the treasury, but they constantly tended to increase to an amount which was considered dangerous. Thus the revenue of each year was spent before it was collected; and loans were contracted, not for any urgent and exceptional necessity of the state, but for ordinary running expenses. Another practice was the issuing by the king in person of drafts on the treasury. Such drafts (*acquits de comptant*) were made payable to bearer, and it was therefore impossible for the controller of the finances to know for what purpose they had been drawn. Originally a device for the payment of the private expenses of the king, these drafts had become favorite objects of the cupidity of the courtiers; because from their form it was impossible to trace them and discover the recipient. Under Louis XVI.

---

[1] Anticipations. "On entendait par là des assignations sur les revenus futurs, remises aux fournisseurs et autres créanciers du Trésor et négociables entre leurs mains." Clamageran, iii. 30. Necker, *Compte rendu*, 20. Stourm (ii. 200) thinks the amount not excessive, while acknowledging that it was so considered. The Anticipations formed in fact the floating debt of the government. Gomel, 287.

they absorbed more money than ever before. It was very easy for that weak prince to give a check to any one who might ask him. Turgot made him promise to stop doing so, but he had not the strength to keep his word.[1]

From an early time the custom of selling public offices had taken root in France. Before the middle of the fourteenth century we find Louis X. selling judicial places to the highest bidder, and less than a hundred years later the practice had extended so that all manner of petty offices were sold by the government. This method of raising money was so easy that, in spite of the remonstrances of estates general and the promises of kings, it was continually extended. In the sixteenth century, as a greater inducement to purchasers, the offices were made transferable on certain conditions, and in 1605 they became subjects of inheritance. Places under government were thus assimilated to other property and passed from the holder to his heirs. The law which established this state of things was called *Edit de la Paulette*, after one Paulet, a farmer of the revenue.

This sale of offices bore a certain resemblance to a loan and to a tax. The services to be performed were often unimportant, sometimes worse than useless. But the salary attached to the office might be considered the interest of money lent to the crown; or if the office-holder were paid by fees, he was enabled to make good to himself the advance made to the government by drawing money from the tax-payers. Very generally the two forms of profit to the incumbent were combined, together with a third, the possession, namely, of privileges, or exemption from taxation, attached to the office.

In managing its revenue from this source, the treasury

---

[1] Clamageran, iii. 380, n. Bailly, i. 221, ii. 214, 259. The foreign office made use of *ordonnances de comptant* to the amount of several millions annually, for subsidies to foreign governments, expenses of ambassadors, secret service, etc. Stourm, ii. 153.

dealt fairly neither with the office holders nor with the public. Places were created only to be sold, and before long were abolished, either without any promise of compensation to the buyers, or with promises destined never to be fulfilled. This want of faith kept down the price, which was often but ten years' purchase of the income of the place. Yet rich and poor were eager to buy. "Sir," said a minister of finance to King Louis XIV., "as often as it pleases your Majesty to make an office, it pleases God to make a fool to fill it."

Thus it came to pass that most places about the royal person, in the courts of justice and in the treasury, and many in the municipal governments, the professions, and the trades, were subject to sale and purchase. Numberless persons waited at the royal table, sat in the high courts of Parliament, weighed, measured, gauged, sold horses, oysters, fish, or sucking pigs, shaved customers or gave hot baths, as public functionaries and by virtue of letters patent sold to them by the crown. The clerk kept his register, not because the information it contained would be useful to the government, but because he or some one else had lent money, on which the public was now paying interest in the form of registration fees. Thus the custom of selling offices was cumbrous and objectionable.[1]

While the taxes of France were thus devised without

---

[1] Montesquieu defends the custom, however. He maintains that the offices in a monarchy should be venal; because people do as a family business what they would not undertake from virtue; every one is trained to his duty, and orders in the state are more permanent. If offices were not sold by the government they would be by the courtiers. Montesquieu, iii. 217 (*Esprit des Lois*, liv. v. cxix.). See also De Tocqueville, iv. 171 (*Anc. Rég.* ch. xi.). In many cases offices were desired more for the sake of distinction and privilege than for profit. The income was often very small. Clamageran, ii. 196, 378, 569, 615, 665; iii. 23, 24, 102, 155, 200, 319. Necker, *De l'Administration*, iii. 147. Thierry, i. 163. Pierre de Lestoile, 390, n.

system and levied without skill, the attention of a thoughtful part of the nation had been turned to financial matters. About the middle of the century arose the Physiocrats, the founders of modern political economy. Their leader, Quesnay, believed that positive legislation should consist in the declaration of the natural laws constituting the order evidently most advantageous for men in society. When once these were understood, all would be well, for the absurdity of all unreasonable legislation would become manifest. He taught two cardinal principles; first, "that the land was the only source of riches, and that these were multiplied by agriculture;" and, second, that agriculture and commerce should be entirely free. The former of these doctrines, after exercising a good deal of influence by calling attention to the injustice and oppression with which the agricultural class in France was treated, has ceased to be believed as a statement of absolute truth. The latter, adopted with great enthusiasm by many generous minds, has exercised a deep influence on modern thought.

Manufactures, according to Quesnay, do no more than pay the wages and expenses of the workmen engaged in them. But agriculture not only pays wages and expenses, but produces a surplus, which is the revenue of the land. He divides the nation into three classes: (1) the productive, which cultivates the soil; (2) the proprietary, which includes the sovereign, the land-owners, and those who live by tithes, in other words the nobility and the clergy; and (3) the sterile, which embraces all men who labor otherwise than in agriculture, and whose expenses are paid by the productive and proprietary classes. Therefore he argues that taxes should be based directly on the net product of real estate, and not on wages nor on chattels. In other words, all taxes should be levied directly on the income derived from land, and indirect taxation in every shape should be abolished.

Liberty of agriculture, liberty of commerce! "Let every man be free to cultivate in his field such crops as his interest, his means, the nature of the ground may suggest as rendering the greatest possible return." "Let complete liberty of commerce be maintained; for the regulation of commerce, both internal and external, which is most safe, most accurate, most profitable to the nation, consists in full liberty of competition." These doctrines of Quesnay, joined with the ideas of property and security, form the basis of the modern school of individualism.[1]

The body of doctrines long known as "political economy," (for the words seem now to be used in a larger sense), bore the mark of their origin in the eighteenth century. Here, as elsewhere, it was the belief of Frenchmen of that age that the application of a few simple rules derived from natural laws would solve the difficulties of a complicated subject. The principles of political economy were conceived as forming "a true science, which does not yield to geometry itself in the conviction which it carries to the soul, and which certainly surpasses all others in its object, since that is the greatest well-being, the greatest prosperity of the human race upon the earth."[2] Quesnay and Gournay founded branches of the economic school. The latter, who printed nothing, is chiefly known through the encomiums of Turgot. Gournay was a merchant, and recognized that commerce and manufactures are hardly less advantageous to a state than agriculture. This is the chief difference of his teaching from that of Quesnay. Gournay is the author of the famous maxim: *Laissez faire; laissez passer;* and his whole system de-

[1] Lavergne, *Les Economistes*, 105. Quesnay, *Œuvres*, 233, 306, 331 (*Maximes du gouvernement économique d'un royaume agricole Maxime*, iii. v. xiii. xxv.). Turgot, iv. 305. Bois-Guillebert appears to have been the principal precursor of the Physiocrats. Horn, *L'Economie politique avant les Physiocrates, passim;* φυσις = nature, κρατος = power.

[2] Abbé Beaudeau, quoted in Lavergne, *Les Economistes*, 179.

pended on the idea "that in general every man knows his own interest better than another man to whom that interest is entirely indifferent;" and that "hence, when the interest of individuals is exactly the same as the general interest, the best thing to do is to leave every man to do as he likes."[1]

The best known member of the economic school in France was Anne Robert Jacques Turgot, born in Paris on the 10th of May, 1727, of a family belonging to the higher middle class. His father was *prévost des marchands*, or chief magistrate of the city. Young Turgot was at first educated for the ecclesiastical life, and indeed pursued his studies in that direction until a bishopric seemed close at hand. But he felt no vocation to enter the priesthood. Turgot was too much the child of his century to be content to put his great powers into the harness of the Roman Church; he was, as he told his friends who remonstrated with him on abandoning his brilliant prospects, too honest a man to wear a mask all his life.

At the age of twenty-four, Turgot turned finally from the study of divinity to that of law and administration. He was rapidly promoted to the place of a *maître des requêtes*, a member of the lowest board of the royal council, and nine years later he became intendant of the district of Limoges. It was the poorest in France, but Turgot soon became so much interested in its welfare that he refused to exchange it for a richer one. In spite of years of dearth and of the extraordinary measures of relief which they made necessary, he went energetically to work at all manner of permanent reforms. He effected improvements in the apportionment and levy of the taille. He abolished the onerous *corvée*. He diminished the terror of compulsory service in the militia, by permitting the engagement of substitutes. He encouraged agricul-

[1] Turgot, iii. 336 (*Eloge de M. de Gournay*).

ture by distributing seeds and offering prizes for the destruction of wolves, which were still numerous in his district, and he waged a successful war on a moth that was ravaging the wheat crop. He assisted in the introduction of the manufacture of pottery, still one of the leading industries of Limoges. His reports are among the most valuable material in existence for the study of the condition of old France.

Soon after the accession of Louis XVI., Turgot was called to the ministry, first, for a very short time, as secretary of the navy, and then as Controller of the Finances. Two courses were open to the new minister. Malesherbes, his close adherent, standing in high official position, urged him to summon the Estates General, or at least the Provincial Estates, and rule constitutionally. Such action would have been a great, a serious innovation, but it was not on this ground that Turgot opposed it. Like most of the economists of his day, he believed at once in freedom and in despotism. "The republican constitution of England," he had said, "sets obstacles in the way of the reform of certain abuses." Turgot had a plan for the benefit of mankind. None but a despot could carry it out for him. France and the world were to be set right; and it would take absolute power to compel them into the best course.

The new Controller of the Finances could not afford to wait. "You accuse me of too great haste," he said to a friend, "and you forget that in my family we die of the gout at fifty." But this haste, combined with his awkward and haughty manners, proved the cause of his ruin. The courtiers, whose perquisites were in danger, were disgusted at his simplicity and economy. Although he was the friend of absolute government, he was accused of republican austerity. And his measures were not more popular than his manners. The harvest of 1774 had been bad, and famine was in the land. Turgot met the situation by declaring commerce in grain free throughout the kingdom. The harvest was again bad in 1775, and riots broke out, for the common people had it firmly in their minds that the price of bread was fixed by the government. Turgot put down disturbances with a high hand, and persevered in his measures. He abolished the *corvée* on roads and public works throughout France. In truth it would have been better to modify and regulate it, for in poor countries many men had rather work on the roads than pay for them, but such considerations as this were foreign to his mind. He, moreover, abolished the trade-guilds (*jurandes*), which possessed the monopoly of most kinds of manufactures and trades, saying that God, in giving man needs and making labor his necessary resource, had made the right to work the property of every man, and that this property is the most sacred and inalienable of all.[1] But Turgot's ideal of freedom was entirely industrial and commercial, and not at all political or social. He forbade all associations or assemblies of masters or workmen, holding that the faculty granted to artisans of the same trade to meet and join in one body is a source of evil. Under Turgot's system, the individual workman would not have escaped the tyranny of the masters' guild only to fall under that of the trades-union; but one of the most essential privileges of a freeman would have been denied him. Individual liberty to work, and political liberty to combine, have not yet been made perfectly to coincide.

The innovations thus introduced were great; the interests threatened were powerful. The Parliament of Paris rallied to the defense of vested rights. It refused to register the edicts issued to enforce the minister's innova-

---

[1] Turgot, viii. 330. Yet the monopolies in certain trades, as those of apothecaries, jewelers, printers, and booksellers, were retained, probably because their strict regulation and supervision was considered necessary. The guilds were reëstablished, with modifications, on the fall of Turgot. *Encyclopédie méthodique, Commerce*, ii. 760, 790.

tions. The king held a bed of justice and forced their registration; but his weak nature was tiring of the struggle. Turgot was unpopular on all sides, and Louis never supported a truly unpopular minister. "Only M. Turgot and I love the people," he cried, in his impotent despair; and then he gave way. Malesherbes, the principal supporter in the royal council of the Controller General of the Finances, was the first to go. Thereupon Turgot wrote the king a long and harsh letter, blaming him for Malesherbes's resignation. "Do not forget, sir," said he, "that it was weakness which put the head of Charles I. on the block; it was weakness which formed the League under Henry III., which made crowned slaves of Louis XIII. and of the present king of Portugal; it was weakness which caused all the misfortunes of the late reign." Kings to whom such language as this can be used are not strong enough to bear it. Turgot was dismissed twelve days after sending the letter.[1]

The financial situation of France was undoubtedly serious. The cause of this was far less the amount of the debt, or the excess of expenditure over revenue, than the total demoralization of the public service. The annual deficit at the accession of Louis XVI. is variously stated at from twenty to forty million livres a year.[2] Such a deficiency would have nothing very appalling for a strong minister of finance, supported by a determined sovereign, and could have been overcome by economy alone. The expenses of the court were not less than thirty millions. Turgot proposed to reduce them by five millions immediately and by nine millions more in the course of a few years. Twenty-eight millions were spent in pensions, and it requires but a superficial knowledge of the state of France to assure us that many of these were bestowed

---

[1] May 12, 1776. Lavergne, *les Economistes*, 219. Turgot, iii. 335; viii. 273, 330. Bailly, ii. 210.

[2] From four to eight million dollars.

without sufficient reason.¹ Important reductions might have been made in the expenditures of most of the departments without impairing their efficiency. But to have done this many interests would have had to be disturbed, many hardships inflicted. Amiable persons, living without labor at the public cost, would have been deprived of their revenues. Other agreeable and influential men and women would have had to live without pleasant things which they had been brought up to expect. The goodnature of the king made him shrink from inflicting pain. He would approve of the best plans of economy, he would promise his minister of finance to adhere to them, he would depart from them secretly at the solicitation of his wife or of his courtiers. The poor man wanted "to make his people happy," and he could not bear to see those of his people who came nearest to him discontented. The successor of Turgot was a mere courtier, not even personally honest, whose career was fortunately cut short by death within a few months of his nomination.

The war of the American Revolution was drawing near, and old Maurepas, the prime minister, felt the need of a competent man to take charge of the finances. A name was suggested to him, — that of Necker, a successful banker. But Necker was a Protestant, a Swiss, a nobody. The title of Controller was too high for him, so a new post was created, and he was made Director-General of the Finances, coming into office in October, 1776.

It has been the fate of Necker to excite strong enthusiasm and violent objurgation; but in fact he was little more than commonplace. An ambitious man, he wanted to make a reputation, to build up the royal credit, to found a national debt, like that of England. Did he really believe that such a debt would pay its own interest, without additional taxes, or did he rely on economy of

---

[1] Stourm sets the pensions at thirty-two millions, and thinks that the improper ones did not exceed six or seven millions, ii. 134.

expenditure and good administration, not only to balance the ordinary accounts, but to cover the interest of the war-loans which he was obliged to contract? How far did his cheerful manifestoes deceive himself? What might he not really have accomplished if the royal support had been anything more solid than a shifting quicksand? These questions cannot be answered satisfactorily. Neither Necker, nor anybody else, knew exactly what the government owed, or what it borrowed. The loans contracted by Necker himself are believed to have amounted to five hundred and thirty million livres. Of this sum it is thought that about two hundred millions were employed in covering the annual deficit for five years, and that three hundred and thirty millions were spent for the extraordinary demands of the war. The money was raised chiefly by state lotteries and by the sale of life annuities, although many other means also were employed.

The royal lottery had been a favorite device earlier in the century. As practiced by Necker and some of his predecessors it combined the features of gambling and of investment. Every ticket, in addition to its chance of drawing a prize, was in itself a pecuniary obligation of the government, either carrying perpetual interest at four per cent., or to be repaid at its full price in seven or nine years without interest. The prizes were sums of money or annuities. Thus the ticket-holder did not lose his whole stake, and ran the chance of winning a fortune. But the operation was not brilliant for the government.

Nor was the sale of annuities more judiciously managed. Here, as in the lotteries, Necker copied old models, without making any improvements of importance. No account was taken of the age of the annuitants, but incomes were sold at a fixed rate of ten per cent. of the capital deposited for one life, nine per cent. for two lives, eight and a half for three, eight for four. The bankers and financiers of the day were shrewd enough to profit by this arrangement.

They bought up the obligations, and named healthy children as the annuitants. The chance of life of these selected persons was more than fifty years, and as the children were usually chosen at about the age of seven, the treasury would be called on to pay its annuities for an average term of between forty and forty-five years. As the current rate of interest on good security was about six per cent. the operation was not a very promising one for the state.

In spite of all these blunders Necker was liked by the nation. He recognized the need of economy and honestly tried to reduce expenses. He succeeded in cutting off a little of the extravagance of the court and in simplifying the collection of the revenue. He tried to establish provincial assemblies and to equalize the incidence of the salt-tax. And above all, in order to sustain the royal credit, he took the country into his confidence to some extent, and prophesied pleasant things. But he did not stop there. The national accounts had long been considered a government secret; Necker resolved to publish them to the world. His famous "Compte rendu au roi" appeared in February, 1781. The portrait of the author, excellently engraved on copper, stares complacently from the frontispiece, above an allegorical picture, where we can make out Justice and Abundance, while Avarice appears to bring her treasures, and a lady in high, powdered hair, and no visible clothing, gazes astonished from the background. The contents of the report are not such as we are in the habit of expecting in financial documents, but are rhetorical and self-complacent. The ordinary revenues of the country are said to exceed the expenditures by ten million livres. As a matter of fact, no such surplus existed, but Necker was an optimist by temperament, and was moreover anxious to bolster credit. The nation was delighted, but Maurepas and the court were shocked. The cupidity of the courtiers was painted in the account in glowing language. Such a publication was dangerous in itself, and the economical measures already taken, with those announced as to follow, threatened many interests. Even the old prime minister trembled for his personal power. Necker had obtained the removal from office of one of the adherents of Maurepas, while the latter was kept in Paris by the gout. So the usual machinery of detraction was put in motion. Letters, pamphlets, and epigrams flew about. While the larger part of the public was singing Necker's praises, the smaller and more influential inner circle was conspiring against him. He might yet have prevailed but for an act of imprudence. Although the most conspicuous and popular man in the kingdom, he had hitherto been excluded from the Council of State. He now asked to be admitted to it. Louis XVI., whose Catholicism was his strongest conviction, replied that Necker, as a Protestant, was inadmissible by law. Thereupon the latter offered to resign his place as Director of the Finances, and the king, by the advice of Maurepas, accepted his resignation.[1]

From this time all real chance of the extrication of Louis XVI. from his financial difficulties, without a radical change of government, disappeared forever. The controllers that succeeded Necker only plunged deeper and deeper into debt and deficit. It is needless to follow them in their flounderings. A long experience of the vacillation of the government both as to persons and as to systems had discouraged the hopes of conscientious patriotism, and strengthened the opposition to reform of all those who were interested in abuses. From the well-meaning king, if left to his own ways, nothing more could be hoped. Pecuniary embarrassment, with Louis, as with many less important people, was quite as much a symptom of weakness as a result of unmerited misfortune.

[1] Gomel, *passim*.

CHAPTER XVI.

"THE ENCYCLOPÆDIA."

WE have seen that the church had an irreconcilable enemy in Voltaire; that the government of France had found a critic of weight and importance in Montesquieu; that the Economists had attacked the financial organization of the country. But the assaults of the Philosophic school were not leveled at the religious and civil administration alone. The very foundations of French thought, slowly laid through previous ages, were made in the reign of Louis XV. the subject of examination, and by a very dogmatic set of thinkers were pronounced to be valueless. Nor were men left at a loss for something to put in the place of what was thus destroyed. The teachings of Locke, explained and amplified by Condillac and many others, obtained an authority which was but feebly disputed. The laws against free speech and free printing, intended for the defense of the old doctrines, deterred no one from expressing radical opinions. Only persons of conservative and law-abiding temperament, the natural defenders of things existing, were restrained by legal and ecclesiastical terrors. The champions of the old modes of thought stood like mediæval men at arms before a discharge of artillery, prevented from rushing on the guns of the enemy by the weight of the armor that protected them no longer. The new philosophy, stimulated and hardly impeded by feeble attempts at persecution, was therefore able to overrun the intellectual life of the nation, until it found its most formidable opponent in one who was half its ally, and who had sprung from its midst, the mighty heretic, Rousseau.

The most voluminous work of the Philosophers is the "Encyclopædia," a book of great importance in the history of the human mind. The conception of its originators was not a new one. The attempt to bring human knowledge into a system, and to set it forth in a series of folio volumes, had been made before. The endeavor is one which can never meet with complete success, yet which should sometimes be made in a philosophic spirit. The universe is too vast and too varied to be successfully classified and described by one man, or under the supervision of one editor. But the attempt may bring to light some relation of things hitherto unnoticed, and the task is one of practical utility.

The great French "Encyclopædia" may claim two immediate progenitors. The first is found in the works of Lord Bacon, where there is a "Description of a Natural and Experimental History, such as may serve for the foundation of a true philosophy," with a "Catalogue of particular histories by titles." The second is Chambers's Cyclopædia, first published in 1727, a translation of which Diderot was engaged to edit by the publisher Le Breton. Diderot, who freely acknowledges his obligation to Bacon, makes light of that to Chambers, saying in his prospectus that the latter owed much to French sources, that his work is not the basis of the one proposed, that many of the articles have been rewritten, and almost all the others corrected and altered. There is no doubt that the whole plan of the "Encyclopædia" was much enlarged by Denis Diderot himself.[1]

This eminent man was born at Langres in 1713, the son of a worthy cutler. He was educated by the Jesuits,

---

[1] Bacon, iv. 251, 265. Morley, *Diderot*, i., 116. Diderot, *Œuvres*, xiii. 6, 8. "If we come out successfully we shall be principally indebted to Chancellor Bacon, who laid out the plan of a universal dictionary of sciences and arts *at a time when there were, so to speak, neither sciences nor arts.*"

and on his refusal to enter either of the learned professions of law or medicine, was set adrift by his father, — who hoped that a little hardship would bring him to reason, — and found himself in Paris with no resource but the precarious one of letters. Diderot lived from hand to mouth for a time, sleeping sometimes in a garret of his own, sometimes on the floor of a friend's room. Once he got a place of tutor to the children of a financier, but could not bear the life of confinement, and soon threw up his appointment and returned to freedom. When any friend of his father turned up on a visit to the town, he would borrow, and the old cutler at Langres would grumble and repay. Gradually the young author rose above want. He became one of the first literary men of his day and one of the most brilliant talkers, rich in ideas, overflowing in language, subtle without obscurity, suggestive, and satisfying; yet always retaining a certain shyness, and "able to say anything, but good-morning." Yet he was soon carried away by the excitement of conversation and of discussion. He had a trick of tapping his interlocutor on the knee, by way of giving point to his remarks, and the Empress Catharine II. of Russia complained that he mauled her black and blue by the use of this familiar gesture, so that she had to put a table between herself and him for protection. Diderot was fond of the young, and especially of struggling authors. To them his purse and his literary assistance were freely given. He was delighted when a writer came to consult him on his work. If the subject were interesting he would recognize its capabilities at a glance. As the author read, Diderot's imagination would fill in all deficiencies, construct new scenes in the tragedy, new incidents, new characters in the tale. To him all these beauties would seem to belong to the work itself, and his friends would be astonished, after hearing him praise some new book, to find in it but few of the good things which he had quoted from it.

Diderot's good nature was boundless. One morning a young man, quite unknown to him, came with a manuscript, and begged him to read and correct it. He prepared to comply with the request on the spot. The paper, when opened, turned out to be a satire on himself and his writings.

"Sir," said Diderot to the young man, "I do not know you; I can never have offended you. Will you tell me the motive which has impelled you to make me read a libel for the first time in my life? I generally throw such things into the waste-paper basket."

"I am starving. I hoped that you would give me a few crowns not to print it."

Instead of flying into a passion, Diderot simply remarked: "You would not be the first author that ever was bought off; but you can do better with this stuff. The brother of the Duke of Orleans is in retreat at Saint Geneviève. He is religious; he hates me. Dedicate your satire to him; have it bound with his arms on the cover; carry it to him yourself some fine morning, and he will help you."

"But I don't know the prince; and I don't see how I can write the dedicatory epistle."

"Sit down; I'll do it for you."

And Diderot writes the dedication, and gives it to the young man, who carries the libel to the prince, receives a present of twenty-five louis, and comes back after a few days to thank Diderot, who advises him to find a more decent means of living.

The people whom the great writer helped were not always so polite. One day he was seeing to the door a young man who had deceived him, and to whom, after discovering it, he had given both assistance and advice.

"Monsieur Diderot," said the swindler, "do you know natural history?"

"A little; I can distinguish an aloe from a head of lettuce, and a pigeon from a humming-bird."

"Do you know the *formica leo*?"

"No."

"It is a very clever little insect. It digs a hole in the ground, shaped like a funnel. It covers the surface with fine, light sand. It attracts silly insects and gets them to tumble in. It seizes them, sucks them dry, and then says: 'Monsieur Diderot, I have the honor to wish you good-morning.'" Whereupon the young man ran downstairs, leaving the philosopher in fits of laughter.[1]

As a writer, the great fault of Diderot is one not common in France. He is verbose. As we read his productions, even the cleverest, we feel that the same thing could have been better said in fewer words. There is also a lack of arrangement. Diderot would never take time to plan his books before writing them. But these faults, although probably fatal to the permanent fame of an author, are less injurious to his immediate success than might be expected. A large part of the public does not dislike a copious admixture of water in its intellectual drink. And Diderot reconciles the reader to his excessive flow of words by the effervescence of his enthusiasm. It is because his mind is overfull of his subject that the sentences burst forth so copiously.

The first writing of Diderot that need engage our attention is his "Letter on the Blind," published in 1749. This letter deals with the question, how far congenital deprivation of one of the senses, and especially blindness, would modify the conceptions of the person affected; how far the ideas of one born blind would differ from the ideas of those who can see. The bearing of this question on Locke's theory that all our ideas are derived from sensation and reflection is obvious. Diderot, in a manner

---

[1] Morley, *Diderot and the Encyclopædists.* Scherer, *Diderot, passim.* Morrellet, i. 29. Marmontel, ii. 313. *Mémoire sur Diderot,* par Mme. de Vandeul, sa fille (a charming sketch only 64 pages long) in Diderot, *Mémoires, Corresp., etc.,* vol. i.

quite characteristic of him, took pains to examine the cases of persons who had actually been blind and had recovered their sight, and where these failed him, supplied their places by inventions of his own.[1]

Diderot's principal witness is Nicholas Saunderson, a blind man with a talent for mathematics, who between 1711 and 1739 was a professor at the University of Cambridge. Diderot quotes at some length the atheistic opinions of Saunderson, giving as his authority the Life of the latter by "Dr. Inchlif." No such book ever existed, and the opinions are the product of Diderot's own reasoning. When an author treats us in this way our confidence in his facts is hopelessly lost. His reasons, however, remain, and the most striking of these, in the "Letter on the Blind," is the answer given to one who attempts to prove the existence of God by pointing out the order found in nature, whence an intelligent Creator is presumed. In answer to this, the dying Saunderson is made to say: "Let me believe . . . that if we were to go back to the birth of things and of times, and if we should feel matter move and chaos arrange itself, we should meet a multitude of shapeless beings, instead of a few beings that were well organized. . . . I can maintain that these had no stomach, and those no intestines; that some, to which their stomach, palate, and teeth seemed to promise duration, have ceased to exist from some vice of the heart or the lungs; that the abortions were successively destroyed; that all the faulty combinations of matter have disappeared, and that only those have survived whose mechanism implied no important contradiction, and which could

[1] Condorcet says of Diderot, "faisant toujours aimer la vérité, même lorsqu'entraîné par son imagination il avait le malheur de la méconnaître. D'Alembert, Œuvres, i. 79 (*Eloge par Condorcet*). There is a great deal in this remark. Unless we can enter into the state of mind of men who tell great lies from a genuine love of abstract truth, we shall never understand the French Philosophers of the 18th century.

live by themselves and perpetuate their species."[1] The step from the idea here conveyed to that of the struggle for existence and of the survival of the most fit is not a very long one.

For his "Letter on the Blind," Diderot was imprisoned at Vincennes. The real cause of this punishment is said to have been a slight allusion in the "Letter" to the mistress of a minister of state. But this may not have been the only cause. There occurred about this time one of those temporary seasons of severity which are necessary under all governments to meet occasional outbursts of crime, but to which weak and corrupt governments are liable with capricious frequency. Diderot sturdily denied the authorship of the "Letter," lying as thoroughly as he had done in that piece of writing itself, when he invented the name of Inchlif and forged the ideas of Saunderson. This time there was more excuse for his untruth; for the disclosure of his printer's name might have sent that unfortunate man to prison or to the galleys. The imprisonment of Diderot himself, at first severe, was soon lightened at the instance of Voltaire's mistress, Madame du Châtelet. Diderot was allowed to see his friends, and even to wander about the park of Vincennes on parole. After three months of captivity he was released by the influence of the booksellers interested in the "Encyclopædia."[2]

The first volume of that great work was in preparation. Diderot, whose untiring energy was unequal to the task of editing the whole, and who was, moreover, insufficiently trained for the work in some branches, and notably in mathematics, gathered about him a band of workers which increased as time went on, until it included a great number of remarkable men. First in importance to the enterprise, acting with Diderot on equal terms, was D'Alembert, an almost typical example of the gentle scholar, who

[1] Diderot, i. 328.   [2] Morley, *Diderot*, i. 105.

refused one brilliant position after another to devote himself to mathematics and to literature. Next, perhaps, should be mentioned the Chevalier de Jaucourt, a man of encyclopædic learning, who helped in the preparation of the book with patient enthusiasm, reading, dictating, and working with three or four secretaries for thirteen or fourteen hours a day. Montesquieu, whose end was approaching, left behind him an unfinished article on Taste. Voltaire not only sent in contributions of his own, but constantly gave encouragement and advice, as became the recognized head of the Philosophic school. Rousseau, whose literary reputation had recently been made by his "Discourses," contributed articles on music for a time; but subsequently chose to quarrel with the Encyclopædists, whose minds worked very differently from his. Turgot wrote several papers on economic subjects, and in the latter part of the work, Haller, the physiologist, and Condorcet were engaged.

The publication of the "Encyclopædia" lasted many years, and met with many vicissitudes. The first volume appeared in 1751, the second in January, 1752. The book immediately excited the antagonism of the church and of conservative Frenchmen generally. On the 12th of February, 1752, the two volumes were suppressed by an edict of the Council, as containing maxims contrary to royal authority and to religion. The edict forbade their being reprinted and their being delivered to such subscribers as had not already received their copies. The continuation of the work, however, was not forbidden. It was believed at the time that the administration took this step in order to silence the Jesuits, to please the Archbishop of Paris, and perhaps to be beforehand with the Parliament, which might have taken severer measures. It was also intimated that certain booksellers, jealous of the success of the undertaking, were exerting influence on the authorities. All these enemies of the "Encyclopædia" were not content with their first triumph. A few days after the appearance of the edict, the manuscripts and plates were seized by the police. They were restored to the editors three months later. The work was one in the performance of which many Frenchmen took pride. It is said that the Jesuits had tried to continue it, but had failed even to decipher the papers that had been taken from Diderot. The attack of the archbishop, who had fulminated against the great book in an episcopal charge, had served the purpose of an advertisement; such was the wisdom and consistency of the repressive police of that age.

From 1753 to 1757 the publication went on without interruption, one volume appearing every year. Seven volumes had now been published, bringing the work to the end of the letter G. The subscription list, originally consisting of less than two thousand names, had nearly doubled. But the forces of conservatism rallied. In 1758 appeared Helvetius's book "De l'Esprit," of which an account will be given in the next chapter, and which shocked the feelings of many persons, even of the Philosophic school. Few things could, indeed, have made the Philosophers more unpopular than the publication by one of their own party of a very readable book, in which the attempt was made to push their favorite ideas to their last conclusions. This is a process which few abstract theories can bear, for the limitations of any statement are in fact essential parts of it. But human laziness so loves formulas, so hates distinctions, that extreme and unmodified expressions are seized with avidity by injudicious friends and exulting foes.

The feeling of indignation awakened in the public by the doctrines of Helvetius gave opportunity to the opponents of the "Encyclopædia." That work was denounced to the Parliament of Paris, together with the book "De l'Esprit." The learned court promptly condemned the latter to the flames. The great compilation, on the other hand, of which the volume of Helvetius was said to be a mere abridgment, was submitted to nine commissioners for examination, and further publication was suspended until they should report. While proceedings before the Parliament were still pending, the Council of State intervened, and the "Encyclopædia" was arbitrarily interdicted, its privilege taken away, the sale of the volumes already printed, and the printing of any more, alike forbidden.

It is characteristic of the condition of things existing under the weak and vacillating government of Louis XV. that the interdict pronounced against the "Encyclopædia" did not stop its printing. The editor and the publishers determined to prepare in private the ten volumes that were still unmade, and to launch them on the world at one time. To this work Diderot turned with boundless energy. D'Alembert, however, was discouraged, and retired from the undertaking. For six years Diderot labored on, never safe from interference on the part of the government, and managing a great enterprise, with its staff of contributors and its scores of workmen, while constantly liable to arrest and imprisonment. Diderot worked indefatigably also with his pen; writing articles on all sorts of subjects, — philosophy, arts, trades, and manufactures. To learn how things were made he visited workshops and handled tools, baffled at times by the jealousy and distrust of the workmen, who were afraid of his disclosing their secret processes, or of his giving information to the tax-gatherer.

The sharpest blow was yet to fall. The "Encyclopædia" was issued by an association of publishers which paid Diderot a moderate salary for his services. Of these publishers one, named Le Breton, was the chief. He is said to have been a dull man, incapable of understanding any work of literature. It was his maxim that literary men labor for glory, and publishers for pay, and consequently he divided the income of the "Encyclopædia" into two parts, giving to Diderot the glory, the danger, and the persecution, and reserving the money for himself and his partners. From his position in Paris he felt sure of being able to foresee any new order launched against the "Encyclopædia" while the printing was in progress, and of providing against it. But the time of publication was likely to be marked by a new storm. Under these circumstances Le Breton resorted to a trick. After Diderot had read the last proof of every sheet, the publisher and his foreman secretly took it in hand, erased and cut out all that seemed rash or calculated to excite the anger of religious or conservative people, and thus reduced many of the principal articles to fragments. Then, to make the wrong irremediable, they burned the manuscripts, and quietly proceeded with the printing. This process would seem to have been continued for more than a year. One day in 1764, when the time of publication was drawing near, Diderot, having occasion to consult an article under the letter S, found it badly mutilated. Puzzled at first, he presently recognized the nature of the trick that had been played him. He turned to various parts of the book, to his own articles and to those of other writers, and found in many places the marks of the outrage. Diderot was in despair. His first thought was to throw up the undertaking and to announce the fraud to the public. The injury that would have been done to Le Breton's innocent partners, the danger of publishing the fact that the "Encyclopædia" was still in process of printing, — a fact of which the officers of the government had only personal and not official knowledge, — determined him to go on with the publication. It may be that Le Breton's changes had been less extensive than Diderot, in his first excitement on making the discovery, had been led to believe. In examining the "Encyclopædia" no alteration of tone is observable between the first seven and the subsequent volumes; and Grimm, to whom we owe the story, acknowledges that none of the authors engaged with Diderot in the work complained or even noticed that their articles had been altered.

In 1765 the ten volumes which completed the alphabet (making seventeen of this part of the work) were delivered to the subscribers. As a precautionary measure, those for foreign countries were sent out first, then those for the provinces, and lastly those for Paris. The eleven volumes of plates were not published until 1772. A supplement of four volumes of text and one of plates appeared in 1776 and 1777, and three years later a table of contents in two volumes.[1]

What was the great book whose history was so full of vicissitudes? Why did the French government, the church, and the literary world so excite themselves about a dictionary? The "Encyclopædia" had in fact two

[1] Several volumes of the original edition have the imprint of Neufchâtel, and the supplement has that of Amsterdam, although all were actually printed in Paris. The *Encyclopædia* was reprinted as a whole at Geneva and at Lausanne. Editions also appeared at Leghorn and at Lucca; besides volumes of selections and abbreviations. Morley, *Diderot*, i. 169. For the *Encyclopædia*, see Morley, *Diderot*, *passim*. Scherer, *Diderot*; the correspondence of D'Alembert and Voltaire in the works of the latter. Diderot, *Mémoires*, i. 431 (Nov. 10, 1760). Grimm, vii. 44, and especially ix. 203–217, an excellent article. Barbier, v. 159, 169; vii. 125, 138, 141; also in the work itself the word *Encyclopédie* in vol. v. Mr. Morley thinks that the article *Genève*, in vol. vii. of the *Encyclopædia*, especially excited the church and the Parliament to desire its suppression. The same article drew from Rousseau his letter to D'Alembert on the theatre at Geneva, which marks the separation between Rousseau and the Philosophers. But in the *Discours préliminaire* D'Alembert had attacked Rousseau's *First Discourse*. For the excitement caused at Geneva by the article, see Voltaire, lvii. 438 (Voltaire to D'Alembert, Jan. 8, 1758). It is perhaps superfluous to remark that Grimm's account of the character and ideas of Le Breton, which has been followed above, is probably not unbiased.

functions; it was a repository of information and a polemical writing. Condorcet has thus stated the purpose of the book. Diderot, he says, "intended to bring together in a dictionary all that had been discovered in the sciences, what was known of the productions of the globe, the details of the arts which men have invented, the principles of morals, those of legislation, the laws which govern society, the metaphysics of language and the rules of grammar, the analysis of our faculties, and even the history of our opinions."[1] So comprehensive a scheme was not without danger to those classes which claimed an exclusive right to direct men's minds. As for the double nature of the book, we have the words of two of the men most concerned in its preparation. First there is an anecdote by Voltaire, certainly inaccurate, probably quite imaginary, but setting forth most clearly one cause of the interest which the "Encyclopædia" excited.

"A servant of Louis XV. has told me that one day when the king his master was supping at Trianon with a small party, the conversation turned on shooting and then on gunpowder. Somebody said that the best powder was made of equal parts of saltpetre, sulphur, and charcoal. The Duke of La Vallière, better informed, maintained that for cannon the proper proportion was one part of sulphur, one of charcoal, and five of well-filtered, well-evaporated, and well-crystallized saltpetre.

" 'It is absurd,' said the Duke of Nivernois, 'that we should amuse ourselves every day with killing partridges in the park of Versailles, and sometimes with killing men or getting ourselves killed on the frontier, and not know exactly what we kill with.'

"'Alas! we are in the same state about all things in the world,' answered Madame de Pompadour. 'I don't know of what the rouge is composed that I put on my cheeks, and I should be much puzzled to say how my stockings are made.'

[1] D'Alembert, Œuvres, i. 79 (Eloge par Condorcet).

"'It is a pity,' then said the Duke of La Vallière, 'that His Majesty should have confiscated our encyclopædic dictionaries, which cost us a hundred pistoles apiece. We should soon find in them the answers to all our questions.'

"The king justified his confiscation. He had been warned that the twenty-one volumes in folio, that were to be found on all the ladies' dressing-tables, were the most dangerous thing in the world for the French monarchy; and he wished to see for himself if that were true before he allowed the book to be read. After supper he sent for a copy, by three servants of his bed-chamber, each of whom brought in seven volumes, with a good deal of difficulty.

"They saw, in the article on gunpowder, that the Duke of La Vallière was right. Madame de Pompadour soon learned the difference between the old-fashioned Spanish rouge, with which the ladies of Madrid colored their cheeks, and the rouge of the ladies of Paris. She learned that the Greek and Roman ladies were painted with the purple that came from the *murex*, and consequently that our scarlet was the purple of the ancients; that there was more saffron in the Spanish rouge and more cochineal in the French.

"She saw how her stockings were made on the loom, and the machine used for the purpose filled her with astonishment. 'Oh, what a fine book, sir!' she cried. 'Have you confiscated this store-house of all useful things in order to own it alone, and to be the only wise man in your kingdom?'

"They all threw themselves upon the volumes, like the daughters of Lycomedes on the jewels of Ulysses. Each found at once whatever he sought. Those that had lawsuits on hand were surprised to find the decision of their cases. The king read all the rights of his crown. 'But, really,' said he, 'I don't know why they spoke so ill of this book.'

"'Do you not see, sir,' said the Duke of Nivernois, 'that it is because it is very good? People do not attack poor and flat things of any kind. When the women try to make a new-comer appear ridiculous, she is sure to be prettier than they are.'

"All this time they were turning over the pages, and the Count of C—— said aloud, 'Sir, you are too happy that men should have been found in your reign able to know all the arts and to transmit them to posterity. Everything is here, from the way of making a pin to that of casting and of aiming your cannon; from the infinitesimal to the infinite. Thank God for having given birth in your kingdom to men who have thus served the whole world. Other nations are obliged to buy the "Encyclopædia," or to imitate it. Take all I have, if you like, but give me back my "Encyclopædia."'

"'But they say,' rejoined the king, 'that this necessary and admirable work has many faults.'

"'Sir,' replied the Count of C——, 'at your supper there were two ragouts that were failures. We did not eat them, but we had a very good supper. Would you have had the whole of it thrown out of the window on account of those two ragouts?' The king felt the force of this reasoning, each one took back his book, and it was a happy day.

"But Envy and Ignorance did not consider themselves beaten; those two immortal sisters kept up their cries, their cabals, their persecutions. Ignorance is very learned in that way.

"What happened? Foreigners bought out four editions of this French work which was proscribed in France, and made about eighteen hundred thousand dollars.

"Frenchmen, try hereafter to understand your own interests."[1]

---

[1] This story is printed among "Facéties." Morley points out that Mme. de Pompadour died before the volumes containing "Poudre" and "Rouge" were published. Voltaire, xlviii. 57.

We see by this anecdote, written probably to puff the book, that the "Encyclopædia" was recommended for the same advantages which have since given value to scores of similar works. No other collection of general information so large and so useful was then in existence. Elaborate descriptions of mechanism abound in it, and are illustrated by beautiful plates. We see before us the simple beginnings of the great manufacturing movement of modern times. There are articles on looms, on cabinet work, on jewelry, side by side with all that the science of that day could teach of anatomy, medicine, and natural history. Nor were more frivolous subjects forgotten. Nine plates are given to billiards and tennis. Choregraphy, or the art of expressing the figures of the dance on paper, occupies six pages of text and two of illustrations, with the remark that it is one of the arts of which the ancients were ignorant, or which they have not transmitted to us. There is a proposal for a new and universal language, based of course on French; and we are reminded by an article on Alcahest, a mysterious drug of the alchemists, to which two columns and a half are devoted, that the eighteenth century was nearer to the Middle Ages than the nineteenth. It was an idea of the compilers of the "Encyclopædia" that if ever civilization should be destroyed mankind might turn to their volumes to learn to restore it.[1]

Yet all this mere learning was not what came nearest to the heart of Diderot and his fellow-workers. In a moment of excitement, when smarting from the excisions of the publisher Le Breton, he was able to write that the success of the book was owing in no degree to ordinary, sensible, and common things; that perhaps there were not

[1] History and geography are almost passed over in the *Encyclopædia*, while the arts and sciences are fully treated. The contempt for history, as the tale of human errors, was common among the Philosophers.

two men in the world who had taken the trouble to read in it a line of history, geography, mathematics, or even of the arts; and that what all sought in the "Encyclopædia" was the firm and bold philosophy of some of its writers.[1]

This philosophy appears in the Preliminary Discourse by D'Alembert; it comes up again time after time throughout the volumes. The metaphysics are founded chiefly on those of Locke, who "may be said to have created metaphysics as Newton created physics," by reducing them to "what in fact they should be, the experimental physics of the soul." Beyond this there is little unity of opinion, although much agreement of spirit. We have articles on government and on taxation, liberally conceived, but not agreeing as to actual measures. We have a prejudice in favor of democracy, as the ideal form of government, and the worship of theoretical equality, but contempt for the populace, "which discerns nothing;" the reduction of religion to the sentiments of morality and benevolence, and great dislike for its ministers and especially for the members of monastic orders; the belief in the Legislator, in natural laws and liberties, including the inalienable right of every man to dispose of his own person and property and to do all things that the laws allow; faith in the Philosopher, a man governed entirely by reason as the Christian is governed by grace. To him, Truth is not a mistress corrupting his imagination. He knows how to distinguish what is true, what is false, what is doubtful, and he glories in being willing to remain undetermined when he has not the material for judgment. The Philosopher understands as well the doctrines that he rejects as those that he adopts. His spirit brings everything to its true principles. The nations will be

[1] When in a cooler mood Diderot boasts that there are people who have read the book through. See the word *Encyclopédie*, vol. v.

happy when kings are Philosophers, or when Philosophers are kings.

There was no uniformity of execution in the "Encyclopædia." The editors were not free to reject all that they did not approve. They had to consider the feelings of their writers, and sometimes, no doubt, to print a poor article by a valued hand. There were many long dissertations where short articles would have been more to the purpose. Diderot was not the man to repress the natural tendency of contributors to wordiness. Then official censors and possible prosecutors had to be considered. "Doubtless," says D'Alembert to Voltaire, in reply to the latter's remonstrances, "doubtless we have bad articles on theology and metaphysics; but with theological censors and a privilege, I defy you to make them better. There are other articles less conspicuous where all is repaired. Time will enable people to distinguish what we thought from what we have said." ... "It is certain," he says in another place, "that several of our workers have put in worthless things, and sometimes declamation; but it is still more certain that I have not had it in my power to alter this state of things. I flatter myself that the same judgment will not be passed on what several of our authors and I myself have furnished for this work, which apparently will go down to posterity as a monument of what we would and what we could not do." On the whole the chief of the Philosophers was satisfied. "Oh, how sorry I am," he exclaims, "to see so much paste among your fine diamonds; but you shed your lustre on the paste."[1]

[1] *Correspondence of Voltaire and D'Alembert* (A. to V., July 21, 1757 ; Jan. 11, 1758 ; V. to A., Dec. 29, 1757). Voltaire, lvii. 296, 444, 421.

CHAPTER XVII.

HELVETIUS, HOLBACH AND CHASTELLUX.

There are two books issuing so directly from what may be called the orthodox school of Philosophers, and so closely connected with the "Encyclopædia" and its authors, that they should be noticed next to the great compilation itself. One of them has already been mentioned. It bears the untranslatable title "De l'Esprit," a word which in this simple and unmodified form means exactly neither wit nor spirit, but something between the two and different from either.

The author, Helvetius, was one of those clever men whose ambition it is to shine. The son of a fashionable physician, he had made a fortune as a farmer of the revenue. He had been addicted, in his youth, to the pursuit of women and of literature, and had subsequently shown moderation in leaving his lucrative office and the dissipations of the town and retiring into the country with a charming wife. For eight months in the year they lived at Voré, not unvisited by Philosophers; for four they kept open house in Paris. Both were good natured, charitable, and benevolent. Among the Philosophers Helvetius held the place of the rich and clever worldling, so often found in literary circles.

The treatise "De l'Esprit" has for its object the setting forth of the doctrine of utility in its extreme form. As a preliminary argument all the operations of the mind are reduced to sensation. "When by a succession of my ideas, or by the vibration which certain sounds cause in the organ of my ears, I recall the image of an oak, then my interior organs must necessarily be nearly in the same situation as they were at the sight of that oak. Now this situation of the organs must necessarily produce a sensation; it is, therefore, evident that memory is sensation.

"Having stated this principle, I say further that it is in the capacity which we have of perceiving the resemblances or the differences, the agreement or the disagreement, which different objects have with each other, that all the operations of the mind consist. Now this capacity is nothing else than physical sensibility; therefore everything is reduced to sensation."

Utility, according to Helvetius, is the foundation of all our moral feelings. Each person praises as just in others only those actions which are useful to himself; every nation or society praises what is useful to it in its corporate capacity. "If a judge acquits a guilty man, if a minister of state promotes an unworthy one, each is just, according to the man protected. But if the judge punishes, or the minister refuses, they will always be unjust in the eyes of the criminal and of the unsuccessful." . . . "The Christians who justly spoke of the cruelties practiced on them by the pagans as barbarity and crime, did they not give the name of zeal to the cruelties which they, in their turn, practiced on these same pagans?" As the physical world is subject to laws of motion, so is the moral world to those of interest. All men alike strive after their own happiness. It is the diversity of passions and tastes, some of which are in accordance with the public interest and others in opposition to it, which form our virtues and our vices. We should, therefore, not despise the wicked, but pity them, and thank heaven that it has given us none of those tastes and passions which would have obliged us to seek our happiness in other people's misfortunes. This opinion, although extravagantly stated, was, as we have seen, but the caricature of the doctrine of utility, as taught by Locke and held by his followers.

Helvetius took great pains to make the treatment of his theme interesting. He labored long over every chapter. His pages overflow with anecdotes, with sneers at monks, and with excuses for lust. They show the belief in the omnipotence of legislation which was common in his day. A large space is devoted to minimizing the natural inequality of mankind, and attributing the differences observable among men to chance or to education. If Galileo had not happened to be walking in a garden in Florence where certain workmen asked him a question about a pump, he would not, according to Helvetius, have discovered the weight of the atmosphere. It was the fall of the apple which gave Newton his theory of gravitation. Such puerilities as these disgust us in the book; yet the theory that greatness is but the result of an inconsiderable accident, was not unnatural in one who had probably hit on an idea which struck him as telling, and believed that he had thereby achieved greatness.[1]

Helvetius had endeavored to carry the doctrines of the French followers of Locke to their last logical conclusions, but the successful accomplishment of that task was reserved for a stronger and steadier hand than his. Baron Holbach was an amiable and good man, the constant friend of the Encyclopædists. At his house they often met, so that it came to be known among them as the Café de l'Europe, and its master as the "maître d'hôtel" of Philosophy. But these nicknames were used in good part. Holbach had none of the flippancy of Helvetius. His book, the

[1] Helvetius, i. 130, 183; ii. 7, and *passim*. For Helvetius, see *Nouvelle Biographie universelle*. Morley, *Diderot*, ii. 141. Grimm, iv. 80. Morellet, i. 71, 140. Morellet represents himself as a tame cat in Helvetius's house. Marmontel, ii. 115 (liv. vi.) an excellent description. Compare Locke, i. 261, ii. 97. The doctrine of utility is probably nearly as old as philosophy itself. It has been well suggested that although not the ultimate motive of virtue, utility may be the test of morals. It was, in a measure, Helvetius that inspired Bentham. Morley, *Diderot*, ii. 154.

"System of Nature," is a solemn, earnest argument, proceeding from a clear brain and a pure heart. Our nature may revolt at his theories, but we cannot question his honesty or his benevolence. The book, published, as the fashion was, under a false name, yet expresses the inmost convictions of the writer.[1]

"Men," he says, "will always make mistakes, when they abandon experience for systems born of the imagination." Man exists in nature and can imagine nothing outside of nature. Let him, therefore, cease to seek beyond the world he inhabits for beings which shall procure for him that happiness which nature refuses to give him. "Man is a being purely physical. Moral man is but that being considered from a certain point of view, that is to say, relatively to some of his ways of acting, due to his particular organization." All human actions, visible and invisible, are the necessary consequences of man's mechanism, and of the impulsions which it receives from surrounding entities.

The universe is made up of matter and motion, cause and effect. Nature is the great whole, resulting from the assemblage of different matters, combinations, and motions. By motion only do we know the existence and properties of other beings and distinguish them from each other. There is continual action and reaction in all things. Love and hate in men are like attraction and repulsion in physics, with causes more obscure. All beings, organic and inorganic, tend to self-preservation. This tendency in man is called self-love.

[1] The name assumed was that of Mirabaud, once secretary to the Academy, who had died before the book appeared. See Morley, *Diderot*, ii. 173, as to the authorship of the *System of Nature*. It has sometimes been attributed to Diderot, but it seems clear from internal evidence that Diderot could not have written it. The style and the thought are both too compact to proceed from that diffuse thinker and writer. But Diderot, who had great influence on many men, may have suggested some of the ideas.

There is in reality no order nor disorder, since all things are necessary. It is only in our minds that there exists the model of what we call order; like other abstract ideas, it corresponds to nothing outside of ourselves. Order is no more than the faculty of coördinating ourselves with the beings that surround us, or with the whole of which we form a part. But if we wish to apply the word to nature, it may stand for a succession of actions or motions which we suppose to contribute to a given end. We call beings intelligent when they are organized like ourselves, and can act toward an end which we understand.

No two beings are exactly alike; differences, whether called physical or moral, being the result of their bodily qualities. These differences are the cause and the support of human society. If all men were alike they would not need each other. It is a mistake to complain of this inequality, by which we are put under the fortunate necessity of combining. In coming together men have made an explicit or implied compact, by which they have bound themselves to render mutual services and not to injure each other. But as each man's nature leads him to seek to satisfy his own passions or caprices without regard to others, law was established to bring him back to his duty. This law is the sum of the wills of the society, united to fix the conduct of its members, or to direct their actions towards the common aim of the association. For convenience, certain citizens are made executors of the popular will, and are called monarchs, magistrates, or representatives, according to the form of the government. But that form may be changed, and all the powers of all persons under it revoked, at the will of the society itself, by which and for which all government is established. Laws, to be just, must have for their invariable end the general interests of society; they must procure for the greatest number of citizens the advantages for which those citizens have combined. A society whose chiefs and whose laws do not benefit its members loses all rights over them. Chiefs who do harm to any society lose the right to command it. By not applying these maxims the nations are made unhappy. By the imprudence of nations, and by the craft of those to whom power had been entrusted, sovereigns have become absolute masters. They have claimed to hold their powers from Heaven and not to be responsible to any one on earth. Hence politics have become corrupt and no more than a form of brigandage. Man unrestrained soon turns to evil. Only by fear can society control the passions of its rulers. It must, therefore, confer but limited powers on any one of them, and divide those forces which, if united, would necessarily crush it.[1]

Government influences alike, and necessarily, the physical and moral welfare of nations. As its care produces labor, activity, abundance, and health, its neglect and its injustice produce indolence, discouragement, famine, contagion, vices, and crimes. It can bring to light, or can smother talents, skill, and virtue. In fact the government, distributing rank, wealth, rewards and punishments; master of the things in which men have learned from childhood to place their happiness, acquires a necessary influence on their conduct, inflames their passions, turns them as it will, modifies and settles their manners and customs.[2] These are, in whole nations, as in individuals, but the conduct, or general system of will and action which necessarily results from their education, their government, their laws, their religious opinions, their wise or foolish institutions. In short, manners and customs are the habits of nations; good when they produce solid and true happiness for society, and detestable in the eyes of reason, in spite of the sanction of laws, usage, religion,

---

[1] Holbach is clearly indebted both to Rousseau and to Montesquieu.
[2] *Mœurs*, a word for which we have no exact equivalent. It includes the idea of morals as well as that of customs.

public opinion or example, when they have the support only of habit and prejudice, which seldom consult experience and good sense. No action is so abominable that it is not, or has not been, approved by some nation. Parricide, infanticide, theft, usurpation, cruelty, intolerance, prostitution, have been allowed and even considered meritorious by some of the peoples of the earth. Religion especially has consecrated the most revolting and unreasonable customs.

The cause of the wickedness and corruption of men is that nowhere are they governed according to their nature. Men are bad, not because they are born bad, but because they are made so. The great and powerful safely crush the poor and unfortunate, who try, at the risk of their lives, to return the evil they have suffered. The poor attack openly, or in secret, that unjust society which gives all to some of its children and takes all from others.

The rights of a man over his fellows can be founded only on the happiness which he procures for them, or for which he gives them cause to hope. No mortal receives from nature the right to command. The authority which the father exercises over his family is founded on the advantages which he is supposed to bestow upon it. Ranks in political society have their basis in real or imaginary utility. The rich man has rights over the poor man solely by virtue of the well-being which he may bestow upon him. Genius, talents, art, and skill have claims only on account of the pleasant and useful things with which they furnish society. To be virtuous is to make people happy.

A society enjoys all the happiness of which it is capable when the greater number of its members is fed, clothed, and lodged; when most men can, without excessive labor, satisfy the cravings of nature. Men's imagination should be satisfied when they are sure that the fruits of their labor cannot be taken from them, and that they are working for themselves. Beyond this all is superfluity, and it is foolish that a whole nation should sweat to give luxuries to a few persons who can never be content because their imaginations have become boundless.

Religion is a delusion. The soul, born with the body, is childish in children, adult in manhood, grows old with advancing years. It is vain to suppose that the soul survives the body. To die is to think, to feel, to enjoy, to suffer, no more. Let us reflect on death, not to encourage fear and melancholy, but to accustom ourselves to look at it with peaceful eyes, and to throw off the false terror with which the enemies of our peace try to inspire us.

Utility is the touchstone of systems, opinions, and actions; it is the measure of our very love of truth. The most useful truths are the most admired; we call those truths great which most concern the human race; those futile which concern only a few men whose ideas we do not share.

The doctrine of utility is combined with that of necessity. Most of the French Philosophers were necessarians, but Holbach expressed the doctrine in a more extreme form than the others. Will, according to him, is a modification of the brain by which it is disposed, or prepared, to set our other organs in motion. The will is necessarily determined by the quality and pleasantness of the ideas which act upon it. Deliberation is the oscillation of the will when moved in different directions by opposing forces; determination is the final prevalence of one force over the other. There is no difference between the man who throws himself out of a window and the man who is thrown out, except that the impulse on the latter comes from something outside of himself, and that of the former from something within his own mechanism.[1]

[1] Chaudon, the Benedictine, probably the cleverest of the clerical writers of the time, thus attacks the doctrine of necessity, as set forth by Holbach. The author of the *System* has certainly given out very fine maxims of morality, very pathetic exhortations to virtue ; but with

Nature has made men neither good nor bad; it has made them machines. Man is virtuous only in obedience to the call of interest. Morals are founded on our approbation of those actions which are advantageous to the race. When good actions benefit others and not ourselves our approbation of them is similar to the admiration we feel for a fine picture belonging to some one else. The good man is he whose true ideas have shown him that his happiness lies in a line of conduct which others are forced by their own interests to like and approve. By virtue we acquire the good will of our neighbors, and no man can be happy without it. Our self-love becomes a hundred times more delightful when to it is joined the love of others for us. Let us remember that the most impracticable of all designs is that of being happy alone.

To this point in his argument Holbach had only repeated with strength, clearness and consistency what the school of the Philosophers from Voltaire to Helvetius had either affirmed or hinted. In his second volume, however, he boldly cut loose from his predecessors and avowed his disbelief in any God. Voltaire and Rousseau were theists, with different sorts of faith, and the Philosophers, although treating all churches, and especially all priests, with contempt, had retained, at least in speech, some remnant of theism. But Holbach declared that God was an illusion, devised by the fears and the ignorance of mankind. "The idea of Divinity," he says, "always awakens afflicting ideas in our minds." By the word "God" men mean the most hidden or remote cause; they use the word only when the chain of material and known causes ceases

his principles this can be but a joke. It is an absurdity, like that of a man who, recognizing that his watch was only a machine, should not fail to exhort it every day to prevent its getting out of order. Grosse, *Dict. d'antiphilosophisme*, 923. Holbach would probably have replied that he was necessarily obliged to exhort, and that Chaudon was fatally forced to answer.

to be visible to them. It is a vague name which they apply to a cause short of which their indolence, or the limits of their knowledge, forces them to stop. Men found nature deaf to their cries; they therefore imagined an intelligent master over it, hoping that he would listen to them.

This theme is elaborated by Holbach throughout his second volume. Here as elsewhere he writes with seriousness and conviction, although some of his logical positions are assailable. Never before in France had materialism, necessarianism and atheism been so clearly and forcibly expounded. The very Philosophers were alarmed. Voltaire hastened to write an article on God so unconvincing, that it can hardly have convinced himself. It amounts to little more than an argument that God is the most probable of hypotheses, and it admits that there may be two or several gods as well as one. It is not unlikely that Voltaire thought it necessary for his peace in the world to protest against so outspoken a book as the "System of Nature."

The true answer to Holbach is to be found in a different order of ideas from any that Voltaire was prepared to accept. Yet Locke might have taught him that if there is no logical reason to believe in the existence of mind, there is as little to believe in the existence of matter. Experience might have shown him that men do not always seek the thing which they believe most useful to themselves. The old and favorite doctrine of utility labors under the disadvantage that it has never shown, nor ever can show, an adequate reason why any man should care for another or for the race. And as for the existence of God, — that can no more be proved by argument than the existence of matter, mind, or the *non-ego*.

Helvetius and Holbach had worked out the theories of the school to their last philosophical conclusion. A younger writer in the last years of the reign of Louis

XV. was to furnish the complete application of them. The Chevalier de Chastellux is well known in America by the book of travels which he wrote when he accompanied the Marquis of Rochambeau in the Revolutionary War. Chastellux was just then at the height of his reputation. He had published in 1772 a book which, although now almost forgotten, is still interesting as a link between the thought of the last century and that of a large school of thinkers to-day. The title is "Of Public Felicity, or considerations on the fate of men in the different Epochs of History," and the motto is *Nil Desperandum*. "So many people have written the history of men," says Chastellux; "will not that of humanity be read with pleasure?" And again: "Several authors have carefully examined if such a Nation were more religious, more sober, more warlike than another; none has yet sought to discover which was the happiest."

The object of inquiry being thus indicated, it becomes of the first importance to consider what test of happiness Chastellux will propose. He leaves us in no doubt on this point. "A happy nation is not one which lives with little; the Goths and Vandals lived with little, and they sought abundance in other regions. A happy nation is not one which is hardened to trouble and labor; the Goths and Vandals were hardened to labor, and they sought elsewhere for softness and rest. A happy nation is not one which is strongest in battle; it fights only to obtain peace and the commodities of life. A happy nation is one which enjoys ease and liberty, which is attached to its possessions, and, above all things, which does not desire to change its condition." And in another place he asks, what are some of the indications, the symptoms of public felicity. Two of them, he says, are naturally presented: agriculture and population. "I name agriculture before population," he continues, "because if it happens that a nation which is not numerous cultivates carefully a great quantity of land, it will result that this nation consumes much, and adds to the food necessary to life the ease and commodity which make its happiness. If, on the other hand, the increase of the people is in proportion to that of the agriculture, what can we conclude except that this multiplication of the human race, as of all other species, comes solely from its well-being. Agriculture is, therefore, an indication of the happiness of the nations anterior and preferable to population." The most certain indication of felicity is a large proportional consumption of products; a high rate of living. The marvelous and even the sublime are to be dreaded; but "all that multiplies men in the nations, and harvests on the surface of the earth, is good in itself, is good above all things, and preferable to all that seems fine in the eyes of prejudice."[1]

And as material good is the only good, so it is in modern times and in civilized countries that the highest point reached by humanity is to be found. "If wisdom be the art of happy living; if philosophy be truly the love of wisdom, as its name alone would give us to understand, the Greeks were never philosophers."

To show that modern nations are increasing the ease and comfort of life to a point unknown before is no difficult task. Chastellux enumerates the discoveries of physical science, and touches on the achievements of learning and the arts, then calls on his readers to look on all these but as payments on account in the progress of our knowledge; as so much of the road already passed in the vast course of the human mind. Here we have the truly mod-

[1] Chastellux finds it hard to stick quite close to his definition of felicity. Of the English he says, "Such are the true advantages of this nation; which, joined to the safety of its property and the inestimable privilege of depending only on the law, would make it the happiest on earth, if its climate, its ancient manners and customs, and its frequent revolutions had not turned it toward discontent and melancholy. But these considerations do not belong to our subject." ii. 144.

ern ideal of progress; the end of government the greatest happiness of the greatest number, and happiness dependent merely on material conditions. Morals under this system are but a branch of medicine. Religion is an old-fashioned prejudice. Let us push on and unite the world in one great, comfortable, well-fed family. Such is the last practical advice of the French Philosophic school of the eighteenth century and of its unconscious followers in this. If the conclusion does not satisfy the highest aspirations of the human race, that is perhaps because of some flaw in the premises.

CHAPTER XVIII.

ROUSSEAU'S POLITICAL WRITINGS.

IN passing from the study of the Philosophers to that of Rousseau, we turn from talent to genius, from system to impulse. The theories of the great Genevan were drawn from his own strange nature, with little regard for consistency. They belong together much as the features of a distorted and changeful countenance may do; their unity is personal rather than systematic. And while Rousseau was, from certain aspects and chiefly in respect to his conduct, the most contemptible of the great thinkers of his day, he surpassed most of the others in constant literary sincerity, and in occasional elevation of thought and feeling. Voltaire, although never swerving long from his own general philosophical scheme, would lie without hesitation for any purpose. Diderot would quote from nonexistent books to establish his theories. But no one can read Rousseau without being convinced that he believed what he wrote, at least at the moment of writing it. Truthfulness of this kind is quite consistent with inaccuracy, and it is probable that some incidents in Rousseau's autobiographical writings have been wrongly remembered, colored by prejudice, or embellished by vanity. Some of them may even be completely fictitious; the author caring little for facts except as the ornaments and illustrations of ideas. But what he thought in the abstract Rousseau was quite ready to write down, caring little for the feelings or the opinions of any sect or party; or even of that great public whose thought was as law to the Philosophers. He deserved to profit by his sincerity, and he has done so. His many and great faults were well known to his contemporaries; they are told in his posthumous "Confessions" in a way to show them more dark than any contemporary could have imagined; yet such is the evident frankness of those evil and repugnant volumes that many decent men have got from them a sneaking kindness for Rousseau, and an inclination to take him at his own estimate, as one no worse than other people.

This estimate of himself is never to be forgotten in reading his books. "You see what I am, " he seems to say at every turn; "now, I am a good man." In the belief in his own comparative goodness he was firmly fixed. His theories of life were largely founded on it. For Rousseau was an introspective thinker, and thus in seeming opposition to the intellectual tendency of his age. Voltaire and Diderot were interested chiefly in the world around them. Locke had viewed his own mind objectively; he had attempted the feat of getting outside of it, in order to take a good look at it; and in so doing he had missed seeing some important parts of it, because they were internal. Rousseau studied himself and the world within himself. Thus while he was as immoral in his actions as any of the Philosophers, he was more religious than any of them. Voltaire's theism was little more than a remnant of early habit, strengthened by a notion that some sort of religion was necessary for purposes of police. To Rousseau, a world without a God would have been truly empty. But as his religion was theistic, and not orthodox; as, with characteristic meanness, he was ready to profess Catholicism or Calvinism as he might find it convenient, he has been classed among atheists by churchmen. In so far as this is mere vituperation it is perhaps deserved, for Rousseau's life deserved almost any conceivable vituperation; but as an historical fact, Rousseau's faith was quite as living as that of many of his revilers.

[1] Rousseau looked on Catholicism and Calvinism rather as civil

Every thinking human being has a philosophy and a theology, — a metaphysical foundation for his beliefs, and an opinion concerning the Deity. The only escape from having these is to think of nothing outside of the daily routine of life. The attempt to be without them on any other terms generally ends in having but crude and contradictory opinions on the most important subjects of human interest. The theology of Rousseau will be considered later. Philosophical systems were his especial bugbear, and it is only incidentally that he formulates his metaphysical ideas. His general tendency of belief was toward intuition. Justice and virtue he believed to be written in the hearts of men, disturbed rather than elucidated by the observation of the learned and the reflection of the ingenious. As to the ground of our actions he was less at one with himself. Sometimes, in agreement with the prevalent philosophy of his day, he assumed that men are moved only by their own interest. At times, however, he recognized two principles of human action anterior to reason; the first of which is care for our own well-being; the second, a natural repugnance to see others suffer. In making this distinction he separated from the school of thinkers to whom pity and affection are but refined forms of self-love. This is characteristic of Rousseau, who was free from that craving for system which is the snare of those minds in which logic and pure reason prevail over acuteness of self-observation.

The society of the eighteenth century had grown very rigid and artificial. The struggle of the Philosophers was to bring men back in one way and another to a life founded rationally on a few simple laws derived from the nature of things. Of these laws the leaders themselves had not always a true perception, nor did they always

systems than as ideas, and accepted them in the same way in which a man may live under a foreign government, of whose principles he does not approve.

derive the right rules from such laws as they perceived. But their struggle was ever for reason, as they understood it, and generally for simplicity. In this work Rousseau was a leader. He was constantly preaching the merits and the charms of a simple life. In his denunciations of elaborateness, of luxury, and even of civilization, he was often mistaken, sometimes absurd. But his authority was great. He set a fashion of simplicity, and he exerted an influence which went far beyond fashion, and has helped to modify the world to this day.

There was another quality beside introspection in which Rousseau was the precursor of the literary men of the nineteenth century, and that is the love of nature. To say that he was the first great writer to enjoy and describe natural scenery would be a gross exaggeration. But most of Rousseau's predecessors valued the world out of doors principally for its usefulness, and in proportion to its fertility. Rousseau is perhaps the first great writer who fairly reveled in country life; for whom lake and mountain, rock and cloud, tree and flower, had a constant joy and meaning. The true enjoyment of natural scenery, generally affected nowadays, is not given in a high degree to most people; in a very few it may be as intense as the enjoyment of music is in many more; but most people can get from scenery, as from other beautiful things, a reasonable and modest enjoyment, if the object for their admiration be well pointed out to them. Rousseau needed no such instruction. To some extent he furnished it to the modern world. The genuineness of his love of nature is partly shown by the fact that she was as dear to him in her simpler as in her grander aspects. The grass filled him with delight as truly as the mountain-peak; indeed, he felt contempt for those who look afar for the beauty that is all about us, and his admiration was not reserved for the unusual. Nor did he fill his pages with description. It is in his autobiographical writings and in reference to its effect on himself that he most often mentions natural scenery. Recognizing instinctively that the principal subjects of language are thought and action, as the chief interests of painting are form and color, this writer so keenly alive to natural beauty is guiltless of word painting.

Jean Jacques Rousseau was born at Geneva on the 28th of June, 1712. His mother, the daughter of a Protestant minister, died at his birth. His father, a clockmaker by trade, a man of eccentric disposition, had little real control over the boy, and, moreover, soon moved away from the city on account of a quarrel with its government, leaving his son behind him. Jean Jacques was first put under the care of a minister in a neighboring village; then passed two or three years with an uncle in the town. At the age of eleven he was sent to a notary's office, whence he was dismissed for dullness and inaptitude. He was next apprenticed to an engraver, a man of violent temper, who by his cruelty brought out the meanness inherent in the boy's weak nature. Rousseau had not been incapable of generosity; perhaps he never quite became so. But, with a cowardly temperament, he especially needed firm kindness and judicious reproof, and these he did not receive. He took to pilfering from his master, who, in return, used to beat him. Rousseau's thefts were, in fact, not very considerable, — apples from the larder, graving tools from the closet. His worst offenses at this time were not such as would make us condemn very harshly a lad of spirit. But Jean Jacques was not such a lad. The last of his scrapes as an apprentice was important only from its consequences. One afternoon he had gone with some comrades on an expedition beyond the city gates. "Half a league from the town," say the "Confessions," "I hear the retreat sounded, and hasten my steps; I hear the drum beat, and run with all my might; I arrive out of breath, all in a sweat; my heart beats; I see from a distance the soldiers at their posts; I rush on; I cry with a failing voice. It was too late. When twenty yards from the outpost I see the first drawbridge going up. I tremble as I see in the air those terrible horns, sinister and fatal augury of that terrible fate which was at that moment beginning for me.

"In the first violence of my grief I threw myself on the glacis and bit the earth. My comrades laughed at their misfortune and made the best of it at once. I also made up my mind, but in another way. On the very spot I swore that I would never go back to my master, and on the morrow, when the gates were opened and they returned to town, I bade them adieu forever."

Thus did Rousseau become a wanderer at the age of sixteen. The duchy of Savoy, into which he first passed, adjoined the republic of Geneva, and was a country as fervently Catholic as the other was ardently Calvinistic. The young runaway soon fell in with a proselytizing priest, who gave him a good dinner and dispatched him, for the furtherance of his conversion, to a singular lady, living not far off, at Annecy. This lady, named Madame de Warens, about twelve years older than Rousseau, was not long after to occupy a large place in his life. She belonged to a Protestant family of Vevay, on the north side of the Lake of Geneva. She, like him, had fled from her country, and apparently for no more serious reason. In her flight she had left her husband and abjured her religion. In morals she had a system of her own, and gave herself to many men, without interested motives, but with little passion. She was a sentimental, active-minded woman, of small judgment; pleasing rather than beautiful, short of stature, thickset, but with a fine head and arms. Madame de Warens received the boy kindly, and on this first occasion of their meeting did little more than speed him on his way to Turin, where he entered a monastery for the express purpose of being converted to

Catholicism. In nine days the farce was completed, and the new Catholic turned out into the town, with about twenty francs of small change in his pocket, charitably contributed by the witnesses of the ceremony of his abjuration. It is needless to dwell on his adventures at this time. He was a servant in two different families. After something more than a year he left Turin on foot, and wandered back to Annecy and to Madame de Warens.

The period of Rousseau's life in which that lady was the ruling influence lasted ten or twelve years. The situation was one from which any man of manly instincts would have shrunk, a condition of dependence on a mistress, and on a mistress who made no pretense of fidelity. In a desultory way Rousseau learned something of music at this time, and made some long journeys on foot, one of them taking him as far as Paris. This man, morally of soft fibre, was able to endure and enjoy moderate physical hardship; and from early education felt most at home in simple houses and amid rude surroundings. At last, disgusted with the appearance of a new rival in Madame de Warens's changeable household, Rousseau left that lady and drifted off to Lyons; then, after once trying the experiment of returning to his mistress and finding it a failure, to Paris.

For more than eight years after his final separation from Madame de Warens, Rousseau did nothing to make any one suppose him to be a man of genius. He obtained and threw up the position of secretary to the French ambassador at Venice; he supported himself as a musician and as a private secretary; he lived from hand to mouth, having as a companion one Thérèse Levasseur, a grotesquely illiterate maid servant, picked up at an inn. Their five children he successively took to the Foundling, losing sight of them forever. To the mother he was faithful for the most part, although not without some amorous vanderings, for many years.

Up to 1749, then, when Rousseau was thirty-seven years old, he had published nothing of importance. He had, however, some acquaintance with literary men, being known merely as one of those adventurers without any settled means of existence, who may always be found in cities, and with whom Paris at this time appears to have been over-furnished. In features he was plain, in manners awkward; much given to making compliments to women, but generally displeasing to them, although at times interesting when roused to excitement. The Swiss Jean Jacques had little of the sparkling wit which the Frenchmen of his day rated very high, but he had much subtlety of observation and many ideas. He constantly applauded himself in his writings on being sensible rather than witty. In fact he was neither, but very ingenious and eloquent. In character he was self-indulgent but not luxurious, sensitive, vain, and sentimental. To this man, — if we may believe his own account, and I think in the main we may do so, — there came by a sudden flash an idea which altered his whole life, and which has materially affected millions of lives since he died. The idea was an evil seed, and it found an evil soil to grow in.

The summer of 1749 was a hot one. Diderot, just rising into notice as a man of letters, had been imprisoned in the Castle of Vincennes, for his "Letter on the Blind," and his friends were allowed to come and see him. Rousseau used to visit him every other afternoon, walking the four or five miles which lie between the centre of Paris and the castle. The trees along the road were trimmed after the dreary French fashion, and gave little shade. From time to time Rousseau would stop, lie down on the grass and rest, and he had got into the habit of taking a book or a newspaper in his pocket. It was in this way that his eye happened to fall on a paragraph in the "Mercure de France," announcing that the Academy of Dijon would give a prize the next year for the best essay on the following subject: "Whether the Progress of the Arts and Sciences has tended to corrupt or to improve Morals."

From that moment, according to Rousseau, a complete change came over him. Struck with sudden giddiness, he was like a drunken man. His heart palpitated and he could hardly walk or draw breath. Throwing himself at the foot of a tree, he spent half an hour in such agitation that when he arose he found the whole front of his waistcoat wet with tears, although he had not known that he was shedding any. Thus did his great theory of the degeneracy of man under civilization burst upon him.[1]

The very question asked by the academy suggests the possibility of an answer unfavorable to civilization, but Rousseau's treatment of it was such as to form the beginning of an epoch in the history of thought. It is under the rough coat of the laborer, he says, and not under the tinsel of the courtier, that strength and vigor of body will be found. Before art had shaped our manners, they were rustic but natural, and men's actions freely expressed their feelings. Human nature was no better, at bottom, than now, but men were safer because they could more easily read each other's minds, and thus they avoided many vices. The advance of civilization brings increase of corruption. Constantinople, where learning was preserved during the dark ages, was full of murder, debauch-

---

[1] Rousseau, xviii. 135 (*Confessions*, Part. ii. liv. viii); xix. 358 (*Seconde Lettre à M. de Malesherbes*). Exaggerated as the above story probably is, we may reasonably believe that it comes nearer the truth than that told by Diderot in after years, when he and Rousseau had quarreled. In that version, Rousseau, desiring to compete for the prize, consulted Diderot as to which side he should take, and was advised to assume that which other people would avoid. Diderot, *Œuvres*, xi. 148. Rousseau's thoughts had been wandering into subjects akin to that of the prize essay before he had seen the announcement in the *Mercure de France*. Musset-Pathay, ii. 363. Moreover, if Rousseau was imaginative, and not always to be believed about facts, Diderot was a tremendous liar.

ery, and crime. Contrast with its inhabitants those primitive nations which have been kept from the contagion of vain knowledge: the early Persians, the Germans described by Tacitus, the modern Swiss, the American Indians, whose simple institutions Montaigne prefers to all the laws of Plato. These nations know well that in other lands idle men spend their time in disputing about vice and virtue, but they have considered the morals of these argumentative persons and have learned to despise their doctrine.

"Astronomy is born of superstition; eloquence of ambition, hatred, flattery, and lying; geometry of avarice; physics of a vain curiosity; all, and morals themselves, of human pride. The arts and sciences, therefore, owe their birth in our vices; we should have less doubt of the advantage to be derived from them if they sprang from our virtues." . . . "Answer me, illustrious philosophers, you from whom we know why bodies attract each other in a vacuum; what are the relations of areas traversed in equal times in the revolutions of the planets; what curves have conjugate points, points of inflection and reflection; how man sees all things in God; how the soul and body correspond without communication, as two clocks would do; what stars may be inhabited; what insects reproduce their kind in extraordinary ways, — tell me, I say, you to whom we owe so much sublime knowledge — if you had taught us none of these things, should we be less numerous, less well-governed, less redoubtable, less flourishing, or more perverse?"

This is the theme of the First Discourse, a theme most congenial to the nature of Rousseau. His ill-health, his dreamy habit of mind, his vanity, all made him long for a state of things as different as possible from that about him.

"Among us," he says, "it is true that Socrates would not have drunk the hemlock; but he would have drunk from a more bitter cup of insulting mockery and of contempt a hundred times worse than death." Such sensitiveness as this belongs to Rousseau himself. With what disdain would the healthy-minded Socrates have laughed at the suggestion that he was troubled by the contempt or the mockery of those about him. How gayly would he have turned the weapons of the mockers on themselves. Rousseau had neither the sense of humor nor the joy of living, which added so much to the greatness of the Athenian. His theories are especially pleasing to the disappointed and the weak, and therein lies their danger; for they tend, not to manly effort for the improvement of individual circumstances or of mankind, but to vain dreaming of impossible ideals. There is a luxury that softens, but there is also a luxury that causes labor. A nation without astronomy, or geography, or physics, is generally less numerous, less redoubtable, less flourishing, and sometimes less well governed than a civilized nation. It is true that in the arts and sciences, in the deeds and in the condition of men, there is an admixture of what is base; but there is no baser nor more dangerous habit of mind than that which for every action seeks out the worst motive, for every state the most selfish reason.[1]

While Rousseau's First Discourse is pernicious in its general teaching, it is rich in eloquent passages, and it contains some of those sensible remarks which we seldom fail to find in its author's works. At the time of writing it, as later, he was interested in education,—the subject on which his influence has been, on the whole, most use-

[1] Long after the publication of the First Discourse, Rousseau insisted that he had never intended to plunge civilized states into barbarism, but only to arrest the decay of primitive ones, and perhaps to retard that of the more advanced, by changing their ideals. Œuvres, xx. 275 (II. Dialogue); xxi. 34 (III. Dialogue). Rousseau's writings generally must be taken as expressions of feeling, quite as much as attempts to change the world. They are growls or sighs, rather than sermons.

ful. "I see on every side," he says, "enormous establishments where youth is brought up at great expense to learn everything but its duties. Your children will be ignorant of their own language, but will speak others which are not in use anywhere; they will know how to make verses which they will hardly be able to understand themselves; without knowing how to distinguish truth from falsehood, they will possess the art of disguising both from others by specious arguments; but those words, magnanimity, equity, temperance, humanity, courage, will be unknown to them; that sweet name of country[1] will never strike their ears; and if they hear of God, it will be less to fear Him than to be afraid of Him. 'I would as lief,' said a sage, 'that my schoolboy had spent his time in a tennis-court; at least his body would be more active.' I know that children must be kept busy, and that idleness is the danger most to be feared for them. What, then, should they learn? A fine question surely! Let them learn what they must do when they are men, and not what they must forget."[2]

The First Discourse not only took the prize at Dijon, but attracted a great deal of notice in Paris, and immediately gave Rousseau a distinguished place among men of letters. Controversy was excited, refutations attempted. In 1753 the Academy of Dijon again offered a prize for an essay on a subject evidently connected with the former one: "What is the Origin of Inequality among Men, and whether it is authorized by Natural Law." Again Rousseau competed, and this time the prize was given to some one else, but Rousseau's essay was published, and takes rank among the important writings of its author and of its time. In the Second Discourse we see the development of the ideas of the First. Rousseau

[1] *Patrie*, — a word seemingly necessary, but which the English language manages to do without.
[2] Compare Montaigne, i. 135 (liv. i. chap. xxv.).

composed an imaginary history of mankind, starting from that being of his own creation, the happy savage. He thinks that man in the primitive condition, having no moral relations nor known duties, could be neither good nor bad; unless these words are taken in a purely physical sense, and those things are called vices in the individual which may interfere with his own preservation, and those are called virtues which may contribute to it. In this case, Rousseau believes that he must be called the most virtuous who least resists the simple impulses of nature; a mistake surely, for what natural impulses are more simple than those which turn a man aside from all sustained exertion, and what impulses tend more than these to the destruction of the individual and of the species?

Rousseau's savage has but few desires, and those of the simplest, and he is dependent on no one for their satisfaction. In him natural pity is awake, although obscure, while in civilized man it is developed, but weak. The Philosopher will not leave his bed although his fellow-beings be slaughtered under his window, but will clap his hands to his ears and quiet himself with arguments. The savage is not so tranquil, and gives way to the first impulse. In street fights the populace assembles and prudent folk get out of the way. It is the rabble and the fishwives who separate the combatants, and prevent respectable people from cutting each other's throats.[1]

Love, he says, is physical and moral. The physical side is that general desire which leads to the union of the sexes. The moral side is that which fixes that desire on one exclusive object, or at least that which gives the ex-

---

[1] Rousseau says in his *Confessions* (*Œuvres*, xviii. 205 *n*. Part. ii. liv. viii.), that this heartless philosopher was suggested to him by Diderot, who abused his confidence, and gave his writings at this time a hard tone and a black appearance. The abuse of confidence is nonsense, but the comic picture of the philosopher, with his hands on his ears, may well have come from Diderot. Rousseau was always in deadly earnest.

elusive desire a greater energy. Now it is easy to see that this moral side of love is a factitious feeling, born of the usage of society, and vaunted by women with much skill and care in order to establish their empire, and to give dominion to the sex which ought to obey. This feeling is dull in the savage, who has no abstract ideas of regularity or beauty; he is not troubled with imagination, which causes so many woes to civilized man. "Let us conclude that the savage man, wandering in forests, without manufactures, without language, without a home, without war, and without connections, with no need of his kind, and no desire to injure it, perhaps never recognizing one person individually, subject to few passions, and sufficient to himself, had only the feeling and the intelligence proper to his state; that he felt only his real needs; he looked only at those things which he thought it was for his interest to see, and his intelligence made no more progress than his vanity. If, by chance, he made some discovery, he could not communicate it, not recognizing even his own children. The art perished with the inventor. There was neither education nor progress; the generations multiplied uselessly; and, as all started from the same point, the centuries went by with all the rudeness of the first age; the species was already old, and man still remained a child."

Inequalities among savage men would be small. Those which are physical are often caused by a hardening or an effeminate life; those of the mind, by education, which not only divides men into the rude and the cultivated, but increases the natural differences which nature has allowed among the latter; for if a giant and a dwarf walk in the same road, every step they take will separate them more widely. And if there are no relations among men, their inequalities will trouble them very little. Where there is no love, what is the use of beauty? What advantage can people who do not speak derive from wit; or those who have no dealings from craft? "I constantly hear it said," cries Rousseau, "that the strong will oppress the weak. But explain to me what is meant by the word "oppression." Some men will rule with violence, others will groan in their service, obeying all their caprices. This is exactly what I observe among us; but I do not see how it could be said of savage men, who could hardly be made to understand the meaning of servitude and domination. One man may well take away the fruit that another has picked, the game he has killed, the cave that was his shelter; but how will he ever succeed in making him obey? And what can be the chains of dependence among men that possess nothing? If I am driven from one tree, I need only go to another; if I am tormented in any place, who will prevent my moving elsewhere? Is there a man so much stronger than I, and moreover so depraved, so lazy, and so fierce as to compel me to provide for his maintenance while he remains idle? He must make up his mind not to lose sight of me for a single moment, to have me tied up with great care while he is asleep, for fear I should escape or kill him; that is to say, he is obliged to expose himself willingly to much greater trouble than that which he wishes to avoid, and than that which he gives me. And after all, if his vigilance is relaxed for a moment, if he turns his head at a sudden noise, I take twenty steps through the forest, my chains are broken, and he never sees me again as long as he lives."

Rousseau recognized that his state of nature was not like anything that had existed on our planet.[1] But that

[1] This concession probably took the form it did, partly to satisfy the censor, or the Academy of Dijon, jealous for Genesis. "Religion commands us to believe that God himself having removed men from the state of nature, immediately after the creation, they are unequal because he has willed that they should be so." Such remarks as this are common in all the writings of the time, although less so in those of Rousseau than in those of most of his contemporaries. They are

consideration troubled him not at all. Let us begin, he says, by putting aside all facts; they do not touch the question. This is the constant practice of the philosophers of certain schools, but few of them acknowledge it as frankly as Rousseau. Had the facts of human nature and human history been seriously considered, we should have no Republic of Plato, no Utopia of More; the world would be a very different place from what it is; for these cloudy cities, the laws of whose architecture seem contrary to all the teachings of physics, yet gild with their glory and darken with their shadows the solid temples and streets beneath them.

In the second part of his essay, Rousseau follows the development of human society. "The first man," he says, "who, having enclosed a piece of ground, undertook to say, 'This is mine,' and found people simple enough to believe him, was the true founder of civil society. How many crimes, wars, murders, how much misery and horror would not he have spared the human race, who, pulling up the stakes or filling the ditch, should have cried to his fellows, 'Beware of listening to that impostor. You are lost if you forget that the fruits belong to all, and the land to none.'"

But this benefactor did not make his appearance. Soon all the land was divided among a certain number of occupiers. Those whose weakness or indolence had prevented their getting a share were obliged to sink into slavery, or to rob their richer neighbors. Then followed civil wars, tumult and rapine. At last those who had the land conceived the most deliberate plot that ever entered into the human mind. They persuaded the poorer people to join with them in establishing an association which should defend all its members and ensure to each one the peaceful possession of his property. "Such was the origin of so-

evidently intended to satisfy the authorities, and to be simply overlooked by the intelligent reader.

ciety and laws, which gave new bonds to the weak, new strength to the rich, irrevocably destroyed natural liberty, established forever the laws of property and inequality, turned adroit usurpation into settled right, and, for the profit of a few ambitious men, subjected thenceforth all the human race to labor, servitude, and misery."

But on the whole the stage of development which seemed to Rousseau the happiest was not the state of complete isolation. He supposes that at one time mankind had assembled in herds, and had made some simple inventions. A rude language had been formed, huts were built. Men had become more fierce and cruel than at first. The condition was intermediate between the indolence of the primitive state, and the petulant activity of self-love now seen in the world. This, he thought, was the stage reached by most savages known to Europeans; it was the most desirable; and he remarks that no savage has yet adopted civilization, whereas many Frenchmen have joined Indian tribes, and taken up a savage mode of life.

In closing the Second Discourse, Rousseau thus sums up his conclusions. "It follows from this exposition that inequality, being almost nothing in the state of nature, draws its force and growth from the development of our faculties and from the progress of the human spirit, and becomes at last stable and legal by the establishment of property and the laws. It follows also that moral inequality, authorized by positive law only, is contrary to natural law whenever it does not coincide in the same proportion with physical inequality; a distinction which shows sufficiently what should be thought in this respect of the kind of inequality which reigns among all civilized nations, since it is manifestly contrary to the law of nature, however defined, that a child should command an old man, a fool lead a wise man, and a handful of people be glutted with superfluity, while the hungry multitude is in want of necessaries."

The Discourse on Inequality was sent by Rousseau to Voltaire, and drew forth a characteristic letter from the pontiff of the Philosophers. "I have received, sir, your new book against the human race. I thank you for it. You will please the men to whom you tell disagreeable truths, but you will not correct them. It is impossible to paint in stronger colors the horrors of human society, from which our ignorance and weakness promise themselves so many consolations. No one ever spent so much wit in trying to make us stupid; when we read your book we feel like going on all fours. Nevertheless, as it is more than sixty years since I lost the habit, I am conscious that it is impossible for me to take it up again, and I leave this natural attitude to those who are more worthy of it than you and I. Nor can I take ship to go out and join the savages in Canada; first, because the diseases which bear me down oblige me to stay near the greatest physician in Europe, and because I should not find the same relief among the Missouris; secondly, because there is war in those regions, and the example of our nations has made the savages almost as cruel as we are." Voltaire then goes on to complain of his own sufferings as an author, but to vaunt the influence of letters. It is not Petrarch and Boccaccio, he says, that made the wars of Italy; the pleasantries of Marot did not cause the massacre of Saint Bartholomew's Day; nor the tragedy of the Cid produce the riots of the Fronde. Great crimes have generally been committed by ignorant great men. It is the insatiable cupidity, the indomitable pride of mankind, which have made this world a vale of tears; from Thamas Kouli-Kan, who could not read, to the custom-house clerk, who only knows how to cipher.[1]

This letter is neither very complimentary nor very conclusive in its treatment of Rousseau's position, but it may be said to mark his official reception into the guild of lit-

[1] August 30, 1755. Voltaire, lvi. 714.

erary men. He was presently engaged in new work. He wrote an article on Political Economy for the great "Encyclopædia," in which, reversing the teaching of the Second Discourse, he maintains that "it is certain that the right of property is the most sacred of all the rights of citizens, and more important in some respects than liberty itself; either because it more closely concerns the preservation of life, or because, property being easier to take away and harder to defend than persons, that should be most respected which is most easily ravished; or again, because property is the true foundation of civil society, and the true guarantee of the engagements of the citizens; for if property did not answer for persons, nothing would be so easy as to elude duties and to laugh at the laws."[1] And further on, in the same article, he calls property the foundation of the social compact, whose first condition is that every one be maintained in the peaceful enjoyment of what belongs to him. We must not wonder at seeing Rousseau thus change sides from day to day. A dreamer and not a philosophic thinker, he perceived some truths and uttered many sophistries, speaking always with the fire of conviction and a fatal eloquence.

It is needless to enter into the detail of Rousseau's life at this time, the time when his most remarkable work was done. Labor was always painful and irritating to him, and it was perhaps the irksomeness of his tasks that drove him into something not unlike madness.[2] Yet he kept on writing with enthusiasm. He speaks of himself as moved in these years by the contemplation of great objects; ridiculously hoping to bring about the triumph of reason

---

[1] Rousseau, *Œuvres*, xii. 41.

[2] There is little doubt that Rousseau was at one time really insane, subject to the delusion that he was being persecuted. His insanity did not become very marked until the time of the real persecutions undergone after the publication of *Emile*. See his Biographies and *Le Docteur Chatelain, La folie de J. J. Rousseau*, Paris, 1890. He

and truth over prejudice and lies, and to make men wiser by showing them their true interests. He learned at this time, he says, to meditate profoundly, and for a moment astonished Europe by productions in which vulgar souls saw only eloquence and wit, but in which those persons who inhabit ethereal regions joyfully recognized one of their own kind.[1]

The best known and probably the most important of Rousseau's political writings is the "Contrat Social," or "Social Compact," which followed the Second Discourse after an interval of eight years, thus coming out near the end of the period of its author's greatest literary activity. In this essay, which is intended to be but a fragment of a larger work on government, Rousseau lays down the conditions which should, as he thinks, govern the lives of men united to form a true state. Indeed, he believes that any government not founded on these principles is illegitimate, resting merely on force and not on right. A nation thus wrongly governed is but an aggregation, not an association. It is without public weal or body politic.

There was nothing original with Rousseau in the idea of a social compact. That idea may be traced in the writings of Plato, who speaks of it as one already familiar. But it did not become a leading doctrine with writers on politics until the publication of Hooker's "Ecclesiastical Polity" in 1594. In that book it was contended that there is no escape from the anarchy which exists before the establishment of law, but by men "growing into composition and agreement amongst themselves, by ordaining some kind of government public, and yielding themselves

was, of course, always eccentric and ill balanced; and was often rendered irritable by a painful disease, caused by a malformation of the bladder. Morley, *Rousseau*, i. 277, etc. *Œuvres*, xviii. 155 (*Conf.* Part. ii. liv. viii.).

[1] Rousseau, *Œuvres*, xx. 275 (II. Dialogue).

subject thereunto." Through the seventeenth century the theory grew and flourished. It was treated as the foundation of absolute government by Hobbes, of free government by Locke; it was recognized by Grotius. It received its embodiment in the cabin of the Mayflower, when the Pilgrims did solemnly and mutually, in the presence of God and one another, covenant and combine themselves together into a civil body politic. By the time of Rousseau the social compact had become one of the commonplaces of political thought.[1] Men recognized, more or less vaguely, that in the case of most countries no definite solemn agreement could actually be shown to have been made, but in their inability to find the record of such a contract writers were willing to assume one, express or implied. What, then, were the exact conditions of the compact? Rousseau put the question as follows: "To find a form of association which shall protect with all the common strength the person and property of each associate, and by which each one, uniting himself to all, may yet obey only himself and remain as free as before." And he undertook to solve the problem by proposing "the total alienation of every associate, with all his rights, to the whole community," which he supported by saying that, as every one gave himself up entirely, the condition was equal for all; and that as the condition was equal for all, no one was interested in making it onerous for others.

It will be noticed that there is a variation between the thing sought and the thing found. Rousseau, having promised that each man shall obey only himself, presently puts us off with a condition equal for all. That is to say, instead of liberty we are given equality. The dif-

[1] See a history of the social compact in A. Lawrence Lowell, *Essays on Government*. Plato, ii. 229 (*The Republic*, Book ii.). Hooker, i. 241. Hobbes, *Leviathan, passim*. Locke, v. 388 (*Of Civil Government*, § 87). Morton's *New England's Memorial*, 37.

ference is one generally recognized by Anglo-Saxons and often invisible to Continentals. It was seldom seen by Frenchmen in the eighteenth century. This confusion of thought was a cause of many of the troubles of the French Revolution. We shall see that Rousseau, who had been carried by the love of liberty beyond the verge of the ridiculous in his Discourses, was brought back, in his "Social Compact," by his love of equality, so far as to become the advocate of an intolerable tyranny, yet was quite unaware that he was inconsistent. He composed, in fact, a description of liberty strangely compounded of truth and falsehood. He reckoned that man to be free who was not under the control of any person, but only of the law, and then he provided for the most arbitrary and capricious kind of law-making.

The first task of Rousseau, after settling the conditions of his compact, is to provide a sovereign power in the state. This he finds in the association of the citizens united, as above described, in a body politic. This sovereign cannot be bound by its own actions or resolves, except in case of an agreement with strangers, for none can make a contract with himself. By the original compact the action of the individual citizens as independent agents was exhausted. They can act henceforth only as parts of the whole. There is no contract possible between one or several of them and the community of which they form a part.[1] The sovereign must not, however, act directly on individuals, for in so doing it would represent a part only of the community acting on another part, and it would thus lose its moral right. It must act in general matters exclusively, by means of general decrees, which

[1] In an epitome of the *Social Compact*, inserted by Rousseau in the fifth book of *Emile*, he thus defines the terms of that compact. "Each of us puts into a common stock his property, his person, his life and all his power, under the supreme direction of the general will, and we receive as a body each member as an indivisible part of the whole." *Œuvres*, v. 254.

only can properly be called laws. "Now the sovereign, being made up only of the individuals which compose it, has and can have no interest opposed to theirs; therefore the sovereign power need not provide its subject with any guarantee, because it is impossible that the body should wish to injure its members," and as the nature of its action is general and not particular, it cannot injure one individual without doing harm to all the others at the same time. "The sovereign, by the very fact of its existence, is always what it ought to be."

The general will is always right and always tends to public utility, says Rousseau, but it does not follow that the decisions of the people are always equally correct. Man always wills his own good, but does not always see it. The people is never corrupt, but often deceived, and in the latter case only does it seem to will what is evil. If there were no parties in the state, the people, if sufficiently informed, would always vote rightly, for the little differences in private interests would balance each other, and the resulting average would be the general will. But through parties and associations this result is prevented. A nation may change its laws when it pleases, even the best of them; for if it likes to hurt itself, who has the right to say it nay?

Sovereignty is inalienable, for power is transmissible, but not will. Sovereignty consists essentially in the general will, and the general will cannot be represented. It is the same, or it is other; there is no intermediate point. The deputies of the people cannot be its representatives; they can only be its agents; they can conclude nothing definitely. Any law that the people has not ratified in its assembly is null; it is not a law. The English nation thinks itself free. It is much mistaken. It is free only during the election of members of Parliament. As soon as these are elected the nation is enslaved; it is nothing. Sovereignty is indivisible, its powers being legislative only, and the executive function of the state being but its emanation.

Such being the essential conditions of the social compact, what are the states to which it may be applied? Although Rousseau gives many directions for the government of larger countries, we see that his system is truly applicable only to nations so small that the whole body of voters can be united in one meeting. These popular assemblies, he says, should be held frequently, at times fixed by law and independent of any summons, and also at irregular times when needed. Let no one object that such frequent meetings would take up too much time. He answers that "as soon as the public service ceases to be the principal business of the citizens, and they prefer to serve with their purses rather than with their persons, the state is already near to ruin. If it be necessary to march to battle, they pay soldiers and stay at home; if it be necessary to attend the council, they choose deputies and stay at home. By laziness and money they have at last got troops to enslave their country and representatives to betray her."

The only law that requires unanimity is the social compact itself. When that is once formed, each citizen consents to every law, even to those which are passed in spite of him. When a law is proposed in the assembly of the people, the question is not exactly whether the proposal is approved or rejected, but whether it is in accordance with the general will, which is the will of the people. Every man by his vote declares his opinion on that point, and by counting the votes the declaration of the general will is ascertained. When, therefore, the opinion which is opposed to mine prevails, it proves nothing more than that I was mistaken, and that what I took to be the general will was not so. If my private opinion had carried the day against the general will, I should have done what I did not wish; and then I should not have been free.

It has been said that the sovereign must not act in particular cases. To do so would be to confound law and fact, and the body politic would soon be a prey to violence. It is, therefore, necessary to institute an executive branch, which Rousseau calls indifferently *government* or *prince*, explaining that the latter word may be used collectively. But, differing in this from older writers, he denies that the establishment of an executive power gives rise to any contract between the body of the people and the persons appointed to govern. He considers these persons to be intermediate between the nation considered as sovereign, and the people considered as subject, and to hold but a delegated power. In this opinion, Rousseau has been followed by most liberal governments instituted since his day. But he carries this theory much farther than it is safe to do in practice. The sovereign, he says, may at any moment revoke the powers of its agents, and the first act of every public assembly should be to answer these two questions: first, whether it pleases the sovereign to maintain the present form of government; and second, whether it pleases the people to leave the administration to those persons who now exercise it.

The chapters on the form of government are far less important than those on sovereignty. Rousseau recognized democracy, aristocracy, and monarchy as applicable respectively to small, middle-sized, and large states. He says that democracy is the most difficult form to manage, requiring for its perfect working a state so small that every citizen can know every other personally, and also great simplicity of manners, great equality of ranks and fortunes, and little luxury. This applies, of course, only to democracy in its extreme form, in which the people exercises all the functions of government without delegating any of them. Rousseau's preference was for what he calls aristocracy, a government of the most wise and experienced. The first societies, he says, were thus governed, and the American Indians are so governed still. It is noticeable that the Indians take in the works of Rousseau a place similar to that taken by the Chinese in those of Voltaire; they are distant people, living in an ideal condition. The freedom of the savage, the literary civilization of the Oriental, were held up to admiration by these two writers, diametrically opposed in their way of looking at life, but similar in their utter want of comprehension of all that was not European and contemporary. Next after the government of the sages and the elders Rousseau placed elective government, which, in common with some other abstract writers, he classes as aristocratic. An hereditary aristocracy he calls the worst of all governments. He intimated that his remedy for the weakness of small countries, as against foreign enemies, would be found in federation, but he postponed the discussion of this subject to a larger treatise, which was never written.[1]

Rousseau pointed out very forcibly the incompatibility with civil government of a religion depending on a priesthood whose organization extends beyond the territory of the country itself and forms a body politic. Yet he did not propose to apply the only true remedy for this condition of things, which is the complete separation of church

[1] Rousseau has himself given two summaries of the Social Compact; one very short, in the Sixth Letter from the Mountain (*Œuvres*, vii. 378). This was written after the condemnation of the book by the authorities of Geneva, and he points out in his remonstrance that he has taken Geneva as the model state, in the Social Compact. The other summary, much fuller, is in the fifth book of *Emile* (*Œuvres*, v. 248). Here we find the following growl at the whole social order: "Nous examinerons si l'on n'a pas fait trop ou trop peu dans l'institution sociale. Si les individus soumis aux loix et aux hommes, tandis que les sociétés gardent entre elles l'indépendance de la nature, ne restent pas exposés aux maux des deux états sans en avoir les avantages, et s'il ne vaudrait pas mieux qu'il n'y eut point de société civile au monde que d'y en avoir plusieurs."

and state, combined with liberty of speech both for the clergy and the laity. He recognized as possible only three sorts of religion, of which the first, without temples, altars, or rites, confined inwardly to the worship of God and externally to the moral duties, was, as he thought, the pure and simple religion of the Gospels, the true theism, and might be called the natural divine law. The next is a national religion, belonging to one country. It has its gods, its rites, its altars, all within its own land, outside of which everything is infidel, strange, and barbarian. Man's duties extend no farther than the boundaries of his own country. Such were the religions of the early nations. The third kind gives to its votaries two systems of legislation, two chiefs, two homes, makes them submit to contradictory duties, prevents their being at once devout worshipers and good citizens. Such a religion is the Roman Catholic.

The Roman clergy, he says, is united, not by its formal assemblies, but by communion and excommunication, which are its social compact, and by means of which it will always retain the mastery over kings and nations. All the priests who are in communion are citizens, although at the ends of the earth. This invention is a masterpiece of politics.

On some religion our author believes that the state has a right to insist. There is a purely civil profession of faith, whose articles the sovereign may fix, not exactly as dogmas of religion, but as principles of sociability. These must be few, simple and clear, and announced without explanation or commentary. The existence of a deity, powerful, intelligent, beneficent, foreseeing, and providing; the life to come, with the happiness of the good and the punishment of the wicked; the sacredness of the Social Compact and of the laws,— these are the positive dogmas. Of things forbidden there should be but one: intolerance. Whosoever says that there is no salvation but in the church should be driven from the state; for such teaching is dangerous to the sovereign, except, indeed, in a theocracy. Any one who does not hold to the simple creed above described may properly be banished, not as impious, but as unsociable, incapable of loving justice and the laws sincerely, or of sacrificing his life to his duty. And if any one, after having publicly accepted these dogmas, behaves as if he did not believe them, let him be put to death; he has committed the greatest of crimes; he has lied before the laws.

In the short essay on the Social Compact, Rousseau has brought together, as we have seen, several of the most dangerous errors which have afflicted modern society. The people, according to him, is not only all powerful, but always righteous; sometimes deceived, but never corrupt. Why the whole community should be better or wiser than the best of the persons who compose it; why our errors should balance or counteract each other and our virtues not do so, Rousseau probably never asked himself; or if the question occurred to his mind, he dismissed it with a merely specious answer. There is hardly a limit to the tyranny which he allows to the multitude. The individual citizen is made free from the interference of a single master only that he may be the more dependent on that corporate despot who is to control his every action and his very thoughts. Manners, customs, above all public opinion, are declared to be the most important of laws. Individuality is, therefore, to be absolutely banished. Nor is security provided for. It is the advantage of a stationary system that a man may know this year what the world will expect of him ten years hence and may lay his plans accordingly. Human laws may sometimes be pardoned for being as inflexible as the laws of physics if they are as surely to be relied on. But Rousseau, while hoping that his state will change very little, carefully reserves for his tyrant the right to be capricious. And lest that right should ever be forgotten he takes care that the whole form of government shall be brought in question at every public meeting. What the multitude has to-day decided it may reverse to-morrow. The unfortunate citizen is not left even the right to protest. The general will, when once proved by the popular vote, is his own will. The very desires of his heart must loyally follow the changing caprices of his many-headed master.

Yet here as elsewhere Rousseau has joined a noble conception to a base one. The law, once promulgated by the sovereign power, is to be universal throughout the state and superior to all human rulers. The idea was not novel, but it was well that it should again be distinctly formulated.

It is quite in accordance with the general spirit of the essay that while intolerance is said to be the only religious crime, it is in fact the foundation of the whole ecclesiastical system of the republic. Whoever dares to say that there is no salvation outside of the church is to be driven from the state. By this means Rousseau would have exiled nearly every Christian of the eighteenth century. On the other hand, whoever doubts the existence of God, His providence, and His rewards and punishments, is to be treated in the same manner. Some of the Philosophers of the age are thus excluded. Verily, few are the just that remain, and Rousseau is quite right in his opinion that those who distinguish between civil and theological intolerance are mistaken. In his system, at least, the two are closely connected.

CHAPTER XIX.

"LA NOUVELLE HÉLOÏSE" AND "ÉMILE."

It was not alone by his political writings that Jean Jacques Rousseau exercised a great influence over Europe. Of all his books, the two which are perhaps most famous take the form of loose and disjointed fiction, and deal not with government, but with life, passion, society, and education. Yet the characters of "La Nouvelle Héloïse," and of "Emile," are not mere frames of scarecrows clothed with abstract qualities and fine sentiments. Saint-Preux, Emile and the Tutor, Julie, Sophie, Claire, and Lord Edward Bomston are live persons, whom the reader may like or dislike. In the first three Rousseau would seem to have incorporated himself, and the result is interesting, but repulsive. In Julie we have Jean Jacques' ideal woman, a being of a noble nature, tinged and defiled with something low and morbid; but Claire and Sophie seem taken only from observation, not introspection, and although far from faultless are often charming.

"La Nouvelle Héloïse" is a novel written in letters, a form of writing more tedious than any other. But it should be remembered that in the early days of fiction novels were so few that to occupy a long time in the reading was not an impediment to the popularity of one of them. If we may believe Rousseau, the "New Heloisa" produced a great sensation. All Paris was impatient for its appearance. When at last it was published, men of letters were divided in opinion, but society was unanimous in its praise, and women were so much delighted with it that there were few even of high rank whose conquest the author might not have achieved had he chosen to undertake it. While making due allowance for the morbid vanity of Jean Jacques, we may entirely believe him when he says that the book captivated the reading public. One lady, he tells us, had dressed after supper for the ball at the Opera House, and sat down to read the new novel while waiting for the time to go. At midnight she ordered her carriage, but did not put down the book. The coach came to the door, but she kept on. At two her servants warned her of the hour. She answered that there was no hurry. At four she undressed, and continued to read for the rest of the night. On the first appearance of the story the booksellers used to let out copies at twelve sous the hour.[1] To-day its charm is gone. Few indeed are the works of pure literature which are read a hundred years after publication, except by the authors of literary histories and the unfortunate pupils of injudicious schoolmistresses (and the "New Heloisa" will not form a part of any scheme of female education); but a good style and a true enthusiasm may lighten the task even of these sufferers.

It is a singular fact that in some matters of feeling no age seems so far from our own as that of our great-grandfathers. The lovers of the Middle Ages and of the sixteenth century appear to us natural and healthy beings. Those of the eighteenth seem sentimental and foolish. In the case of Rousseau's great novel this effect is increased by the morbid strain of the author's mind. With him all passion tends to assume unhealthy shapes, and the very breezes of Lake Leman come laden with close and sickly odors.

It is not worth while to deal here with the story of the "New Heloisa," — a story of illicit passion in the first part; and in the second, of the happy marriage of the heroine to a man who is not her lover. The visit paid by

[1] Rousseau, xix. 101 (*Confessions*, liv. xi.).

that lover to his old mistress and her husband in their home at Clarens, with all the trials of virtue which it involves, is a disagreeable piece of sentimentality. The members of the trio fall on each other's necks with unpleasant frequency and fervor. But the picture of that home itself, with its well-ordered housekeeping, its liberality and its plainness, is interesting and attractive. "Since the masters of this house have taken it for their dwelling, they have turned to their use all that served only for ornament; it is no longer a house made to be seen, but to be lived in. They have built up the long lines of doors by which rooms opened one out of another, and made new doorways in convenient places; they have cut up rooms that were too large, and improved the arrangement; they have substituted simple and convenient furniture for what was old and expensive. Everything is agreeable and smiling, everything breathes abundance and cleanliness; nothing shows costliness or luxury; there is no room where you do not feel yourself in the country and where you do not find all the conveniences of town. The same changes are noticeable outside; the poultry-yard has been enlarged at the expense of the carriage-house. In the place of an old broken-down billiard-table they have built a fine winepress, and they have got rid of some screeching peacocks to make room for a dairy. The kitchen garden was too small for the kitchen; a second one has been made of the parterre, but so neat and so well laid out that thus transformed it is more pleasing to the eye than before. Good espaliers have been substituted for the doleful yews that covered the wall. Instead of the useless horse-chestnut tree, young black mulberries are beginning to shade the courtyard, and two rows of walnut trees, running to the road, have been planted in place of the old lindens which bordered the avenue. Everywhere the useful has been substituted for the agreeable, and almost everywhere the agreeable has gained by it." The description is masterly, but we cannot quite forgive Rousseau for sacrificing the horse-chestnut and the lindens.[1]

But not quite all the land is treated in this utilitarian manner. The heroine has an "Elysium." This place is near the house, but separated from the rest of the grounds by a thick hedge. It is full of native plants forming a deep shade, yet the ground is covered with grass like velvet, and flowers spring up on all sides. Vines climb from tree to tree, rooted, it may be, in the trunks of the trees themselves. A stream of clear water meanders through the place, sometimes divided into several channels, sometimes united in one, rippling here over a bed of gravel, there reflecting the trees and the sky. A colony of birds, protected from all disturbance, charms the solitude with song. Nature is here encouraged, not thwarted; little is left to the gardener; much to the intelligent and loving care of the mistress.

The account of the garden covers many pages of the "New Heloisa," pages at once eloquent and interesting. Artificial as are many of its details, the letter is a plea for nature against artificiality. The readers in the eighteenth century were charmed, and hastened to imitate Rousseau's heroine. The straight gravel walks, the formal flower-beds, the clipped hedges of old France, became tiresome in the eyes of their possessors. A dreamer had told them that all these things made a very fine place, where the owner would scarcely care to go, and they believed him. The new fashion brought with it a new affectation, perhaps the most offensive of all, the affectation of simplicity. The garden, as truly a product of man's hand and brain as the house or the picture-gallery, was made to mimic the forest, losing, in too many cases, its own peculiar beauty, without gaining the true charm of wild nature. On the other hand, the eyes of Rousseau's admirers were opened to many things not noticed

[1] Rousseau, ix. 235 (*Nouv. Hél.* Part. iv. Let. x.).

before. The real woods received their appropriate worship. The novel of Jean Jacques combined with the exhortations of the economists to turn the attention of the educated classes to rural matters.

The life led by the model couple in the "New Heloisa" is one of humdrum, conscientious respectability. It is a country life, fairly simple and without ostentation; but it is as far removed as possible from all that can be connected with the noble savage. Julie and Monsieur de Wolmar, her husband, rule their little world strictly and kindly. They try to make life profitable and pleasant to their children and their servants. To the poor they are patronizing and benevolent. Apart from their overflowing sentimentality they are honest, self-sufficient, commonplace people. Rousseau, born in the middle class, had a middle-class, respectable ideal, lying beside many very different ideals in his ill-ordered brain. And this novel which begins with passion ends with something not far removed from priggishness.

It is quite needless to discuss here how much Rousseau owed in his "Emile" to the teachings of Locke, of Montaigne, or of others. His ideas, wherever he may have got them, were always sufficiently colored by his own personality. "Emile," which has even less structure of fiction than the "New Heloisa," is a treatise on education, or rather on the ideal education, for Rousseau distinctly disclaims the intention of writing a handbook. It is on the whole the most agreeable and the most useful of the works of its author; although not without deplorable marks of his baseness. The book shows an amount of careful observation of children not a little astonishing in a man who sent his own infants to the Foundling lest they should disturb him; it contains remarks about good women equally remarkable in one whose dealings in life were principally with bad ones.

"All is good coming from the hands of the Author of

things; everything degenerates in the hands of man;" thus begins "Emile." "He makes one land nourish the productions of another, one tree bear another's fruit; he mixes and confounds the climates, the elements, the seasons; he mutilates his dog, his horse, his slave; he overturns, he disfigures everything; he loves deformity and monstrosities; he wants nothing such as nature made it, not even man, who has to be trained for him like a managed horse, trimmed to his fashion, like a tree of his garden."

Ignorance is harmless; error only is pernicious. Men do not go astray on account of the things of which they are ignorant, but of those which they think they know. The time which we spend in learning what others have thought is lost for learning to think ourselves; we have more information and less vigor of mind.

Let us seek out the kind of education proper for the formation of a vigorous and, above all, of an independent man. We will call our pupil Emile. The author himself shall be his tutor and shall devote himself exclusively to the education of this single boy. A father, however, is the best of tutors, for zeal is far more valuable in this place than talent. But whoever it be that undertakes the education, he must be always the same and always absolute. If a child ever gets the idea that there are grown people that have no more reason than children, the authority of age is lost, the education has failed.

The position of the tutor is one of the most curious and one of the most mistaken things in "Emile." While in many respects the training described in the book would tend to make a manly and independent boy, the pervading presence of the tutor would perhaps undo all the good of the system. It is true that absolute truth is recommended, that "a single lie which the master was shown to have told the pupil would ruin forever the fruit of the education." Yet the tutor is to interfere openly or secretly in every part of Emile's life. "It is important that the disciple shall do nothing without the master's knowing and willing it, not even what is wrong; and it is a hundred times better that the governor approve of a fault and be mistaken, than that he should be deceived by his pupil and the fault committed without his knowledge." Let the tutor, therefore, be the pupil's confidant, even, if necessary, his companion in vice. You must be a man to speak strongly to the human heart. The tutor is constantly deceiving Emile, and some of his tricks are so transparent that it is wonderful that Rousseau could have expected the simplest of boys to be taken in by them. Here is an instance.

The object is to show Emile the origin of property, and to give him the first idea of its obligations. "The child, living in the country, will have got some notion of fieldwork; for that he will need only eyes and leisure, and both of these he will have. It belongs to every age, and especially to his, to wish to create, to imitate, to produce, to show signs of power and activity. He will not twice have seen a garden dug, vegetables sown, sprouting and growing, before he will want to be gardening too.

"On the principles heretofore established, I do not oppose his desire; on the contrary, I favor it, I share his taste, I work with him, not for his pleasure, but for mine; at least he thinks so; I become his under-gardener; as his arms are not strong yet, I dig the earth for him; he takes possession of it by planting a bean; and surely that possession is more sacred and worthy of respect than that which Nunès Balbao took of South America, in the name of the king of Spain, by planting his standard on the shores of the South Sea.

"We come every day to water the beans, we see them sprout with ecstasies of joy. I increase that joy by telling him, 'This belongs to you;' and by explaining to him this term, 'to belong,' I make him feel that he has spent here his time, his labor, his pains, his very person; that in this earth there is something of himself, which he can claim against every one, as he could draw his arm from the hand of a man who should try to hold it in spite of him.

"One fine day he comes out eagerly, with his watering-pot in his hand. Oh horrible sight! Oh grief! All the beans are torn up, all the ground is turned over; you could not recognize the very place. 'Oh, what has become of my labor, my work, the sweet fruit of my care and of my sweat? Who has robbed me of my property? Who has taken my beans?' His young heart rises; the first feeling of injustice comes to pour its sad bitterness into it; tears flow in streams; the desolate child fills the air with groans and cries. I share his pain, his indignation; we seek, we inquire, we examine. At last we discover that the gardener has done the deed; we summon him.

"But here we are very far out of our reckoning. The gardener, learning of what we complain, begins to complain louder than we. 'What! gentlemen; it is you that have thus spoiled my work! I had sown in that place some Maltese melons, whose seed had been given me as a treasure, and which I hoped to serve up to you for a feast when they were ripe; but now, to plant your miserable beans, you have destroyed my melons after they had sprouted, and I can never replace them. You have done me an irreparable injury, and you have deprived yourselves of the pleasure of eating delicious melons.'

"*Jean Jacques.* Excuse us, my poor Robert. You had put there your labor and your pains. I see that we were wrong to spoil your work; we will get you some more Maltese seed, and we will dig no more in the ground, without knowing if some one has not set his hand to it before us.

"*Robert.* Well, gentlemen, at that rate you may take

your rest, for there is very little wild land left. I work on what my father improved; everybody does the same by his own, and all the land you see has long been occupied.

"*Emile.* In that case, Robert, is melon seed often lost?

"*Robert.* I beg your pardon, my young sir; little gentlemen do not often come along who are so thoughtless as you. No one touches his neighbor's garden; each man respects the work of others, so that his own may be safe.

"*Emile.* But I have no garden.

"*Robert.* What difference does that make to me? If you spoil mine, I will no longer let you walk in it; for, you see, I do not want to lose my labor.

"*Jean Jacques.* Could we not make an arrangement with our good Robert? Let him grant my young friend and me a corner of his garden to cultivate, on condition that he shall have half the produce.

"*Robert.* I grant it without conditions. But remember that I shall go and dig up your beans if you touch my melons."

It is perhaps wrong to hold Rousseau in any part of his writings to any approach to consistency. We have seen some of the mistakes in Emile's education. Let us look at some of its strong points. Yet we shall find the tares so thoroughly mixed with the wheat that to separate them entirely may be impossible. Rousseau insists that from the earliest infancy the child's body shall be free. The swaddling bands, common all over the continent in the last century, in which the poor little being was bound and bundled so that he could not move hand or foot, were to be absolutely discontinued. The child, nursed if possible by its own mother, was to have free limbs. It was to be brought up in the country, and as it grew older was to run about bareheaded and barefoot. Too much clothing, thought Rousseau, makes the body tender; and he seems to have carried the theory unreasonably far.

Cleanliness and cold baths were recommended to a generation singularly in need of them. Emile was brought up to enjoy fresh air, perhaps to be almost a slave to the need of it. He was given plenty of sleep, but his bed was hard, his food coarse. Everything was done to make him strong, hardy, and active.

"The only habit which the child should be allowed to form is that of forming none." He should not use one hand more than the other; he should not be accustomed to want to eat or to sleep at the same hours every day, nor should he fear to be alone. He should be gradually taught not to be afraid of masks, to overcome his fright at firearms. He should be helped in all that is really useful, but not encouraged to indulge vain fancies. Children should be given as much real liberty as possible, and as little dominion over others as may be. They should do as much as possible by themselves, and ask as little as they can of others. "The only person who does his own will is he who does not need, in doing it, to put another's arms at the end of his own; whence it follows that the first of all good things is not authority, but liberty."

Emile's desire to learn is to be excited. He is to see the reason for the steps he takes. The talent of teaching is that of making the pupil pleased with the instruction. Something must be left to the boy's own mind and reflection. He is not to be given much to read. For a long time, let "Robinson Crusoe" be his only book. But Emile shall learn a trade, a good mechanical trade, which is always needed, in which there is always employment. He shall also learn to draw; less for the art itself than to make his eye accurate and his hand obedient; for in general it is less important for him to know this or that than to acquire the clearness of sense and the good habit of body which the various studies give.

Having brought up Emile to manhood, it becomes necessary to provide him with a wife. Here the tutor is still active, and prepares the meeting with Sophie which Emile takes for accidental. It is needless to remark again on the young man's gullibility. He is Rousseau's creature, and fashioned as his maker pleases. Nothing is more disturbing than to submit the dreams of such a man as Jean Jacques to the unsympathetic rules of common sense. Our concern is with the effect they produced on the minds of other people, who undertook in some measure to live them out. Let us then pause over some of the considerations suggested by the necessity of admitting into the scheme of education a being so disturbing as a woman.

Rousseau saw more, I think, than most persons who have undertaken to deal with the subject in a reforming spirit, what is the true and proper relation between the sexes. While boys are to exercise the manly trades that require physical strength, he would leave to women the lighter employments, and more especially those connected with dress and its materials. It is the usual mistake of those who in our day set themselves up as champions of woman, to seek to make the sexes not coördinate and mutually helpful, but identical and competing. "It is perhaps one of the marvels of nature," says Rousseau, "to have made two beings so similar while forming them so differently." [1]

On the whole, Sophie is a more attractive person than Emile; perhaps because she has been brought up by her mother, and not given over in her babyhood to the vigilance of Jean Jacques. The artistic quality of the author's mind has obliged him to make his heroine more true to nature than his theories have allowed him to make his hero. And his theories about girls are quite as good and quite as different from the fashionable practice of his day as those about boys. It is curious how his ideas

[1] *Œuvres*, v. 5 (*Emile*, liv. v.). Compare viii. 203 (*Nouv. Hél.* Letter). "A perfect man and a perfect woman should not resemble each other any more in their souls than in their faces."

approach the American customs. A certain coquetry, he says, is allowable in marriageable girls; amusement is their principal business. Married women have the cares of home to occupy them, and have no longer to seek husbands. Rousseau would let the girls appear in public, would take them to balls, entertainments, the theatre. Sophie is not only more vivacious than Emile, she has also more self-control than he; who, in spite of his virile education, is entirely overcome when the ever-meddling tutor insists on two years of travel for his pupil, in order that the young people may grow older and that Emile may learn to master his passions. The day of parting arrives, and Emile, in true eighteenth century style, utters shrieks, sheds torrents of tears on the hands of Sophie's father, of her mother, of the heroine herself, embraces with sobs all the servants of the family, and repeats the same things a thousand times with a disorder which, even to Jean Jacques's rudimentary sense of humor, would be laughable under circumstances less desperate. Sophie, on the other hand is quiet, pale and sad, without tears, insensible to the cries and caresses of her lover.

It is in "Emile" that Rousseau gives the most elaborate expression of his religious opinions, putting them in the mouth of a poor curate in Savoy.[1] The pupil has been kept ignorant of all religion to the age of eighteen, "for if he learns it earlier than he should, he runs the risk of never knowing it." Without stopping to consider the dangers of this course, let us see what answer Rousseau gives to the greatest questions that perplex mankind. We may expect much sublime feeling, some moral perversion, little logical thought.

The Roman Church, he says, by calling on us to believe too much, may prevent our believing anything. We

[1] The passage is known as "Profession de Foi du Vicaire savoyard" and is found in the fourth book of *Emile*, *Œuvres*, iv. 136-254.

know not where to stop. But doubt on matters so important to us is a state unbearable to the human mind. It decides one way or another in spite of itself, and prefers to make a mistake rather than to believe nothing.

Motion can originate only in will. "I believe, then, that a will moves the universe and animates nature." . . . "How does a will produce a physical and corporeal action? I do not know, but I feel within myself that it does produce it. I will to act, and I act; I wish to move my body, and my body moves; but that an inanimate body in repose should move itself, or should produce motion, is incomprehensible and without example." . . . "If matter moved shows me will, matter moved according to certain laws shows me intelligence; this is my second article of faith." We see that the universe has a plan, although we do not see to what it tends. I cannot believe that dead matter has produced living and feeling beings, that blind chance has produced intelligent beings, that what does not think has produced what thinks. "Whether matter is eternal or created, whether or not there is a passive principle, it is certain that all is one and proclaims a single intelligence; for I see nothing which is not ordered in the same system, and which does not concur to the same end, namely, the preservation of the whole in the established order. This Being who wills and who can, this Being active in Himself, this Being, whatever he may be, who moves the universe and orders all things, I call God. I attach to this name the ideas of intelligence, power and will, which I have united [to form the conception], and that of goodness which is their necessary consequence; but I know no better the Being to whom I have given it; He hides Himself alike from my senses and my understanding; the more I think of it, the more I am confused; I know very certainly that He exists and that He exists by himself; I know that my existence is subordinated to His, and that all things that I know of are in the same case. I perceive God everywhere in His works; I feel Him in myself, I see Him about me; but as soon as I want to contemplate Him in Himself, as soon as I want to seek where He is, what He is, what is His substance, He escapes from me, and my troubled spirit perceives nothing more."

Having considered the attributes of God, the Savoyard curate turns to himself. He finds that he can observe and govern other creatures; whence he infers that they may all be made for him. But mankind differs from all other things in nature by being inharmonious, disorderly, and miserable. Man has in himself two distinct principles, one of which lifts him to the study of eternal truth, to the love of justice and moral beauty; the other enslaves him under the rule of the senses, and the passions which are their servants. "No!" cries the curate, "man is not one; I will, and I will not; I feel myself at once enslaved, and free; I see good, I love it, and I do evil; I am active when I listen to reason, passive when my passions carry me away; my worst torture, when I fail, is to feel that I could have resisted."

Man is free in his actions, and, therefore, animated by an immaterial substance. This is the third article of the curate's faith. Conscience is the voice of the soul; the passions are the voices of the body. Immortality of the soul is a pleasing doctrine and there is nothing to contradict it. "When, delivered from the illusions caused by the body and the senses, we shall enjoy the contemplation of the Supreme Being, and of the eternal truths whose source He is, when the beauty of order shall strike all the powers of our soul, and we shall be solely occupied in comparing what we have done with what we ought to have done, then will the voice of conscience resume its force and its empire; then will the pure bliss which is born of self-content, and the bitter regret for self-debasement, distinguish by inexhaustible feelings the fate which each man will have prepared for himself. Ask me not, O my good friend, if there will be other sources of happiness and of misery; I do not know, and the one I imagine is enough to console me for this life and to make me hope for another. I do not say that the good will be rewarded; for what other reward can await an excellent being than to live in accordance with his nature; but I say that they will be happy, because the Author of their being, the Author of all justice, having made them to feel, has not made them to suffer; and because, not having abused their liberty on the earth, they have not changed their destiny by their own fault; yet they have suffered in this life, and so they will have it made up to them in another. This feeling is less founded on the merit of man than on the notion of goodness which seems to me inseparable from the divine essence. I only suppose the laws of order to be observed, and God consistent with Himself."[1]

"Neither ask me if the torments of the wicked will be eternal, and whether it is consistent with the goodness of the Author of their being to condemn them to suffer forever; I do not know that either, and have not the vain curiosity to examine useless questions. What matters it to me what becomes of the wicked? I take little interest in their fate. Nevertheless I find it hard to believe that they are condemned to endless torments. If Supreme Justice avenges itself, it avenges itself in this life. You and your errors, O nations, are its ministers! It employs the ills which you make to punish the crimes which brought them about. It is in your insatiable hearts, gnawed with envy, avarice, and ambition, that the avenging passions punish your crimes, in the midst of your false prosperity. What need to seek hell in the other life? It is already here, in the hearts of the wicked."

[1] "Non pas pour nous, non pas pour nous, Seigneur,
Mais pour ton nom, mais pour ton propre honneur,
O Dieu! fais nous revivre! Ps. 115."
(Rousseau's note).

Revelation is unnecessary. Miracles need proof more than they give it. As soon as the nations undertook to make God speak, each made Him speak in its own way. If men had listened only to what He says in their hearts, there had been but one religion upon earth. "I meditate on the order of the universe, not to explain it by vain systems, but to admire it unceasingly, to adore the wise Author who is felt in it. I converse with Him, I let His divine essence penetrate all my faculties, I tenderly remember His benefits, I bless Him for His gifts; but I do not pray to Him. What should I ask Him? That He should change the course of things on my account; that He should perform miracles in my favor? I, who should love more than all things the order established by His wisdom, and maintained by His Providence, should I wish to see that order interfered with for me? No, that rash prayer would deserve to be punished rather than to be answered. Nor do I ask Him for the power to do good; why ask Him for what He has given me? Has He not given me a conscience to love the good; reason, to know it; liberty, to choose it? If I do evil, I have no excuse; I do it because I will; to ask him to change my will is to ask of Him what He demands of me; it is wanting Him to do my work, and let me take the reward; not to be content with my state is to want to be a man no longer, it is to want things otherwise than they are, it is to want disorder and evil. Source of justice and truth, clement and kind God! in my trust in Thee the supreme wish of my heart is that Thy will may be done. In uniting mine to it, I do what thou doest, I acquiesce in Thy goodness; I seem to share beforehand the supreme felicity which is its price."

This appears to have been Rousseau's deliberate opinion on the subject of prayer. He has, however, expressed in the "New Heloisa" quite another view, which is found in a letter from Julie to Saint-Preux, and is inserted principally, perhaps, to give the latter an opportunity to answer it. Yet Rousseau, as we have often seen, although unable to understand that any one could honestly differ from himself, was quite capable of holding conflicting opinions. And the value of any one of his sayings is not much diminished by the fact that it is contradicted in the next chapter. "You have religion," says Julie,[1] "but I am afraid that you do not get from it all the advantage which it offers in the conduct of life, and that philosophical pride may disdain the simplicity of the Christian. I have seen you hold opinions on prayer which are not to my taste. According to you, this act of humility is fruitless for us; and God, having given us, in our consciences, all that can lead us to good, afterwards leaves us to ourselves and allows our liberty to act. That is not, as you know, the doctrine of Saint Paul, nor that which is professed in our church. We are free, it is true, but we are ignorant, weak, inclined to evil. And whence should light and strength come to us, if not from Him who is their source? And why should we obtain them, if we do not deign to ask for them? Beware, my friend, lest to your sublime conceptions of the Great Being, human pride join low ideas, which belong but to mankind; as if the means which relieve our weakness were suitable to divine Power, and as if, like us, It required art to generalize things, so as to treat them more easily! It seems, to listen to you, that this Power would be embarrassed should It watch over every individual; you fear that a divided and continual attention might fatigue It, and you think it much finer that It should do everything by general laws, doubtless because they cost It less care. O great philosophers! How much God is obliged to you for your easy methods and for sparing Him work."

Enough has been said of the theism of Rousseau to show its great difference from that of Voltaire and of his

[1] *Nouvelle Héloïse*, Part. vi. Let. vi. (*Œuvres*, x. 261).

followers. His attitude toward them is not unlike that of Socrates toward the Sophists. Indeed, Jean Jacques, by whomever inspired, is far more of a prophet than of a philosopher. He speaks by an authority which he feels to be above argument. In opposition to Locke and to all his school, he dares to believe in innate ideas, although he calls them feelings.[1] These innate ideas are love of self, fear of pain, horror of death, the desire for well-being. Conscience may well be one of them.

"My son," cries the Savoyard curate, "keep your soul always in a state to desire that there may be a God, and you will never doubt it. Moreover, whatever course you may adopt, consider that the true duties of religion are independent of the institutions of men; that a just heart is the true temple of Divinity; that in all countries and all sects, to love God above all things, and your neighbor as yourself, is the sum of the law; that no religion dispenses with the moral duties; that these are the only duties really essential; that the inward worship is the first of these duties, and that without faith no true virtue exists.

"Flee from those who, under the pretense of explaining nature, sow desolating doctrines in the hearts of men, and whose apparent skepticism is a hundred times more affirmative and more dogmatic than the decided tone of their adversaries."

At the time when "Emile" was written, Jean Jacques had quarreled personally with most of his old associates of the Philosophic school. Diderot, D'Alembert, Grimm, and their master, Voltaire, — Rousseau had some real or fancied grievance against them all. But the difference between him and them was intrinsic, not accidental. By

---

[1] "When, first occupied with the object, we think of ourselves only by reflection, it is an idea ; on the other hand, when the impression received excites our first attention and we think only by reflection on the object which causes it, it is a sensation." *Œuvres*, iv. 195 *n*. (*Emile*, liv. iv.).

nature and training they belonged to the rather thin rationalism of the eighteenth century; a rationalism which was so eager to believe nothing not acquired through the senses that it preferred to leave half the phenomena of life not only unaccounted for but unconsidered, because to account for them by its own methods was difficult, if not impossible. Rousseau, at least, contemplated the whole of human nature, its affections, aspirations, and passions, as well as its observations and reflections, and this was the secret of his influence over men.

CHAPTER XX.

THE PAMPHLETS.

THE reign of Louis XVI. was a time of great and rapid change. The old order was passing away, and the Revolution was taking place both in manners and laws, for fifteen years before the assembling of the Estates General. In the previous reigns the rich middle class had approached social equality with the nobles; and the sons of great families had consented to repair their broken fortunes by marrying the daughters of financiers; — "manuring their land," they called it.

Next a new set of persons claimed a place in the social scale. The men of letters were courted even by courtiers. The doctrines of the Philosophers had fairly entered the public mind. The nobility and the middle class, with such of the poor as could read and think, had been deeply impressed by Voltaire and the Encyclopædists. All men had not been affected in the same way. Some were blind followers of these leaders, eager to push the doctrines of the school to the last possible results, partisans of Helvetius and Holbach. These were the most logical. Beside them came the sentimentalists, the worshipers of Rousseau. They were not a whit less dogmatic than the others, but their dogmatism took more fanciful and less consistent forms. They believed in their ideal republics or their social compacts with a religious faith. Some of them were ready to persecute others and to die themselves for their chimeras, and subsequently proved it. And in not a few minds the teachings of Holbach and those of Rousseau were more or less confused, and coexisted with a lingering belief in the church and her doctrines. People still went to mass from habit, from education, from an uneasy feeling that it was a good thing to do; doubting all the while with Voltaire, dreaming with Rousseau, wondering what might be coming, believing that the world was speedily to be improved, having no very definite idea as to how the improvement was to be brought about, but trusting vaguely to the enlightenment of the age, which was taken for granted.

For this reign of the last absolute king of France was a time of hope and of belief in human perfectibility. One after another, the schemers had come forward with their plans for regenerating society. There were the economists, ready to swear that the world, and especially France, would be rich, if free trade were adopted, and the taxes were laid — they could not quite agree how. There were the army reformers, burning to introduce Prussian discipline; if only you could reconcile blows and good feeling. There were people calling for Equality, and for government by the most enlightened; quite unaware that their demands were inconsistent. There were the philanthropists, perhaps the most genuine of all the reformers, working at the hospitals and prisons, and reducing in no small measure the sum of misery in France.[1]

These changes in men's minds began to bear fruit in action. The attempted reforms of Turgot, of Necker,

[1] Among other instances of this spirit of hopefulness, notice those volumes of the *Encyclopédie Méthodique* which were published as early as 1789. They are largely devoted to telling how things ought to be. See also the correspondence of Lafayette, who was thoroughly steeped in the spirit of this time. The feeling of hope was not the only feeling, there was despondency also. But we must be careful not to be deceived by the tone of many people who wrote long afterward, when they had undergone the shock of the great Revolution. In the study of this period, more perhaps than in that of any other, it is important to distinguish between contemporary evidence and the evidence of contemporaries given subsequently.

of the Notables; the abolition of the *corvée*, of monopolies in trade, of judicial torture, the establishment of provincial assemblies, the civil rights given to Protestants, have been mentioned already. These things were done in a weak and inconsistent manner because of the character of the king, who was drawn in one direction by his courtiers and in another by his conscience, and satisfied neither.

Man must always look outside of himself for a standard of right and wrong. He must have something with which to compare the dictates of his own conscience, some chronometer to set his watch by. In the decay of religious ideas, the Frenchmen of the eighteenth century had set up a standard of comparison independent of revelation. They had found it in public opinion. The sociable population of Paris was ready to accept the common voice as arbiter. It had always been powerful in France, where the desire for sympathy is strong. A pamphlet published in 1730 says that if the episcopate falls into error it should be "instructed, corrected, even judged by the people." "A halberd leads a kingdom," cried a courtier to Quesnay the economist. "And who leads the halberd?" retorted the latter. "Public opinion." "There are circumstances," say the venerable and conservative lawyers of the Parliament, "when magistrates may look on their loss of court favor as an honor. It is when they are consoled by public esteem." Poor Louis himself, catching the fever of longing for popularity, proposes to "raise the results of public opinion to the rank of laws, after they have been submitted to ripe and profound examination."[1] The appeal is constantly made from old-fashioned prejudice to some new notion supposed to be generally current, as if the one proved more than the other. From this worship of public opinion come extreme irritation under criticism and cowardly fear of ridicule;

[1] *Rocquain*, 54.   Lavergne, *Economistes*, 103.   Chérest, i. 454 (May 1, 1788).

Voltaire himself asking for *lettres de cachet* against a literary opponent. Seldom, indeed, do we find any one ready to say: "This is right; thus men ought to think; and if mankind thinks differently, mankind is mistaken." Such a tone comes chiefly from the mouth of that exception for good and evil, Jean Jacques Rousseau.

This dependent state of mind is far removed from virtue. But human nature is often better than it represents itself to be. Both Quesnay and the magistrates had in fact a higher standard of right and wrong than the average feeling of the multitude. Every sect and every party makes, in a measure, its own public opinion, and the consent for which we seek is chiefly the consent of those persons whose ideas we respect. The thinkers of the eighteenth century, after appealing to public opinion, were quite ready to cast off their allegiance to it when it decided against them.

Yet Frenchmen paid the penalty for setting up a false god. Having agreed to worship public opinion, without asking themselves definitely who were the public, they fell into frequent and fatal errors. The mob often claimed the place on the pedestal of opinion, and its claims were allowed. The turbulent populace of Paris, clamorous now for cheap bread, now for the return of the Parliament from exile, anon for the blood of men and women whom it chose to consider its enemies, was supposed to be the voice of the French nation, which was superstitiously assumed to be the voice of God.

The inhabitants of great cities love to be amused. Those of Paris, being quicker witted than most mortals, care much to have something happening. They detest dullness and are fond of wit. In countries where speech and the press are free, a witticism, or a clever book, is seldom a great event. But under Louis XVI., as has been said, you could never quite tell what would come of a paragraph. A minister of state might lose his temper.

A writer might have to spend a few weeks in Holland, or even in the Bastille. This was not much to suffer for the sake of notoriety, but it gave the charm of uncertainty. There was just enough danger in saying "strong things" to make them attractive, and to make it popular to say them. With a free press, men whose opinions are either valuable or dangerous get very tired of "strong things," and prefer less spice in their intellectual fare.

The most famous satirical piece of the reign is also its most remarkable literary production. The "Mariage de Figaro," of Beaumarchais, has acquired importance apart from its merits as a comedy, both from its political history and from its good fortune in being set to immortal music. The plot is poor and intricate, but the dialogue is uniformly sparkling, and two of the characters will live as typical. In Chérubin we have the dissolute boy whose vice has not yet wrinkled into ugliness, best known to English readers under the name of Don Juan, but fresher and more ingenuous than Byron's young rake. Figaro, the hero of the play, is the comic servant, familiar to the stage from the time of Plautus, impudent, daring, plausible; likely to be overreached, if at all, by his own unscrupulousness. But he is also the adventurer of the last age of the French monarchy, full of liberal ideas and ready to give a decided opinion on anything that concerns society or politics; a Scapin, who has brushed the clothes of Voltaire. He is a shabby, younger brother of Beaumarchais himself, immensely clever and not without kindly feeling, a rascal you can be fond of. "Intrigue and money; you are in your element!" cries Susanne to Figaro, in the first act. "A hundred times I have seen you march on to fortune, but never walk straight," says the Count to him, in the third. We laugh when the blows meant for others smack loud on his cheeks; but we grudge him neither his money nor his pretty wife.

It is through this character that Beaumarchais tells the nobility, the court, and the government of France what is being said about them in the street. He repays with bitter gibes the insolence which he himself, the clever, ambitious man of the middle class, has received, in his long struggle for notoriety and wealth, from people whose personal claims to respect were no better than his own. "What have you done to have so much wealth?" cries Figaro in his soliloquy, apostrophizing the Count, who is trying to steal his mistress, "You have taken the trouble to be born, nothing more!" "I was spoken of, for an office," he says again, "but unfortunately I was fitted for it. An accountant was needed, and a dancer got it." And in another place: "I was born to be a courtier; receiving, taking and asking, are the whole secret in three words."

As for the limitations on the liberty of the press: "They tell me," says Figaro, "that if in my writing I will mention neither the government, nor public worship, nor politics, nor morals, nor people in office, nor influential corporations, nor the Opera, nor the other theatres, nor anybody that belongs to anything, I may print everything freely, subject to the approval of two or three censors." "How I should like to get hold of one of those people that are powerful for a few days, and that give evil orders so lightly, after a good reverse of favor had sobered him of his pride! I would tell him, that foolish things in print are important only where their circulation is interfered with; that without freedom to blame, no praise is flattering, and that none but little men are afraid of little writings."

The "Marriage of Figaro" was accepted by the great Parisian theatre, the Comédie Française, toward the end of 1781. The wit of the piece itself and the notoriety of the author made its success almost inevitable. The permission of the censor was of course necessary before the play could be put on the boards; but the first censor to whom the work was submitted pronounced that, with a few alterations, it might be given. The piece was already exciting much attention. As an advertisement, Beaumarchais had read it aloud in several houses of note. It was the talk of the town and of the court. The nobles were enchanted. To be laughed at so wittily was a new sensation. Old Maurepas, the prime minister, heard the play and spoke of it to his royal master. The king's curiosity was excited. He sent for a copy, and the queen's waiting woman, Madame Campan, was ordered to be at Her Majesty's apartment at three o'clock in the afternoon, but to be sure and take her dinner first, as she would be kept a long time.

At the appointed hour, Madame Campan found no one in the chamber but the king and the queen. A big pile of manuscript, covered with corrections, was on the table. As Madame Campan read, the king frequently interrupted. He praised some passages, and blamed others as in bad taste. At last, however, near the end of the play, occurred the long soliloquy in which Figaro has brought together his bitterest complaints. Early in the scene there is a description of the arbitrary imprisonment which was so common in those days. "A question arises concerning the nature of riches," says Figaro, "and as you do not need to have a thing in order to talk about it, I, who have not a penny, write on the value of money and its net product. Presently, from the inside of a cab, I see the drawbridge of a prison let down for me; and leave, as I go in, both hope and liberty behind." On hearing this tirade, King Louis XVI. leaped from his chair, and exclaimed: "It is detestable; it shall never be played! Not to have the production of this play a dangerous piece of inconsistency, we should have to destroy the Bastille. This man makes sport of everything that should be respected in a government."

"Then it will not be played?" asked the queen.

"Certainly not!" answered Louis; "you may be sure of it."

For two years a contest was kept up between the king of France and the dramatic author as to whether the "Marriage of Figaro" should be acted or not. The king had on his side absolute power to forbid the performance or to impose any conditions he pleased; but he stood almost alone in his opinion, and Louis XVI. never could stand long alone. The author had for auxiliaries some of the princes, most of the nobility, the court and the town. Public curiosity was aroused, and no one knew better than Beaumarchais how to keep it awake. He continued to read the play at private parties, but it required so much begging to induce him to do so that the favor never became a cheap one. Those people who heard it were loud in its praise, and less favored persons talked of tyranny and oppression, because they were not permitted to see themselves and their neighbors delightfully laughed at by Figaro. Poor Louis held out against the solicitations of the people about him with a pertinacity which he seldom showed in greater matters. At last his resolution weakened, and permission was accorded to play the piece at a private entertainment given by the Count of Vaudreuil. After that, the public performance became only a question of time and of the suppression of obnoxious passages. On the 27th of April, 1784, the theatre-goers of Paris thronged from early morning about the doors of the Comédie Française; three persons were crushed to death; great ladies dined in the theatre, to keep their places. At half past five the curtain rose. The success was unbounded, in spite of savage criticism, which spared neither the play nor the author.[1]

As the people of Paris liked violent language, they also enjoyed opposition to the government, whatever form that opposition might assume. The Parliament, as we have seen, although contending for privileges and against mea-

---

[1] Campan, i. 277. Loménie, *Beaumarchais*, ii. 293. Grimm, xiii. 517. La Harpe, *Corresp. litt.* iv. 227.

sures beneficial to most people in the country, was yet popular, for it was continually defying the court. But many privileged persons went farther than the conservative lawyers of the city. It was indeed such people who took the lead both in proclaiming equality and in denouncing courtiers. From the nobility and the rich citizens of Paris, discontent with existing conditions and the habit of opposition to constituted authorities spread to the lower classes and to the inhabitants of provincial towns.

Louis XVI. had not been long on the throne when a series of events occurred in a distant part of the world which excited in a high degree both the spirit of insubordination and the love of equality in French minds. The American colonies of Great Britain broke into open revolt, and presently declared their independence of the mother country. The sympathy of Frenchmen was almost universal and was loudly expressed. Here was a nation of farmers constituting little communities that Rousseau might not have disowned, at least if he had looked at them no nearer than across the ocean. They were in arms for their rights and liberties, and in revolt against arbitrary power. And the oppressor was the king of England, the monarch of the nation that had inflicted on France, only a few years before, a humiliating defeat. Much that was generous in French character, and much that was sentimental, love of liberty, admiration of equality, hatred of the hereditary enemy, conspired to favor the cause of the "Insurgents." The people who wished for political reforms could point to the model commonwealths of the New World. Their constitutions were translated into French, and several editions were sold in Paris.[1] The people that adored King Louis could cry out for the

[1] *Recueil des loix constitutives. Constitutions des treize Etats Unis de l'Amérique.* Franklin to Samuel Cooper, May 1, 1777. *Works*, vi. 96.

abasement of King George. A few prudent heads in high places were shaken at the thought of assisting rebellion. The Emperor Joseph II., brother-in-law to the king of France, was not quite the only man whose business it was to be a royalist. Ministers might deprecate war on economical grounds, and advise that just enough help be given to the Americans to prolong their struggle with England until both parties should be exhausted. But the heart of the French nation had gone into the war. It was for the sake of his own country that the Count of Vergennes, the foreign minister of Louis XVI., induced her to take up arms against Great Britain, and in the negotiations for peace he would willingly have sacrificed the interests of his American to those of his Spanish allies; yet the part taken by France was the almost inevitable result of the sympathy and enthusiasm of the French nation. Never was a war not strictly of defense more completely national in its character. Frenchmen fought in Virginia because they loved American ideas, and hated the enemy of America.[1]

Thus France, while still an absolute monarchy, undertook a war in defense of political rights. Such an action could not be without results. Writers of a later time, belonging to the monarchical party, have not liked the results and have blamed the course of the French upper classes in embarking in the war. But it was because they were already inclined to revolutionary ideas in politics that the nobility did so embark. Poor Louis was dragged along, feebly protesting. He was no radical, and to him change could mean nothing but harm; if it be harm to be deprived of authority beyond your strength, and of responsibility exceeding your moral power. The war, in its turn, fed the prevailing passions. Young Frenchmen, who had first become warlike because they were adventurous and high-spirited, adopted the cries of "liberty" and

[1] Rosenthal, *America and France*, — an excellent monograph.

"equality" as the watchwords of the struggle into which they entered, and were then interested to study the principles which they so loudly proclaimed. Voltaire, Rousseau, d'Alembert, even Montesquieu, became more widely read than ever. Officers returning from the capture of Yorktown were flushed with success and ready to praise all they had seen. They told of the simplicity of republican manners, of the respect shown for virtuous women. Even Lauzun forgot to be lewd in speaking of the ladies of Newport. So unusual a state of mind could not last long. A reaction set in after the peace with England. Anglomania became the ruling fashion. The change was more apparent than real. London was nearer than Philadelphia and more easily visited. Political freedom existed there also, if not in so perfect a form, yet in one quite as well suited to the tastes of fashionable young men. Had not Montesquieu looked on England as the model state?[1]

Thus English political ideas were adopted with more or less accuracy and were accompanied by English fashions: horses and horseracing, short stirrups, plain clothes, linen dresses, and bread and butter. Clubs also are an English invention. The first one in Paris was opened in 1782. The Duke of Chartres had recently cut down the trees of his garden to build the porticoes and shops of the Palais Royal. The people who had been in the habit of lounging under the trees were thus dispossessed. A speculator opened a reading-room for their benefit, and provided them with newspapers, pamphlets, and current literature. The duke himself encouraged the enterprise,

[1] Ségur, i. 87. The French officers who were in the Revolutionary war often express dissatisfaction with the Americans, but their voices appear to have been drowned in France in the chorus of praise. See Kalb's letters to Broglie in Stevens's MSS., vii., and Mauroy to Broglie, *ibid.*, No. 838. The foreign politics of the reign of Louis XVI. are admirably considered by Albert Sorel, *L'Europe et la Révolution française,* i. 297.

and overcame the resistance which the police naturally made to any new project. The reading-room, which seems to have had a regular list of subscribers, was called the Political Club. In spite of the name, the regulations of the police forbade conversation within its walls on the subjects of religion and politics; but such rules were seldom enforced in Paris. Other clubs were soon founded, some large and open, some small and private. A certain number of them took the name of literary, scientific, or benevolent associations. Some appear to have been secret societies with oaths and pledges. The habit of talking about matters of government spread more and more.[1]

It was on the approach of the meeting of the Estates General that the habit of political reading assumed the greatest importance. In the latter part of 1788 and the earlier months of 1789 a deluge of pamphlets, such as the world had not seen and is never likely to see again, burst over Paris. The newspapers of the day were few and completely under the control of the government, but French heads were seething with ideas. In vain the administration and the courts made feeble attempts to limit the activity of the press. From the princes of the blood royal (who issued a reactionary manifesto), to the most obscure writer who might hope for a moment's notoriety, all were rushing into print. The booksellers' shops were crowded from morning until night. The price of printing was doubled. One collector is said to have got together twenty-five hundred different political pamphlets in the

[1] Chérest, ii. 101. Droz, i. 326. See in Brissot ii. 415, an account of a club to discuss political questions, under pretense of studying animal magnetism. Lafayette, d'Esprésmenil, and others were members. Their ideas were vague enough. Brissot was for a republic, D'Esprésmenil for giving the power to the Parliament, Bergasse for a new form of government of which he was to be the Lycurgus. Morellet, i. 346. Lameth, i. 34 n. Sainte-Beuve, x. 104 (Sénac de Meilhan).

last months of 1788, and to have stopped in despair at the impossibility of completing his collection.[1]

In most political crises there is but one great question of the hour; but in France at this time all matters of government and social life were in doubt; and every man believed that he could settle them all by the easy and speedy application of pure reason, if only all other men would lay down their prejudices. And a special subject was not wanting. The question which called loudest for an answer was that of representation. Should there be one chamber in the Estates General, in which the Commons should have a number of votes equal to that of the other two orders combined, or should there be three chambers? This matter (which is more particularly discussed in the next chapter) and the general political constitution occupied the chief attention of the pamphleteers, but law reform and feudal abuses were not forgotten.

The pamphlets came from all quarters and bore all sorts of titles. "Detached Thoughts;" "The Forty Wishes of the Nation;" "What has surely been forgotten;" "Discourse on the Estates General;" "Letter of a Burgundian Gentleman to a Breton Gentleman, on the Attack of the Third Estate, the Division of the Nobility, and the Interest of the Husbandmen;" "Letter of a Peasant;" "Plan for a Matrimonial Alliance between Monsieur Third Estate and Madam Nobility;" "When the Cock crows, look out for the Old Hens;" "Ultimatum of a Citizen of the Third Estate on the Mémoire of the Princes;" "Te Deum of the Third Estate as it will be sung at the First Mass of the Estates General, with the Confession of the Nobility;" "Creed of the Third Estate;" "Magnificat of the Third Estate;" and "Requiem of the Farmers General."

[1] Droz, ii. 93. "Thirteen came out to-day, sixteen yesterday, and ninety-two last week." A. Young, i. 118 (June 9, 1789). Chérest, ii. 248, etc.

The pamphlets are generally anonymous, from a lingering fear of the police. The place of printing is seldom mentioned; at least, few of the pamphlets bear the true one. The imprint, where one appears, is London, Ispahan, or Concordopolis. One humorous and distinctly libelous publication is "sold at the Islands of Saint Margaret, and distributed gratis at Paris." The pamphlet entitled "Diogenes and the Estates General" is "sold by Diogenes in his Tub."

In spite of the stringent orders against printed attacks on the government, in spite of the spasmodic activity of the police, the boldness of some of the pamphlets is remarkable. One of them, for instance, begins as follows: "There was once, I know not where, a king born with an upright spirit and a heart that loved justice, but a bad education had left his good qualities uncultivated and useless." The king is then accused of eating and hunting too much, and of swearing. And when we pass from personal to political subjects there is almost no limit to the rashness of the pamphleteers. It was not the most sane and judicious part of the nation which became most conspicuous by its writings at this time and in this manner. The pamphlets are noticeably less conservative than the *cahiers*, which were likewise produced in the spring of 1789.

Yet the subversionary writers were not left to occupy the field alone. Nobles and magistrates took up their pens to defend old institutions. Moderate men tried to get a hearing in behalf of peace and good will. But, alas, the old constitution was a dream. France was in fact a despotism with civilized traditions and with a few customs that had almost the force of fundamental laws, and her people wanted a liberal government. As to the form of that government they were not entirely agreed; although they were not quite so subversionary as many of the pamphleteers wished them to be, or as their subsequent history would lead us to believe them to have been. But no leader appeared, for a long time, strong enough to dominate the factions and to keep the peace.

Of the mass of political literature which saw the light in 1788 and 1789, three lines only are commonly remembered. They are on the first page of a pamphlet by the famous Abbé Sieyès. Of the many persons who in our own time have wondered how to pronounce his name, all are aware that he asked and answered the following questions: —

"(1.) What is the Third Estate? Everything.

"(2.) What has it been hitherto in the political order? Nothing.

"(3.) What does it ask? To become something."

Few have followed him farther in his inquiries. Yet his pamphlet excited great interest and admiration in its day. It is an eloquent and well-written paper, as strong in rhetoric as it is weak in statesmanship.

In agriculture, manufactures, and trade, and in those services which are directly useful and agreeable to persons, and which include the most distinguished scientific and literary professions and the most menial service, the Commons, according to Sieyès, do all the work. In the army, the church, the law, and the administration of government, they furnish nineteen twentieths of the men employed, and these do all that is really onerous. Only the lucrative and honorary places are occupied by members of the nobility. These upper places would be infinitely better filled if they were the rewards of talents and services recognized in the lower ranks. The Third Estate is quite able to do all that is needful. Were the privileged orders taken away, the nation would not be something less than it is, but something more.

"What is a nation?" asks Sieyès; and he answers that it is "a body of associates living together under a common law and represented by the same legislature." But the order of the nobility has privileges, dispensations, different rights from the great body of the citizens. It is outside of the common order and the common law. It is a state within a state.

The Third Estate, therefore, embraces everything which belongs to the nation; and all that is not a part of the Commons cannot be considered a part of the nation. What, then, is the Third Estate? Everything.

What has the Third Estate hitherto been? Nothing. It is but too true that you are nothing in France if you have only the protection of the common law. Without some privilege or other, you must make up your mind to suffer contempt, contumely, and all sorts of vexation. The unfortunate person who has no privileges of his own can only attach himself to some great man, by all sorts of meanness, and thus get the chance, on occasion, to demand the assistance of *somebody*.

What does the Third Estate ask? To become something in the state. And in truth the people asks but little. It wants true representatives in the Estates, taken from its own order, able to interpret its wishes, and defend its interests. But what would it gain by taking part in the Estates General, if its own side were not to prevail there? It must, therefore, have an influence at least equal to that of the privileged orders; it must have half the representatives. This equality would be illusory if the chambers voted separately; therefore, the voting must be by heads. Can the Third Estate ask for less than this? And is it not clear that if its influence is less than that of the privileged orders combined, there is no hope of its emerging from its political nullity and becoming something?

Sieyès goes on to argue that the Third Estate should be allowed to choose its representatives only from its own body. He has persuaded himself, by what seems to be a process of mental juggling, that men of one order cannot be truly represented by men of another. Suppose, he says, that France is at war with England, and that hostilities are conducted on our side by a Directory composed of national representatives. In that case, I ask, would any province be permitted, in the name of freedom, to choose for its delegates to the Directory the members of the English ministry? Surely the privileged classes show themselves no less hostile to the common order of people, than the English to the French in time of war.

Three further questions are stated by Sieyès.

(4.) What the ministers have attempted and what the privileged classes propose in favor of the Third Estate?

(5.) What should have been done?

(6.) What is still to be done?

Under the fourth head, Sieyès considers the Provincial Assemblies recently established, and the Assembly of Notables, both of which he considers entirely incapable of doing good, because they are composed of privileged persons. He scorns the proposal of the nobility to pay a fair share of the taxes, being unwilling to accept as a favor what he wishes to take as a right. He fears that the Commons will be content with too little and will not sweep away all privilege. He attacks the English Constitution, which the liberal nobles of France were in the habit of setting up as a model, saying that it is not good in itself, but only as a prodigious system of props and makeshifts against disorder. The right of trial by jury he considers its best feature.

He then passes to the question: What should have been done? and here he gives us the foundation of his system. Without naming Rousseau he has adopted the Social Compact as the basis of government. A nation is made up of individuals; these unite to form a community; for convenience they depute persons to represent them and to exercise the common power.[1] The constitution of the

[1] It need hardly be pointed out that Sieyès falls short of the full

state is the body of rules by which these representatives are governed when they legislate or administer the public affairs. The constitution is fundamental, not as binding the national will, but only as binding the bodies existing within the state. The nation itself is free from all such bonds. No constitution can control it. Its will cannot be limited. The nation assembling to consider its constitution is not controlled by ordinary forms. Its delegates meeting for that especial purpose are independent of the constitution. They represent the national will, and questions are settled by them not in accordance with constitutional laws, but as they might be in a meeting of the whole nation were it small enough to be brought together in one place; that is to say, by a vote of the majority.[1]

But where find the nation? Where it is: in the forty thousand parishes which comprise all the territory and all the inhabitants of the country. They should have been arranged in groups of twenty or thirty parishes, and have thus formed representative districts, which should have united to make provinces, which should have sent true delegates, with special power to settle the constitution of the Estates General.

This correct course has not been followed, but what now remains to be done? Let the Commons assemble apart from the other orders. Let them join with the Nobility and the Clergy neither by orders, as a part of a legislature of three chambers, nor by heads, in one common assembly. Two courses are open. Either let them appeal to the nation for increased powers, which would

measure of Rousseau's doctrine when he allows the law-making, or more correctly the constitution-making power, to be delegated at all.

[1] Sieyès and his master do not see that if unanimity cannot be secured, and if constitutional law be once done away, men are reduced under their system to a state of nature, and the will of a majority has no binding force but that of the strong arm.

be the most frank and generous way; or let them only consider the enormous difference that exists between the assembly of the Third Estate and that of the other two orders. "The former represents twenty-five millions of men and deliberates on the interests of the nation. The other two, were they united, have received their powers from but about two hundred thousand individuals, and think only of their privileges. The Third Estate alone, you will say, cannot form the Estates General. So much the better! It will make a *National Assembly*."

I have considered this famous pamphlet at some length, because it was eminently timely, expressing, as it did, the doctrines and the aspirations of the subversionary party in France. I believe, and principally on the evidence of the cahiers, that this party did not form a majority, or even, numerically, a very large minority, of the French nation. A constitutional convention, organized from the Commons alone as Sieyes would have had it, if left to itself and uncontrolled by the Parisian mob, would undoubtedly have settled the question of a single chamber in a popular sense, but it would have preserved the privileges of the nobility to an extent which would have disgusted the extremists, and perhaps have saved the country from years of violence and decades of reaction. But the people of violent ideas were predominant in Paris and in some of the towns, and were destined, for a time, to be the chief force in the French Revolution. The passions of this party were love of equality and hatred of privilege. To men of this stamp despotism may be comparatively indifferent; liberty is a word of sweet sound, but little meaning. Sieyès hardly refers to the king in his pamphlet. "The time is past," he says, "when the three orders, thinking only of defending themselves from ministerial despotism, were ready to unite against the common enemy." This comparative indifference to the tyranny of the court was not the feeling of the country, but it was that of the enthusiasts. Nothing is too bad according to these last, for men who hold privileges. They have no right to assemblies of their own, nor to a voice in the assemblies of the people. To ask what place they should occupy in the social order "is to ask what place should be assigned in a sick body to the malignant humor which undermines and torments it."

CHAPTER XXI.

THE CAHIERS.

It is seldom, indeed, that a great nation can express fully, frankly, and yet officially, all its complaints, wishes, and hopes in respect to its own government. Our knowledge of national ideas must generally be derived from the words of particular classes of men: statesmen, politicians, authors, or writers in the newspapers. The ideas of these classes are more or less in accord with those of the great mass of the people which they undertake to represent; yet their expressions are necessarily tinged by their own professional way of looking at things. But in the spring of 1789 all Frenchmen, with few exceptions, were called on to unite, not merely in choosing representatives, but in giving them minute instructions. The occasion was most solemn. The Estates General, the great central legislature of France, which had not met for nearly two centuries, was summoned to assemble at Versailles. It should be the old body and something more. It was to partake of the nature of a constitutional convention. It was not only to legislate, but to settle the principles of government. It was called by the king to advise and consent to all that might concern the needs of the state, the reform of abuses, the establishment of a fixed and lasting order in all parts of the administration, the general prosperity of his kingdom, and the welfare of all and each of his subjects.[1]

[1] *Royal Letter of Convocation*, January 24, 1789, *A. P.* i. 611. The principal printed collection of cahiers, together with much preliminary matter, may be found in the first six volumes of the *Archives Parle-*

The three orders of men, the Clergy, the Nobility, and the Commons, or Third Estate, were to hold their elections separately in every district,[1] unless they should, by separate votes, agree to unite.[2] In accordance with ancient custom they were to draw up petitions, complaints, and remonstrances, which were intended to form a basis for legislation. These complaints were to be brought to the Estates, and were to serve as instructions, more or less positive, to the deputies who brought them. They were known in French political language as *Cahiers*.

The cahiers of the Clergy and of the Nobility were drawn up in the electoral meetings which took place in every district. To these local assemblies of the Clergy, all bishops, abbots, and parish priests, holding benefices, were summoned. Chapters and monasteries sent only representatives. The result of this arrangement was that the parish priests far outnumbered the regular ecclesiastics and dignitaries, and that the clerical cahiers oftenest express the wishes of the lower portion of the secular clergy. This preponderance of the lower clergy appears

mentaires, edited by MM. Mavidal et Laurent, Paris. The seventh volume consists of an index, which, although very imperfect, is necessary to an intelligent study of the cahiers. The cahiers printed in these volumes occupy about 4,000 large octavo pages in double column. These volumes will be referred to in this chapter and the next as *A. P.* Many cahiers and extracts from cahiers are also found printed in other places. I have not undertaken to give references to all the cahiers on which my conclusions are founded, but only to a few typical examples. The letters *C.*, *N.*, and *T* indicate the three orders. Where no such letter occurs the cahier is generally that of a town or village.

[1] *Baillage, sénéchaussée*.
[2] The three orders did not often unite, but there is often evidence of communication between them. They all united at Bayonne, *A. P.* iii. 98. Montfort l'Amaury, *A. P.* iv. 37. Rozières, *A. P.* iv. 91. Fenestrange, *A. P.* v. 710. Mohon, *A. P.* v. 729. The Clergy and the Nobility united at Lixheim, *A. P.* v. 713 ; the Nobility and the Third Estate at Péronne, *A. P.* v. 355.

to have been foreseen and desired by the royal advisers. The king had expressed his wish to call to the assemblies of the Clergy "all those good and faithful pastors who are occupied closely and every day with the poverty and the assistance of the people and who are more intimately acquainted with its ills and its apprehensions."[1]

To the local assemblies of the nobles, all Frenchmen of the order, not less than twenty-five years of age, were summoned. Men, women, or children possessing fiefs might appear by proxy. The latter provision did not suffice to take the meetings out of the control of the more numerous part of the order, — the poorer nobility. To pride of race and intense loyalty to the king, these country gentlemen united distrust and dislike of the court, and the desire that all nobles at least should have equal rights and chances. Their cahiers differ somewhat from place to place, but are wonderfully alike in general current.[2]

For the Third Estate a more complicated system was adopted. The franchise extended to every French subject, neither clerical nor noble, twenty-five years of age, and entered on the tax rolls.[3] Every town, parish, or village, drew up its cahier and sent it, by deputies, either to the assembly of the district or to an intermediate assembly. Here a committee was appointed to consider all the local cahiers and consolidate them; those of the intermediate assemblies being again worked over for the general cahier of the Third Estate of each electoral district. Thus the cahiers of the Commons finally carried to the Estates General at Versailles were less directly the expression of the opinions of the order from which they

[1] *Règlement du* 24 *Jan.* 1789, *A. P.* i. 544. Parish priests were not allowed to leave their parishes to go to the assemblies if more than two leagues distant, unless they left curates to do their work. But this provision did not keep enough of them away to alter the character of the assemblies.

[2] *N.*, Périgord, *A. P.*, v. 341.

[3] In Paris only, a small property qualification was exacted.

came than were the cahiers of the Clergy and of the Nobility. Fortunately, however, large numbers of the primary or village cahiers have been preserved and printed.

The cahiers of the Third Estate differ far more among themselves than do those of the upper orders. Some of them, drawn up in the villages, are very simple, dealing merely with local grievances and the woes of peasant life. The long absence of the lord of the place causes more loss to one village than even the price of salt, or than the taille, with which the people are overburdened. Then follows the enumeration of broken bridges, of pastures overflowed because the bed of the stream is obstructed, of robbery and violence and refusal of justice, with no one to protect the poor, nor to direct repairs and improvements.[1]

In another place we have the touching humility of the peasant. "The inhabitants of this parish have no other complaints to make than those which are common to folk of their rank and condition, namely, that they pay too many taxes of different kinds already; that they would wish that the disorder of the finances might not be the cause of new burdens upon them, because they were not able to bear any more, having a great deal of trouble to pay those which are now levied, but that it much rather belonged to those who are rich to contribute toward setting up the affairs of the kingdom.

"As for remonstrances, they have no other wishes nor other desires than peace and public tranquillity: that they wish the assembly of the Estates General may restore the order of the finances, and bring about in France the order and prosperity of the state; that they are not skillful enough about the matters which are to be treated in the said assembly to give their opinion, and they trust to the intelligence and the good intentions of those who will be sent there as deputies.

"Finally, that they know no means of providing for

[1] Paroisse de Longpont, *A. P.*, v. 334.

the necessities of the state, but a great economy in expenses and reciprocal love between the king and his subjects."[1]

Not many of the cahiers are so modest as this one. Some of them are many pages long, arranged under heads, divided into numbered paragraphs. These contain a general scheme of legislation, and often also particular and local petitions. They ask that such a lawsuit be reviewed, that such a dispute be favorably settled. Many localities complain, not only that the country in general is overtaxed, but that their particular neighborhood pays more than its share. Their soil is poor, they say, water is scarce or too plenty. The cahiers of the country villages contain more complaints of feudal exactions, while those of the towns and of the electoral districts give more space to political and social reforms.

Many models of cahiers were prepared in Paris and sent to the country towns. Thus the famous Abbé Sieyès, whose violent doctrines were considered in the last chapter, composed and distributed a form. It was brought to Chaumont in Champagne by the Viscount of Laval, who undertook to manage the election in that town in the interest of democracy and the Duke of Orleans. Dinners and balls were given to the voters; promises were made. The badges of an order of canonesses, which the duke proposed to found, were distributed among the ladies. The abbé's cahier was accepted, but the peasants of Champagne appended to its demands for constitutional reforms the petition that their dogs might not be obliged to carry a log fastened to their collars to prevent their running after game, and that they themselves might be allowed to have guns to kill the wolves.[2]

Some of the cahiers were entirely of home manufacture,

[1] Paroisse de Pas-Saint-Lomer, *A. P.*, v. 334.
[2] Beugnot, *Mémoires*, i. 110.

drawn up by the lawyer or the priest of the village. The people of Essy-lès-Nancy, in Lorraine, describe the process. "Each one of us proposed what he thought proper, and then we chose our deputies, Imbert Perrin and Joseph Jacques, whom we thought best able well to represent us. The only thing left was to express our wishes well, and to draw up the official report of the meeting. But our priest, in whom we trust, who feels our woes so well, and who expresses our feelings so rightly, had been obliged to go away. We said: 'We must wait for him; we will first beg his assistant to begin, and then, when the priest comes back, we will give him the whole thing to correct, and have our affairs ready to be taken to the assembly of the district.' He came back in fact; we asked him to draw it all up. We told him all we wanted. He kept writing, and scratching out, and writing over, until we saw that he had got our ideas. Everything seemed ready for the fifteenth. But we heard that the district assembly would be put off until the thirtieth. We said to him: 'Sir, wait again, let us profit by the delay, we shall think of something more, you will add it;' he consented."[1]

There was evidently some concert among the different districts, but also much freedom and originality. There are many protests on the part of minorities. Bishops or chapters complain of clauses which attack their rights; monasteries remonstrate against the proposed diversion of their funds to pay parish priests. Individuals take this opportunity to give their views on public matters. An old officer would have nobility of the sword confined to families in which the men bear arms in every generation. A commoner, having bought noble lands, complains of the additional taxes laid on him on this account. The peasants of Ménil-la-Horgne say that the lawyers have captured the electoral assembly of their district, and cut

[1] Mathieu, 423.

out their remonstrances from the general cahier; that although there are thirty-two rural communities in the bailiwick, and all agreed, the six deputies of the towns have managed things in their own way; and that thus the poor inhabitants of the country can never bring their wishes to the notice of their sovereign, who desires their good, and takes all means to accomplish it.[1]

The meetings in which the cahiers were composed were sometimes stormy. At Nemours the economist Dupont was one of the committee especially engaged in the task. The question of abolishing the old courts of law was a cause of strong feeling. The excitement rose so high that the crowd threatened to throw Dupont out of the window. Matters looked serious, for the room was a flight above ground, the window was already open, and angry men were laying hands on the economist. The latter, however, picked out one inoffensive person, a very fat man, who happened to be standing by. Dupont managed to get near him and suddenly grasped him round the body. "What do you want?" cried the startled fat man. "Sir," answered Dupont, "every one for himself. They are going to throw me out of the window, and you must serve as a mattress." The crowd laughed, and not only let Dupont alone, but came round to his opinion, and chose him deputy.[2]

The agreement of general ideas in the cahiers is all the more striking on account of the diversity in their details, and of the freedom of discussion and protest enjoyed by those concerned in composing them. They have been constantly referred to by writers on history, politics, and

[1] No strict line appears to have been drawn as to who might and who might not properly issue a cahier. Jean Baptiste Lardier, seigneur de Saint-Gervais de Pierrefitte, *A. P.* v. 17. Messire Carré, *A. P.*, v. 21; *A. P.* ii. 224.

[2] Another politician under similar circumstances was frightened out of the room, and lost all political influence. Beugnot, i. 118.

economics for information as to the state of France at the time when they were written. They are, indeed, capable of teaching a very great deal, but they will prove misleading if the purpose for which they were composed be forgotten. This purpose was to express the complaints and desires of the nation. It appears in their very name, "Cahiers of Lamentations, Complaints, and Remonstrances."[1] We must not, therefore, look to the cahiers for mention of anything good in the condition of old France; and we must remember that people who are advocating a change are likely to bring forward the worst side of the things they wish to see altered. Two political ideas coexisted in the minds of Frenchmen in 1789 as to what they and their Estates General were to do and to be. They were to resume their ancient constitution. They were to make a new one, in accordance with reason and justice. Both of these desires may well be present in the minds of practical legislators, even if their reconciliation be at the expense of strict logic and historical accuracy. But unfortunately the historical and the ideal constitutions in France were too far separated to be easily united. The chasm between the feudal monarchy gradually transformed into a despotism, which had existed, and the well governed limited monarchy, which the most judicious Frenchmen desired, was too wide to be bridged. "The throne of France is inherited only in the male line;" to that all men agreed. They agreed also that all existing taxes were illegal, because they had not been allowed by the nation, and that such taxes should remain in force only for convenience, and for a limited time, unless voted by the legislature. The legislative power resides, or is to reside in the king and the nation, the latter being represented by its lawful assembly or Estates General;[2] here also they were in accord. But how are those Estates

---

[1] The titles vary, but generally bear this meaning.
[2] Some say in the Estates General, without mentioning the king.

General to be composed? "Of three orders, deliberating and voting separately, the concurrence of all three being necessary to the passage of a law," said the nobles. "Of one chamber," answered the Third Estate, "in which our numbers are to be equal to those of the other orders united, and in which the vote is to be counted by heads." Here was the first and most dangerous divergence of opinion, on a question which should have been answered before it was even fairly asked, by the king who called the assembly. But neither Louis nor Necker, his adviser, had the strength and foresight to settle the matter on a firm basis while it was yet time. Were the old form of voting by three chambers intended, it was folly to make the popular one as numerous as the other two together. Were a new form of National Assembly, with only one chamber, to be brought into being, it was culpable to allow the old orders to misunderstand their fall from power. "We are an essential part of the monarchy," said the nobles. "We are twenty-three twenty-fourths of the nation, and the more useful part at that," retorted the Commons. "Our claim rests on law and history," cried the one. "And ours on reason and justice," shouted the other. And many of the deputies on either side held the positive instructions of their constituents not to yield in this matter. But while the Commons were practically a unit on this question, the nobles were more divided. About half of them insisted on their ancient rights, declaring, in many instances, that should the vote by heads be adopted their deputies were immediately to retire from the Estates. Others wavered, or allowed discussion by a single, united chamber under certain circumstances, or on questions which did not concern the privileges of the superior Orders. In a few provinces the nobles frankly took the popular side. The Clergy joined in some cases with one party, in some with the other, but oftenest gave no opinion.[1]

[1] I have found one cahier of the Third Estate asking for the vote

The cahiers on both sides took this question as settled, and proceeded, with a tolerable agreement, to the other parts of the constitution. The king, in addition to his concurrence in legislation, was to have nominally the whole executive power. Many are the expressions of love and gratitude for Louis XVI. He is requested to adopt the title of "Father of the People," of "Emulator of Charlemagne." In the latter connection we are treated to a bit of history. It appears that Egbert, King of Kent, came to France in the year 799, to learn the art of reigning from Charlemagne himself. He bore back to England the plan of the French constitution. The next year he acquired the kingdom of Wessex, in 808 that of the Mercians, and in time his reputation brought under his rule the four remaining kingdoms of Great Britain. Thus it is the basis of our French constitution which for nearly a thousand years has made the happiness and strength of all England, and which is the true origin of the rightful privileges of the province of Brittany.[1]

The royal power was to be exercised through responsible ministers, but we must not be misled by words. The ministerial responsibility contemplated by Frenchmen in the cahiers was something quite different from what is

by orders. *T.*, Mantes et Meulan, *A. P.*, iii. 666, art. 4, § 3. A suggestion of two coördinate chambers, in one cahier of the Clergy and Nobility, and in one of the Third Estate. *T.*, Bigorre, *A. P.*, ii. 359, § 3.

[1] *T.*, Ballainvilliers, *A. P.*, iv. 336, art. 35. Triel, *A. P.* v. 147, art. 104. For the title of *Père du Peuple*, St. Cloud, *A. P.* v. 68. Montaigut, *A. P.* v. 577. *T.*, Rouen, *A. P.* v. 602. *T.*, Vannes, *A. P.*, vi. 107. For blessings on the king and on Necker, see Mathieu, 425. The sole expression of disrespect for Louis XVI. which I have found is given in Beugnot, i. 116. "Let us give power to our deputies to solicit from our lord the king his consent to the above requests ; in case he accords them, to thank him ; in case he refuses, to *unking* him" (*déroiter*). This, according to Beugnot, was in a rural cahier and he seems to quote from memory. The pamphlets, as has been said, were much more violent than the cahiers.

known by that name in modern times. Under the system of government which was forming in England in the last century, and which has since been extensively copied on the Continent, the ministers, although nominally the advisers of the king, form in fact a governing committee, selected by the legislature among its own members. The ministers are at once the creatures and the leaders of the Parliament from which they spring. To it they are responsible not only for malfeasance in office, but for matters of opinion or policy. As soon as they are shown to be in disagreement with the majority of their fellow-members, they fall from power; but their fall is attended with no disgrace, and no one is shocked or astonished to see them continue to take part in public life, and regain, by a turn of popular favor, those places which they may have lost almost by accident.

The idea of such a system as this had not entered the minds of the Frenchmen of 1789. They knew ministers only as servants of a monarch, chosen by him alone, to carry out his orders, or to advise him in affairs of which the final decision lay with him. They knew but too well that kings and their servants are sometimes law-breakers. They knew, moreover, that their own actual king was weak and well-meaning. The pious fiction by which the king was always spoken of as good, and his aberrations were ascribed to defective knowledge or to bad advice, had taken some real hold on the popular imagination. The nation felt that the person of a king should be inviolable. But the breaches of law committed by the king's unaided strength could not be far-reaching. Frenchmen, therefore, desired to make all those persons responsible who might abet the king in illegal acts, or who might commit any such acts under his orders or in his name. They feared the levy of illegal taxes, and it was against malfeasance of that sort that they especially wished to provide. They therefore asked in their cahiers that the ministers should be made responsible to the civil tribunals or to the Estates General. The voters did not conceive of royal ministers as members of their legislature. In fact, some cahiers carefully provided that deputies should accept no office nor favor of the court either during the continuance of their service in the Estates, or for some years thereafter. The demand for ministerial responsibility was a demand that ministers, and their master through them, should be amenable to law; and was in the same line with the demand, also made in some cahiers, that soldiers should not be used in suppressing riots, except at the request of the civil power.[1]

It was universally demanded that the Estates General should meet at regular intervals of two, three, or five years, and should vote taxes for a limited time only. Thus it was hoped to keep power in the hands of the nation. And all debates were to be public; the proceedings were to be reported from day to day.[2] Such provisions were not unnatural, for jealousy and distrust are common in political matters, and the less the experience of the people, the greater their dread of plots and cabals. But only two years before the cahiers were drawn up, another nation, which it had recently been the fashion much to admire in France, had appointed its deputies to draw up its constitution. This nation was at least as superior to the French in political experience as it was inferior in the arts and sciences that adorn life. Its attempts at constitution making might, therefore, well have served as a guide. The American convention of 1787 had many difficulties to encounter and many jealousies to excite; but these were less threatening than those which confronted the French Estates. Yet in Philadelphia precautions had been taken which were scorned

---

[1] T., St-Gervais (Paris), A. P., v. 308, § 3. N. Agenois, A. P., i. 680, § 15. Chérest, ii. 475.

[2] Chérest, ii. 461.

at Versailles. The American deputies did not number twelve hundred, but less than sixty. The Americans sat with closed doors, and exacted of each other a pledge, most religiously kept, that their proceedings should be secret. The French admitted all manner of persons, not only to listen to their debates, but to applaud and hiss them. Their chamber came in a short time to be influenced, if not controlled, by its galleries; so that France was no longer governed by her chosen representatives, but by the mob of her capital. The American deputies, for the most part, came unpledged to their work. The French in many instances were commanded by their constituents to retire unless such and such of their demands were complied with. The American constitution was accepted with difficulty, and could probably never have been accepted at all if the public mind had been inflamed by discussion of each part before the whole was known. That constitution, with but few important amendments, is to-day regarded with a veneration incomprehensible to foreigners, by a nation twenty times as large as that which originally adopted it.[1] The French constitution made by the body which met in 1789, with the name of Estates General, Constituent, or National Assembly, was hailed with clamorous joy by a part of the nation, and met with angry incredulity by another part. Many of its provisions have remained; but the constitution itself did not last two years. Could the sober deliberation of a small body of authorized men, sitting with closed doors, have produced in France in 1789 a constitution under which the nation could have prospered, and which could have been gradually improved and adapted to modern civilization? Was the enthusiasm and rush of a large popular assembly ne-

[1] An eminent foreign historian would almost seem to have written his book on the Constitutional History of the United States for the purpose of showing that a man may know all about a subject without understanding it.

cessary to overcome the interested opposition of the court and the weak nervelessness of the monarch? It will never be known. Louis XVI. was too feeble to try the experiment, and no one else had the legal authority.

While the Estates General were to have the exclusive right of legislation, and France was thus to remain a centralized monarchy, Provincial Estates were to be established all over the country, unless where local bodies of the same character already existed. These Provincial Estates were to exercise large administrative powers, in the assessment and levy of taxes, in laying out roads, granting licenses, encouraging commerce and manufactures. It was the prayer of many of the cahiers that offices of one sort and another, civil or military, or that nobility itself, should be granted only on the nomination of the Provincial Estates. Many cahiers ask for elective municipal or village authorities. Many would sweep away the old officers of the crown, the intendants and military governors, the farmers general, and the very clerks. These men were hated as tax-gatherers, and distrusted as members of the old ring which had misgoverned the country. There are, says one cahier, more than forty thousand of them in the kingdom, whose sole business it is to vex and molest the king's subjects, by false declarations and other means, and all for the hope of a share in the fines and confiscations that may be exacted.[1]

It is a mistake to assume that the Frenchmen of 1789 cared chiefly for civil and social reforms, and only incidentally for reforms of a political character. In most of the cahiers the political reforms are first mentioned and are as elaborately insisted on as any others. If there be any

[1] *T.*, Perche, *A. P.*, v. 325, § 13. Several cahiers ask that the rights and privileges of the old Estates of the *Pays d' Etats* be retained. *N.*, Amont, *A. P.*, i. 764. Officers of government called "vampires." Domfront. *A. P.*, i 724, § 21. See also *T.*, Amiens, *A. P.*, i. 751, § 40. Desjardins, xxxix.

difference in this respect among the Orders, it is that the Nobility are more urgent for the political part of the programme than either the Clergy or the Third Estate. The priests were much occupied with their own affairs. The peasantry were thinking of the hardships they suffered. But all intelligent men felt that social and economic reforms would be unstable unless an adequate political reform were made also. The deputies of the three orders were in many cases instructed not to consider questions of state debt or taxation until the proposed constitution had been adopted.[1]

Having thus fixed the legislative power in the Estates General, and divided the executive and administrative branches of the government between the king with his responsible ministers and the Provincial Estates, the cahiers turned to the judicial function. On the reforms to be here accomplished there was substantial agreement; although the Third Order was most emphatic in its demands, as the expensive and complicated machinery of law weighs more heavily on the poor than on the rich, on the commercial class than on the land-owner. The great influence of lawyers among the Commons at this time was also a cause of the attention given to legal matters in the cahiers of the Third Estate. The common demand was for the simplification of courts and jurisdictions, the abolition of the purchase of judicial place, more uniform laws and customs. The codification of the laws, both civil and criminal, was sometimes called for. It was an usual request that there should be only two degrees in the administration of justice: a simple court in every district of sufficient size to warrant it, and parliaments in reasonable numbers, with final appellate jurisdiction. Commercial courts (*consulats*) were, however, to be retained. The nation was unanimous that the writ of *com-*

[1] *T.*, Briey, *A. P.*, ii. 204. *N.*, Ponthieu, *A. P.*, v. 431. *N.*, Agenois, *A. P.*, i. 680.

mittimus, by which cases could be removed by privileged persons from the regular courts to be tried by exceptional tribunals, or by distant parliaments, should be totally abolished. Justices of the peace, or informal courts with summary processes, were to have the settlement of small cases. The jurisdiction of the lords' bailiffs was to be much abridged or entirely done away.[1]

In the criminal law, changes were recommended in the direction of giving a better chance to accused persons. Trials were to be prompt and public, and counsel were to be allowed. The prisons were to be improved. The Third Estate desired that punishment should be the same for all classes, and that the death penalty should be decapitation, a form of execution which had previously been reserved for the nobility. The thoroughness with which this reform was carried out some years later is very noticeable. The guillotine treated all sorts of men and women alike. It was a common request of the cahiers that the family of a man convicted and punished for crime should not be held to be disgraced, nor the relations of the culprit shut out from preferment. The former request shows a curious ignorance of what can and what cannot be done by legislation. Persons acquitted were to receive damages, either from the accuser, or from the state. Judges were to give reasons for their decisions. Arbitrary imprisonment by *lettre de cachet* was, according to some cahiers, to be suppressed altogether; according to others it was to be regulated, but the practice retained where public policy or family discipline might require it.[2]

---

[1] *T.*, Alençon, *A. P.*, i. 717, § 4. *T.*, Amiens, *A. P.*, i. 747, § 1. This cahier gives a very full statement of existing judicial abuses. Desjardins, xxxv. Poncins, 286. Desjardins (xl.) says that the Nobility tried to save the jurisdiction of the bailiffs, and in some cases persuaded the Third Estate. I do not find the instances.

[2] Domfront, *A. P.*, i. 723, § 6. Amiens, *A. P.*, i. 747, § 7. The

cahiers show that everybody was opposed to the use of *lettres de cachet* as they then existed ; but most of the cahiers that had anything to say about them expressed a desire to keep something of the kind. They are considered necessary for reasons of state, or in the interest of families. Desjardins, 407. The author of the *Histoire du gouvernment de France depuis l'Assemblée des Notables*, a good, sensible, middle-class man, approves of them (260). Mercier (viii. 242) considers them useful and even necessary.

CHAPTER XXII.

SOCIAL AND ECONOMICAL MATTERS IN THE CAHIERS.

As we pass from political and administrative questions to social and economical ones, the difficulty of an amicable arrangement is seen to increase. All agree that property is sacred; but the greater part of the nation is firmly persuaded that privilege must be destroyed; and in a vast number of cases, privilege is property. This difficulty will not stand long in the way of the Commons of France. It is just where privilege has this private character that it is the most odious to some classes of the population. The possession of land is connected with feudal obligations of all sorts; a violent separation must be made between them. The services to be rendered by the tenant to the landlord may be the most important part of the latter's ownership; and by the system of tenure maintained for centuries over the greater part of Christendom, every landholder has been some one's tenant. With the exception of a very few sovereign princes there has been no man in possession of an acre of land who has not rendered therefor, theoretically if not practically, some rent or service. The service might be merely nominal; in the case of noble lands in the eighteenth century, it generally was so; but nominal or real, the right to exact it was some one's property. If such a right did not put money in his purse, it yet added to his dignity and self-satisfaction. But such rights as this had come to be looked on with deep distrust by a large part of the French nation. Ideas of independence and of the abstract rights of man had struck deep root. It was felt that land should be owned absolutely, — by allodial possession, as the phrase is. The feudal services, in fact, were often more onerous to those who paid them than they were beneficial to those who received them. It was time that they should be abolished. Those which were purely honorific, although valued by the nobility, who possessed them, outraged the sense of equality in the nation. They were felt to be badges and marks of the inferiority of the tenant to the landlord, of the poor to the rich. There is but one king, and we cannot all be noble, but let every man hold his farm in peace; such was the impatient cry of the common people. The feudal rights, which are merely honorific, offend man as man; some of them are degrading, some ridiculous. They must be abolished as fast as possible.[1]

Relief from the operation of one set of privileges, neither strictly pecuniary nor entirely honorific, was almost unanimously demanded by the farmers. These were the rights of the nobles concerning the preservation of game, and the cognate right of keeping pigeons. The country-folk speak of doves as "the scourge of laborers," and ask that they may be destroyed, or at least shut up during seed-time and harvest. One gentleman answers with the remonstrance that, being very warm, they are used in medicine, but that sparrows devour every year a bushel of grain apiece, and that each village should be obliged to kill a certain quantity of them. The peasants ask that wild boars and rabbits be alike destroyed. The royal preserves are particularly hated by all the agricultural population living near Paris. Land naturally of the

[1] *T.*, Aix en Provence, *A. P.*, i. 697, § 8. *T.*, Draguignan, *A. P.*, iii. 260. Chérest (ii. 424) points out that the cahiers of the districts (*bailluges*) are more moderate than those of the villages in matters concerning feudal rights, and thinks that this moderation was assumed from politic motives, not to frighten the privileged orders too much at this stage. But it seems improbable that such a piece of policy could have been so widely practiced.

first class is said to be made almost worthless by the abundance of the game. The hare feeds on the tender shoots of the growing grain. The partridge half destroys the wheat. Rabbits and other vermin browse on the vines, fruit-trees, and vegetables. Farmers are not allowed to destroy weeds for fear of disturbing game. Mounted keepers ride all over the fields, trampling down the crops. The king is begged to reduce his preserves, in so far as he can do so without interfering with his own amusement, or even to suppress them altogether.[1]

As for the feudal rights which brought in money to their owners, it was generally felt, at least by the Commons, that they must be redeemable; that the persons liable to pay on their account must be allowed to buy them off by the payment of a certain sum down, where the ownership was true and fair. Here, however, a great trouble seemed likely to arise from an important divergence of ideas. The French nobles believed, as the vast mass of property holders has believed in all ages, that prescription or ancient use was sufficient evidence of property. If it could be shown that a man, or his predecessors in title, had held a certain piece of land or a certain right over the land of another, from time immemorial, or for a very long time, nothing more was needed to establish his property. Unless this theory be admitted, at least to some extent, it would seem that all rights of property must perish. In respect therefore to land in actual possession the French nation held firmly to prescription. But in respect to those more subtle rights in land which had been enormously favored by the feudal system, another theory came

[1] *T.*, Pecqueuse (Paris, *extra muros*), *A. P.*, v. 11, § 36. *T.*, Alençon, *A. P.*, i. 719, ch. viii. § 3. Exmes, *A. P.*, i. 728, §§ 20, 21. Verneuil, *A. P.*, i. 731, § 44. Seigneur de Pierrefitté, *A. P.*, v. 19, § 16. Port au Pecq (Paris, *ex. m.*), *A. P.*, v. 12, § 18. Plaisir (Paris, *ex. m.*) *A. P.* v. 25. Amont-Gray, *A. P.*, i. 780. Périgny en Brie (Paris, *ex. m.*) *A. P.*, v. 14, § 5–11, and many others.

in. Those rights were thought in the eighteenth century to be unnatural in themselves, and therefore abusive. It was believed, moreover, that many of them had been usurped without reason or justice.[1] It was commonly held by the Third Estate that unless an express charter or agreement could be shown establishing such rights, they should be abolished without compensation, and that some of them were so unjust and objectionable that not even an agreement or a charter could sanction them. Such were many feudal payments and monopolies; common bulls, common ovens, rights to labor and to services. Such above all, where it lingered, was serfdom.[2]

When we pass from the property of private persons to that of clerical corporations, whether sole or aggregate, we find the case still stronger. It has been said that the greater number of the cahiers of the clergy were composed under the prevailing influence of the parish priests. These men felt themselves to be wronged in the distribution of church property. They thought it outrageous that the working part of the clergy should receive but a pittance, while useless drones fattened in idleness.[3] Their proposals were radical. They would take from the few who had much and give to the many who had little. The salaries of those who ministered in parishes should be increased, by fixing a minimum, and the money should come out of the pockets of abbots, chapters, and monasteries. Not only are future appointments to be made so

---

[1] *T.*, Béarn, *A. P.*, vi. 500. Rennes, *A. P.*, v. 546.

[2] For the desire to retain feudal rights, see *N.*, Condom, *A. P.*, iii. 38, § 5. *N.*, Dax, *A. P.*, iii. 94, § 21. *N.*, Etain, *A. P.*, ii. 215, § 10. *N.*, Bas Vivarais, *A. P.*, vi. 180, § 19. For the desire to abolish them, *T.*, Avesnes, *A. P.*, ii. 153, §§ 34–40. *T.*, Bar-le-duc, *A. P.*, ii. 200, §§ 49, 50. *T.*, Beaujolais, *A. P.*, ii. 285, § 22. *T.*, Cambrai, *A. P.*, ii. 520, §§ 14–16. *C.*, Clermont en Beauvoisis, *A. P.*, ii. 746. *T.*, Crépy, *A. P.*, iii. 74, § 21. *T.*, Linas, *A. P.*, iv. 649, § 17. *T.*, Ploermel, *A. P.*, v. 379, §§ 14–20 (a very full exposition), and many others.

[3] *C.*, Paroisse de St. Paul, *A. P.*, v. 270, § 11.

as to favor the parish priests, but for their benefit the present incumbents of fat livings are to be dispossessed. The schemes for this purpose were not identical everywhere, but the spirit was the same throughout the popular part of the order.

While the Third Estate agreed with the Clergy in wishing to readjust clerical incomes, an attack was made in some quarters on the payment of the tithe itself. This, however, was not general. The people were willing to pay a reasonable tithe, although some of them would have preferred that the priests should receive salaries, paid from the product of ordinary taxation. Compulsory fees for religious ceremonies, such as weddings and funerals, were very unpopular. It was repeatedly asked that such fees should be abolished, when the incomes of the priests were made sufficient.[1]

Thus the cahiers do not attack the right of property in the abstract; on the contrary, they maintain it. But they shake its foundations by blows aimed at vested rights and at prescription.

The question of taxation is postponed in the cahiers to that of constitutional rights. But financial necessities were the very cause of the existence of the Estates General, the opportunity for all reforms. On the most important principle of taxation the country was almost unanimous. Thenceforth the burdens were to be borne by all. Only here and there did some privileged body contend for old immunities, some chapter put in a claim that the Clergy should still pay only in the form of a voluntary gift. The privileged orders generally relinquish their freedom from taxation. Sometimes they applaud themselves for so doing. The Clergy, in many cases, undertake to bear their share of taxation only on condition that their corporate debt shall be made a part of the debt of the nation.

[1] Poncins, 179. *T.*, Ploermel, *A. P.*, v. 380, § 22. Soissy-sous-Etioles, *A. P.*, v. 121, § 16.

The Third Estate, on the other hand, maintains that it is but fair and right that all citizens shall be taxed alike. Its cahiers demand as a right what those of the higher orders offer as a gift.[1]

As to the method of taxation to be employed there was some approach to agreement. Many of the old taxes were utterly condemned, at least in their old forms. The salt tax was to be equalized, if it were not entirely done away. The monopoly of tobacco, that "article of first necessity," was to receive the same treatment. Many demands were made concerning the excise on wine. "We find it hard to believe," cry the people of the village of Pavaut, "that all this multitude of duties goes into the king's strong-box; we rather believe that it serves to fatten those who are at the head of the excise; and that at the expense of the poor vine-dresser." All the taxes were to be converted as fast as possible into one on land and one on personal property. But the minds of the reformers had not grasped the real difficulties of the subject. They were in that stage of thought in which great questions are answered off-hand because the thinker has not fully apprehended them. Should the personal tax be based on capital or on incomes, and how should these be ascertained? It is far easier to formulate general principles of taxation than to apply them successfully.[2]

A common demand is for the taxation of luxuries, such as servants, carriages, or dogs. The people of Segonzac propose a charge on rouge, "which destroys beauty," and strike at a fashionable folly of the day by suggesting a special payment by those "who allow themselves to wear two watches." This is perhaps not the place to mention the

---

[1] A few cahiers of the Nobility request that a certain part of the property of poor nobles be exempt from taxation. *N.*, Clermont-Ferrand, *A. P.*, ii. 767, § 23. *N.*, Bas Limousin, *A. P.*, iii. 538, § 14.

[2] Salt and tobacco, *T.*, Perche, *A. P.*, v. 327, § 38. Loisail, *A. P.* v. 334, § 7. Wine, Pavaut, *A. P.*, v. 9.

proposal to impose an additional tax on persons of both sexes who are unmarried after "a certain age." The great movement from the country to the cities was already exciting alarm. The people of Albret think that a tax on luxuries will have the double advantage of weighing on the richest and least useful citizens, and of sending the population back to the country from the cities, which will receive just limits. And the people of Domfront speak of Paris as an "awful chasm," in which the wealth, population, and morals of the provinces are swallowed up together.[1]

Theoretical attacks on luxury are common in all ages, and not very significant. Far more so are proposals for progressive taxation. These are of occasional occurrence in the cahiers. The Third Estate of Rennes, whose cahier is considered typical of the more revolutionary aspirations of the times,[1] asks that "the tax on persons shall be established and assessed with reference to their powers, so that he that is twice as well off as the well to do people of his class shall pay three times the tax, and so following." The spirit of this demand is more clear than its application. The town of Bellocq, in the province of Béarn, is more explicit. It would pay the public debt by a special tax, justly assessed, first on farmers general and other collectors of the revenue, who have made fortunes quickly for themselves and their relations, by money drawn from the nation; next on all persons who have an income exceeding two hundred pistoles, whether from lands, contracts, or manufactures; then on the feoffees of tolls, where the amount of the tolls is more than double the rent paid for them; and lastly, if the above do not

---

[1] Taxation of luxuries in general, C., Douai, A. P., iii. 174, § 19. N., Alençon, A. P., i. 715. C., Amiens, A. P., i. 735. T., Aix, A. P., i. 696. T., Langon, A. P., ii. 270, §§ 26, 27, and many others. Bachelors, T., Rennes, A. P., v. 544, § 115. Vicheray, A. P., vi. 24, § 30. Cities, T., Albret, A. P., i. 706, § 38. Domfront, A. P., i. 724, § 14.

suffice, it is proposed to obtain a sum of money by seizing a part of all articles of luxury and superfluity, wherever found; and it is explained that the plate of the rich and the ornaments of churches are especially intended.[1]

The financial scheme outlined in the cahiers is, in the main, as follows. As soon as the constitution shall have been settled, the deputies shall call on the royal ministers for accounts and estimates. The latter shall be furnished in two parts. First shall come those for the necessary, current expenses of the government, including those of the king and his family and court, to be maintained in a style suitable to the splendor of a great monarchy. It shall then be considered what economies can be introduced into every department. Among these economies, the suppression or reduction of extravagant pensions, especially of such as are bestowed for mere favor, and not for service to the state, shall take a prominent place. When the estimates have been duly considered, special appropriations shall be made by the Estates, and ministers shall be held to a strict responsibility in expending them.

Next, concerning the debts of the state, a separate and detailed account shall be rendered to the Estates General. This also shall be scrutinized, the justice of the various claims considered, and means provided for their gradual payment. It is taken for granted that, henceforth, the French nation is usually to live within its income; but if debts are contracted at any time, special provision must be made for the repayment of principal and interest.[2]

Having considered the general matters of constitutional government, law, property, and taxation, we may pass to those questions which more particularly interested one of the great orders of the state, or on which the opinions of one order might be expected to differ from those of another. In general policy the clergy agreed with the

---

[1] *A. P.*, ii. 275, § 42 *n.*
[2] *N.*, Amont, *A. P.*, i. 766. *N.*, Agenois, *A. P.*, i. 682.

nobility and the Third Estate, but in some matters they differed. Yet the differences were greater in degree than in kind. I mean that the clergy, as was natural, had most to say about ecclesiastical, religious, and moral questions, and differed from the nobility and the commons more by the relative prominence which it gave to these, than by the nature of its opinions concerning them.

The Roman Catholic and Apostolic Religion is the religion of the state; and the public worship of no other shall be allowed in France. This was the universal demand of the clergy, and in it the other orders usually acquiesced. As for the granting of civil rights to those who are not Catholic, the clergy is of opinion that quite enough, perhaps too much, has already been done in that direction. Such rights as have already been granted must be limited and defined, and a stop put to the encroachments of heresy. Sometimes the lay orders would go farther in toleration. One cahier of the nobility proposes a military cross for distinguished Protestant officers, another that non-Catholics may be electors, but not elected, to the Estates General. The inhabitants of some of the central provinces would restore the property of exiles for religion's sake to their families. The people of one quarter of Paris would allow the free worship of all religions. Expressions of approval of the recent concession of a civil status to Protestants are not unusual in the cahiers. But the country and all the orders are undoubtedly and overwhelmingly Catholic.[1]

The clergy asks that the observance of Sundays and holidays be enforced. The Third Estate, in some places, thinks that there are too many holidays already. It would

---

[1] For toleration, Bellocq, *A. P.*, ii. 276, § 59. N., Agen, *A. P.*, i. 684, § 14. *T.*, Périgord, *A. P.*, v. 343, § 45. *T.*, Poitou, *A. P.*, v. 414. Vouvant, *A. P.*, v. 427, § 18. T. Paris-Théatins, *A. P.*, v. 316, § 29. *T.*, Montargis, *A. P.*, iv. 23, § 10.

abolish many of them, transferring their religious observances to the Sunday to which they fall nearest.[1]

In regard to the liberty of the press the clergy is at variance with the other orders. It would maintain a stricter censorship than heretofore, and is inclined to attribute all the immorality of the age to the unbridled license of authors. The nobility and the Third Estate, on the other hand, would generally allow the press to be free, but would exact responsibility on the part of authors and printers, one or both of whom should always be required to sign their publications. Thus anonymous libels should no longer be suffered to appear, and bad books generally should bring down punishment on their authors.

The cahiers of the clergy, more, perhaps, than any others, insist on the importance of education; and the ecclesiastics generally wish to control it themselves. Here the commons sometimes go farther than they; asking that all monks and nuns be obliged to give free instruction.[2]

As for the administration of their own order the clergy, under the lead of the parish priests, demand extensive reforms. There must be no more absenteeism; no bishops and abbots drawing large incomes and amusing themselves in Paris or Versailles. There must be no more pluralities, which are contrary to the decrees of the Council of Trent. Promotion must be thrown open to the parochial clergy. Faithful clergymen must be provided for in their old age. Frequent synods and provincial councils must be held. The laity agree with the clergy in calling for these reforms, and would in many cases go a great way in the suppression and consolidation of monasteries.[1]

[1] *T.*, St. Pierre-le-Moutier, *A. P.*, v. 640, §63.   *T.*, Paris-hors-les-murs, *A. P.*, 241, § 2.

[2] *C.*, Aix, *A. P.*, i. 692, § 6.   *C.*, Labourt, iii. *A. P.*, 424, § 27.   Ornans, *A. P.*, iii. 172, § 4.   *T.*, Douai, *A. P.*, iii. 181, §§ 28, 29.

Both clergy and laity are intensely Gallican. They do not wish to pay tribute to Rome, but desire that the church of France shall preserve her privileges and immunities. Dispensations for the marriage of relatives should, they think, be granted by French bishops, and the fees payable therefor should be kept in the country. Annats, or payments to the Pope on the occasion of appointment to French benefices, should be discontinued. An importance far beyond what their amount alone would seem to justify was attached in French minds to these payments to the Holy See. They were repugnant to the national sense of dignity. In some places the idea that the church of France was to govern herself went so far as to threaten orthodoxy. The clergy of the province of Poitou ask for the composition by the French bishops, "who would doubtless think proper to consult the universities," of a body of theology, "divested of all useless questions," which shall be exclusively taught in all seminaries, schools, and monasteries. We have here an instance of that impatience of all complicated and difficult thought, of that simple faith that all questions admit of short and sensible answers, which characterized the eighteenth century. The clergy of Poitou ask also for a great and little catechism, common to all dioceses. "Uniform instruction throughout all the Gallican Church," they say, "would have so many advantages that the bishops will not fail to apply themselves to obtain it. A common breviary and a common liturgy would be equally desirable."[2]

The election of bishops is asked for in several cahiers, and many parishes wish to elect their priests. These requests were not as radical as they may now seem to have been, — at least they did not interfere with the prerogatives of Rome, — for the bishops in France were nominated by the crown, as they still are by the French gov-

[1] Poncins, 190, *A. P.*, *passim*. N., Agenois, *A. P.*, i. 682, § 8.
[2] *A. P.*, v. 391, § 19.

ernment, and the appointment of the priests, then in France as now in England, was often in the hands of lay patrons.[1]

The French nation in general wished to retain its nobility as a distinct part of the state. In but few cahiers do we find so much as a hint of the suppression of the order.[2] The Third Estate would, however, reduce the advantage of the nobility to little more than a distinction and a political weight. The nobles, being in numbers perhaps one hundredth part of the nation, are to be allowed one quarter of the representatives in the Estates General and in the Provincial Estates. They are to have a large share of honors, offices, and emoluments. Their order is to be made more exclusive than it has been. Nobility is no longer to be bought and sold, but shall be accorded only for merit or long service, perhaps only on the nomination of the Provincial Estates. Except in the most democratic cahiers, these concessions are not disputed.

On the other hand, the Commons ask for a share of the chances hitherto reserved for the nobles. The exclusive right held by the upper order, of serving as judges in the higher courts of justice, or as officers in the army, is to disappear. To the latter right the nobles strongly cling. The career of arms, they say, is their natural, their only vocation. In some cases, however, they ask to be allowed to practice other means of earning a livelihood without derogating from their nobility. But they join with the other orders in the cry for reforms in the army.[3]

[1] Poncins, 168.
[2] Poncins, 111. Hippeau, p. x., etc. My own study of the cahiers confirms this opinion. See, however, a long, argumentative article in the cahier of the Third Estate of Rennes, A. P., v. 540, §§ 48–50. See also that of Bellocq, A. P., ii. 276, § 61. T. Aix, A. P., i. 697. Villiers-sur-Marne, A. P., v. 216. Carri, A. P., vi. 280 § 35, etc.
[3] T., Perche, A. P., 326, § 17. N., Agenois, A. P., i. 683, § 14.

The general irritation caused by the new military regulations has been noticed in another chapter. The cahiers unanimously give it voice. The French soldier shall no longer be insulted with blows. The organization of the army shall be amended. It must not be subjected "to the versatility of the spirit of system and to the caprice of ministers." Many are the requests that the soldier be better treated. Not a few, that his necessary leisure be turned to good account by employment in road-building or in other public works.[1] More numerous, perhaps, are those for fairness of promotion. It was in this matter that the poorer nobility was most bitter in its jealousy of the great court families. With but one path for their ambition, the country nobles saw their way blocked by the glittering figures of men no better born than themselves. The wrinkled old soldier, descended from Crusaders, personally distinguished in twenty battles, stood on his wounded legs and presented his halberd as a captain at fifty; while a Noailles, or a Carignan, with no more quarterings and no service at all, perhaps hardly a Frenchman and only twenty years old, but with a duke for an uncle, or a queen's favorite for a sister, pranced on his managed charger at the head of the regiment as its colonel. Nor was this all. The worthy veteran might, on some trifling quarrel, be deprived of the rank he had won with his sweat and his blood, and sent back to his paternal hawk's nest, a broken and disgraced man. The cahiers demand that there shall be no more dismissals without trial; and many of them ask that particular cases of hardship may be rectified. For now the world is to be set right again; commissions and appoint-

---

[1] *N.*, Ponthieu, *A. P.*, v. 434, §§ 40–42. *T.*, Perche, *A.P.*, v. 326, § 19. Soldiers to work on roads, etc., Poncins, 212. Arles, *A. P.*, ii. 61, § 3. *T.*, Bourbonnais, *A. P.*, ii. 449, § vi., 1. *N.*, Chateau-Thierry, *A. P.*, ii. 665, § 56. *T.*, Etampes, *A. P.*, iii. 287, § 12, etc.

ments to the military school are to be fairly distributed; promotion is to be by merit and term of service; and the loyal nobility of France is once more to be the bulwark of an adored king and a grateful nation.

The Commons also have their particular wishes. They desire not only to be rid of feudal oppression, but of administrative regulations. These are sometimes so combined with privileges, or with taxation, that it is not easy to distinguish their cause. The fishermen of Albret, for instance, ask to be allowed to use any kind of boat that may suit their convenience.[1] We can only guess why any one should have interfered with their boats. Was it a corporation of boat-builders having a monopoly that restricted them, or was it only the paternal fussiness of Continental police regulations?

In matters of commerce the national feeling was far from unanimous. Most of the cahiers asked that trade be free within the kingdom; although some of the border provinces, which had enjoyed a comparatively free trade with Germany and had been cut off from France, preferred the maintenance of that state of things,[2] and although the retention of the *octrois*, or custom-houses at the town gates, was sometimes contemplated. Uniformity of weights and measures was also desired; but was sometimes asked for in a half hopeless tone, as if so great a change could hardly be expected. The request was made that all loans with interest be not considered usurious; a request resisted in some cases by the clergy, which clung to the old laws of usury. The abolition of monopolies is generally called for; certain odious restrictions, such as the mark on leather and on iron, are condemned, but rather as taxes than as commercial regulations. On economic questions the nation has no very fixed opinions, nor

---

[1] *A. P.*, i. 706, § 57.

[2] Alsace, Lorraine, and the Three Bishoprics. Poncins, 282. Mathieu, 441. *C.*, Verdun, *A. P.*, vi. 130.

have definite parties been formed. Free trade and free manufactures commend themselves to the ear; but regulations as to quality and protection against English competition may be highly desirable. Agriculture needs more hands, and is the first, the most necessary, the noblest of arts. Furnaces and foundries use wood, and make fuel dear. Trade should be entirely free, — but peddlers are nuisances, and interfere with regular shop-keepers. Manufactures are a source of wealth, — but dangerous unless well managed; none of them should be established without the consent of the Provincial Estates. If only our king and "his august companion" would wear none but French stuffs, and set a fashion that way, our languishing factories would soon be active again.[1]

Certain demands of the cahiers excite surprise by their frequent recurrence. Among them is that for the more severe treatment of bankrupts, who were able in old France to evade the law of the land and even to take sanctuary. Some cahiers go so far as to ask that those convicted of fraud be made habitually to wear a green cap in public, or that they be whipped, or sent to the galleys for life, or even put to death.[2]

All orders ask for the suppression of begging. The demand is commonly accompanied by one looking to some humane provision for the poor, sometimes by a request for a regular poor-law, or even for regulation of wages. The people of the parish of Pecqueuse ask that there be public works always going on, where the poor may earn wages

---

[1] Concerning usury, *T.*, Agenois, *A. P.*, i. 690. *T.*, Comminges, *A. P.*, iii. 27, § 24. St.-Jean-des-Agneaux, *A. P.*, iii. 65, § 4. *C., N.*, and *T.*, Dôle, *A. P.*, iii. 152, § 14; 158, § 57; 165, § xiv. 6. Paris, St. Eustache, *A. P.*, v. 301, § 52. *C.*, Soule, v. 774, § 17, etc. See also *N.*, Agenois, *A. P.*, i. 684, § 7. *T.*, Paris, *A. P.*, v. 285, §§ 3, 4, and *n*.

[2] Poncins, 285. *T.*, Pont-à-Mousson, *A. P.*, ii. 232, § 11. *N.*, Lille, *A. P.*, iii. 531, § 54. *T.*, Lyon, *A. P.*, iii. 613. *T.*, Mantes et Meulan, *A. P.*, iii. 672, § ix. 2. *C.*, Lille, *A. P.*, iii. 524, §§ 35, 37.

calculated on the price of grain; and, what is more significant, the Third Estate of Paris makes a similar request for public work-shops.[1] Yet the universal cry for the suppression of mendicity, and the form in which it was made, show that begging was considered a great evil on its own account, whether mendicant monks or less authorized persons were the beggars. The begging monks, indeed, were either to be abolished, or their maintenance in their own monasteries was to be provided for in the general readjustment of ecclesiastical benefices.

Another common request is that letters in the post-office be not tampered with. All readers who are familiar with the history, and particularly with the diplomatic history of the last century, know how common was the practice of breaking open and taking copies of political correspondence. The letters of Franklin and Silas Deane, and of many less prominent persons, were continually opened in the mail, both in France and in England. Regular ambassadors were driven to the habitual use of bearers of dispatches; and even these might be waylaid and robbed, by the agents of friendly governments disguised as highwaymen.[2] But it is astonishing to find that the evil had gone so far as to excite the fears of private persons for the maintenance of that privacy of which all decent Frenchmen, with their strong feeling of the sanctity of the family and their great dread of ridicule, are peculiarly jealous.[3]

---

[1] *A. P.*, v. 11, §§ 17, 18. *A. P.*, v. 287, § 28.

[2] Ciphers were in common use, and governments employed decipherers. Great skill had been attained in opening letters and closing them again so that they might not appear to have been tampered with. "This institution, if well directed, has the property of serving as a compass to those who hold the reins of government," writes, with a fine jumbling of metaphors, one who has been a clerk in the post-office. Sorel, i. 77. The *Facsimiles of MSS. in European Archives relating to America*, now in process of publication by Stevens, furnish numerous examples of these practices.

[3] *T.*, Agenois, *A. P.*, i. 690.

Again, the frequent recurrence of the request for the restraint of quack doctors is somewhat surprising. The need of competent surgeons and midwives was much felt in the country, and recourse was had to the Estates General to provide them. In calling for legislation to prohibit quackery and to forbid lotteries, the people asked to be protected against themselves, any extravagant theories of the liberty of man to the contrary notwithstanding.[1]

Such were the desires of the French nation in the spring of 1789. In them we may note several important points of agreement. First, government by the nation and the king together. France was still to be a monarchy; not a republic, open or disguised; but it was to be a limited and not an absolute monarchy. In this all the orders were agreed, and the king, by the mere summoning of the Estates General, as well as by his whole attitude, seemed to acquiesce.

Then, the desires of the nation included a diminution of the privileges of the upper orders, not a complete abolition of them. Like all Catholics, Frenchmen wished to leave the control of religious affairs largely in the hands of the clergy. To the nobility, all but a few extremists were willing to concede many privileges, honors, and advantages.

But while retaining a government of limited monarchy and moderate aristocracy, the nation in all its branches had determined that public burdens and public benefits should be more equally divided than they had ever been before. Proportionate equality of taxation, and a chance to rise — these the Commons were determined to have, and the higher orders were ready to concede.

In another feeling all France shared. Churchmen,

---

[1] Quack doctors, *C.*, Nemours, *A. P.*, iv. 108, § 31. Corneilles-en-Parisis, *A. P.*, iv. 463, § 17. *N.*, Troyes, *A. P.*, vi. 79, § 80. *T.*, Chalons-sur-Marne, *A. P.*, ii. 595, § 24.

nobles, and common people alike dreaded and hated the little ring of courtiers. These had grown great on the substance of the nation. They should be restrained hereafter, and obliged as far as possible to surrender their ill-gotten gains.

And all men wanted administrative reforms. The courts of justice, the army, the finances, were to be put in order and improved. Here all agreed as to the end sought, and if there was much difference of opinion as to the methods, parties had not yet formed, nor had feeling run very high on these subjects.

What, then, were the dangers threatening France? They were to be looked for in the very magnitude of the changes proposed, changes which could not fail to startle and alarm all Europe. They were to be seen in the opposition of the nobles, who were ready to give up much, but were asked to give up more. They were to be feared most of all in a monarch so weak and an administration so faulty, that the first attempt at reform was likely to destroy them altogether.

CHAPTER XXIII.

CONCLUSION.

FRANCE had become a despotism in the attempt to escape from mediæval anarchy. What she asked of her kings was security from external enemies, and good government at home. The first of these they had given her. No country in Europe was more respected and feared. In spite of occasional and temporary reverses, her borders had been enlarged from reign to reign, and her fields, for nearly three centuries, had seldom been trodden by foreign armies.

Within the country the house of Capet had been partially successful. It had put down armed opposition, it had taken away the power of the feudal nobility, it had maintained tolerable security against violent crime. But here its zeal had slackened. Civilization was advancing rapidly, and the French internal government was not keeping pace with it.

This better performance of its external than of its internal tasks is almost inevitable in a despotism. To protect his country, and to add to it, is the obvious duty and the natural ambition of a despot. His dignity is concerned; his pride is flattered by success; and whether he has succeeded or failed is obvious to himself and to every one else. To control and improve the internal administration is a hard and ungrateful labor, in which mistakes are sure to occur; and the greatest and truest reform when accomplished will injure and displease some persons. The most beneficent improvements are sometimes those which involve the most labor and bring the least reputation.

Moreover, it is not the people who surround kings that are chiefly benefited by the good administration of a country. Courtiers are likely to be interested in abuses, and in the absence of a free press courtiers are the public of monarchs. If we compare the facilities possessed by Louis XVI. for ascertaining the true condition of his country with those possessed by the sovereigns of our own day, an emperor of Germany or of Austria, or even a Russian Czar, we shall find that the king of France was far worse off than they are. There were no undisputed national accounts or statistics in France. There was no serious periodical press in any country, watching events and collecting facts. There were no newspapers endeavoring at once to direct and to be directed by public opinion. True, the satirists were everywhere, with their epigrams and their songs; but who can form a policy by listening to the jeers of the splenetic?

The absolute monarchy, therefore, while it protected the French nation, was failing to secure to it the reasonable and civilized government to which it felt itself to be entitled. It was failing partly from lack of information, but largely also from lack of will. The kings in the sixteenth and seventeenth centuries had beaten down the power of the nobility and of the Parliaments; the kings of the eighteenth century shrank before the influence of the very bodies which their ancestors had defeated. It is vain to try to eliminate the personal element from history. France would have been a very different country in 1789 from what she was, had Louis XV. and Louis XVI. been strong and able men. The education of a prince is not necessarily enfeebling. Perhaps the commonest vice of despots is willfulness; but the last absolute king of France might have known a far happier fate if he had had a little more of it.

The French government was not aristocratic. There was no class in the country, unless it were the clergy, that was in the habit of exercising important political rights. But the nobility comprised all those men and all those families which were trained to occupy high administrative place. The secretaries of state, the judges of the higher courts, the officers in the army, were noblemen. The order also included a large proportion of the educated men and the possessors of a considerable part of the wealth of the country. It was, therefore, a true power, which might appropriately be considered. Moreover, it was popularly supposed to have political rights, although in fact these were mostly obsolete. Could a good deal of weight have been given, for a time at least, to the nobility, the result would probably have been favorable to the national order and prosperity.

Government, to be stable, should represent the true forces of the state. In a country where all men are of the same race, and where a large portion of the population has some property and some education, numbers should be given weight in government; for the simple reason that, in such a country, many men are stronger than a few, and may choose to use their strength rather than that a few should govern them. What a large majority of the people desires, it can enforce. It is often agreed, in favor of peace and to end controversy, that what a small majority decides shall be taken as decided for all. On this agreement rests the legitimacy of democracy. The compromise is an arbitrary one in itself, but reasonable and sensible; and in a nation that has a good deal of practical good sense, a feeling of loyalty may gather about it. But sensible and practical as it may be, it remains a compromise after all. There is no divine right in one half the voters plus one. Some other proportion may be, and often is agreed on; or some compromise entirely different may be found to be more in accordance with the national will.

In old France the conditions required for democratic

government were but partially fulfilled. The population was fairly homogeneous. Property and education were more or less diffused. But of political experience there was little, and the democratic compromise, to be thoroughly successful, requires a great deal. It was rightly felt that a proper regard was not had to the desires of the more numerous part of the inhabitants of the country; that a few persons had privileges far beyond their public deserts or their true powers; but how was this state of things to be remedied? What new relations were to take the place of the old? No actual compromise had been effected, and the idea of the rights of a majority, with the limitations to which those rights are subject, was not clearly defined in men's minds.

A government should represent the sense of duty of a country. All men believe that something better is imaginable than that which exists, and that the better things would be attainable if only men would act as they ought. Most men strive somewhat to improve their own condition and conduct. Every man believes at least that others should do so. But in making laws men are trying to regulate the conduct of others, and are willing, therefore, that the laws should be a little nearer to their ideals than their own practice is. All sensible men believe that they ought to obey the laws, and that if they suffer for not doing so their suffering is righteous. This opinion is one of the forces in the world that makes for good.

Now what were the qualities considered really moral and desirable by the Frenchmen of 1789, and how far did the government of the Bourbons tend toward them? The duty first recognized by the whole country was patriotism. The love of France has never grown cold in French hearts. It is needless to insist on this, for no one who has ever met a Frenchman worthy of the name, or read a French book of any value, can doubt it. With all its noble and all its petty incidents, patriotism is a French virtue.

Under the kings of France its aspirations were satisfied. The country was great and glorious.

That loyalty was held to be a duty will perhaps be less generally recognized, but I think that enough has been written in this book to show it. The evidence of the cahiers is chiefly on that side. Most Frenchmen believed that a king should govern, and that they had a good and well-meaning king. Toward him their hearts were still warm and their sense of duty alive. He was misled, thwarted, overruled, by selfish and designing courtiers. If he could but have his way all would be well. Only a very few persons had eyes strong enough to see that they were worshiping a stuffed scarecrow. A man inside those clothes could really have led them.

Next among the ideals of France, and far above loyalty in many bosoms, came liberty and equality. They were not very clearly comprehended. By liberty was chiefly meant a share of political power; few Frenchmen believed then, or ever have believed, in letting every man do what seemed good in his eyes. Such a theory of liberty does not take a very strong hold on a race so sociable as theirs; nor does such unbridled liberty seem consistent with civilization to men accustomed to the rigid system of Continental police. Equality of rights was an ideal, but most people in France were not prepared to demand its entire carrying out. Equality of property and of enjoyment many persons, especially such as considered themselves Philosophers, — persons who had read Rousseau or Montesquieu, — considered desirable; but no one of any weight had the most distant intention of trying to bring about such a state of things in the work-a-day world. Communistic schemes were not quite unknown in the eighteenth century, but they belong to the nineteenth.[1]

With the general growth of comfort, with the general

[1] See for eighteenth century communism the curious essay of Morelly.

hope of an improved world, *humanity*, the hatred of seeing others suffer, had begun to bestir itself. For many ages people had believed that another life, and not this one, was really to be considered. Kind-hearted men had tried to draw souls to heaven, stern men to drive them thither. The effort had absorbed the energy and enthusiasm of a great proportion of those persons who were willing to think of anything but their own concerns. But in the eighteenth century heaven was clouded. Men's eyes were fixed on a promised land nearer their own level. This world, which was known by experience to be but too often a vale of tears, was soon, very soon, by the operation of the fashionable philosophy, to be turned into something like a paradise. To bring about so desirable a condition of things, the tears must be stopped at their source. Nor was this all. The world had acquired a new interest. It was capable of improvement. Hope in temporal matters had led to Faith, — Faith in progress and happiness here below. The new direction given to Faith and Hope was followed by Charity. The task of relieving human pain was fairly undertaken. Sickness and insanity were better cared for; torture was abolished, punishment lightened. In these matters the government rather followed than led the popular aspirations. In its general inefficiency, it came halting behind the good intentions of the people.

The virtues toward which the government of old France tried to lead the French nation were not, as we have seen, exactly the virtues toward which the national conscience led. The government upheld loyalty and humanity, and the people agreed with it; the government upheld a centralized despotism and privileges, and the popular conscience called for liberty and equality. In religion there was both agreement and divergence. The country, in spite of Voltaire and the Encyclopædists, believed itself to be fervently Catholic; but its ideal of Catholicism was of a reformed and regenerated type; while that maintained by the government was corrupt and lifeless in high places. The country wanted provincial councils, resident bishops, a purified church.

And in so far as the ideals of the government differed from those of the people, the monarchy did not stand for something nobler and higher than the moral forces that attacked it. The French nation was in fact better than its government, more honest and more generous. The country priests were more self-devoted than the bishops who ruled over them; the poorer nobles were more public-spirited and more moral than the favored nobility of the court; the citizens of the Third Estate conducted their private business more honorably than the administration conducted the business of the country.

If the stability and legitimacy of government depend on its correspondence with the real powers of the nation and with the national conscience, the functions of government embrace something harder to attain even than this agreement. No sovereign power, be it that of an autocrat on his throne or of a nation in its councils, can directly carry out the policy which it desires to adopt. The sovereign must act through agents; and on the proper selection of these the success of his undertakings will largely depend. Jurists must draft the laws, judges must interpret them, officers must enforce obedience. Generals, commanding soldiers, must defend the land. Engineers must construct forts and roads; marine architects must furnish plans for practical ship-builders. Financiers must devise schemes of taxation, to be submitted to the sovereign; collectors of various kinds must levy the taxes on the people. All these should be experts, trained to do their especial work. The choice of experts, then, is one of the most important functions of government.

In this respect the administration of King Louis XVI. and his immediate predecessor was usually, although not uniformly bad. The army and navy, until the last years of disorganization, were reasonably efficient, the naval engineers in particular being the best then at work in the world. The civil and criminal laws were chaotic, more from a defect of legislation than of administration. Old privileges and anomalies were supported by the government, but good jurists and magistrates were produced. Those lawyers can hardly have been incompetent in whose school were trained the framers of the Code Napoleon, the model of modern Europe. Internal order and police were maintained with a thoroughness that was remarkable in an age when the possession of a good horse put the highwayman very nearly on an equality with the officer. The worst experts employed by the government appear to have been those connected with taxation and expenditure, from the Controller of the Finances to the last clerk in the Excise. The schemes of most of them were blundering, their actions were too often dishonest. They never reached the art of keeping accurate accounts.

The condition of the people of France, both in Paris and in the provinces, was far less bad than it is often represented to have been. The foregoing chapters should have given the impression of a great, prosperous, modern country. The face of Europe has changed since 1789 more through the enormous number and variety of mechanical inventions that have marked the nineteenth century than through a corresponding increase in mental or moral growth. While production and wealth have advanced by strides, education has taken a few faltering steps forward. Pecuniary honesty has probably increased, honesty and industry being the virtues especially fostered by commerce and manufactures. Bigotry, the unwillingness to permit in others thought and language unpalatable to ourselves, has become less virulent, but has not disappeared. It is shown alike by the church and by her enemies. Yet the tone of controversy has softened even in France. There are fewer Voltairean sneers, fewer episcopal anathemas. Humanity has been growing; the rich and prosperous becoming more alive to the suffering around them. But it is the material progress that is most striking, after all. The poor are better off than they were a hundred years ago, and the rich also. The minimum required by custom for the decent support of life has risen. The earners of wages are better housed, fed, and clothed in return for fewer hours of labor. In France, as in the world, there are many more things to divide, and things are, on the whole, more evenly divided.

If we compare the France of 1789 no longer with the France of 1892, but with the other countries of Continental Europe as they were in the days preceding the great Revolution, we find that she was worse governed than a few of them. The administration of Prussia while the great King Frederick sat on the throne was probably better than that of France. After his death it rapidly fell off, until a series of defeats had been earned by misgovernment at Berlin. In a few of the smaller states, such as Holland, the Swiss cantons, or Tuscany, the citizen was perhaps better governed than in France. But in general, life and property appear to have been less safe beyond the French border than within it. A small despotism, when it is bad, is more searching and interfering than a large one. The lords of France were tyrannous enough at times, but there were always courts of law and a royal court above them, and appeals for justice, although doubtful, might yet be attempted with a hope of success.

The intellectual leadership of France in Europe was very clearly marked under Louis XV. French was unquestionably the language of the well-born and the witty as it was the favorite language of the learned all over the Continent. The reputation of Voltaire, Diderot, d'Alembert, and Rousseau, was distinctly European. Frederick of Prussia was glad to compose his academy at Berlin of second-rate French men of letters, and to make his own attempts at literary distinction in the French language. Smaller German princes modeled their courts on that of Versailles, and ruined themselves in palaces and gardens that were distant copies of those of that famous suburb. This spirit lasted well down to 1789, although the masterpieces of Lessing were already twenty years old, and those of Goethe and Schiller had begun to appear.

But while France was great, prosperous, and growing, and a model to her neighbors, she was deeply discontented. The condition of other countries was less good than hers, but the minds of the people of those countries had not risen above their condition. France had become conscious that her government did not correspond to her degree of civilization. The fact was emphasized in the national mind by the mediocrity of Louis XV. as a sovereign and by the utter incompetence of his well-meaning successor. In hands so feeble, the smallest excess of expenditure over income was important as a symptom of weakness, and for many years the deficit had in fact been increasing. The financial situation gave the nation a ground of attack against its government; it was not the cause of the Revolution, but its occasion. All the machinery of the state needed to be inspected, repaired, or renewed. The people entered into the task with good will, and the warmest interest. But they were entirely without experience. They knew and believed that old forms were to be respected as far as might be compatible with new conditions; they thought that the improvements needed were so obvious that nothing but fairness was required to recognize them. In their ignorance of the working of popular assemblies they supposed them to be inspired with wisdom and virtue beyond that of the individuals who compose them.

This is a mistake not likely to occur to any one who has experience of public meetings; but among the twelve hundred deputies to the Estates General, and among their constituents all over France, no one had much experience. A hundred and forty Notables, in 1787 and 1788, had deliberated on public questions; but their work had been done principally in committee, and their conclusions were without binding force on anybody, their functions being merely advisory. A good many delegates had been members of provincial assemblies or provincial estates; but these, in most of the provinces, had met but a few times, and their powers had been very limited. Such assemblies could do some good, and were carefully hedged from doing much harm. As training for membership in a body which was to discuss all sorts of questions and possess almost absolute power, experience among the Notables or in the provincial assemblies and estates, although valuable, was insufficient, and comparatively few of the members had even so much. Nor was foreign example of avail. No great scholar had published in French a study of the parliamentary history of England, nor were Frenchmen prepared to profit by English experience. Absolute right, according to his own ideas, was what every man expected to obtain.

A public body, although less wise than the best of its members, has one great advantage over a natural person, and experience has taught the nations that have made self-government successful to profit by this advantage. A public body may be so tied by its own rules that it can act but slowly. Thus the hot desire of to-day may be moderated by the cool reflection of to-morrow. To this end are arranged the three readings of bills and the various other dilatory devices of most parliaments and congresses. But when great constitutional changes are to be attempted, such measures as these are insufficient. Great changes should be introduced one by one, separately debated and fought over. Elections should be repeated during the process; much time should be allowed and many tedious forms observed. Under these circumstances the legislature may be no wiser than a common man, but how often would a common man do anything very foolish if he took several years to think about it?

The French assembly did not and could not take the necessary time and precautions. The country was seething and bubbling. The deputies were honest and patriotic. They were generally men of local reputation who had pushed themselves forward by political agitation and by activity in the elections. It is probable that the proportion of violent men among them was larger than in the nation, for they were chosen in a time of excitement, when violence of thought and language was likely to be popular; yet the assembly comprised also most of the truly distinguished men in France. What was wanting was not natural ability, but experience, calmness, and patience.

It is not the purpose of this book to follow them in their great undertaking. They accomplished for France much that was good; they prepared the way for much that was evil. Enough if the condition of the country before the great Revolution began has been here set down.

INDEX OF EDITIONS CITED.

ALEMBERT, d'. Œuvres. 18 vols. Paris, 1805.
ALLONVILLE, Cte d'. Mémoires secrets de 1770 à 1830. 6 vols. Paris, 1838-45.
AMBERT, La Calotte. Un régiment peu connu. In Moniteur Universel, Nov. 25th to 30th, 1864.
ANCIENNES LOIS FRANÇAISES, Recueil général des. Depuis l'an 420 jusqu'à la révolution de 1789. 30 vols. Paris, 1821-33.
ARCHIVES PARLEMENTAIRES de 1787 à 1860. Recueil complet de débats législatifs et politiques des chambres françaises imprimé par ordre du Sénat et de la Chambre des Députés sous la direction de M. J. Mavidal et de M. E. Laurent. 1^{ière} Série ; tome 1-37, 1787-92. 2de Série ; tome 1-81, 1800-33. 119 vols. Paris, 1862-91.
ARGENSON, Marquis d'. Journal et Mémoires. 9 vols. Paris, 1859-67.

BABEAU, Albert. Les artisans et les domestiques d'autrefois. Paris, 1886.
—— Les Bourgeois d'autrefois. Paris, 1886.
—— L'école de village pendant la révolution. Paris, 1881.
—— Paris en 1789. Paris, 1890.
—— La vie militaire sous l'ancien régime. 2 vols. Paris, 1890.
—— La vie rurale dans l'ancienne France. Paris, 1883.
—— Le village sous l'ancien régime. Paris, 1878.
—— La ville sous l'ancien régime. Paris, 1880.
(BACHAUMONT.) Mémoires secrets pour servir à l'histoire de la république des lettres en France, 1762-88. 33 vols. Londres (Paris) 1784-88.
BACON, Francis. Works. Ed. Spedding, Ellis, and Heath. 7 vols. London, 1857-59.
BAILLY, A. Histoire financière de la France. 2 vols. Paris, 1830.
BARBIER. Chronique de la régence et du règne de Louis XV. (1718-63) ou Journal de. 8 vols. Paris, 1857.
BARRERE, B. Mémoires. Publiés par H. Carnot et E. David (d'Angers). 4 vols. Paris, 1842.
BARTHÉLEMY, Ch. Erreurs et mensonges historiques. 15 vols. Paris, 1863-82.
BASTARD-D'ESTANG, Vicomte de. Les Parlements de France. 2 vols. Paris, 1857.

390 INDEX OF EDITIONS CITED.

BAYLE, *Pierre.* Œuvres diverses. 4 vols. A la Haye, 1725-31.
BEAUMARCHAIS. Œuvres complètes. 6 vols. Paris, 1826.
BECCARIA. An essay on crimes and punishments. London, 1770.
BENGESCO, *Georges.* Voltaire, — Bibliographie de ses Œuvres. 4 vols. Paris, 1882-90.
BERTRAND DE MOLEVILLE, *A. F.* Histoire de la révolution de France, pendant les dernières années du règne de Louis XVI. 14 vols. Paris, 1801-1803.
—— Mémoires particuliers pour servir à l'histoire de la fin du règne de Louis XVI. 2 vols. Paris, 1816.
BESENVAL, *Baron de.* Mémoires. 2 vols. Paris, 1821. In Collection des mémoires rélatifs à la révolution française of MM. Berville et Barrière. Vols. 6 and 7.
BEUGNOT, *Cte Albert.* Mémoires. 2 vols. Paris, 1866.
BLACKSTONE'S COMMENTARIES. 4 vols. Philadelphia, 1803.
BOIS-GUILLEBERT. Le détail de la France, 1695. In Archives curieuses de l'histoire de France depuis Louis XI. jusqu'à Louis XVIII. 27 vols. Paris, 1834-40. Vol. 12.
BRISSOT DE WARVILLE. Mémoires sur les contemporains et la Révolution française. 4 vols. Paris, 1830-32.
BROC, *Vte de.* La France sous l'ancien régime. 2 vols. Paris, 1887-89.
BOITEAU, *Paul.* Etat de la France en 1789. Paris, 1861.
BOS, *Emile.* Les avocats au conseil du roi. Paris, 1881.
(BURKE, *Edmund.*) Observations on a late State of the Nation. London, 1769.

CAMPAN, *Mme.* Mémoires sur la vie privée de Marie Antoinette. 3 vols. Paris, 1822. In Collection des mémoires relatifs à la révolution française of MM. Berville et Barrière. Vols. 10-12.
CARNÉ, *Le Cte Louis.* La monarchie française au dix-huitième siècle. Paris, 1859.
CHABAUD-ARNAULT, *C.* Histoire des flottes maritimes. Paris and Nancy, 1889.
CHARNOCK, *John.* An History of Marine Architecture. 3 vols. London, 1800-2.
CHASSIN, *Ch. L.* Les cahièrs des curés. Paris, 1882.
(CHASTELLUX.) De la félicité publique ou considérations sur le sort des hommes dans les différentes époques de l'histoire. 2 vols. Amsterdam, 1772.
CHATELAIN, *Le docteur.* La folie de J. J. Rousseau. Paris, 1890.
CHEREST, *Aimé.* La chute de l'ancien régime (1787-1789). 3 vols. Paris, 1884-86.
CHEVALIER, *E.* Histoire de la marine française pendant la guerre de l'indépendance américaine. Paris, 1877.
CLAMAGERAN, *J. J.* Histoire de l'impôt en France. 3 vols. Paris, 1867-76.
(COGNEL.) La vie parisienne sous Louis XVI. Paris, 1882.

INDEX OF EDITIONS CITED. 391

COLLIER, *Sir George*. France on the Eve of the Great Revolution. France, Holland, and the Netherlands a Century Ago. London, 1865.
CONDORCET. Œuvres. 12 vols. Paris, 1847–49.
CONSTITUTIONS des Treize Etats-Unis de l'Amérique. A Philadelphie et se trouve à Paris. 1783.
(CONSTITUTIONS.) Recueil des loix constitutives des colonies, anglaises conféderées sous la dénomination d'Etats-Unis de l'Amérique-septentrionale. A Philadelphie, et se vend à Paris, 1778.
COQUEREL, *Athanase, Fils*. Les Forçats pour la foi. Paris, 1866.

DARESTE, *C*. Histoire de France. 8 vols. Paris, 1865–73.
DESJARDINS, *Albert*. Les cahiers des Etats Généraux en 1789 et la législation criminelle. Paris, 1883.
DESMAZE, *Charles*. Les pénalités anciennes. Supplices, prisons et grace en France. Paris, 1866.
DESNOIRESTERRES, *Gustave*. La jeunesse de Voltaire. Paris, 1867.
—— Voltaire au chateau de Circy. Paris, 1868.
—— Voltaire et J. J. Rousseau. Paris, 1874.
DIDEROT. Mémoires, correspondance et ouvrages inédits de 1759 à 1780. 4 vols. Paris, 1830–31.
—— Œuvres. 21 vols. Paris, 1821.
DROZ, *Joseph*. Histoire du règne de Louis XVI. pendant les années ou l'on pouvait prévenir ou diriger la révolution française. 3 vols. Paris, 1860.
DU BOYS, *Albert*. Histoire du droit criminel de la France, depuis le XVI. jusqu'au XIX siècle, comparé avec celui de l'Italie, de l'Allemagne, et de l'Angleterre. 2 vols. Paris, 1874.
DUFORT, *J. N., Cte de Cheverny*. Mémoires sur les règnes de Louis XV. et Louis XVI. et sur la révolution. 2 vols. Paris, 1886.
DUMOURIEZ. La vie du général. 3 vols. Hamburg, 1795.

ENCYCLOPÉDIE ou dictionnaire raisonné des sciences, des arts, et des métiers, par une société de gens de lettres. 35 vols. Paris, 1751–80. See p. 254 n.
ENCYCLOPÉDIE MÉTHODIQUE. 159 vols. and 43 vols. of plates. Paris, 1782–1830.

FELICE, *G. de*. History of the Protestants of France. Translated by Philip Edw. Barnes. London, 1853.
FÉNELON. Œuvres completes. 10 vols. Paris, 1851–52.
FERSEN, *Le Cte de*, et la cour de France. 2 vols. Paris, 1877–78.
FOURNEL, *Victor*. Les rues du vieux Paris. Paris, 1879.
FRANKLIN, *Alfred*. La vie privée d'autrefois. L'hygiène. Paris, 1890.
—— La vie privée d'autrefois. Les soins de toilette. Paris, 1887.
FRANKLIN, *Benjamin*, The complete works of. Edited by John Bigelow. 10 vols. New York and London, 1887–88.
FRÉRON, *Les confessions de*. (1719–1776.) Receuillies et annotés par Ch. Barthélemy. Paris, 1876.

GEFFROY, *G. A.* Gustave III. et le cour de France. 2 vols. Paris, 1867.
GENLIS, C*tesse de.* Dictionnaire critiqué et raisonné des Etiquettes de la Cour. 2 vols. Paris, 1818.
GOMEL, *Charles.* Les causes financières de la révolution française. Les ministères de Turgot et de Necker. Paris, 1892.
GROSSE, *L'Abbé E.* Dictionnaire d'antiphilosophisme, ou réfutation des erreurs du 18ᵉ siècle d'après Nonnotte et Chaudon. Paris, 1856. In Encyclopédie théologique, vol. 18.
(GRENVILLE, *George.*) The Present State of the Nation; particularly with respect to its trade, finances, etc., etc. London, 1769.
GRIMM, DIDEROT, *etc.* Correspondance, littéraire, philosophique, et critique. 16 vols. Paris, 1877–82.

HELVÉTIUS. Œuvres completes. 5 vols. Paris, 1795.
HIPPEAU, *C.* Les élections de 1789 en Normandie. Paris, 1869.
HOBBES, *Thomas.* Leviathan, or the Matter, Forme, & Power of a Commonwealth Ecclesiastical and Civil. London, 1651.
(HOLBACH.) Système de la nature, par M. Mirabaud. 2 vols. Londres (Paris), 1770.
HOOKER, *Richard.* Works. 3 vols. Oxford, 1841.
HORN, *J. E.* L'économie politique avant les Physiocrates. Paris, 1867.
HOWARD, *John.* An Account of the Principal Lazzarettos of Europe. Warrington, 1789.
——— The State of the Prisons in England and Wales; with . . . an account of some foreign prisons and hospitals. Warrington, 1784.

JULLIANY, *Jules.* Essai sur le commerce de Marseille. 3 vols. Marseilles and Paris, 1842.

LA BRUYÈRE. Œuvres. 4 vols. Paris, 1865–78.
LAFAYETTE, *Le général.* Mémoires. 2 vols. Brussels, 1837–39.
LAFAYETTE, Vie de Mᵐᵉ· de, par Mᵐᵉ· de Lasteyrie, sa fille, précédée d'une notice sur la vie de sa mère, Mᵐᵉ· la Duchesse d'Ayeu, 1737–1807. Paris, 1869.
LAFERRIERE. Histoire du droit français. 2 vols. 1838.
LAHARPE, *Jean-François.* Correspondance littéraire addressée à son altesse impériale, Mgr. le Grand-Duc aujourd'hui Empereur de Russie, etc. 4 vols. Paris, 1804.
LAMETH, *Alex.* Histoire de l'assemblée constituante. 2 vols. Paris, 1828–29.
LANFREY, *P.* L'Eglise et les Philosophes au 18 siècle. Paris, 1879.
LAROUSSE, *Pierre.* Grand dictionnaire universel du XIX siècle, 15 and 2 vols. Paris, 1866–90.
LAUZUN, *Duc de.* Mémoires. Paris, 1862. In Barrière, Bibliothèque des mémoires relatifs à l'histoire de France pendant le 18ᵉ siècle. Vol. 25.
LAVERGNE, *Léonce de.* Les assemblées provinciales sous Louis XVI. Paris, 1864.
——— Les économistes français du 18ᵉ siècle. Paris, 1870.

LEA, *Henry C.* Superstition and Force. Philadelphia, 1878.
LEFRANC DE POMPIGNAN, *Jean Georges.* Œuvres complètes. 2 vols. Paris, 1855.
LEMOINE, *Alfred.* Les derniers fermiers généraux 1774, 1793. Paris, 1872. (Published in a small volume with *Clément M. de Silhouette* and Bouret.)
LESTOILE, *Pierre de.* Supplément au régistre-journal du règne de Henri IV. In *Michaud* and *Poujolat,* Nouvelle collection de mémoires relatifs à l'histoire le France. 34 vols. Paris, 1854. Vol. 15.
LEVASSEUR, *E.* Histoire des classes ouvrières en France. 2 vols. Paris, 1859.
LOCKE, *John.* Works. 10 vols. London, 1823.
LOMENIE, *Louis de.* Beaumarchais et son temps. 2 vols. Paris, 1856.
LOWELL, *A. Lawrence.* Essays on Government. Boston and New York, 1889.
LUCAY, *Vicomte de.* Les assemblées provinciales sous Louis XVI. et les divisions administratives de 1789. Paris, 1871.
—— Des origines du pouvoir ministériel en France. — Les secrétaires d'état depuis leur institution jusqu'à la mort de Louis XV. Paris, 1881.

MACHIAVELLI, *Niccolo*, The Historical, Political, and Diplomatic Writings of. Translated by Christian E. Detmold. 4 vols. Boston, 1882.
MARMONTEL. Œuvres posthumes. Mémoires. 4 vols. Paris, 1804.
MARTENS, *Geo. Fréd. de.* Recueil de traités, etc., depuis 1761 jusqu'à présent. 2d ed., 8 vols. Gottingen, 1817-35.
MARTIN, *Henri.* Histoire de France. 16 vols. Paris, 1855-60.
MATHIEU, *L'abbé D.* L'ancien régime dans la province de Lorraine et Barrois. Paris, 1879.
MERCIER, *Louis Sébastien.* Tableau de Paris. 12 vols. Amsterdam (Paris?), 1782-88.
MERCY-ARGENTEAU, *Cte de.* Marie Antoinette. — Correspondance secréte entre Marie-Thérèse et le Cte de M. A., avec les lettres de Marie Thérèse et de Marie Antoinette. Edited by D'Arneth and Geffroy. 3 vols. Paris, 1874.
MIOT DE MELITO, *Cte de.* Mémoires. 3 vols. Paris, 1858.
MIRABEAU, *Marquis de*, L'ami des Hommes, ou Traité de la Population. Paris, 1883.
MONIN, *H.* L'Etat de Paris en 1789. Paris, 1889.
MONITEUR UNIVERSEL du soir. Journal officiel de l'Empire français.
MONTAGU, *Anne-Paule-Dominique de Noailles, Marquise de.* Paris, 1866.
MONTAIGNE, Les Essais. 4 vols. Paris, 1873-75.
MONTBAREY, *Prince de.* Mémoires. 2 vols. Paris, 1826.
MONTESQUIEU. Œuvres complètes. Notes par Edouard Laboulaye. 7 vols. Paris, 1875-79.
MOORE, *John, M. D.* A View of Society and Manners in France, Switzerland, and Germany. 2 vols. London, 1783.
MORELLET, *L'Abbé.* Mémoires inédits. 2 vols. Paris, 1822.

MORELLY. Code de la nature, ou le véritable Esprit des Loix, de tout temps négligé, ou méconnu. Published as by Diderot in vol. ii. of his Works, ed. London (Paris), 1773.

MORLEY, *John*. Diderot and the Encyclopædists. 2 vols. London, 1878.

—— Rousseau. 2 vols. London, 1873.

—— Voltaire. New York, 1872.

MORTON, *Nathaniel*. New England's Memorial. Boston, 1826.

MUIRHEAD, *Lockhart*. Journals of Travels in Parts of the late Austrian Low Countries, France, the Pays de Vaud, and Tuscany, in 1787 and 1789. London, 1803.

(MUSSET-PATHAY.) Histoire de la vie et des ouvrages de J. J. Rousseau. 2 vols. Paris, 1822.

NECKER, *Jacques*. De l'administration des finances de la France. 3 vols. n. p. 1784.

—— Compte rendu au roi au mois de Janvier, 1781. Paris, 1781.

—— Mémoire de M. Necker au roi sur l'établissement des administrations provinciales. n. p. 1785.

NISARD, *Charles*. Les ennemis de Voltaire. Paris, 1853.

(NOTABLES.) Histoire du gouvernement français depuis l'Assemblée des Notables tenue le 22 Février, 1787, jusqu'à la fin de Décembre de la même année; suivie de l'action de l'opinion sur les gouvernemens, à Londres. (Paris), 1789.

NOUVELLE BIOGRAPHIE UNIVERSELLE (*générale*). Edited by *Hoefer*. 46 vols. Paris, 1852-66.

OLIVIER, *Edouard*. La France avant et pendant la Révolution. Paris, 1880.

PALISSOT DE MONTENOY. Les Philosophes: comédie. Paris, 1760.

(PAMPHLETS OF 1788 AND 1789.) Avis au public et principalement au Tiers-Etat, de la part du Commandant du Château des îles de Sainte-Marguerite, et du médecin, et du chirurgien, etc., du même lieu. Du 10 Novembre, 1788. Se vend aux Iles Ste-Marguerite; et se distribue gratis à Paris.

—— Bien-né. Nouvelles et anecdotes. Apologie de la Flatterie. Paris, 1788.

—— Ce qu'on a surement oublié. 1789.

—— Crédo du Tiers-Etat, ou Symbole politico-moral. A l'usage de tous les amis de l'Etat et de l'Humanité. 1789.

—— Diogène aux Etats Généraux. Se vend chez Diogène dans son tonneau.

—— Discours sur les Etats Généraux, par M. de la Boissière, Conseiller, Avocat Général au Parlement du Dauphiné. 1789.

—— Lettre d'un gentilhomme bourguignon à un gentilhomme breton, sur l'attaque du Tiers-Etat, la division de la Noblesse et l'intérêt des Cultivateurs. 1789.

(PAMPHLETS OF 1788 AND 1789.) Lettre d'un paysan; à Messieurs les Censeurs du Caveau, au Palais-Royal. (1789.)

—— Le Magnificat du Tiers-Etat, Tel qu'on doit le chanter le 26 Avril aux premières Vêpres des Etats Généraux. 1789.

—— Le monstre déchiré. Vision prophétique d'un Persan qui ne dort pas toujours. A Ispahan et se trouve à Paris chez les MARCHANDS de vérité. 1789.

—— Pensées détachées à l'usage de la nation française depuis le 1ᵉʳ Mai, 1788.

—— Projet d'alliance matrimoniale entre M. Tiers-Etat et Madame Noblesse. (1789.)

—— Quand le coq chantera, gare aux vieilles poules. L. C. D. S. F. Harangue de Gros-Jean sur les lettres de convocation des Etats Généraux. Prononcée le 9 Mars, 1789.

—— Les quarante voeux principaux de la nation. 1789.

—— Qu'est-ce que le Tiers-Etat, par Emmanuel Sieyès. Paris, 1888.

—— Le Requiem des Fermiers Généraux, ou plan de révolution dans les finances. (Lyon, 29 Mars, 1789.)

—— Le retour de Babouc à Persépolis, ou la suite du monde comme il va. A Concordopolis. 1789.

—— Le Te Deum du Tiers-Etat. Tel qu'il sera chanté à la première messe des Etats Généraux. Le confiteor de la Noblesse Envoyé à Notre Saint-Père le Pape, Suivie de la contrition tardive ; avec des notes tirées du Texte Parisien. 1789.

—— Ultimatum d'un citoyen du Tiers-Etat au mémoire des princes. 1789. Présenté au Roi.

PLATO, The Dialogues of. Translated by B. Jowett, M. A. 5 vols. Oxford, 1875.

PONCINS, *Leon de*. Les cahiers de 1789, ou les vrais principes libéraux. Paris, 1887.

PROUDHOMME. Traité des droits appartenans aux seigneurs sur les biens possédés en roture. Paris, 1781.

QUESNAY, *F*. Œuvres économiques et philosophiques. Frankfort and Paris, 1888.

RAMBAUD, *Alfred*. Histoire de la civilization française. 3 vols. Paris, 1887–88.

RANDALL, *H. S*. Life of Thomas Jefferson. 3 vols. New York, 1858.

REVUE DES DEUX MONDES.

REVUE DES QUESTIONS HISTORIQUES.

RIBBE, *Charles de*. Les familles et la société en France avant la révolution. 2 vols. Tours, 1879.

RIGBY, *Dr*. Letters from France, etc., in 1789. London, 1880.

ROCHAMBEAU. Mémoires militaires, historiques et politiques. 2 vols. Paris, 1809.

ROCQUAIN, *Félix*. L'Esprit révolutionnaire avant la révolution (1715–1789). Paris, 1878.

ROSENTHAL, *Lewis.* America and France. The Influence of the United States on France in the 18th Century. New York, 1882.
ROUSSEAU, *J. J.* Œuvres complètes. 27 vols. Paris, 1824–25.

SADLIER's Catholic Directory, Almanac, and Ordo for 1885. New York.
SAINTE-BEUVE, *C. A.* Causeries du Lundi. 15 vols. Paris, 1851–62.
SALLIER, *Guy-Marie.* Annales françaises depuis le commencement du règne de Louis XVI., jusqu'aux Etats Généraux, 1774 à 1789. Paris, 1813.
SAXE, *Maurice Cte de.* Les rêveries, ou Mémoires sur l'art de la guerre. 2 vols. The Hague, 1756.
SCHERER, *Edmond.* Diderot. Paris, 1880.
SCIOUT, *Ludovic.* Histoire de la constitution civile du clergé, 1790–1801. 4 vols. Paris, 1872–81.
SEGUR, *Cte de.* Mémoires. 2 vols. Paris, 1859. In Barrière, Bibliothèque des Mémoires relatifs à l'histoire de France pendant le 18e siècle. Vols. 19 and 20.
SIEYÈS, *Emmanuel.* Qu'est ce que le Tiers-Etat. Paris, 1888. (See Pamphlets of 1788 and 1789.)
SOREL, *Albert.* L'Europe et la révolution française; 1^{ière} partie. Les moeurs polit. et les traditions. Paris, 1887.
STEVENS, *B. F.* Fac-similes of Manuscripts in European Archives Relating to America, 1773–1783. 12 vols. London, 1889. (Still in course of publication.)
STOURM, *René.* Les finances de l'ancien régime et de la révolution. 2 vols. Paris, 1885.
STUBBS, *William.* Seventeen Lectures on the Study of Mediæval and Modern History, and Kindred Subjects. London, 1886.
SUSANE. Histoire de l'ancienne infanterie française. 9 vols. Paris, 1849–53.
SWINBURNE, *Henry.* The Courts of Europe at the Close of the Last Century. 2 vols. London, 1841.
SYBEL, *Heinrich von.* History of the French Revolution. 4 vols. London, 1867.

TAINE. Les Origines de la France contemporaine: L'ancien régime.
THIERRY, *Augustin.* Essai sur l'histoire de la formation et des progrès du Tiers-Etat. 2 vols. Paris, 1856.
TILLY, *Cte Alexandre de.* Souvenirs. In Bibliothèque des Mémoires relatifs à l'histoire de France pendant le 18e siècle, par M. Fs. Barrière. Vol. 25.
TOCQUEVILLE, *Alexis de.* Œuvres complètes. 9 vols. 1864–66.
TURGOT. Œuvres. 9 vols. Paris, 1808–11.

VAUBAN. Dime royale. Paris, n. d.
VIAN, *Louis.* Histoire de Montesquieu. Paris, 1878.
VOLTAIRE. Collection complette des œuvres. 45 vols. Geneva and

Paris, 1768-96. (One reference only to this edition; all others to Beuchot's edition.)
—— Œuvres, ed. Beuchot. 72 vols. Paris, 1829-40.

WALPOLE, *Horace*. Letters. 9 vols. London, 1866.
WASHINGTON, *George*, The Writings of. Edited by *Jared Sparks*. 12 vols. Boston, 1837.
WRAXALL, *Sir Nathaniel William*. Memoirs, 1772-1784. 5 vols. New York (Scribner), 1884.

YOUNG, *Arthur*. Travels during the Years 1787, 1788, and 1789, undertaken more particularly with a view of ascertaining the Cultivation, Wealth, Resources, and Natural Prosperity of the Kingdom of France. 2 vols. London, 1794. (The only complete edition of this much-quoted book.)

INDEX.

Acquits de comptant, abuse of, 230.
Aguesseau, d', helps to introduce Roman law, 108.
Aides, 224. See *Excise*.
Aiguillon, duke of, disliked by Marie Antoinette, 24; supersedes Choiseul, 91; appoints the Count of Bréhan, 96.
Alembert, d', his version of the story of Montesquieu and Cardinal de Fleury, 136; assists in editing the Encyclopædia, 249; retires from the editorship, 252; his Preliminary Discourse, 259; correspondence with Voltaire, 260; quarrel with Rousseau, 320; more widely read on account of the American war, 332; his reputation was European, 385. See *Encyclopædia*, *Philosophers*.
Alsace, how taxed, 209; prefers to have free trade with Germany rather than with France, 372 and n.
American colonies, approached the French ideal as to equality of condition, 120; adopted Montesquieu's theory of the division of powers, 140; their attachment to it, 150; causes of the aid rendered them by France, 330; and its results, 331. See *United States*.
American Indians, their place in the works of Rousseau, 299.
Annuities, sale of, under Necker, 240.
Anticipations, or floating debt, 230.
Argenson, marquis of, his account of the taille, 216.
Aristocracy. See *Nobility*.
Aristotle, his "Politics" the model for Montesquieu's "Spirit of the Laws," 141, 143.
Army, 83; *Officers* must be noble, 83; higher and lower, 84; military schools, 86; numbers, relation to soldiers, 87. *Privates*, recruiting, 88; nom de guerre, 88; uniforms, 89; food, pay and barracks, 90; general condition, 91. *Reforms*, Choiseul, 91; Saint Germain, 92; the Viscount de Noailles's flogging, 93. *Discipline*, 95; the Count of Bréhan's duels, 96; the Calotte, 98. *Militia*, 100. Reforms demanded by the *cahiers*, 371. See *Militia*, *Navy*.
Arouet, family name of Voltaire, 51; in the quarrel with Chabot, 52. See *Voltaire*.
Artisans, in Paris, 166; in the Provinces, 176, 179. See *Guilds*.
Artois, count of, his speech to the Parliament, 15; carries the petition of the Notables in favor of the Protestants to the King, 45.
Assemblies. See *Clergy*, *Electoral Assemblies*, *Lands of Estates*, *Notables*, *Provincial Assemblies*.
Atheism, how far held by Voltaire, 63; of Holbach, 269; Holbach answered by Voltaire, 270; atheism condemned by Rousseau, 320.
Ayen, duchess of, her family life, 79.

Babeau, M. Albert, iv., 389.
Bachelors, proposed tax on, 365.
Bacon, Francis, an originator of the French philosophic movement, 56; and of the Encyclopædia, 244.
Bailli, the lord's steward, 203; attempt to save his jurisdiction, 357 n.
Bailly, M. V., 379; his estimate of the gross amount of taxation, 207.
Bankrupts, the cahiers call for severity against them, 373.
Bastille under Louis XVI., 117. See *Lettre de cachet*.
Bayle, advocates toleration, 42; a predecessor of the French philosophic movement, 56.
Beaumarchais, his "Marriage of Figaro," the plot and characters, 326; cutting speeches, 327; the King opposes the acting of the piece, 328; but is overcome, 329.
Beaumont, Elie de, Archbishop of Paris, defends the church, 66, 67; condemns Emile, 67.
Beccaria, his book on crime and punishment, 112.
Bees destroyed for fear of the taille, 217.
Begging orders, 34; the cahiers ask for the suppression of begging, 373.
Benedictines, of Saint Claude, demand quarterings for admission, 33; of Saint Maur, devoted to learning, 31.
Bergasse aspires to be a Lycurgus, 333 n.
Berry, Provincial Assemblies established by Necker, 211. See *Provincial Assemblies*.
Boats, regulations concerning them, 372.
Boiteau, M., v., 390.
Books. See *Censorship*.
Bolingbroke, Lord, a friend of Voltaire, 53.
"Boston" as an imprint on French books, 47. Name of a cap, 160.
Boulevards under Louis XVI. 156.
Boufflers, duke of, throws his son over the parapet, 85.
Bréhan, count of, discipline by duels, 96.

Brienne, Loménie de, establishes Provincial assemblies, 212.
Broc, Vicomte de, v., 390.
Broglie, a great family at court, carries on the secret diplomacy of Louis XV., 14; the count disrespectful to Marie Antoinette, 22.
Bureaucracy under Louis XVI., 8.
Bureaux, under the royal councils, 6; exercise great powers, 8.
Burke, Edmund, answers Grenville concerning French taxes, 208 n.

Cahiers, of Provincial Estates, 211.
Cahiers of the Estates General, 342; how drawn up, 343, 347; a cahier of the Third Estate, 345; models, Abbé Sieyès, 346; stormy electoral meetings, general agreement of the cahiers, 348; they are complaints, 349. *Question* of one or three chambers, 350; of the royal power; praise of Louis XVI.; responsible ministers, 351; meetings of the Estates, publicity, 353; Provincial Estates, elective village officers, the dismissal of old officials, political and social reforms, 355; judicial reforms, 356; property and privilege, 359, 362; game, 360; prescription, 361; tithes, taxation, 363; luxuries, 364; progressive taxation, 365; finance, 366. *Questions interesting particular orders*, 366; *the clergy*, religion and holidays, 367; liberty of the press, education, ecclesiastical reforms, 368; Gallican tone, election of bishops and priests, 369. *Nobility* and its privileges, 370; army reforms, 371. *Third Estate*, freedom from regulations, commerce, 372; bankrupts, begging, 373; post office, 374; doctors, 375. *General summary* of the cahiers, 375. See *Electoral Assemblies, Estates General*.
Calonne, dismissed, 17.
Calotte, the, a military society, 98.
Campan, Mme., her account of the queen's toilet, 19; she reads the "Marriage of Figaro" to the king and queen, 328. See *Genet*.
Capitaineries, royal preserves, injuries done by them to agriculture, 194; complaints of the cahiers, 360.
Capitation, or poll tax, 219.
Caroline, Queen, an edition of the "Henriade" dedicated to her, 53.
Carrousel, Place du, under Louis XVI., 155.
Catharine II. of Russia, Diderot taps her knee, 245.
Catholic Church, its constitution and power, 40; identified in men's minds with religion, 41; Voltaire always its enemy, 51; the strength of the church in its saints, 68; attacked in the "Persian Letters," 128; Rousseau considers it incompatible with freedom in the state, 299; its maintenance demanded by the cahiers, 367; France Catholic, 382. See *Clergy, Pope, Protestants, Toleration*.
Cens, a feudal rent, 194.
Censorship of the press, 46; its effect on style, 47; Voltaire's "English Letters,"
54, 60; books condemned by the Parliament, 115; Montesquieu's "Persian Letters," 135; Diderot's "Letter on the Blind," 249; the "Encyclopædia," 250; Helvetius's "de l'Esprit," 251; censorship in the cahiers, 368. See *Malesherbes*.
Chabot, M. de, his quarrel with Voltaire, 52.
Chambers' Cyclopædia a progenitor of the Encyclopædia, 244.
Champart, a feudal rent, 194.
Champs Elysées under Louis XVI., 156.
Chartres, duke of, builds the porticoes of the Palais Royal, and encourages clubs, 332.
Chastellux, Chevalier de, his opinion concerning taxation in France, 208; accompanies Rochambeau to America, his book "Of Public Felicity," material comfort the test of public happiness, 271; the modern ideal of progress, 272.
Châtelet, Mme. du, procures the release of Diderot from Vincennes, 249.
Chaudon, defends the church, 66; his dictionary, 68.
Chérest, M. Aimé, v. 390.
Chinese, the, admired at a distance by Voltaire, 299.
Choiseul, duke of, favored by Marie Antoinette, an able minister, 24; remedies abuses in the army, superseded by d'Aiguillon, 91.
Church of France. See *Catholic Church, Clergy*.
Clergy, numbers and property, 25; tithes; "Clergy of France" and "Foreign Clergy," 26; assemblies; immunities and powers, 27, 37, 40; free gift; demands the suppression of the works of Voltaire; debt, 28; distribution of income; bishops, 29; abbots, 30; convents, 31; noble chapters, 33; secular clergy, parish priests, 35; *décimes*, 36; propositions of 1682, 37; the clergy and the Protestants, 43; condemnation of books, 46; attacks of the Philosophers, 48; Voltaire always an enemy of the church, 51; he attacks the clergy in the "English Letters," 54; Montesquieu in the "Persian Letters," 65, 128; replies of the clergy, 66; the strength of a church is in its saints, 68; quarrel of the clergy with the Parliament, 104; the clergy generally appoints the schoolmaster in towns, 183; supervises him in the country, 204; how represented in Provincial Estates, 210; and in Provincial Assemblies, 211; elections to the Estates General, preponderance of the lower clergy, 343; divided on the question of one or three chambers, 350; the cahiers of the clergy ask for a redistribution of church property, 362; generally agree to equal taxation, 363; maintain Catholic supremacy; Sundays and holidays, 367; oppose liberty of the press, ask for education, ecclesiastical reforms, 368; Gallican tone, election of bishops and priests, 369; usury, 372; the *Third Estate* and tithe, 363; the Third Estate asks for the suppression of men-

dicant orders, 374. See *Catholic Church, Censorship, Protestants, Monks.*
Clothes. See *Costume.*
Clubs in Paris, 332.
Coigny, duke of, his scene with the King, 15.
Collectors of taxes, elected by village communities, their work and their pay, 203, 215. See *Taxes.*
Commerce, external and internal; with England long prohibited, smuggling, treaty of 1786, 225; *octrois*, 226; free trade demanded by the Physiocrats, 233; commerce in the cahiers, 372. See *Octrois.*
Committimus, writ of, 109; the cahiers demand its abolition, 356.
Common lands, large tracts still held in the 18th century, 201.
Commons. See *Third Estate.*
Concordat, the, its provisions, 27.
Condillac amplifies the teachings of Locke, 243.
Condorcet, his criticism of Montesquieu, 152; he contributes to the Encyclopædia, 250; his statement of its purpose, 255.
Confessions in criminal law, 111 n.
Consuls, town officers, 181. See *Syndic.*
Consulats, commercial courts, 356.
Controller General of the Finances, sits in the councils, 6; his contract with the Farmers General, 220; Turgot, 236; his successor, 239. See *Necker.*
Convents, their property and rules, 31. See *Monks.*
Corvée, described, 226; abolished by Turgot, 227, 237. See *Feudal tenures.*
Costume, in Paris, 159; in provincial towns, 177; of peasants, 200; uniforms, 89.
Councils, royal, their composition and functions, 6; legislation by them, 104; Council of Commerce, 6; of Despatches, 6, 8; of Finance, 6; of Parties, or Privy Council, 6; of State, 6, 7; it suppresses the Encyclopædia, 250, 252.
Counsel, in criminal cases in France, 110; in England, 111 n.
Country, the, general description, 186; prosperity slowly increasing, 190. See *Farms, Land, Métayers, Game, Roads, Villages, Feudal tenures, Peasant.*
Court. See *Courtiers, Courts of Law.*
Courtiers, form a ring, 11; composition of the Court, 13; great families, Sunday ladies, 14; offices at court, 16; etiquette, 17; court of Marie Antoinette, 21; ecclesiastical courtiers, 30; *noblesse de cour*, manners and morals, 72; courtier colonels, 84, 371; share of the court and of the Parliament in making laws, 104; luxurious life of the courtiers, 162; the court conspires against Necker, 242; is defied by the Parliament, 330; hated and dreaded by the nation, 376; courtiers interested in abuses, are the public of monarchs, 378.
Courts of Law, 103; Parliaments, 103; lower courts, 108 and n.; comparison of English and Continental systems, corruption, writ of *committimus*, 109; reforms demanded in the cahiers, 356. See *Law, Parliament of Paris.*

Criminal Law. See *Law, Torture.*
Croupiers on the General Farm, 221.

Deane, Silas, his letters opened in the postoffice, 374.
Décimes, 36 and n.
Deficit, under Louis XVI., 238; the occasion, not the cause of the Revolution, 386. See *Finance.*
Democracy, in the 18th century, 1; Montesquieu, on its danger, 139; on its motive principle, which is virtue, 144; on the importance to it of conservatism, 146; the conditions on which democracy rests, and how far they were fulfilled in old France, 379. See *Equality, Liberty, Rousseau.*
Desjardins, M., vi., 391.
Desnoiresterres, M., vi., 391.
Diderot, Denis, ridiculed by Palissot, 67; imprisoned by a *lettre de cachet*, 117; editor of the Encyclopædia, his history and character, 244; anecdotes of a libel and of the *formica leo*, 246; verboseness, the "Letter on the Blind," 247; Diderot a great liar, 248, 274, 282 n.; imprisonment, publication of the Encyclopædia, 249; Diderot interested in external matters, 275; his connection with Rousseau's "First Discourse," 281; with his "Second Discourse," 286 n.; quarrel with Rousseau, 320; his reputation was European, 385. See *Encyclopædia.*
Director General of the Finances. See *Necker.*
Dixième, equal to two *vingtièmes*, 218 n.
Doctors, surgeons in Paris better taught than physicians, 168; of Marseilles in morocco and masks, 183; the cahiers ask for the suppression of quacks, 375. See *Hospitals.*
Dogs, petition in a cahier that they be not obliged to carry weights, 346; proposed tax on them, 364.
Dol, bishop of, warns Louis XVI. not to grant a civil status to Protestants, 45.
Domat, influential in introducing Roman Law, 108.
Don gratuit, or tax of the clergy, 28.
Du Marsais, the grammarian, gets into trouble, 170.
Dupont de Nemours in danger of being thrown out of a window, 348.
Duties. See *Commerce, Taxes.*

Echevins, town officers, 181. See *Syndic.*
Edit de la Paulette, 231.
Education of middle class better than of nobles, 184; Rousseau in the "First Discourse," 284; in "Emile," 307; the clergy in the cahiers, 368. See *Schoolmasters, Schools.*
Election, a district, 10. See *Lands of Election.*
Electoral Assemblies, for the Estates General, of the clergy, 343; of the nobility and of the Third Estate, 344; an assembly captured, 347; stormy, 348. See *Cahiers, Estates General.*
Encyclopædia, the, its origin, 244; Diderot, 244; d'Alembert, 249; other contributors; vicissitudes of publication, 250;

402   INDEX.

bibliographical note, 254 n.; nature of the book, 254, 258; anecdote of Louis XV., 255; philosophy, 259; uneven execution, 260; Rousseau's article on Political Economy, 292. See *Alembert, Diderot, Jaucourt, Montesquieu, Voltaire, Turgot, Haller, Condorcet. Helvetius.*
Encyclopédie méthodique, its didactic tendency, 323 n.
England, the most free country, according to Montesquieu, 137; one of his models for a monarchy, and for a republic, 145 and n.; adoption of English forms of government in the 19th century, 150; commerce with France prohibited; treaty of 1786, 225; war with American colonies, 330; English ideas in France in 18th century, 332; constitution attacked by Rousseau, 296; and by Sieyès, 338.
Enquêtes, cour des, a department of the Parliament, 103 n.
Equality, of many kinds, 120; equality and liberty naturally opposed to each other, 125; difference of equality in England and Holland, according to Montesquieu, 137; Rousseau on inequality, 285; equality, how desired in France, 381. See *Liberty.*
Espréménil, d', protests against granting civil status to Protestants, 46; member of a club, 333 n.
Estaing, count of, no sailor, 101.
Estates. See *Lands of Estates.*
Estates General, question of one or three chambers, in the pamphlets, 334, 337; in the cahiers, 350; in 1789, a constitutional convention, 342; composition and elections, 343; what they were to be and to do, 349; meetings, publicity, 353; influenced by their galleries, 354; to make special appropriations, 366; want of experience of the members, their qualifications and difficulties, 387. See *Cahiers, Electoral Assemblies.*
Etiquette, its uses, 17; that of the French court antiquated, 18; Marie Antoinette, her chemise, 19; her attempts to evade etiquette, 20, 22.
Excise on wine and cider, 224; in the cahiers, 364. See *Taxes.*

Family, the tie close in France, but loosening, 76; among the country nobles, 82; command of a company almost hereditary, 87; judicial place inherited, 105; request of the cahiers that the family of a criminal be not disgraced, 357. See *Marriage, Married women, Morals.*
Farmers General, their financial operations, 220; their social position, 221. See *Financiers.*
Farms, small, large, and of moderate size, 191. See *Country, Land, Métayers, Villages, Feudal tenures, Peasant.*
Fatalism of the Philosophers, 49; of Holbach, 268. See *Philosophers.*
Fénelon advocates toleration, 42, 43.
Feudal tenures, described, 194; their origin, 196; in the cahiers, 359. See *Cens, Champart, Lods et ventes.*
Finance, anticipations, or floating debt, acquits de comptant, 230; sale of public offices, Paulette, 231; the Physiocrats, Quesnay, 233; Gournay, 234; Turgot, 235; the deficit, 238; Necker, 239; lotteries and annuities, 240; compte rendu, 241; finance in the cahiers, 366; finance the occasion, not the cause, of the Revolution, 386. See *Commerce, Taxes, Necker, Turgot.*
Financiers, regarded with jealousy, 164. See *Farmers General.*
Flanders, how taxed, 209; anomalous position of Walloon de Flanders, 210 n.
Fleury, Cardinal, and Montesquieu's election to the Academy, 135.
Flogging in the army, 92; anecdote, 93; in the navy, 102.
Food, of soldiers, 90; sailors, 102; in Paris, 162; of journeymen in provincial towns, 179; of peasants, 200.
Foundlings in Paris, 169. See *Hospitals.*
Francis I., King of France, makes the Concordat, 27.
Franklin, Benjamin, his letters opened in the mail, 374.
Frederick the Great, as a commander, 86; one half his soldiers are foreigners, 90; composes his Academy of Frenchmen, 386.
Free-trade. See *Commerce, Smuggling.*
French Guards, regiment of, loses its discipline, 100.
Fréron, defends the church, 66.
Friendship, close among the nobility, 74.
Furniture, in noblemen's country houses, 193; in peasants' cottages, 199.

Gabelle, or salt-tax, 222.
Galleys at Toulon, last prisoner for Protestantism released, 43; condition of the galleys, 110.
Gallican Church. See *Catholic Church, Clergy.*
Game, the French idea of sport, 78; abundance of game, 193; hated by the peasants, 194; complaints of the cahiers, 360.
Gay, associates with Voltaire, 53.
Garrison, to collect the poll-tax, 219.
Généralité, a district, 8, 208. See *Lands of Election.*
Genet, Mlle., snubbed by Louis XV., 76. See *Mme. Campan.*
Geneva, books printed there for the French market, 46; an article on Geneva in the Encyclopædia makes trouble, 254 n.; the model for Rousseau's Social Compact, 299 n.
Gomel, M. Charles, v., 392.
Gournay, de, and his doctrines, 234.
Governor of a province, 10.
Grand' Chambre, a department of the Parliament, 103 n.
Grenville, George, his comparison of taxation in France and in England, 208.
Grimm, tells the story of Diderot and Le Breton, 252; quarrel with Rousseau, 320.
Grotius, a predecessor of the French Philosophic movement, 56.
Guémenée, Princess of, her house called a gambling hell, 22.
Guibert, count of, hated in the army, 100.

INDEX.   403

Guilds, described, 179; abolished by Turgot, 237; reëstablished, 237 n.

Haller, contributes to the Encyclopædia, 250.
Haute Guyenne, Provincial Assemblies established by Necker, 211.
Hedonism, a doctrine of the Philosophers, 49. See *Utility, Philosophers.*
Helvetius, his book "de l'Esprit," compromises the Encyclopædists, 251; character of the man and of the book, the doctrine of utility, 261. See *Utility.*
Henry IV. the model of Louis XVI., 12.
Hobbes, influences the French Philosophic movement, 56.
Holbach, Baron, his character, 263; the "System of Nature," materialism, 264; government, 265; happiness, 267; religion a delusion, utility, fatalism, 268; atheism, 269; alarm of the Philosophers, the answer to Holbach, 270.
Holidays, frequent, 179, 205; in the cahiers, 367.
Holland, books printed there for the French market, 46; torture obsolete, 113; compared with England by Montesquieu, 137; and with France, 385.
Hooker, Richard, influences the French Philosophers, 56.
Horn, M., v., 392.
Hospitals, in Paris, 168; in provincial towns, 182. See *Doctors.*
Houses, in Paris, 157; in provincial towns, 176; in the country, of nobles, 192; of peasants, 199.
Howard, John, story of tortured men sweating blood, 111 n.; his book on the "State of the Prisons," 112; he considers the Hôtel Dieu a disgrace to Paris, 168.
Humanity, an ideal in France, 382; its growth since 1789, 385. See *Hospitals, Beccaria, Howard.*

Indians. See *American Indians.*
Inequality, Rousseau's discourse on, 285; Voltaire's answer, 291. See *Equality, Philosophers.*
Intendants, their functions, 8; *maîtres des requêtes* and members of the Privy Council, 9; supervision of Provincial Assemblies, 211.
Itch, common early in the 18th century, disappears, 182.

Jansenist quarrel, 38; its effect on the church, 68; its nature, 104.
Jaucourt, Chev. de, assists in editing the Encyclopædia, 250.
Jefferson, Thomas, his opinion of Paris, 157.
Jesuits, their quarrel with the Jansenists, 38; its nature, 104; they try to continue the Encyclopædia, 251.
Journeymen. See *Artisans.*

King, the, his powers, 4; he sits in the councils, 5; the fountain of justice, 7; his powers in the cahiers, 349, 351; to be maintained in suitable splendor, 366; successes and failures of the kings of France, 377; their inability to get information, 378. See *Louis X., Francis I., Louis XIV., Louis XV., Louis XVI.*
Knights of Malta, 33.

La Barre, his crime and punishment, 114.
La Bruyère, description of the French peasant, 186; comment on it, 187.
Lafayette, marquis of, connected with the family of Noailles, 14; would begin history with 1787, 119; hopeful tone of his letters, 323 n.; member of a club, 333 n.
Lamballe, faction rapacious, 17.
Land, how divided, 191; price, rent and product, according to A. Young, 192 n. See *Farms, Métayers, Villages, Peasant.*
Lands of Election, what they were and how taxed, 208.
Lands of Estates, what they were and how taxed, 209; Estates, 210. See *Provincial Estates.*
La Trappe, account of the monastery, 34.
Lauzun, duke of, fond of adventure, 85; speaks respectfully of American women, 332.
Laval, viscount of, manages the election at Chaumont, 346.
Lavergne, M. Léonce de, v., vi. 392.
Law, method of passing a law, 104; variety of laws and jurisdictions, 107, 384; the civil and the customary law, 107; comparison of Continental and Anglo-Saxon systems, 109; criminal law, torture, death penalty, the wheel, 111; Beccaria, 112; reforms, 113; *lettres de cachet,* police, 116; reforms demanded by the cahiers, 356. See *Lawyers, Parliament of Paris, Parliaments, Torture.*
Lawyers, in Paris, 173; not incompetent, 384. See *Law, Parliament of Paris.*
Le Breton, the publisher, engages Diderot to edit the Encyclopædia, 244; his trick, 252. See *Encyclopædia.*
Lecouvreur, Mlle., present at the quarrel between Voltaire and Chabot, 52.
Lefranc de Pompignan, pastoral letter on toleration, 44; a defender of the church, 66.
Legislator, the, 124; in the Encyclopædia, 259; aspirations of Bergasse, 333 n.
Leprosy, disappeared from France, 183.
Letters, the cahiers ask that they be not opened in the mail, 374.
Lettres de cachet, described, 116, in the cahiers, 357.
Leo X., pope, makes the Concordat, 27.
Liberty, not a simple idea, political rights, 122; absence of interference, 123; liberty and equality naturally opposed to each other, 125; Montesquieu on liberty in England, 137; his definition, 148; Rousseau, the Social Compact, 294; liberty of agriculture and of commerce, 233; of the press in the cahiers, 363; how desired, 381. See *Equality, Inequality, Free-trade, Physiocrats, Censorship.*
Licentiousness, in Paris, 72, 79; regarded by the Philosophers as an artificial wrong, 130. See *Morals.*
Locke, John, advocates toleration, 42, 43; the fountain-head of the French Philo-

sophic movement, 56; his doctrines, 57; Voltaire on Locke, 60; authority of Locke's teachings in France, 243; the Encyclopædia, 259; views his own mind objectively, 275.
Lods et ventes, a feudal due, 195.
Loménie, M. de, vi., 393.
Lorraine, said to have lost prosperity, 191; how taxed, 209; prefers to have free trade with Germany rather than with France, 372.
Lotteries, how drawn in Paris, 173; state lotteries, how managed, 240; cahiers ask for the suppression of lotteries, 375.
Louis X., sells public offices, 231.
Louis XIV., his absolute power, 40; law for compulsory education, 183; poverty of France in his latter years, 190; sale of offices, 232.
Louis XV., led by his mistresses, 13; his secret diplomacy, 14; rudeness to Mlle. Genet, 76; refuses to commute La Barre's sentence, 114; statue, 156; kneels to a religious procession, 172; recuperation of France under his reign, 190; anecdote concerning him and the Encyclopædia, 255; effects of his mediocrity, 386.
Louis XVI., his accession, position, 4; character, 12; mumbles the coronation oath, 44; an awkward man, 76; place of his execution, 156; distrust of Necker, 165; promises Turgot not to issue *acquits de comptant*, 231; weakness in dealing with the deficit, 238, 242; public opinion, 324; attempt to suppress the "Marriage of Figaro," 328; dragged into the American war, 331; attacked in a pamphlet, 335; fails to arrange the composition of the Estates General, 350; praised in the cahiers, 351; threatened in a cahier, 351 n.; requested to wear French stuffs, 373; his want of opportunity of knowing the true condition of France, 378; effects of his incompetence, 386.
Louvre, under Louis XVI., 155.
Lucay, comte de, vi., 393.
Luxembourg, palace and garden, 155.
Luxuries, of the rich in Paris, 162; cahiers demand the taxation of luxuries, 364.

Macchiavelli, comparison of his "Discourses" with Montesquieu's "Greatness of the Romans," 138.
Macaulay, Lord, quoted ("liars by a double right"), 144.
Madame. See *Provence, Countess of*.
Maîtres des requêtes, sit in the Privy Council, 6; the intendants chosen among them, 9.
Malesherbes, does not remain long in office, 17; opposed by Marie Antoinette, 24; conduct as censor, 47; dismissed from the council, 17, 238.
Mansfield, Lord, enlarges the common law of England, 108.
Manufactures. See *Guilds*.
Maria Theresa, Empress, fears too much simplicity, 16; never treated without respect, 22.
Marie Antoinette, the Polignacs her favorites, injured by a Rohan, 14; her first baby and its attendants, 16, 19 n.; etiquette, 17; her chemise, 19; her character and influence, 20; place of her execution, 156; hears the "Marriage of Figaro," 328; requested to wear French stuffs, 373. See *Louis XVI., Etiquette*.
Marriage, of country nobles, 82; in Paris, 165; in provincial towns, 178. See *Family, Married women, Morals*.
Married women, their business education, 165, 182. See *Marriage*.
Materialism, a doctrine of the Philosophic school, 49; Locke inclines to it, 59; Voltaire, 63; Holbach, 264. See *Philosophers*.
Marmontel at school, 184.
Marseilles, doctors with masks, 183.
Maurepas, his selfishness, his influence, 17; advises Louis XVI. not to change the coronation oath, 44; quarrel with Necker, 241; mentions the "Marriage of Figaro," 328.
Maurice de Saxe, commands at Raucoux, 85; as a commander, 86.
Medicine. See *Doctors, Hospitals*.
Memoires de Trévoux, defend the church, 66.
Métayers, farmers, 70, 192.
Military schools described, 86.
Militia, numbers, composition, and term of service, 100; drawing for the militia, 201. See *Army*.
Ministers, their seats in the council, 6; the cahiers demand that they be responsible; what this means, 351.
Mirabaud, secretary of the Academy, his name assumed by Holbach, 262 n.
Mirabeau the elder, kneels before his mother, 82; his opinion of peasant life, 187.
Mirabeau the younger, confined by a *lettre de cachet*, 117.
Molinist. See *Jesuit*.
Monarchy. See *King*.
Monks, their property and rules, 31; policy of allowing them, 32; hated by Voltaire and the Philosophers, 32, 62, 263.
Montaigne, a predecessor of the French Philosophic movement, 56; opposes torture, 112.
Montesquieu, on toleration, 41; may rival Voltaire in influence, 51; remarks on condition of the clergy, 65; opposed to torture, 112; failed to grasp the continuity of history, approves of equality of condition, 120; the work of Montesquieu, his character, 126; the "*Persian Letters*," 65, 127; the church, 128; licentiousness, 130; the monarchy, 132; republics, 133; sacredness of laws; large assemblies, 134; origin of society; Montesquieu and the Academy, 135; in England, 136; liberty and equality in England, Holland, and Venice, 137; the "*Greatness and Decadence of the Romans;*" Montesquieu compared with Macchiavelli, 138; danger to republics; danger of change, 139; the division of powers, 140, 148; the *Spirit of the Laws*, 141; relation of laws to circumstances, 142; Montesquieu sometimes misled by ignorance of foreign customs; the nature

and principle of government, 144; liberty and the division of powers, 148; religion, 151; moderation, uniformity, criticism by Condorcet, 152; difference between Montesquieu and the Philosophers, 153; Montesquieu defends the sale of offices, 232 n.; contributes to the Encyclopædia, 250; more widely read, 332. See *American Colonies, England, United States, Venice.*

Morals, of Louis XVI., 12; of Marie Antoinette, 22; of the bishops and clergy, 30; of French and English priests, according to Voltaire, 54; of the nobility, 72, 79, 81; independence and honesty of judges, 106; sexual morals considered conventional, 130; relation of laws to morals, according to Montesquieu, 142; morals of the middle classes, 166; in the Encyclopædia, 255; reduced to utility, by Helvetius, 262; dependent on government, Holbach, 266; spoiled by civilization, Rousseau, 282; American morals admired, 332; the clergy in the cahiers, 367; the government and the country on moral questions, 380. See *Humanity, Licentiousness.*

Morley, Rt. Hon. John, his books on the French Philosophers, v., 394.

National Assembly, proposed by Sieyès, 340; fate of the constitution made by it, 354; inexperience of its members, 387. See *Estates General.*

Navy, its composition, officers, 101; naval architects excellent, 101, 384; men, flogging, administration, 102.

Necker, does not remain long in office, 17; opposed by Marie Antoinette, 24; a Protestant but important, 44; popularity, 165; estimate of taxation, 207, 227; comparison of taxes in France and England, 208; his Provincial Assemblies, 211; his book on the Administration of the Finances, 212; story about bees, 217; contract with the Farmers General, 221; figures concerning taxation, 227; Director General of the Finances, character and financial devices, 239; *compte rendu*, 241; fall, 242; fails to determine the composition of the Estates General, 350; blessed in the cahiers, 351 n.

Newton, Sir Isaac, influences the French Philosophic movement, 56.

Noailles, a great family at court, 14; *viscount of,* fond of adventure, 85; insists on being flogged, 93.

Nobility, bishops generally noblemen, 29; numbers and property of the nobles, 70; privileges and distinctions; nobility easily acquired; of the sword and of the gown, 71, of the court, manners, 72, 76; friendship, 74; leisure, 78; vice and virtue, 79; country nobles, 81; a military class, 83; of the gown, 103; the nobility hated chiefly on account of its privileges, 119; luxurious life, 162; how represented in Provincial Estates, 210; and in Provincial Assemblies, 211; exemption from taxation, 213, 228; the nobility and the middle class approach each other socially; influence of the Philosophers, 322; nobility

attacked by Sieyès, 336; the feeling not shared by the bulk of the nation, 340; elections to the Estates General, predominance of the poorer nobility, 344; *in the cahiers,* question of one or three chambers, 350; the nobility urgent for political reforms, 356; respective attitude of the nobility and the Third Estate, 370; army reform, 371; the nobility not a governing class, but contains most men trained to govern, 378. See *Army, Parliament of Paris.*

Nom de guerre of private soldiers, 88.

Nonnotte, a defender of the church, 66; his dictionary, 68.

Normandy, rich peasants, 201.

Notables, petition the King about Protestants, 45; establish Provincial Assemblies, 212; Sieyès considers them useless, 338; their work merely advisory, 387.

Octrois, their operation, 226; in the cahiers, 372.

Offices, at court, 16; judicial, 105; municipal, 181; rural, 202; sale of offices, 231.

Officers. See *Army.*

Orders, three in France, 25. See *Clergy, Nobility, Third Estate.*

Orleans, duke of, election at Chaumont, 346.

Orleans, duchess of, and the Queen's chemise, 20.

Osmont, count of, his peculiar manners, 77.

Palais Royal, a centre of gossip, 173; the porticoes and shops built, 332.

Palissot, his comedy, "The Philosophers," 67.

Pamphlets, enormous number, 333; subjects and titles, 334, 394; Sieyès's "What is the Third Estate," 336.

Paris, importance, size, and growth, 154; buildings and streets, 155; dress, 159; food, 162; classes of population, 164; marriage and married women, 165; police, 167; hospitals and doctors, 168; foundlings, religious processions, 169; Sundays, 171; the viaticum, a day in Paris, 172; public opinion, love of excitement, 325; an "awful chasm," 365.

Paris-Duverney, founds the military school, 86.

Parlement Maupeou, its unpopularity, 5; under Louis XV., 104.

Parliament of Paris, trouble under Louis XV., restored by Louis XVI., 5; refuses to interfere in behalf of Protestants, 44; condemns Voltaire's "English Letters," 54; composition, origin, political powers, 103; legislation, remonstrance, bed of justice, struggle with the church, 104; struggle for privileges, venal offices, 105; love of applause, 106; administration of justice, Roman and Feudal law, 107; condemnation of books, 115; the Encyclopædia, 250, 252; Helvetius's "de l'Esprit," 251; worship of opinion, 324; popular because it opposes the court, 329.

Parliaments browbeaten by Louis XIV. and dissolved by Louis XV., 4; new courts in their place, 104; judges, 105.

See *Courts of Law, Law, Parliament of Paris, Censorship.*
Patriotism a French virtue, 380.
Paulet, the edict named after him, 231.
Pays d'Election, described, 209.
Pays d'Etats, 209.
Peasant, La Bruyère's description, 186; Dr. Rigby, 187; A. Young and others, 189; mode of life, 199; political rights, 201; chance in life, 204; amusements, 205; comparative condition, 206. See *Country, Farms, Land, Métayers, Game, Roads, Villages, Feudal tenures.*
Peers of France sit in Parliament of Paris, 103.
Pensions excessive, 238; in the cahiers, 366.
"Philadelphia" as an imprint for French books, 47; name of a cap, 160.
Philosophers of the 18th century, propose to reconstitute society, 1; ambiguity of the word "Philosopher," 48; the Philosophers form a sect, 49; their masters, 56; their ideals, 119; secured equality for Frenchmen, 122; in the Encyclopædia, 259; alarmed by Holbach, 270; difference between them and Rousseau, 274, 320; struggle for simplicity, 276; their hold on the public mind, 322. See *Voltaire, Montesquieu, Rousseau, Diderot, Alembert, Helvetius, Holbach, Chastellux, Turgot, Jaucourt, Haller, Condorcet, Condillac, Sieyès, Beaumarchais, Quesnay, Gournay, Hooker, Bacon, Hobbes, Newton, Locke, Descartes, Bayle, Grotius, Howard, Beccaria, Atheism, Fatalism, Democracy, Equality, Hedonism, Humanity, Legislator, Liberty, Materialism, Toleration, Utility, Encyclopædia, Physiocrats, Clergy, Catholic Church, Monks, Censorship, Lefranc de Pompignan, Beaumont, Chaudon, Nonnotte, Fréron, Trublet, Palissot, Mémoires de Trévoux, Malesherbes.*
Physiocrats, their doctrines, 233. See *Quesnay, Gournay.*
Place de la Concorde, or Place Louis XV., execution of the King and Queen there, 156.
Plague, the, and precautions, 183.
Police, its nature, 116; in Paris, 167; in France, 384.
Polignac, family dependent on the favor of Marie Antoinette, 14; rapacious, 17.
Political Economy, its origin, 234; Rousseau in the Encyclopædia, 292.
Poll tax (*capitation*) described, 219.
Pompadour, Mme. de, anecdote concerning her and the Encyclopædia, 255.
Poncins, M. de, vi., 395.
Pope, the, Leo X. makes the Concordat, 27; election of the pope, 40; sneers of Montesquieu, 128, 132.
Pope, Alexander, associates with Voltaire, 53.
Post-office, the cahiers ask that letters be not opened, 374.
Pothier, introduces Roman law, 108.
Prescription, as a ground of property, 361.
Prime minister, the, sits in the councils, 6.
Princes as generals, 86.

Princesses of the Royal Family and of the Blood, distinction, 19.
Prisons, filthy, the galleys, 110.
Privileges, of the Church of France, 27; Gallican liberties, 37; privileges of the nobility, 71; of the magistrates, efforts of the Parliament of Paris in behalf of privileges, 105; of persons and bodies in the Third Estate, 154; of municipal officers, 181; of persons and places concerning taxation, 208; privileges attacked by Sieyès, 336; some of the nobles ready to vote with the other orders as one chamber on questions which do not concern privileges, 350; privilege and property in the cahiers, 359; readiness to abandon privileges concerning taxation, 363; other privileges, 370. See *Clergy, Nobility, Feudal tenures, Equality.*
Privy council, 6.
Processions in Paris, 169.
Progress, material, asserted by Chastellux, 272; more noticeable than moral progress since 1789, 385.
Progressive taxation. See *Taxes.*
Property, how regarded in the cahiers, 359.
Protestants, their precarious condition, their intolerance, 41; gradual adoption of toleration, 42; persecuted, 43; measures proposed in their favor, 44; civil status granted them, 46; law to bring their children under Catholic teaching, 183; in the cahiers, 367. See *Toleration.*
Provence, Countess of, and the queen's chemise, 20.
Provincial Assemblies, established by Necker, 211; and by the Notables, 212; Sieyès thinks them useless, 338; the cahiers demand them, 355. See *Lands of Estates.*
Provincial Estates. See *Lands of Estates.*
Provincial towns, streets and houses, 175; dress, a thrifty family, 177; marriage, amusements, 178; journeymen, guilds, 179; masters, business education of women, town government, 181; hospitals and diseases, 182; schools, 183; changes in the national life, 184.
Prussia, torture restricted there, 113; compared with France, 385.
Public opinion, as a standard of right and wrong, 324.

Quack doctors, the cahiers ask for their suppression, 375.
Quakers, in Voltaire's "English Letters," 54.
Quesnay, his doctrines, 233; the halberd and public opinion, 324.

Rambaud, M., v. 395.
Recruiting, of soldiers, 88.
Remiremont, wealth of the chapter, 33.
Rennes, its cahier typical; asks for progressive taxation, 365.
Requêtes, cour des, 103 n.
Rigby, Dr., description of France, 187.
Roads, fine but little traveled, 194.
Rochambeau, marquis of, praises discipline of his troops in America, 95; has Chastellux with him there, 271.
Rocquain, M., vi., 395.

INDEX. 407

Rohan, a great family, one member injures Marie Antoinette, 14. See *Chabot.*
Rouge, in the Encyclopædia, 256; proposed tax on, 364.
Rousseau, Jean Jacques, may rival Voltaire in influence, 51; originality, 56; approves of equality of condition, 120; his opinion of Paris, 157; praises rural life, 187; story of the peasant hiding food, 216; Rousseau an opponent of the new philosophy, 243; contributes to the Encyclopædia an article on Political Economy, 250, 292; sincerity of Rousseau, 274; the "Confessions," introspection and religion, 275; philosophy, 276; simplicity, love of nature, 277; early life, 278; Mme. de Warens, 279; Thérèse Levasseur, 280; mode of life and character of Rousseau, sudden inspiration, the "*First Discourse,*" degeneracy of man under civilization, 281; education in the "First Discourse," 284; "*Second Discourse,*" inequality, 285; the happy savage, 286; the development of society, 289; Voltaire on the "Second Discourse," 291; madness of Rousseau, 292 and n.; the "*Social Compact,*" the idea not original, 293; sovereignty, 295; form of government, 298; an official religion, 299; equality in tyranny, 301. Fiction, Rousseau's characters; the "*New Heloisa,*" sensation caused by the book, 303; sentimentality, 304; the country-house and the garden, 305; respectability, 307; "*Emile,*" on education, conformity to nature, 307; the tutor, 308; a lesson on the origin of property, 309; the hardening process, 311; Sophie and female education, 313; religion, the Savoyard Curate, 314; Rousseau's quarrel with the Philosophers, difference, 320; he dares to oppose public opinion, 325; more widely read on account of the American war, 332; the "Social Compact" taken by Sieyès as the basis of government, 338; Rousseau's reputation European, 385. See *American Indians.*
Royal Chamber, established by Louis XV., 104.

Saint-Germain, count of, minister of war, his measures, 92.
Sale of public offices, 231.
Salons, why attractive, 75.
Salt tax (*gabelle*), its operation, 222; in the cahiers, 364.
Saunderson, Nicholas, opinions attributed to him by Diderot, 248.
Scherer, M., vi., 396.
School, of surgery in Paris, 168; school in provincial towns, 183; Marmontel at school, 184; country schools, 204. See *Education.*
Schoolmasters, boys in Paris too much left to them, 165; in towns generally appointed by the clergy, 183; in villages paid by the community, 201; and elected, 202; mode of life, 204.
Ségur, count of, fond of adventure, 85; story about flogging, 93; of the Calotte, 99.

Ségur, viscount of, his account of the education of a young nobleman, 73.
Servants, thieving, might be executed, 111; proposed tax, 364.
Shopkeepers, in Paris, 165; in the provinces, 176. See *Guilds.*
Sieyès, Abbé, his pamphlet, "What is the Third Estate," 336; draws up a form for a cahier, 346.
Smuggling, how regarded, 130; of salt, 223; between France and England, 225.
Social compact, the idea an old one, Rousseau's essay, 293.
Socinians in Voltaire's "English Letters," 55.
Socrates and ridicule, 283.
Soldiers. See *Army.*
Stourm, M., v., 396.
Streets, of Paris, 157; of provincial towns, 175.
Sub-delegates, subordinate to intendants, 10.
Sulli, duke of, refuses to take up Voltaire's quarrel with Chabot, 52.
Sunday, observed in Paris, 171; in the cahiers, 367.
Sunday ladies, at court, 14.
Surgeons. See *Doctors, Hospitals.*
Swift, associates with Voltaire, 53.
Swiss of the rue aux Ours, 170.
Switzerland, its government compared with that of France, 385.
Syndic, a town officer, 181; a village officer, paid by the community, 201; his functions, 202; distributes the corvée among the peasants, 227.

Taille, the, its nature and operation, 213.
Taine, M. Henri, v., 396; his figures concerning taxation considered, 228.
Taxes, paid by the clergy, 27; *décimes,* 36; amount of taxes paid by the nation, 207; unequally assessed, 208; Lands of Election and Lands of Estates, privileges, 209; Provincial Assemblies, 211; persons taxed unequally, *direct taxes,* taille, 213; twentieths, 218; poll-tax, 219; indirect taxes, the Farmers General, 220; salt tax, 222; tobacco, 223; excise, duties, 224; internal duties, 225; *corvée,* 226; proportion of income paid in taxes, 227; arbitrariness and publicity, 229; *in the cahiers,* 363; luxuries, 364; progressive taxation, 365; incompetence of officials, 384. See *Décimes, Tithe, Farmers General.*
Terray, Abbé, his contract with the Farmers General, 220.
Thérèse Levasseur, Rousseau's mistress, 280.
Third Estate, one of the three orders, 25; variety of persons included in it, 154; how represented in Provincial Estates, 210; and in Provincial Assemblies, 211; Sieyès's pamphlet, "What is the Third Estate," 336; elections to the Estates General, *in the cahiers,* 344; desire that the Estates General meet as one chamber, 350; law reform, 356; abolition of privilege and of feudal dues, 359; tithe, 363; equal taxation, 364; fewer holidays, 367; free and responsible press,

369; attitude toward the nobility, 370; *particular wishes of the order*, freedom from administrative regulations, commerce, 372; bankrupts, suppression of begging, 373; public workshops, 374; more doctors, 375.
Three Bishoprics, the, how taxed, 209; prefer to have free trade with Germany rather than with France, 372 and n.
Tithes, how levied, 26; in the cahiers, 363.
Tobacco in common use, 201; monopoly, 223; snuff, 224; in the cahiers, 364.
Tocqueville, M. Alexis de, v., 396.
Toleration, spreads in the 18th century, 41. See *Protestants*.
Torture, its methods, 110; the wheel, 111; protests; Beccaria, 112; defense of torture, 114; preparatory and previous, abolition, 115.
Towns. See *Paris, Provincial Towns*.
Traites (duties), 225.
Trublet, Abbé, defends the church, 66.
Tuileries, palace and garden, 155.
Turgot, Anne Robert Jacques, does not remain long in office, 17; opposed by the queen, 24; tries to induce the king to modify the coronation oath, 44; makes him promise not to issue *acquits de comptant*, 231; life of Turgot, 235; he contributes to the Encyclopædia, 250.
Tuscany, its government compared with that of France, 385.
Twentieths (*vingtièmes*), 218.

Uniforms, described, 89.
United States, their attachment to Montesquieu's theory of the division of powers, 150; their constitutional convention, 353. See *American Colonies*.
Utility, doctrine of, taught by Voltaire, 64; by Helvetius, 261; its antiquity; not the motive but the test of morals, 263 n.; taught by Holbach, 268. See *Hedonism, Philosophers*.

Vassy, Mme. de, and her snuff-box, 77.
Vaudreuil, Count of, the "Marriage of Figaro" played at his house, 329.
Vénalité des charges, 231.
Venice, the liberty of debauchery, 137; one of Montesquieu's models for an aristocratic republic, 145, 149 n.
Vergennes, Count of, retains his office, 17; induces France to make war on England, 331.
Villages, 194; political rights, 201. See *Peasant, Country*.
Villein service. See *Corvée*.
Vingtième, droit de, distinguished from vingtièmes, 218, n.
Vingtièmes, their operation, 218.
Voltaire, the clergy demand the suppression of his works, 28; on toleration, 42; chiefly an enemy of the church; his early history, 51; quarrel with Chabot, 52; stay in England, 53; "English Letters," Quakers, French and English priests, 54; Socinians, 55; Voltaire a popularizer of thought, 56; his eulogy of Locke, 60; his philosophy, 61; hatred of the clergy, and of the supernatural, 62; his religious opinions, 63; he opposes torture, 112; La Barre, 114; imprisoned by *Lettre de cachet*, 117; said to have procured a *lettre de cachet*, 117, 325; his story of Montesquieu and Cardinal de Fleury, 135; he is often led astray by ignorance of foreign nations, 144; thinks the French peasants well off, 187; contributes to the Encyclopædia, 250; tells an anecdote about it, 255; correspondence with d'Alembert about it, 260; answers Holbach's "System of Nature," 270; a great liar, 274; interested in external matters, 275; letter to Rousseau on the "Second Discourse," 291; quarrel with Rousseau, 320; more widely read on account of the American war, 332; his reputation European, 385.

Wages, in the provinces, 179.
Warens, Mme. de, 279. See *Rousseau*.
Wheel, the, punishment described, 111.
Women. See *Marriage, Married women, Education, Rousseau* (Sophie).
Workshops, public, asked for in a cahier, 374.

Young, Arthur, his opinion of Paris, 157; his description of treading out the corn, 189; on the revenue of arable land, 192 n.; clear accounts of French finances not to be expected, 207 n.; taxes in England and in France, 208.
Young, Edward, writes an epigram on Voltaire, 53.